translucent

1

STORY AND ART BY
KAZUHIRO OKAMOTO
岡本一広

TRANSLATION BY
HEIDI PLECHL

LETTERING BY
JIM KEPLINGER

CONTENTS

translucent

STORY AND ART BY
KAZUHIRO OKAMOTO
岡本一広

TRANSLATION BY
HEIDI PLECHL

LETTERING BY
JIM KEPLINGER

Okamoto Kazuhiro

PART 1 Translucent Syndrome

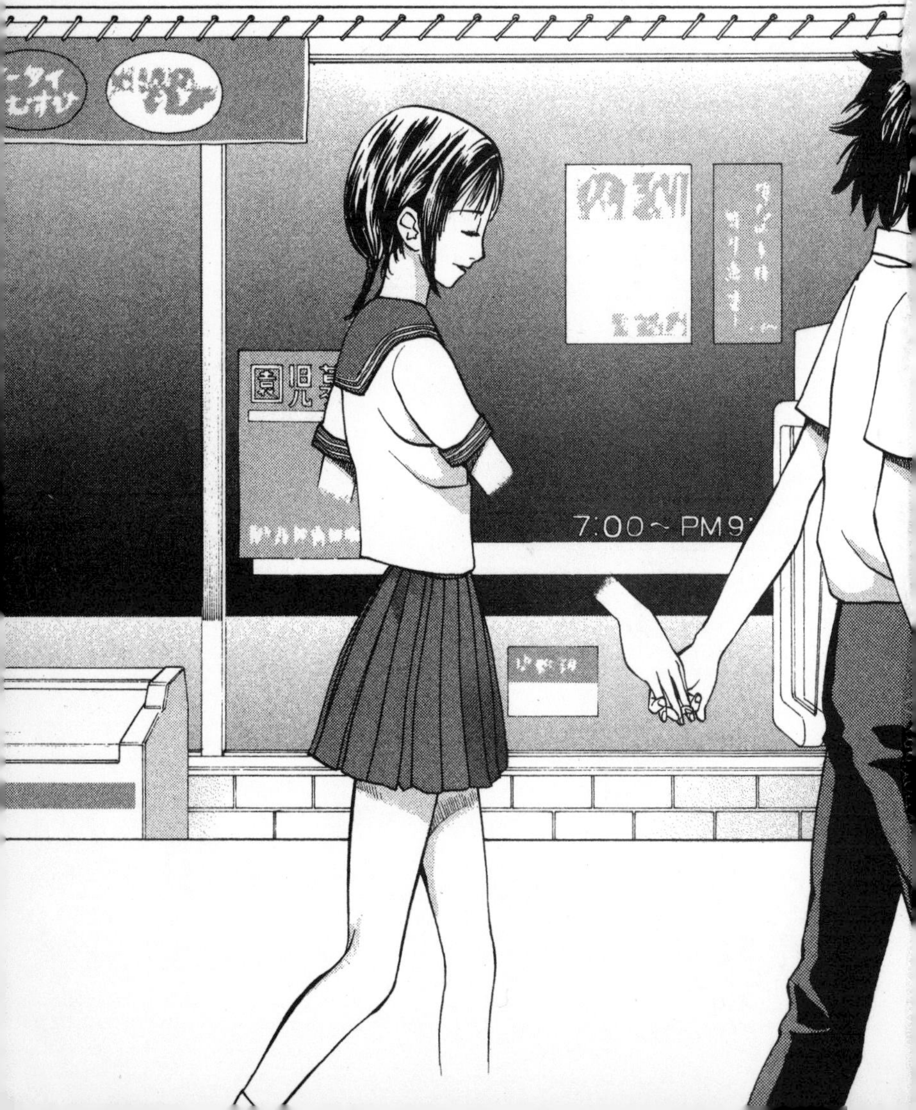
7:00~ PM9

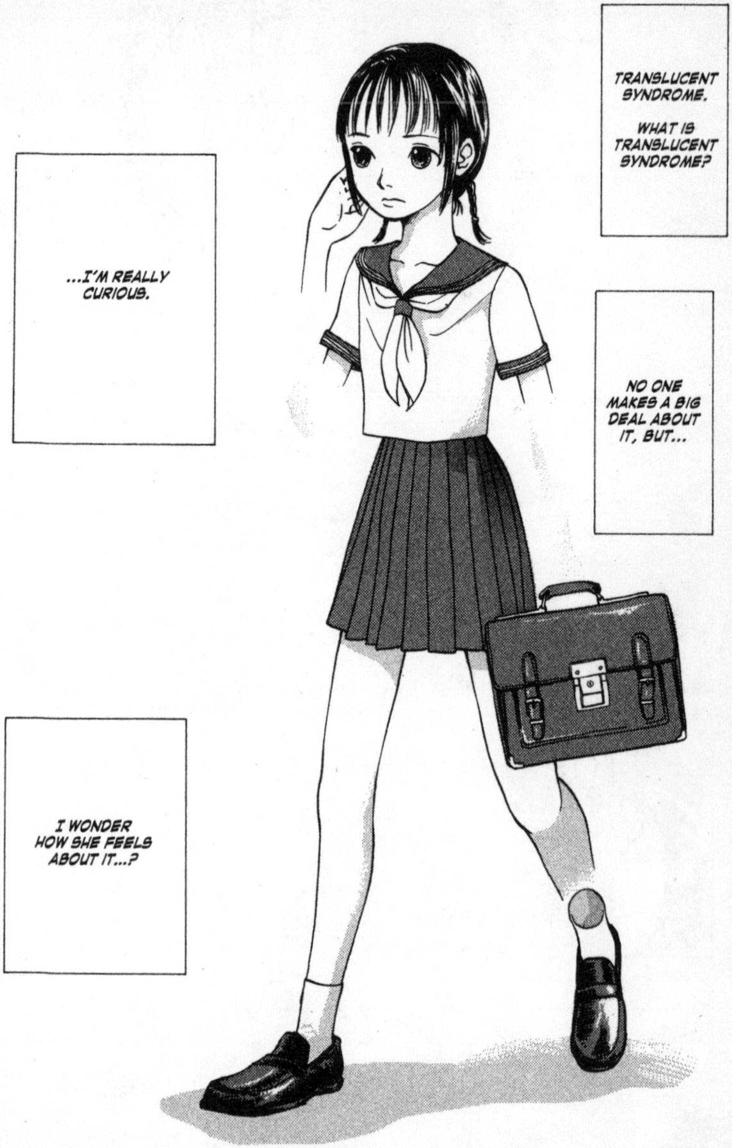
TRANSLUCENT SYNDROME.
WHAT IS TRANSLUCENT SYNDROME?
NO ONE MAKES A BIG DEAL ABOUT IT, BUT...
...I'M REALLY CURIOUS.
I WONDER HOW SHE FEELS ABOUT IT...?

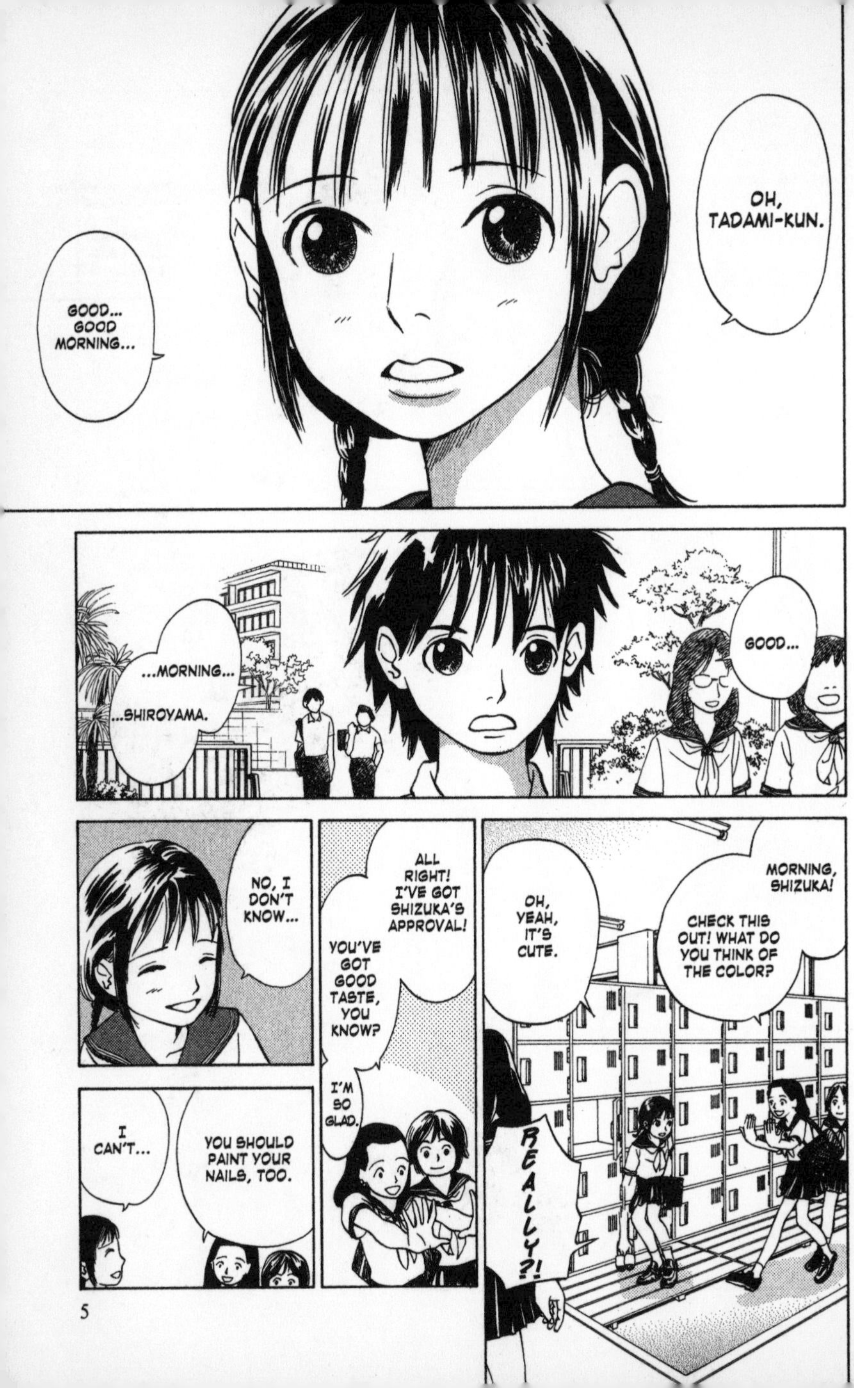
OH, TADAMI-KUN.
GOOD... GOOD MORNING...
GOOD...
...MORNING...
...SHIROYAMA.
MORNING, SHIZUKA!
CHECK THIS OUT! WHAT DO YOU THINK OF THE COLOR?
OH, YEAH, IT'S CUTE.
REALLY?!
ALL RIGHT! I'VE GOT SHIZUKA'S APPROVAL!
YOU'VE GOT GOOD TASTE, YOU KNOW?
I'M SO GLAD.
NO, I DON'T KNOW...
YOU SHOULD PAINT YOUR NAILS, TOO.
I CAN'T...

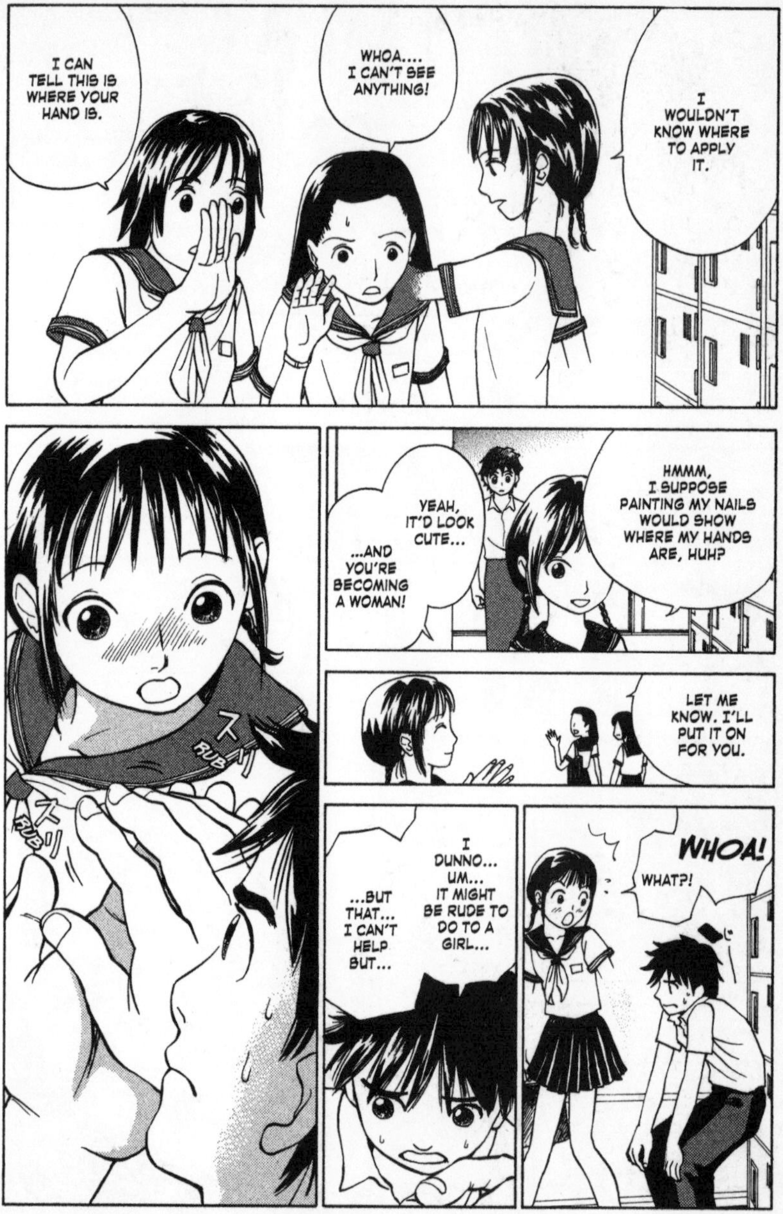
I WOULDN'T KNOW WHERE TO APPLY IT.
WHOA.... I CAN'T SEE ANYTHING!
I CAN TELL THIS IS WHERE YOUR HAND IS.
HMMM, I SUPPOSE PAINTING MY NAILS WOULD SHOW WHERE MY HANDS ARE, HUH?
YEAH, IT'D LOOK CUTE...
...AND YOU'RE BECOMING A WOMAN!
LET ME KNOW. I'LL PUT IT ON FOR YOU.
WHOA!
WHAT?!
I DUNNO... UM... IT MIGHT BE RUDE TO DO TO A GIRL...
...BUT THAT... I CAN'T HELP BUT...
RUB
RUB

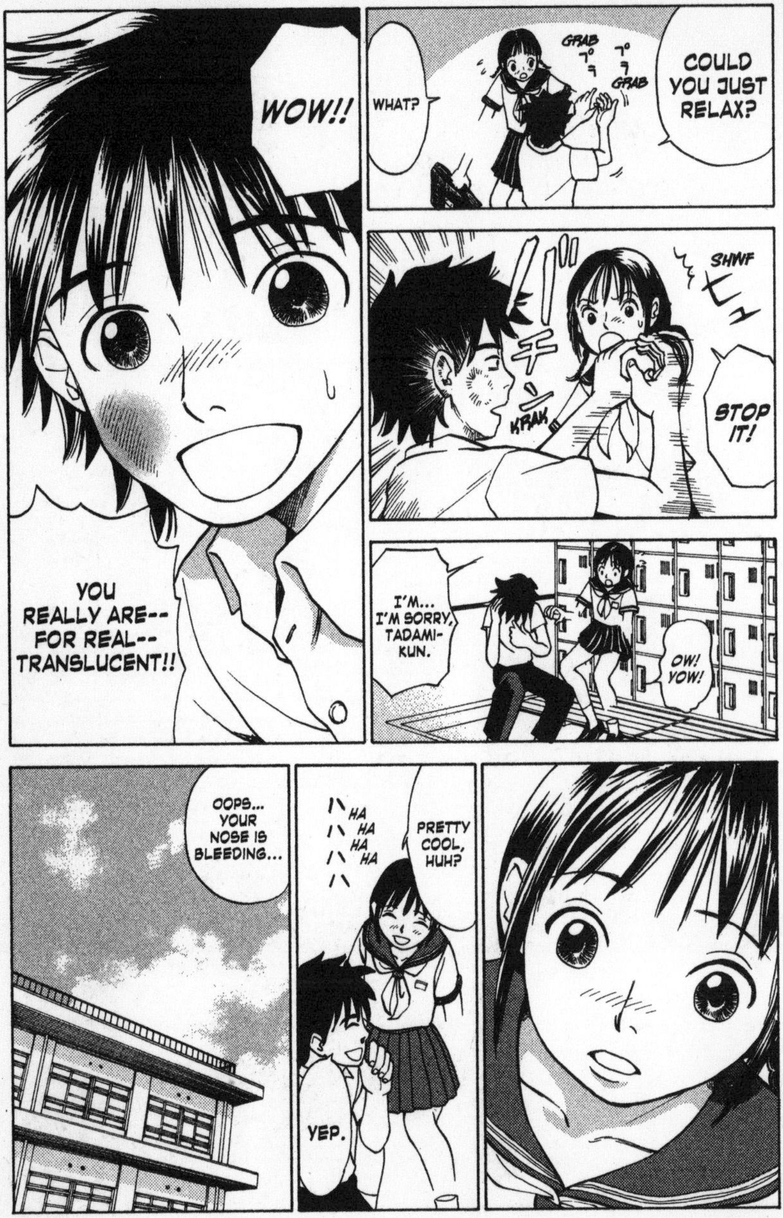
COULD YOU JUST RELAX?
GRAB
GRAB
WHAT?
SHWF
STOP IT!
KRAK
OW! YOW!
I'M... I'M SORRY, TADAMI-KUN.
WOW!!
YOU REALLY ARE-- FOR REAL-- TRANSLUCENT!!
PRETTY COOL, HUH?
HA HA HA HA
YEP.
OOPS... YOUR NOSE IS BLEEDING...

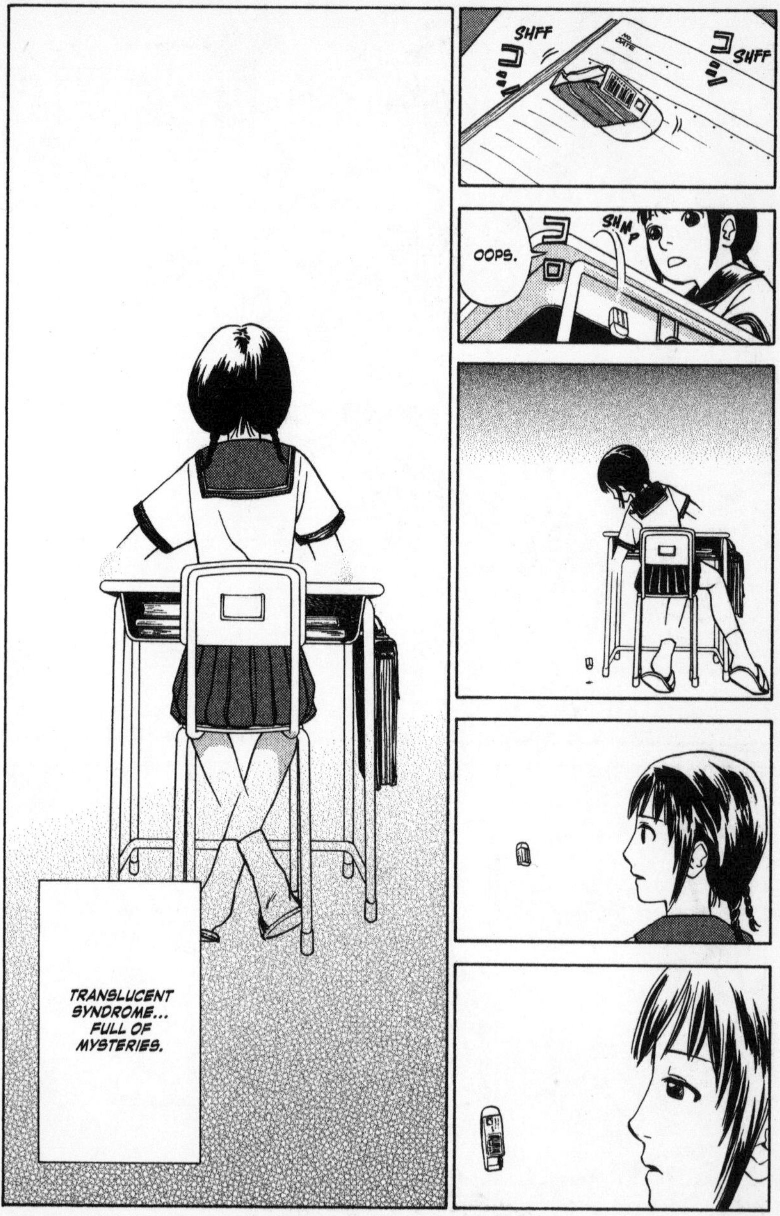
SHFF
SHFF
SHMP
OOPS.
TRANSLUCENT SYNDROME... FULL OF MYSTERIES.

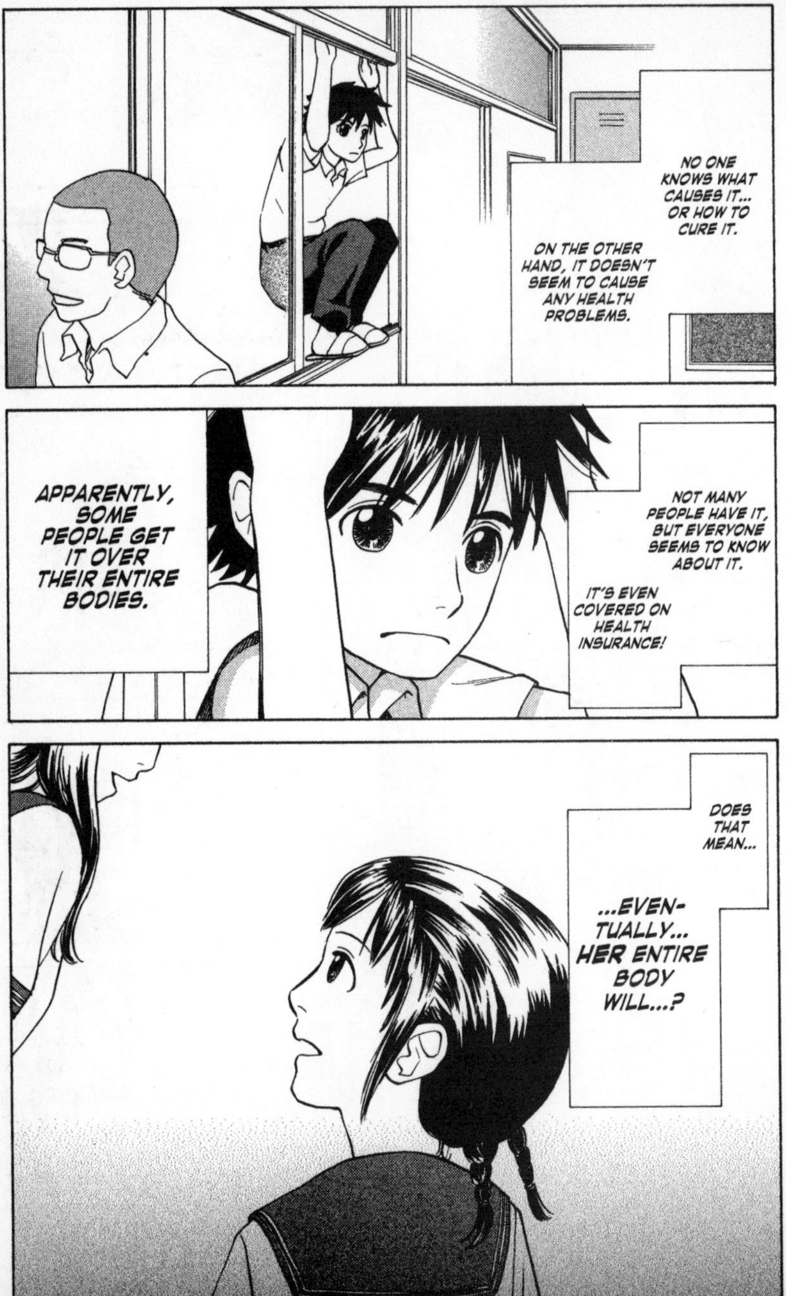
NO ONE KNOWS WHAT CAUSES IT... OR HOW TO CURE IT.
ON THE OTHER HAND, IT DOESN'T SEEM TO CAUSE ANY HEALTH PROBLEMS.
NOT MANY PEOPLE HAVE IT, BUT EVERYONE SEEMS TO KNOW ABOUT IT.
IT'S EVEN COVERED ON HEALTH INSURANCE!
APPARENTLY, SOME PEOPLE GET IT OVER THEIR ENTIRE BODIES.
DOES THAT MEAN...
...EVEN-TUALLY... HER ENTIRE BODY WILL...?

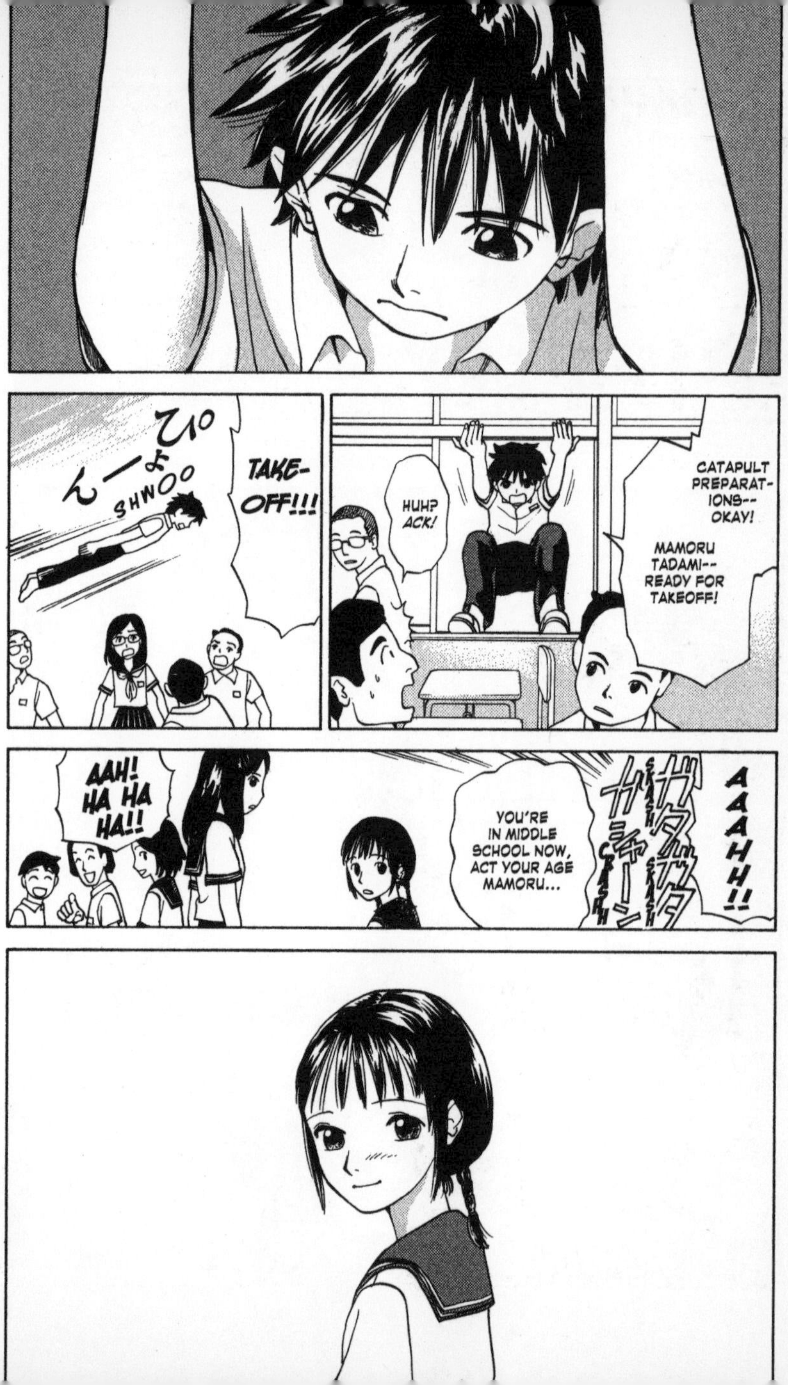
CATAPULT PREPARATIONS--OKAY!
MAMORU TADAMI--READY FOR TAKEOFF!
HUH? ACK!
TAKE-OFF!!!
SHWOO
AAAAHH!!
SKASH SKASH
CRASH
YOU'RE IN MIDDLE SCHOOL NOW, ACT YOUR AGE MAMORU...
AAH! HA HA HA!!

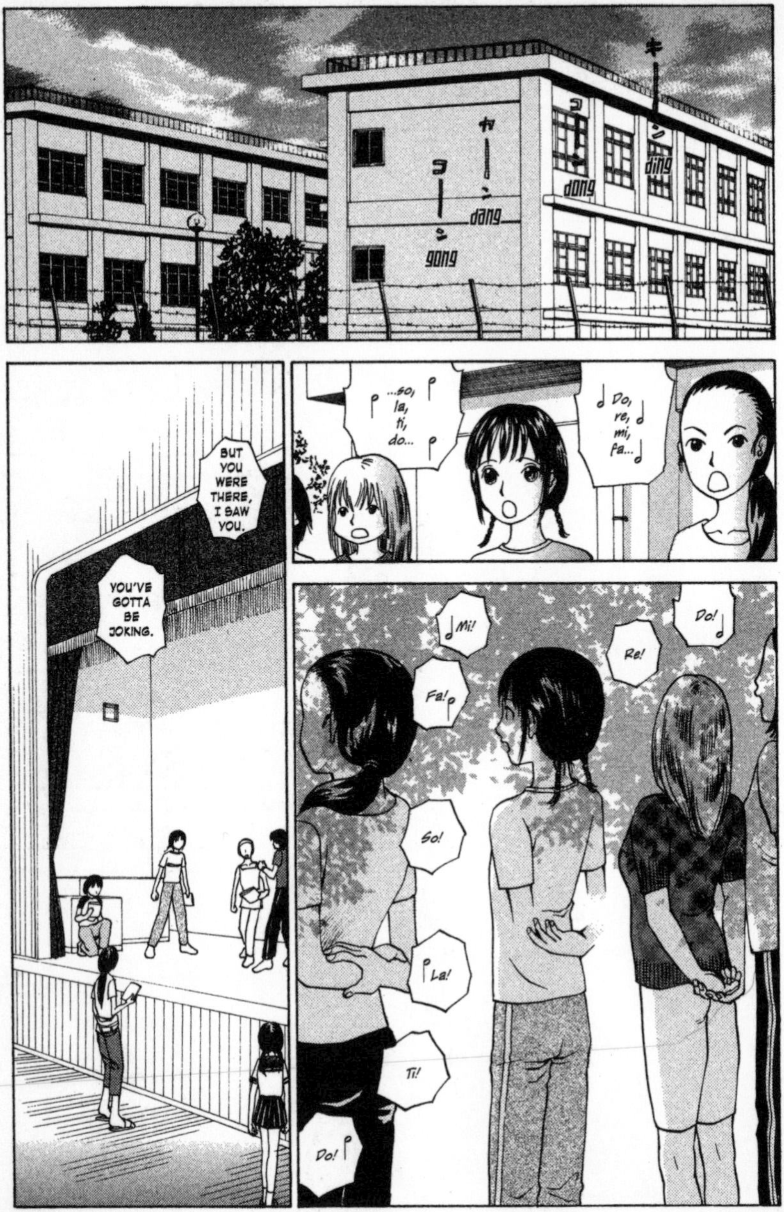
キーン ding
コーン dong
カーン dang
コーン gong
Do, re, mi, fa...
...so, la, ti, do...
Do!
Re!
Mi!
Fa!
So!
La!
Ti!
Do!
BUT YOU WERE THERE, I SAW YOU.
YOU'VE GOTTA BE JOKING.

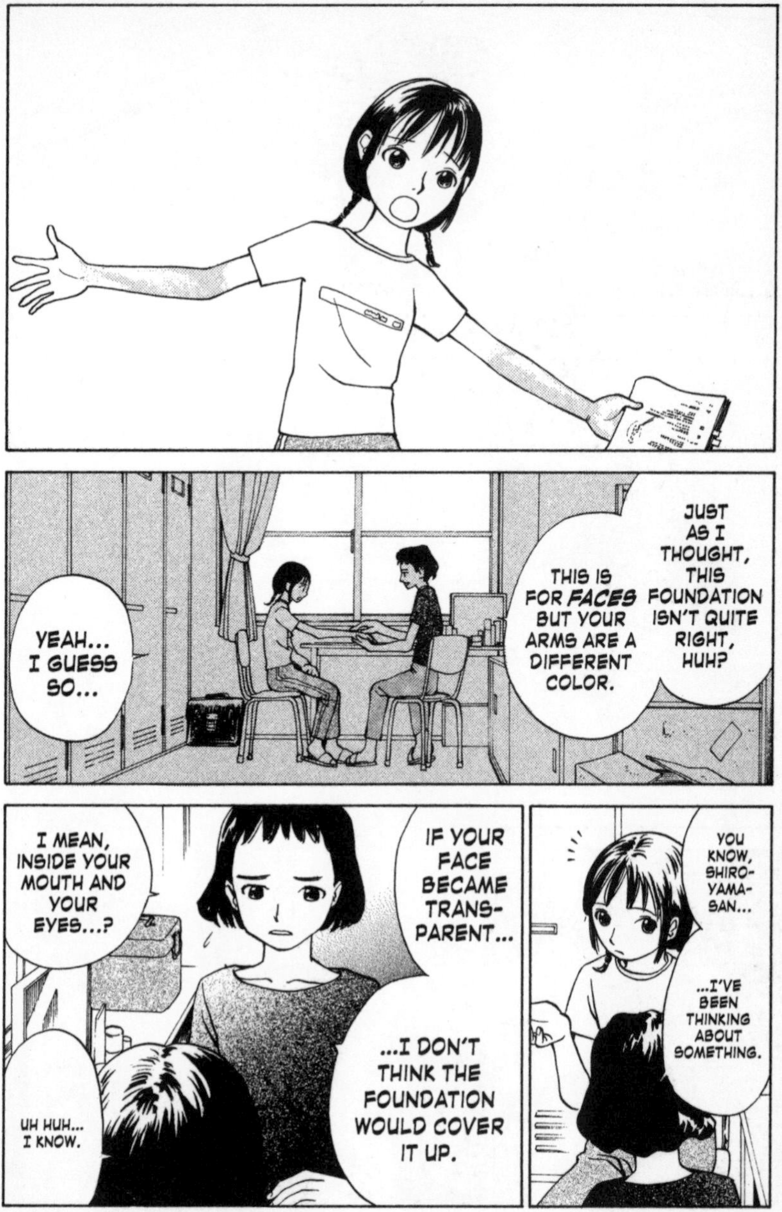
JUST AS I THOUGHT, THIS FOUNDATION ISN'T QUITE RIGHT, HUH?
THIS IS FOR *FACES* BUT YOUR ARMS ARE A DIFFERENT COLOR.
YEAH... I GUESS SO...
YOU KNOW, SHIRO-YAMA-SAN...
...I'VE BEEN THINKING ABOUT SOMETHING.
IF YOUR FACE BECAME TRANS-PARENT...
I MEAN, INSIDE YOUR MOUTH AND YOUR EYES...?
...I DON'T THINK THE FOUNDATION WOULD COVER IT UP.
UH HUH... I KNOW.

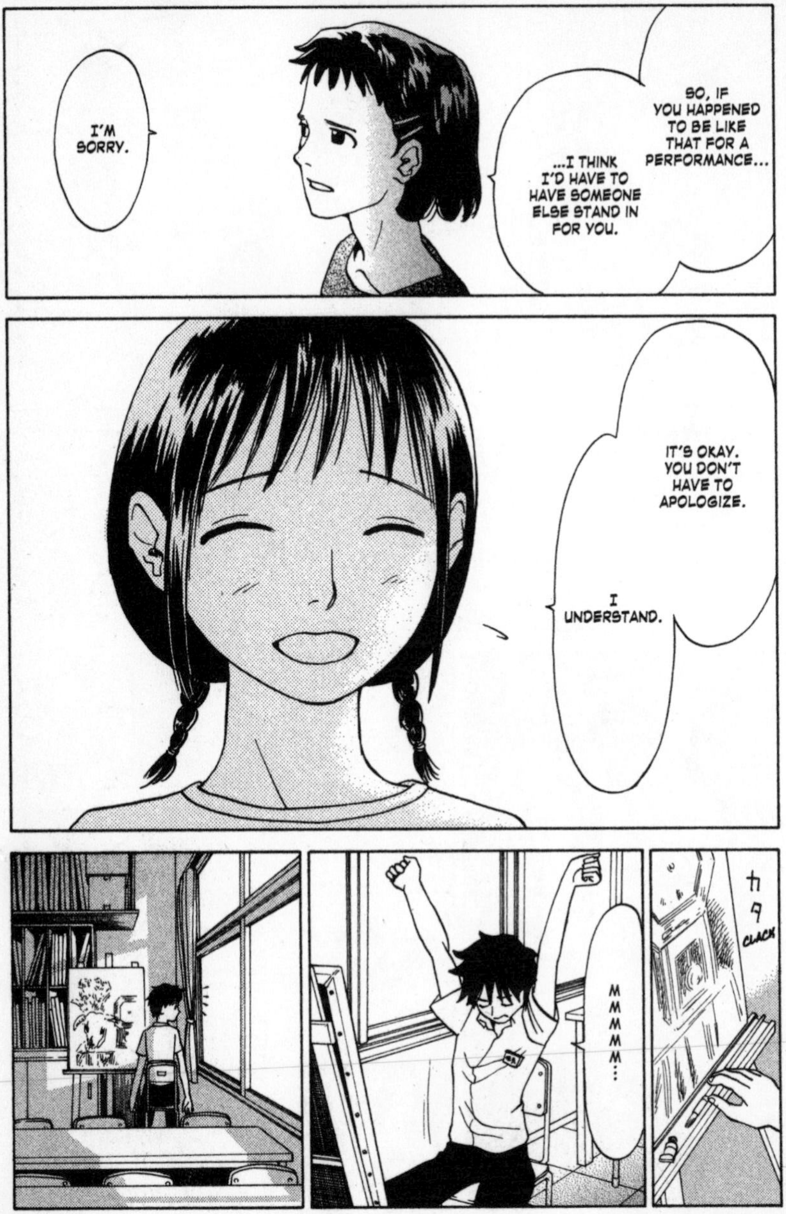

SO, IF YOU HAPPENED TO BE LIKE THAT FOR A PERFORMANCE...
...I THINK I'D HAVE TO HAVE SOMEONE ELSE STAND IN FOR YOU.
I'M SORRY.
IT'S OKAY. YOU DON'T HAVE TO APOLOGIZE.
I UNDERSTAND.
カタ
CLACK
MMMMM...

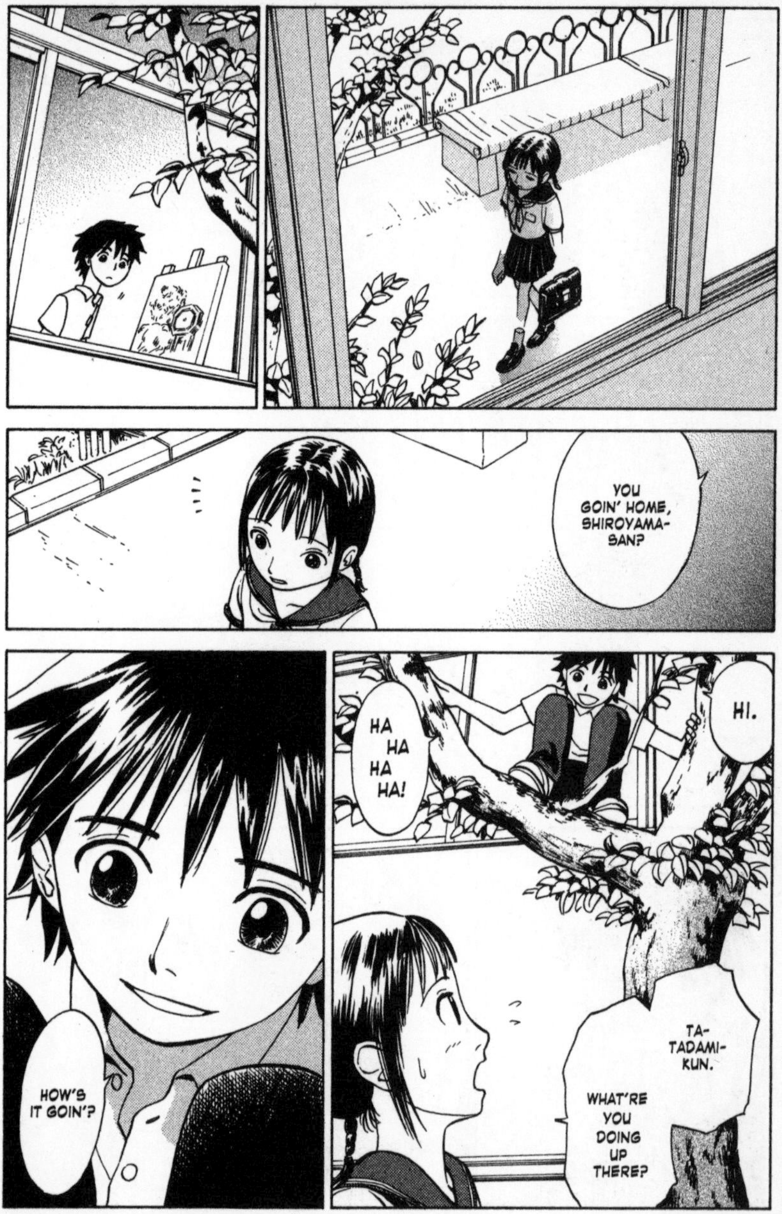
YOU GOIN' HOME, SHIROYAMA-SAN?
HI.
HA HA HA HA!
TA-TADAMI-KUN.
WHAT'RE YOU DOING UP THERE?
HOW'S IT GOIN'?

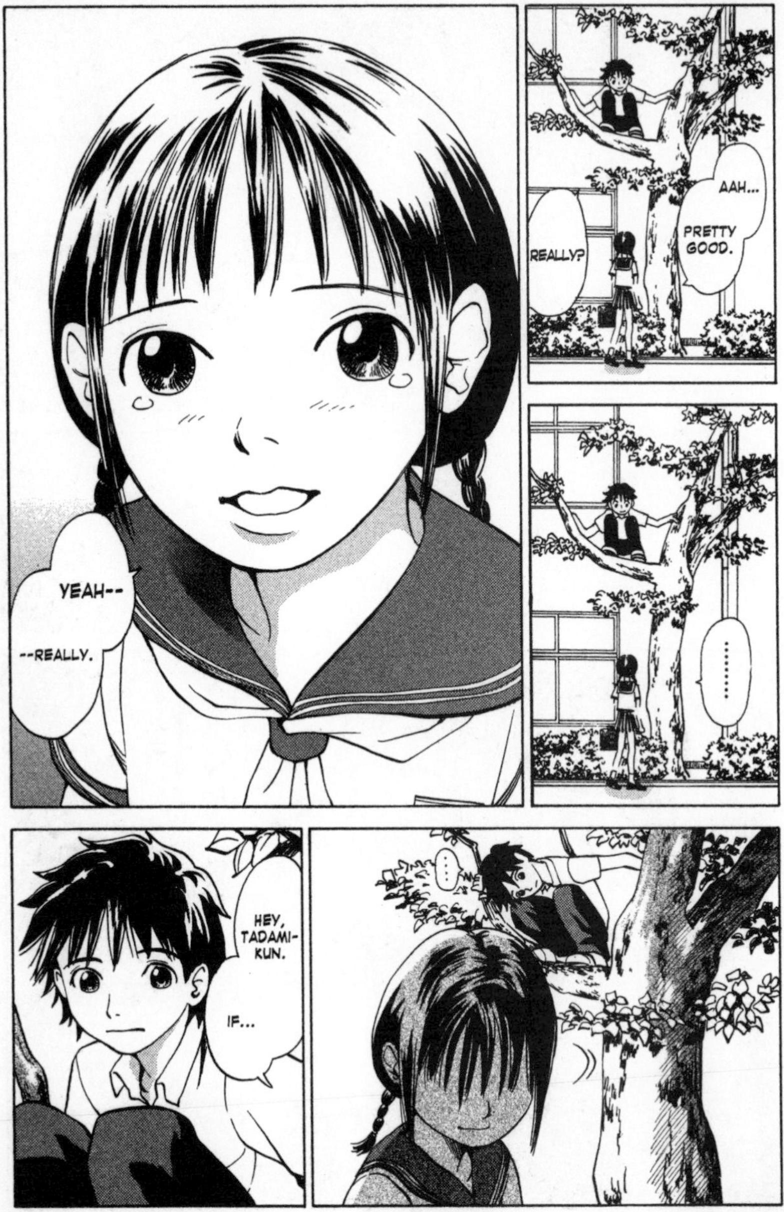
AAH... PRETTY GOOD.
REALLY?
....
YEAH-- --REALLY.
...
HEY, TADAMI-KUN. IF...

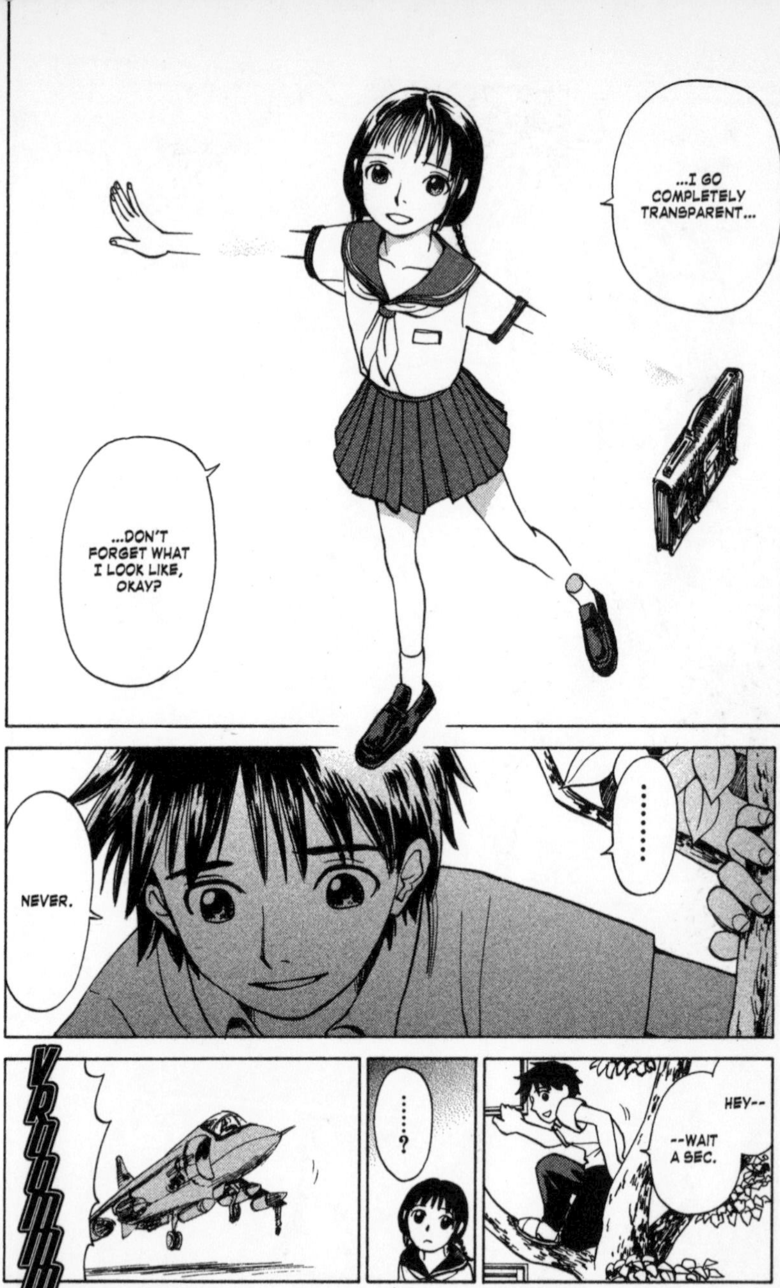
...I GO COMPLETELY TRANSPARENT...
...DON'T FORGET WHAT I LOOK LIKE, OKAY?
....
NEVER.
HEY--
--WAIT A SEC.
......?
VROOMMM

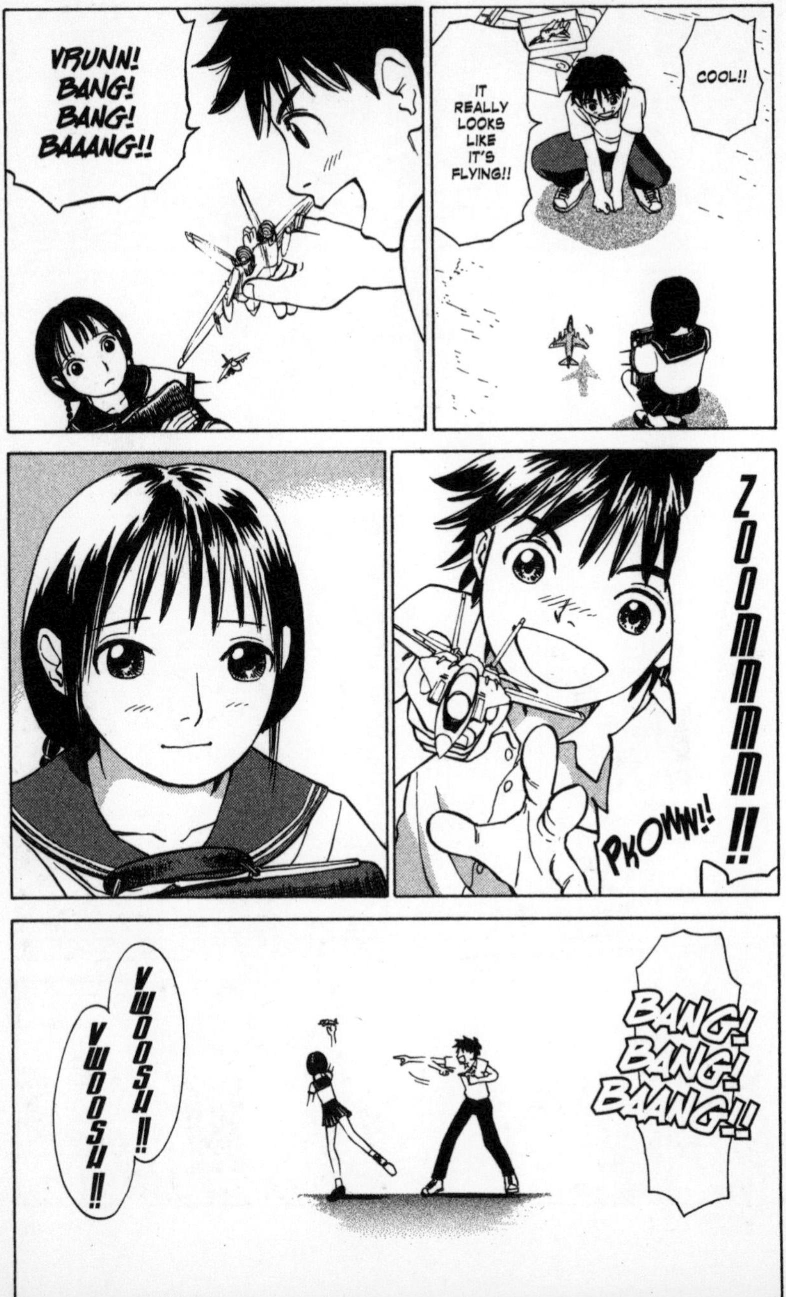
COOL!!
IT REALLY LOOKS LIKE IT'S FLYING!!
VRUNN! BANG! BANG! BAAANG!!
ZOOMMMM!!
PKOWW!!
BANG! BANG! BAANG!!
VWOOSH!!
VWOOSH!!

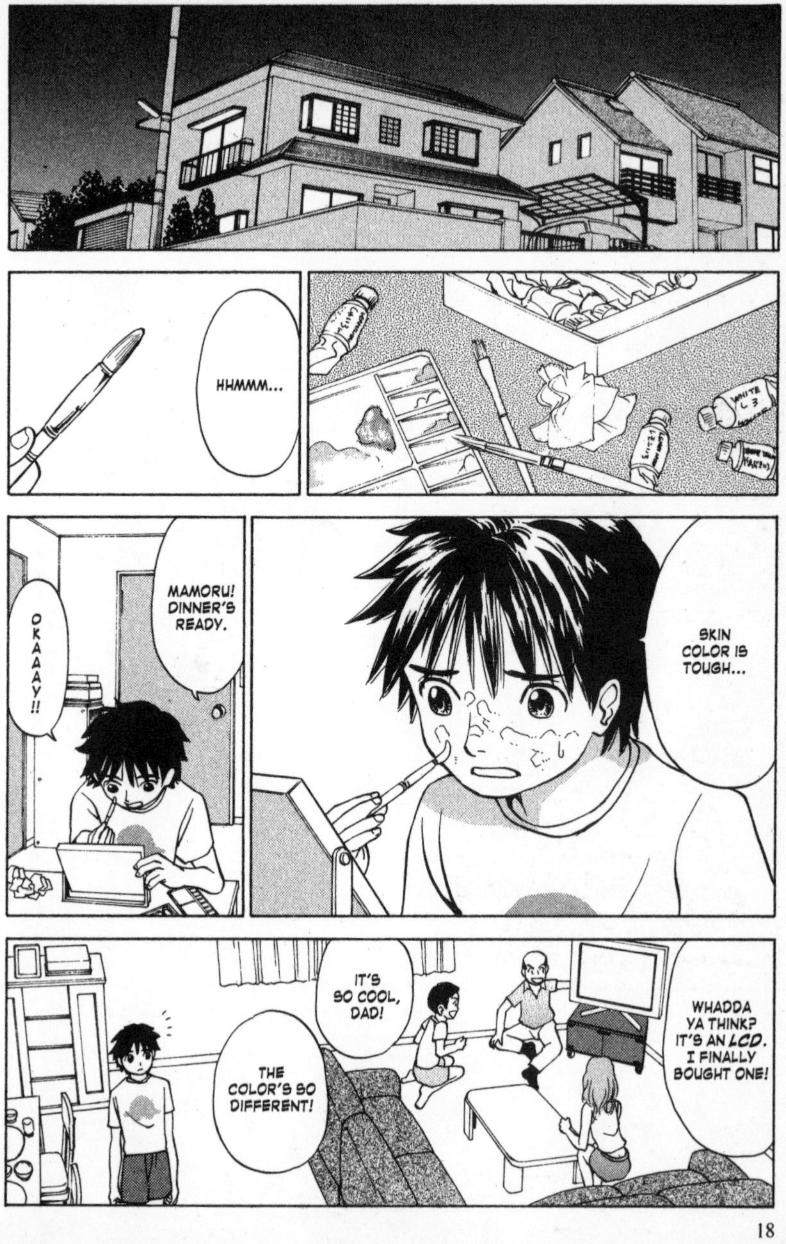
WHITE
HHMMM...
SKIN COLOR IS TOUGH...
MAMORU! DINNER'S READY.
OKAAAAY!!
WHADDA YA THINK? IT'S AN LCD. I FINALLY BOUGHT ONE!
IT'S SO COOL, DAD!
THE COLOR'S SO DIFFERENT!

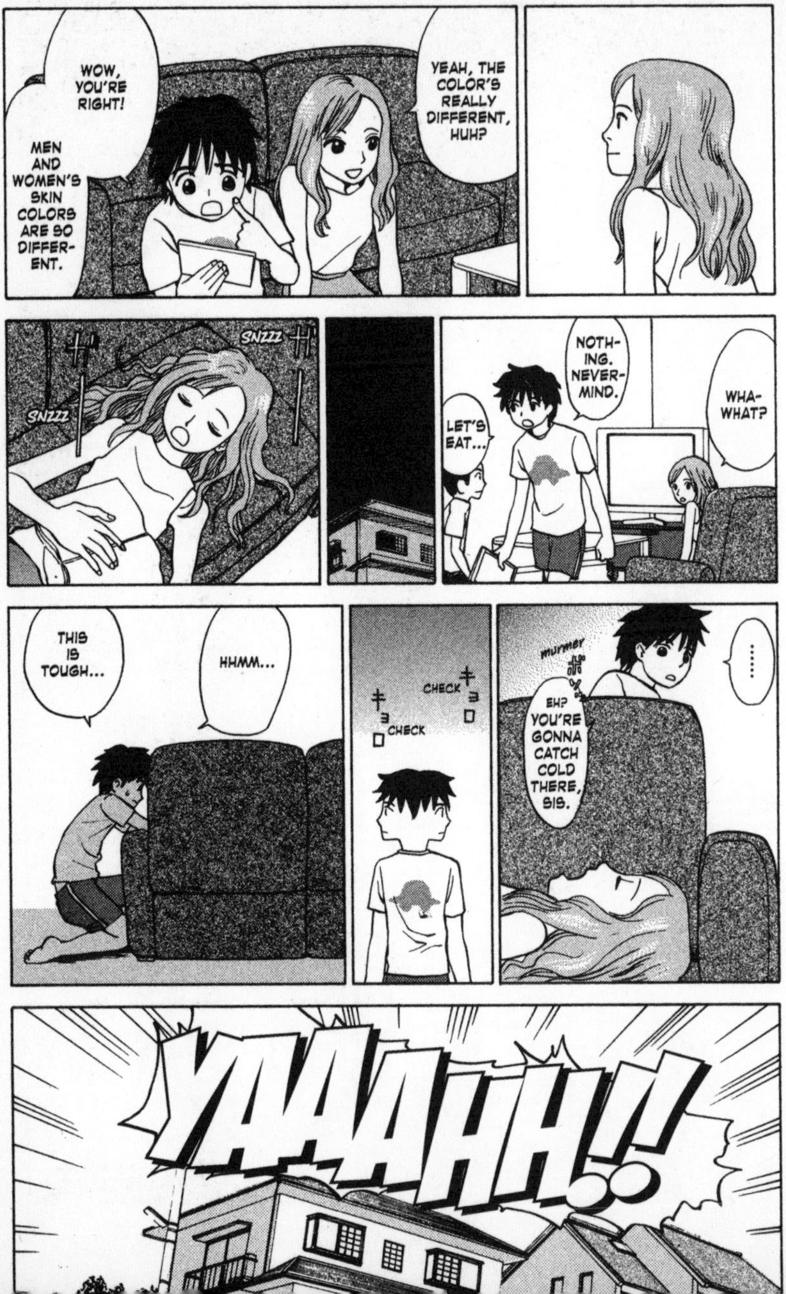
YEAH, THE COLOR'S REALLY DIFFERENT, HUH?
WOW, YOU'RE RIGHT!
MEN AND WOMEN'S SKIN COLORS ARE SO DIFFER-ENT.
WHA-WHAT?
NOTH-ING. NEVER-MIND.
LET'S EAT...
SNZZZ
SNZZZ
......
murmer
EH? YOU'RE GONNA CATCH COLD THERE, SIS.
CHECK
CHECK
HHMM...
THIS IS TOUGH...
YAAAHH!!

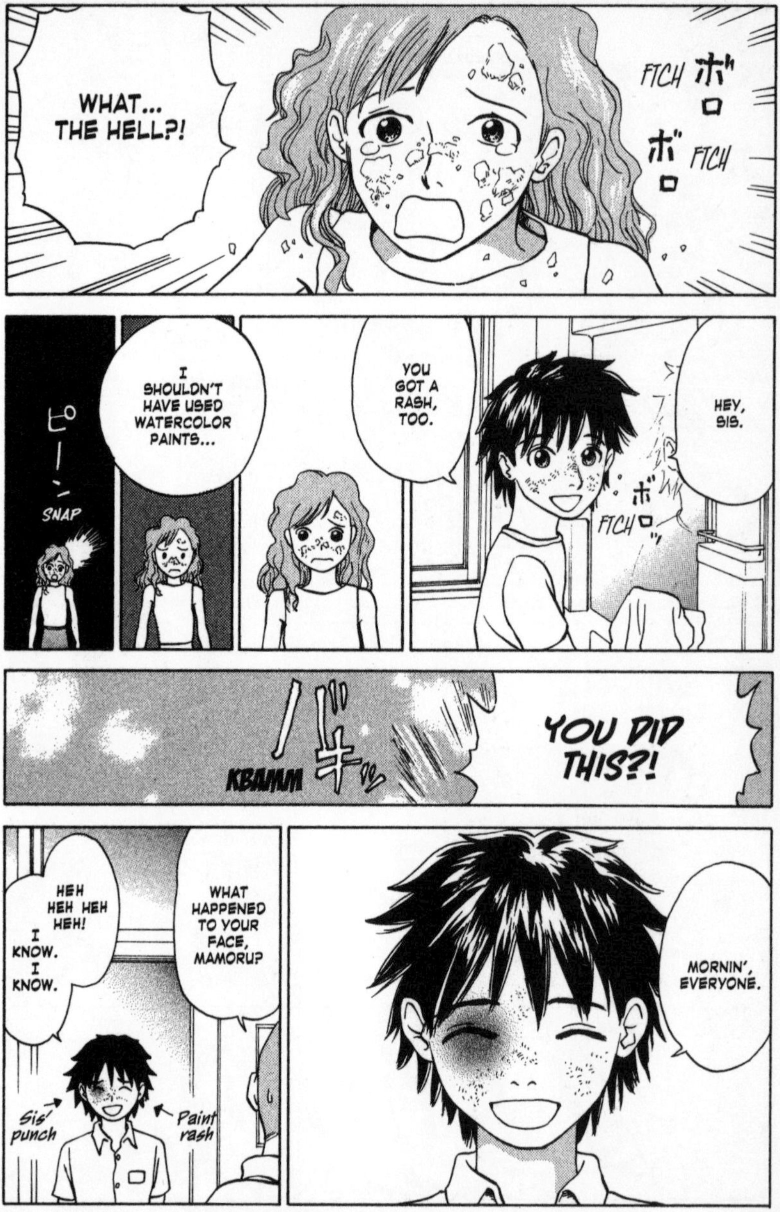
WHAT... THE HELL?!
ボロ
FITCH
ボロ
FITCH
HEY, SIS.
ボロッ
FITCH
YOU GOT A RASH, TOO.
I SHOULDN'T HAVE USED WATERCOLOR PAINTS...
ピーン
SNAP
YOU DID THIS?!
バキッ
KBAMM
MORNIN', EVERYONE.
WHAT HAPPENED TO YOUR FACE, MAMORU?
HEH HEH HEH HEH! I KNOW. I KNOW.
Paint rash
Sis' punch

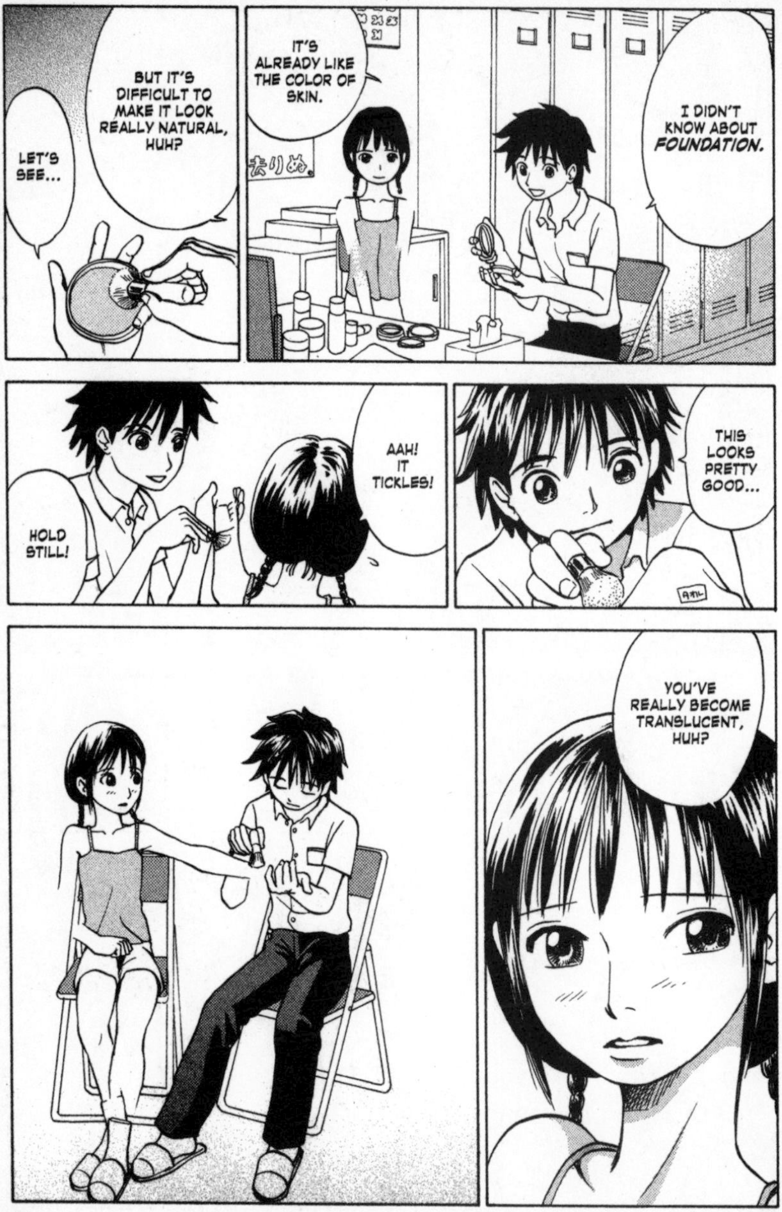
I DIDN'T KNOW ABOUT *FOUNDATION.*
IT'S ALREADY LIKE THE COLOR OF SKIN.
BUT IT'S DIFFICULT TO MAKE IT LOOK REALLY NATURAL, HUH?
LET'S SEE...
THIS LOOKS PRETTY GOOD...
AAH! IT TICKLES!
HOLD STILL!
YOU'VE REALLY BECOME TRANSLUCENT, HUH?

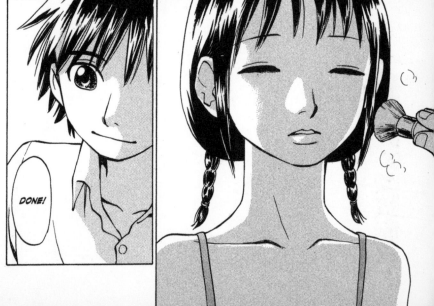

DONE!

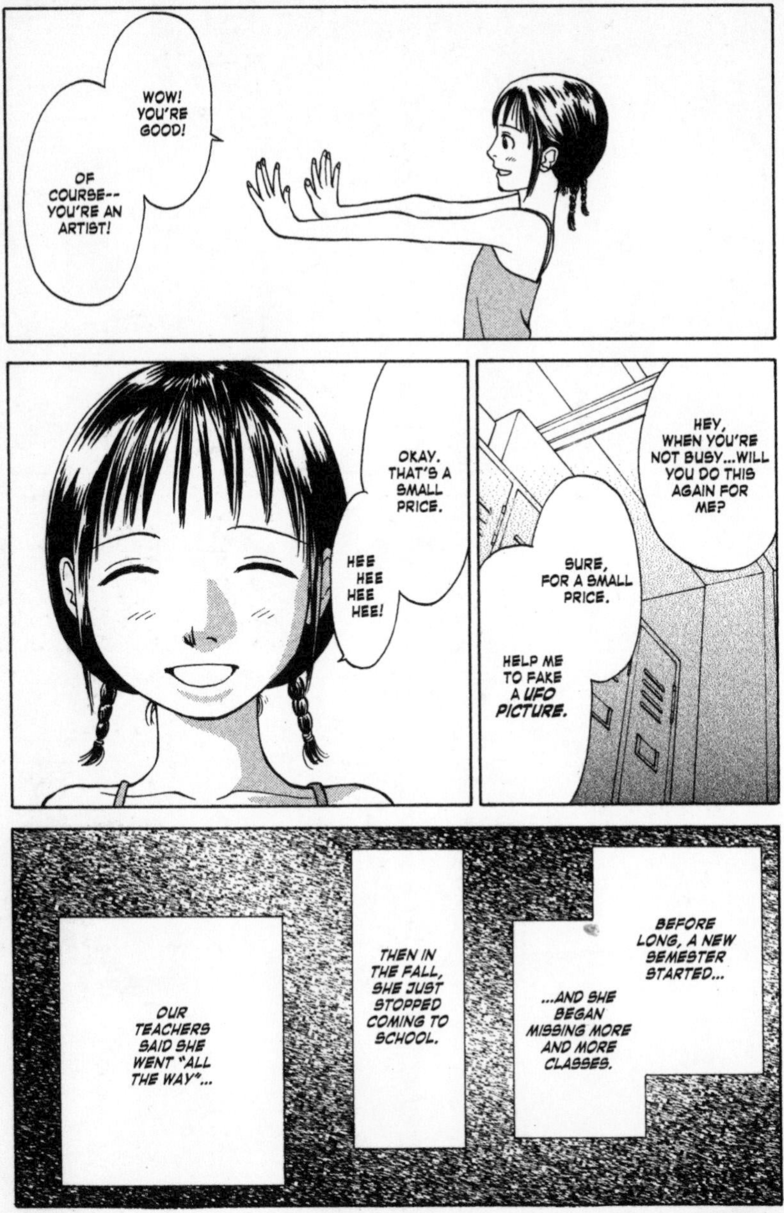
WOW! YOU'RE GOOD!
OF COURSE-- YOU'RE AN ARTIST!
HEY, WHEN YOU'RE NOT BUSY...WILL YOU DO THIS AGAIN FOR ME?
SURE, FOR A SMALL PRICE.
HELP ME TO FAKE A UFO PICTURE.
OKAY. THAT'S A SMALL PRICE.
HEE HEE HEE HEE!
BEFORE LONG, A NEW SEMESTER STARTED...
...AND SHE BEGAN MISSING MORE AND MORE CLASSES.
THEN IN THE FALL, SHE JUST STOPPED COMING TO SCHOOL.
OUR TEACHERS SAID SHE WENT "ALL THE WAY"...

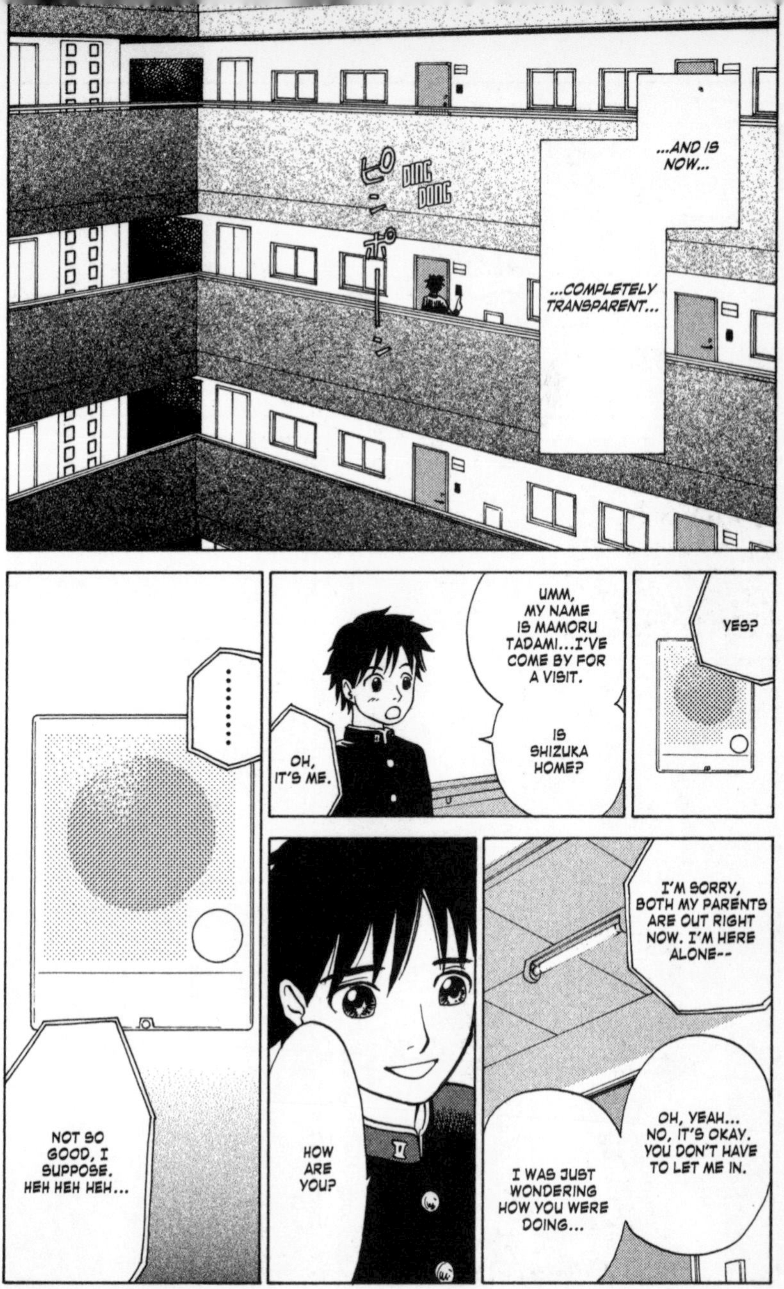

...AND IS NOW...
...COMPLETELY TRANSPARENT...
ピンポーン
DING DONG
YES?
UMM, MY NAME IS MAMORU TADAMI...I'VE COME BY FOR A VISIT.
IS SHIZUKA HOME?
OH, IT'S ME.
I'M SORRY, BOTH MY PARENTS ARE OUT RIGHT NOW. I'M HERE ALONE--
OH, YEAH... NO, IT'S OKAY. YOU DON'T HAVE TO LET ME IN.
I WAS JUST WONDERING HOW YOU WERE DOING...
HOW ARE YOU?
....
NOT SO GOOD, I SUPPOSE. HEH HEH HEH...

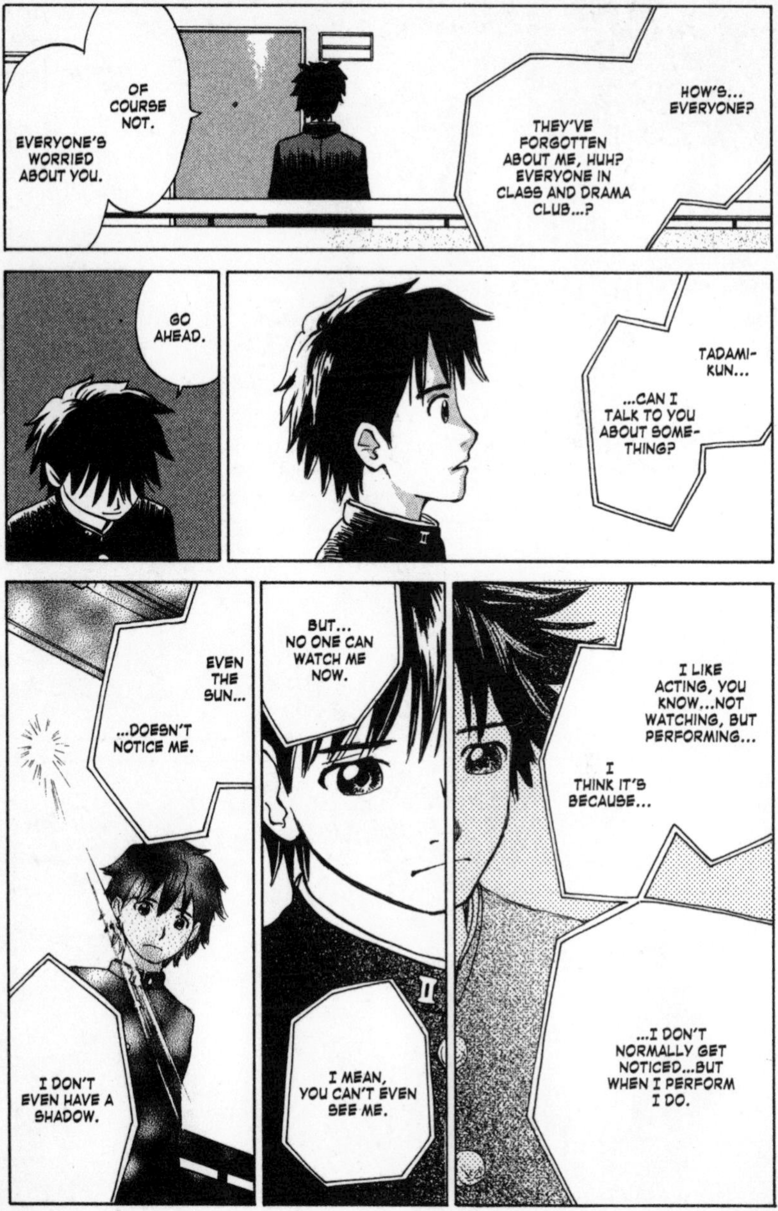
HOW'S... EVERYONE?
THEY'VE FORGOTTEN ABOUT ME, HUH? EVERYONE IN CLASS AND DRAMA CLUB...?
OF COURSE NOT.
EVERYONE'S WORRIED ABOUT YOU.
TADAMI-KUN...
...CAN I TALK TO YOU ABOUT SOME-THING?
GO AHEAD.
I LIKE ACTING, YOU KNOW...NOT WATCHING, BUT PERFORMING...
I THINK IT'S BECAUSE...
...I DON'T NORMALLY GET NOTICED...BUT WHEN I PERFORM I DO.
BUT... NO ONE CAN WATCH ME NOW.
I MEAN, YOU CAN'T EVEN SEE ME.
EVEN THE SUN...
...DOESN'T NOTICE ME.
I DON'T EVEN HAVE A SHADOW.

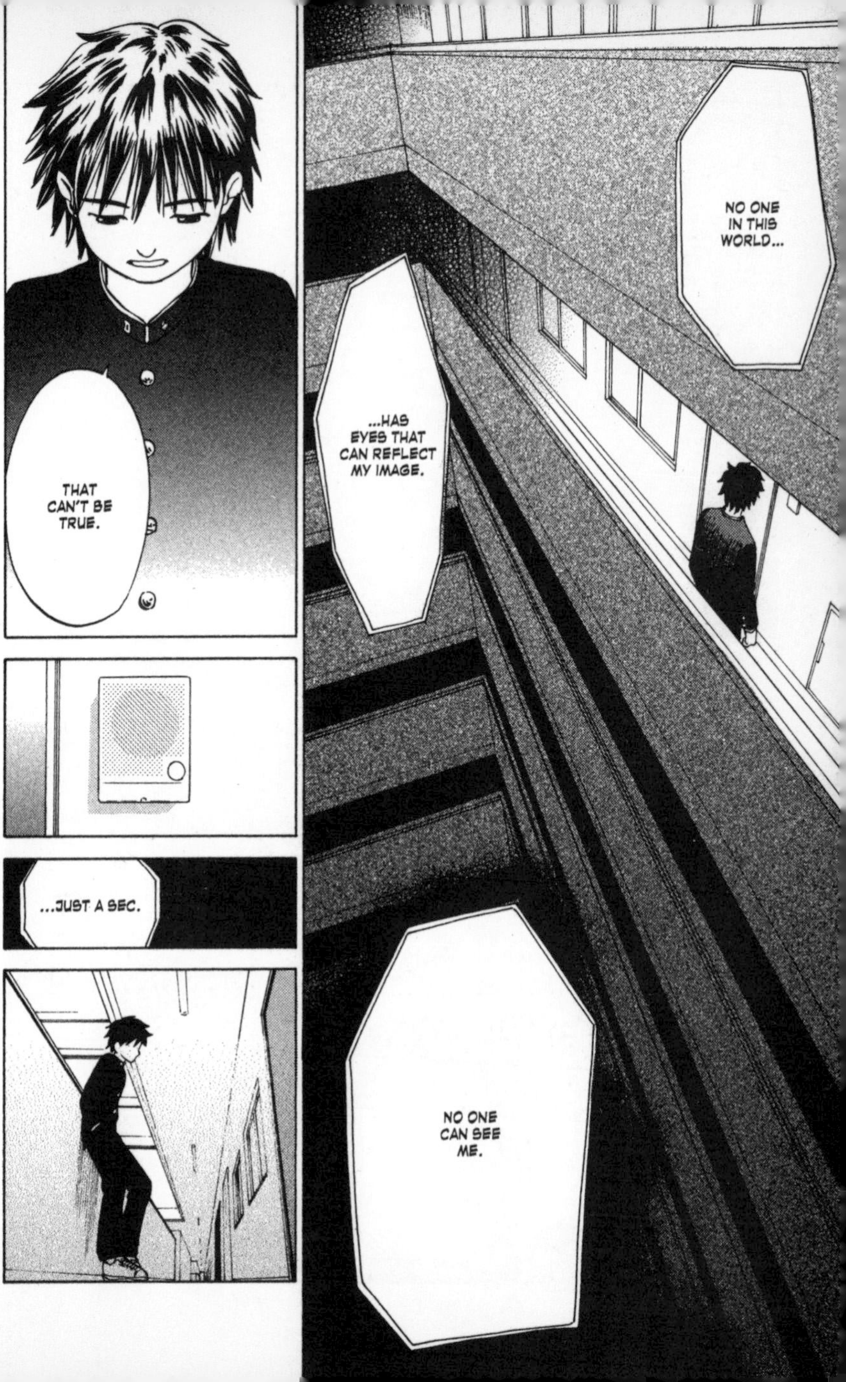
NO ONE IN THIS WORLD...
...HAS EYES THAT CAN REFLECT MY IMAGE.
NO ONE CAN SEE ME.
THAT CAN'T BE TRUE.
...JUST A SEC.

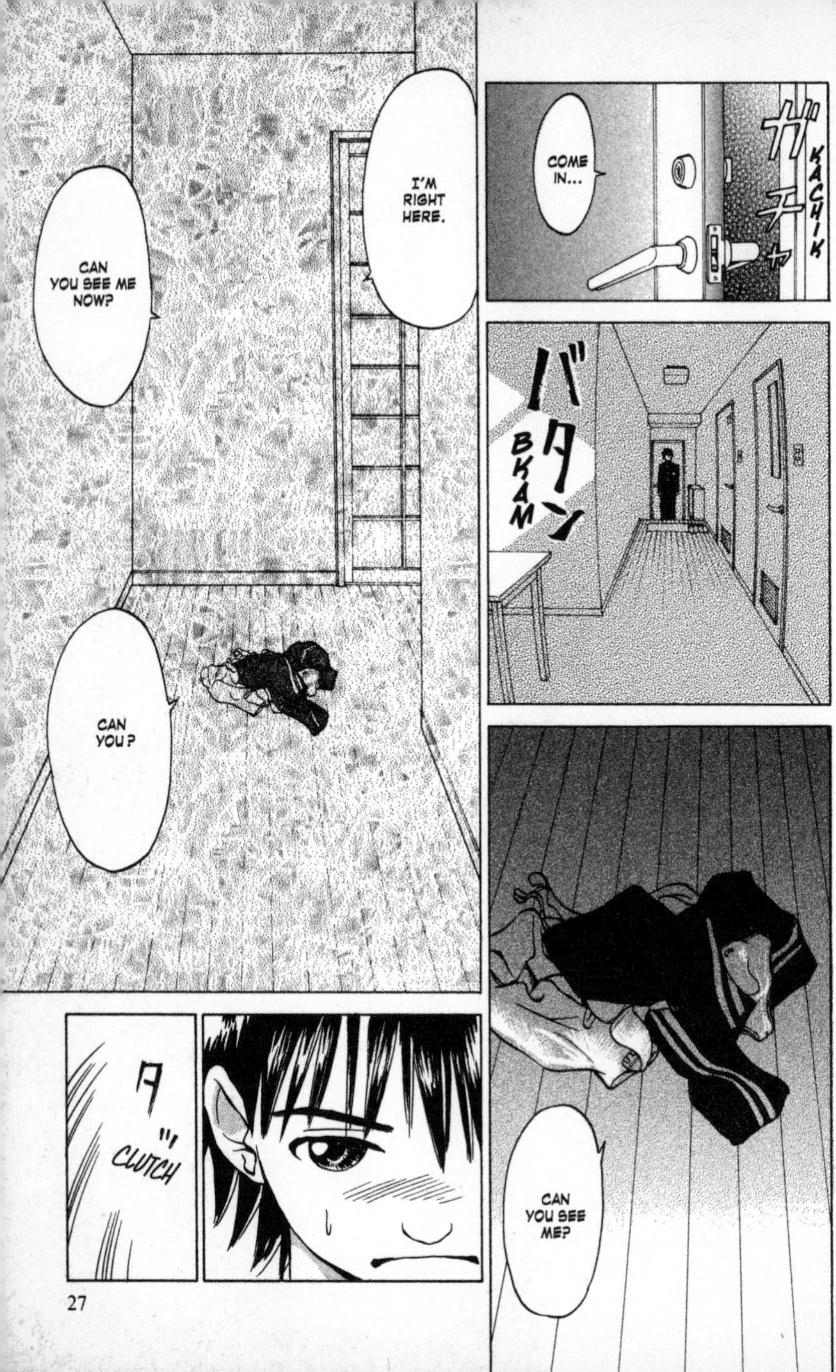
COME IN...
ガチャ
KACHIK
バタン
BKAM
CAN YOU SEE ME?
I'M RIGHT HERE.
CAN YOU SEE ME NOW?
CAN YOU?
タッ
CLUTCH

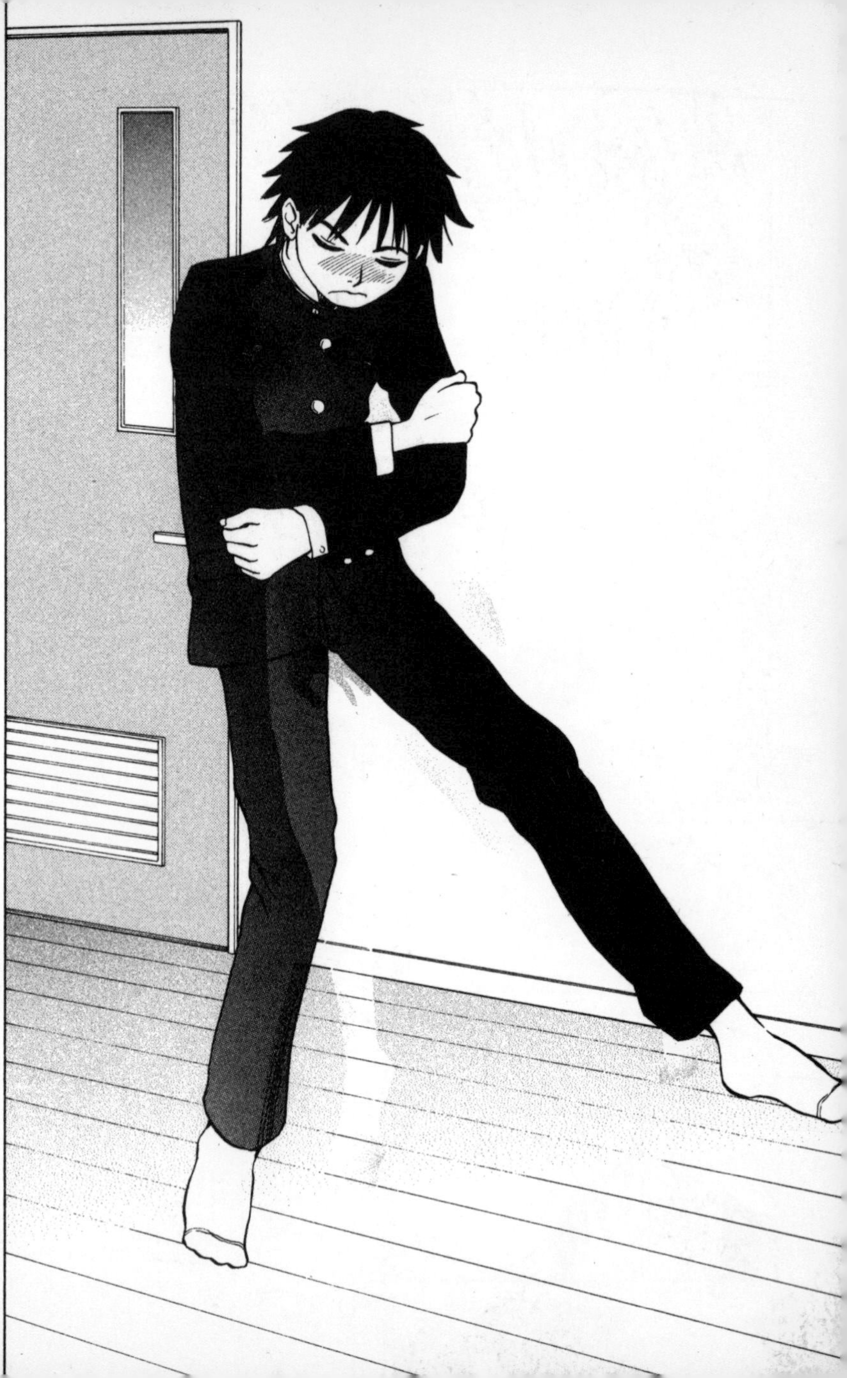

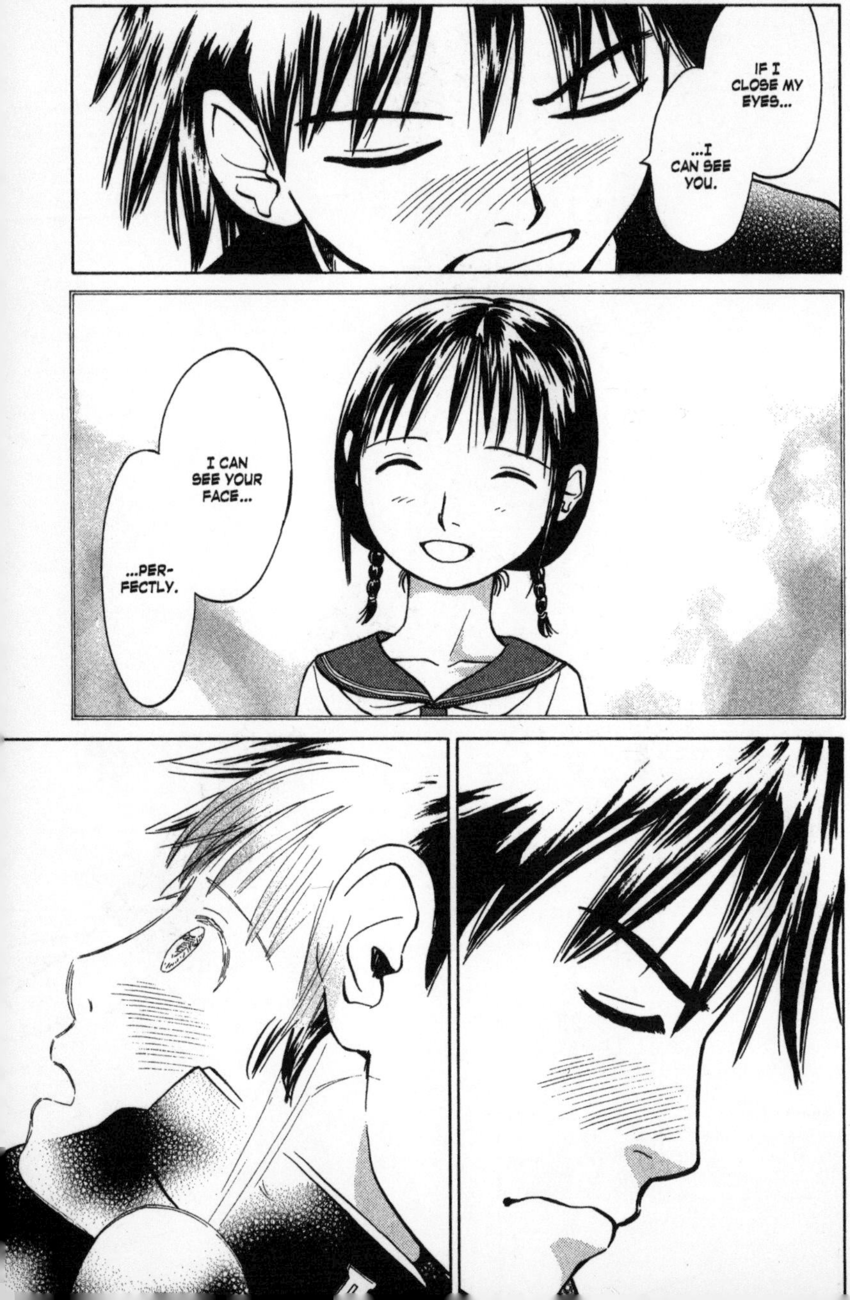
IF I CLOSE MY EYES...
...I CAN SEE YOU.
I CAN SEE YOUR FACE...
...PER-FECTLY.

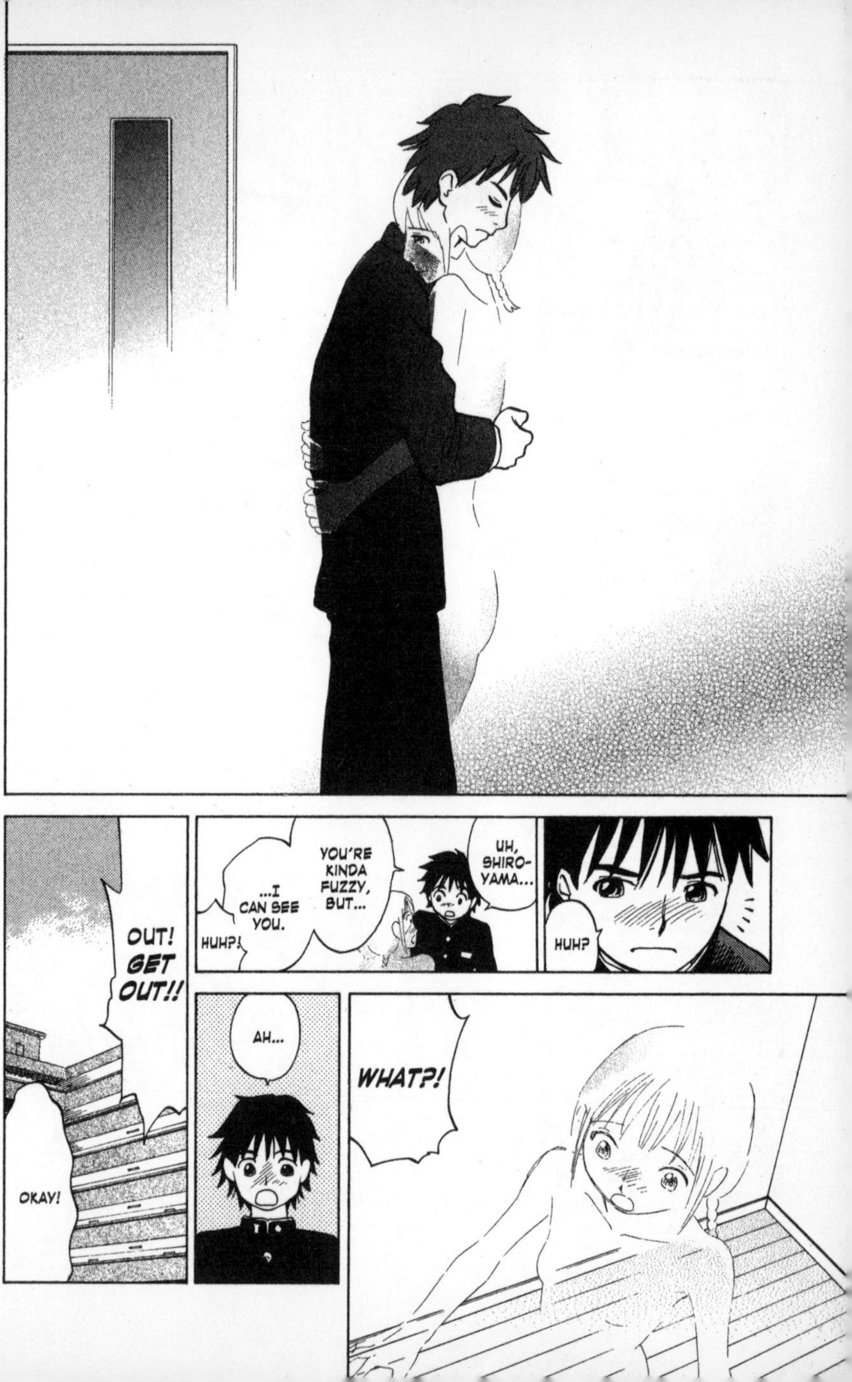
HUH?
UH, SHIRO-YAMA...
YOU'RE KINDA FUZZY, BUT...
...I CAN SEE YOU.
HUH?!
WHAT?!
AH...
OUT! GET OUT!!
OKAY!

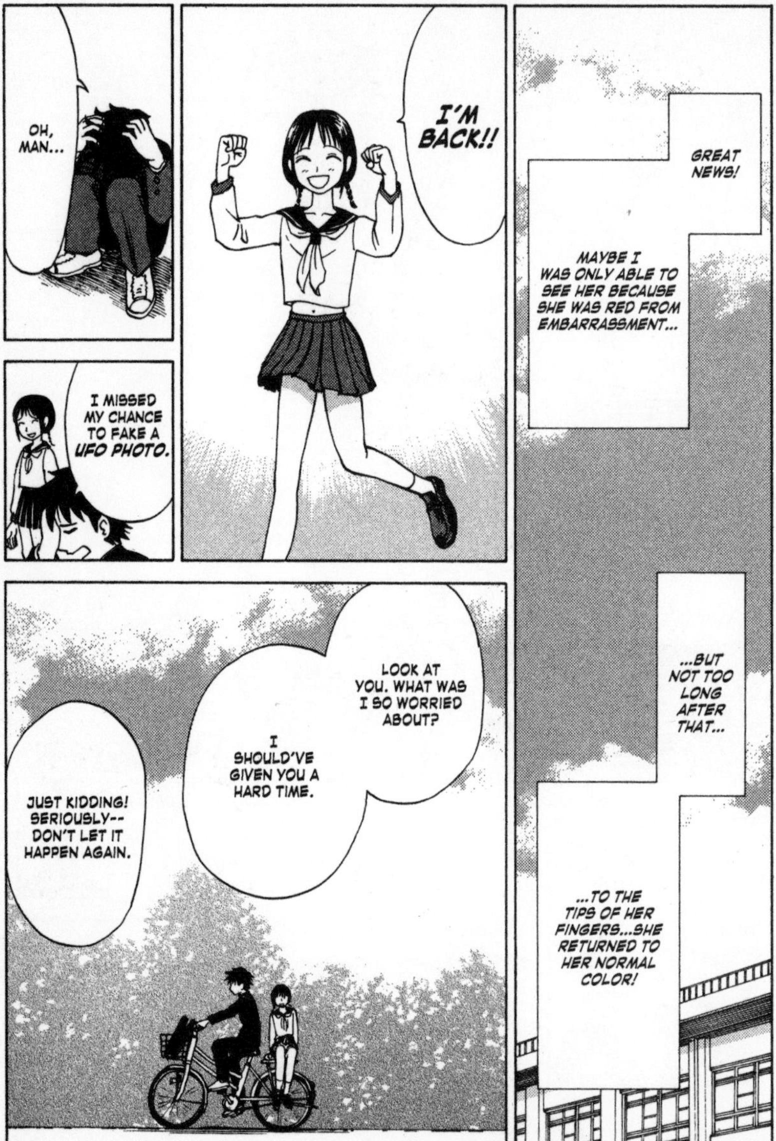
GREAT NEWS!
MAYBE I WAS ONLY ABLE TO SEE HER BECAUSE SHE WAS RED FROM EMBARRASSMENT...
...BUT NOT TOO LONG AFTER THAT...
...TO THE TIPS OF HER FINGERS...SHE RETURNED TO HER NORMAL COLOR!
I'M BACK!!
OH, MAN...
I MISSED MY CHANCE TO FAKE A UFO PHOTO.
LOOK AT YOU. WHAT WAS I SO WORRIED ABOUT?
I SHOULD'VE GIVEN YOU A HARD TIME.
JUST KIDDING! SERIOUSLY-- DON'T LET IT HAPPEN AGAIN.

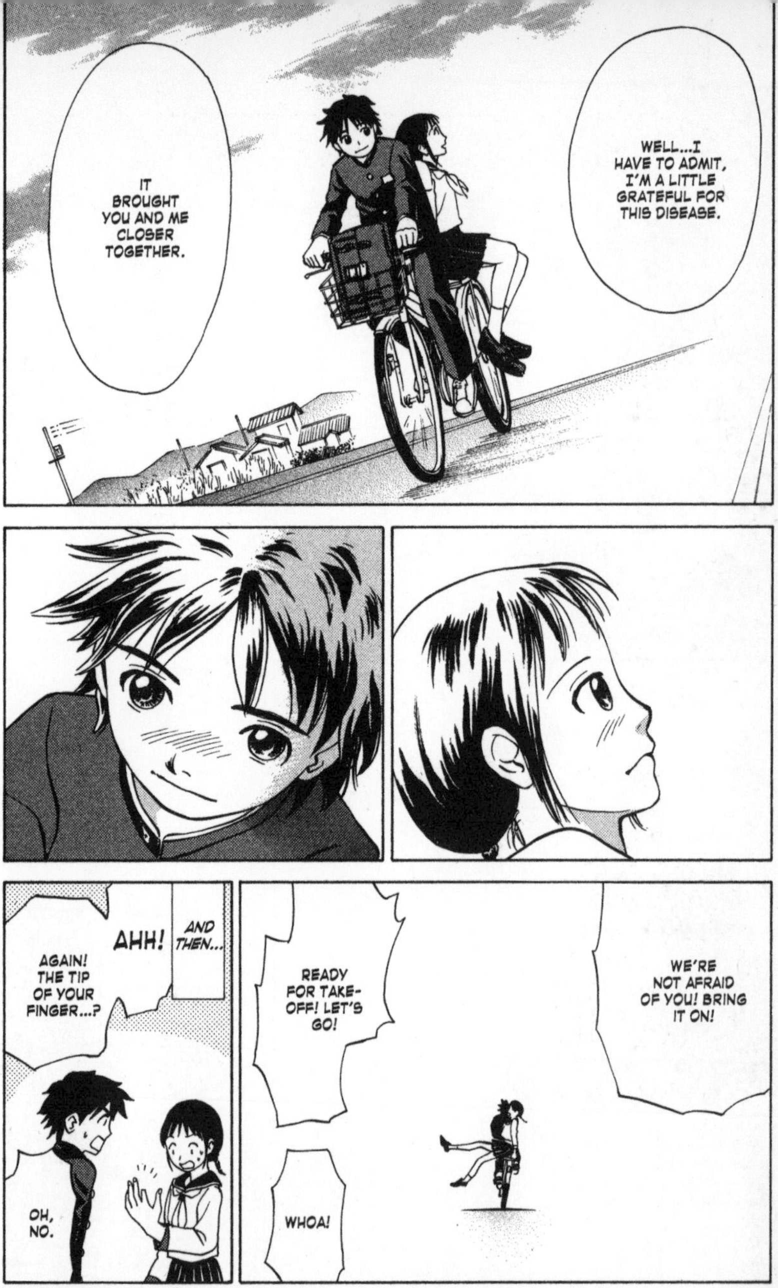
WELL...I HAVE TO ADMIT, I'M A LITTLE GRATEFUL FOR THIS DISEASE.
IT BROUGHT YOU AND ME CLOSER TOGETHER.
WE'RE NOT AFRAID OF YOU! BRING IT ON!
READY FOR TAKE-OFF! LET'S GO!
WHOA!
AND THEN...
AHH!
AGAIN! THE TIP OF YOUR FINGER...?
OH, NO.

PART 2 Introducing Okouchi-san

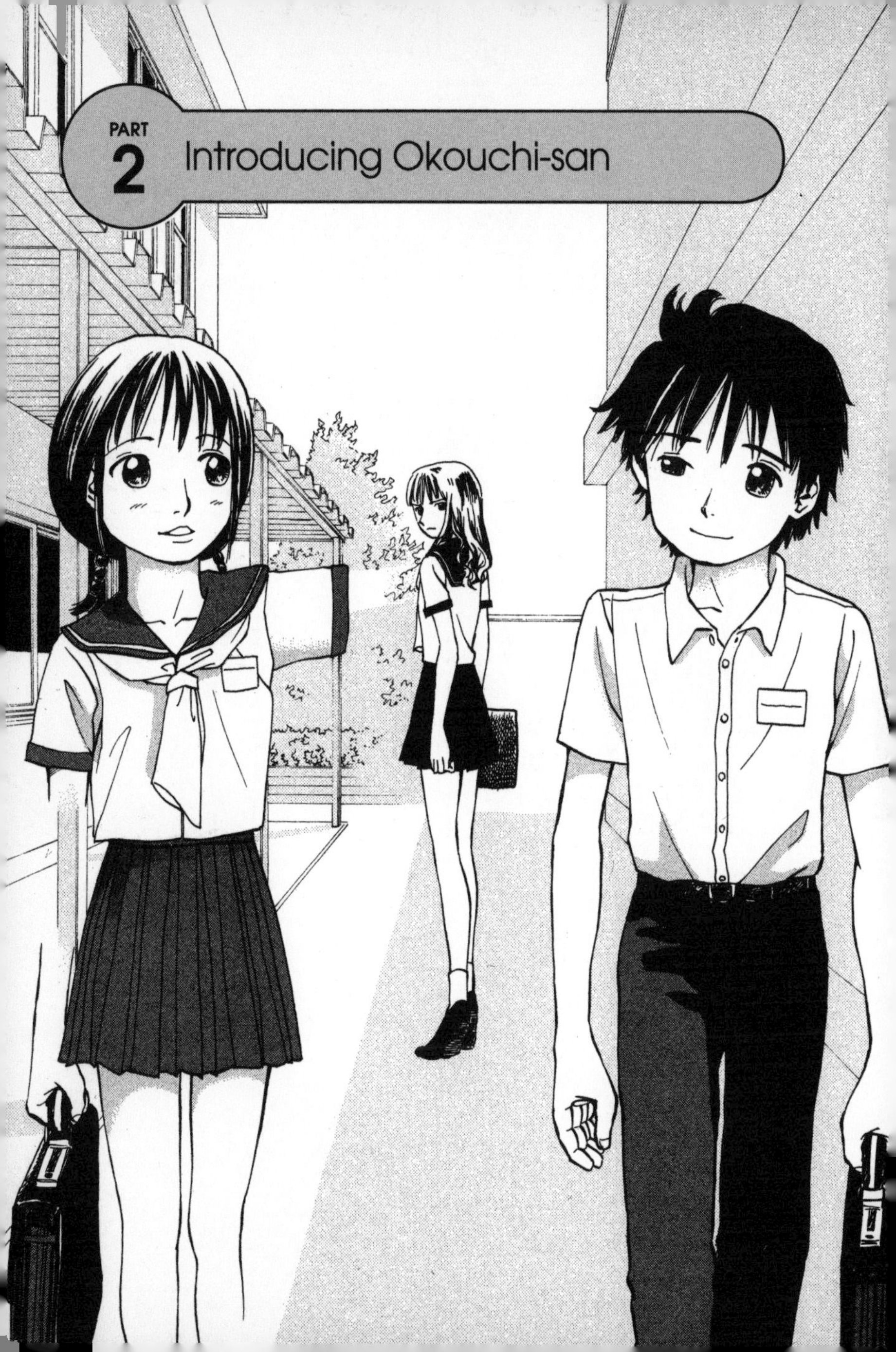

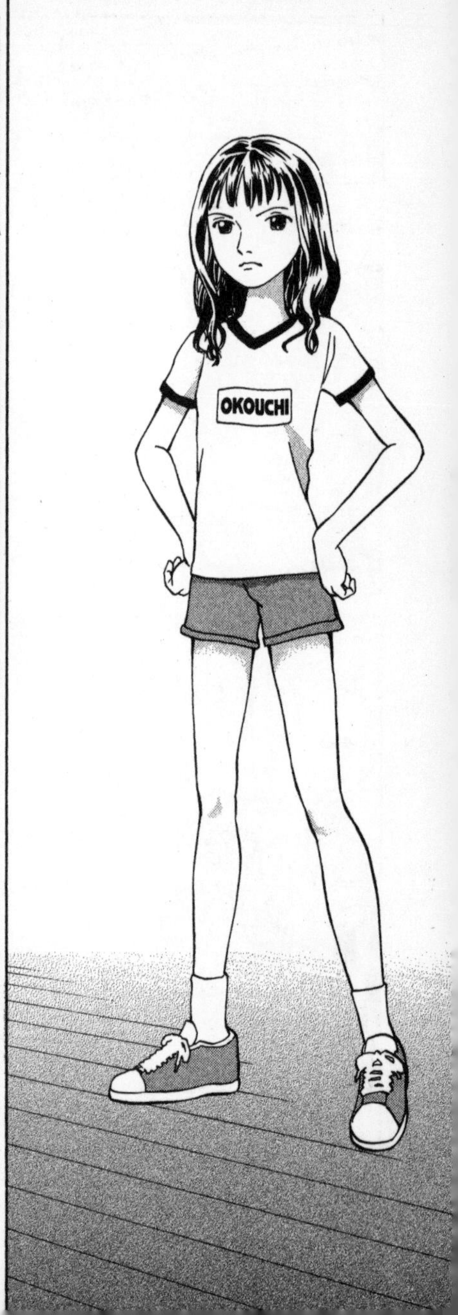
OKOUCHI
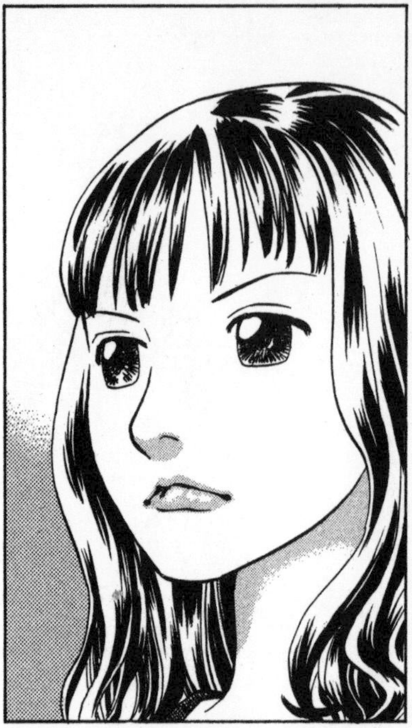
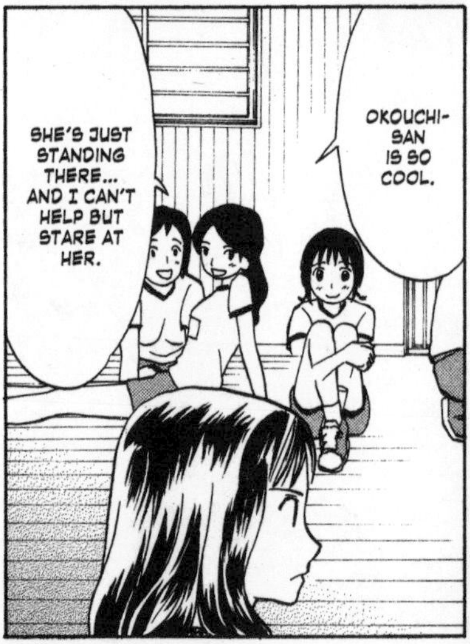
OKOUCHI-SAN IS SO COOL.
SHE'S JUST STANDING THERE... AND I CAN'T HELP BUT STARE AT HER.

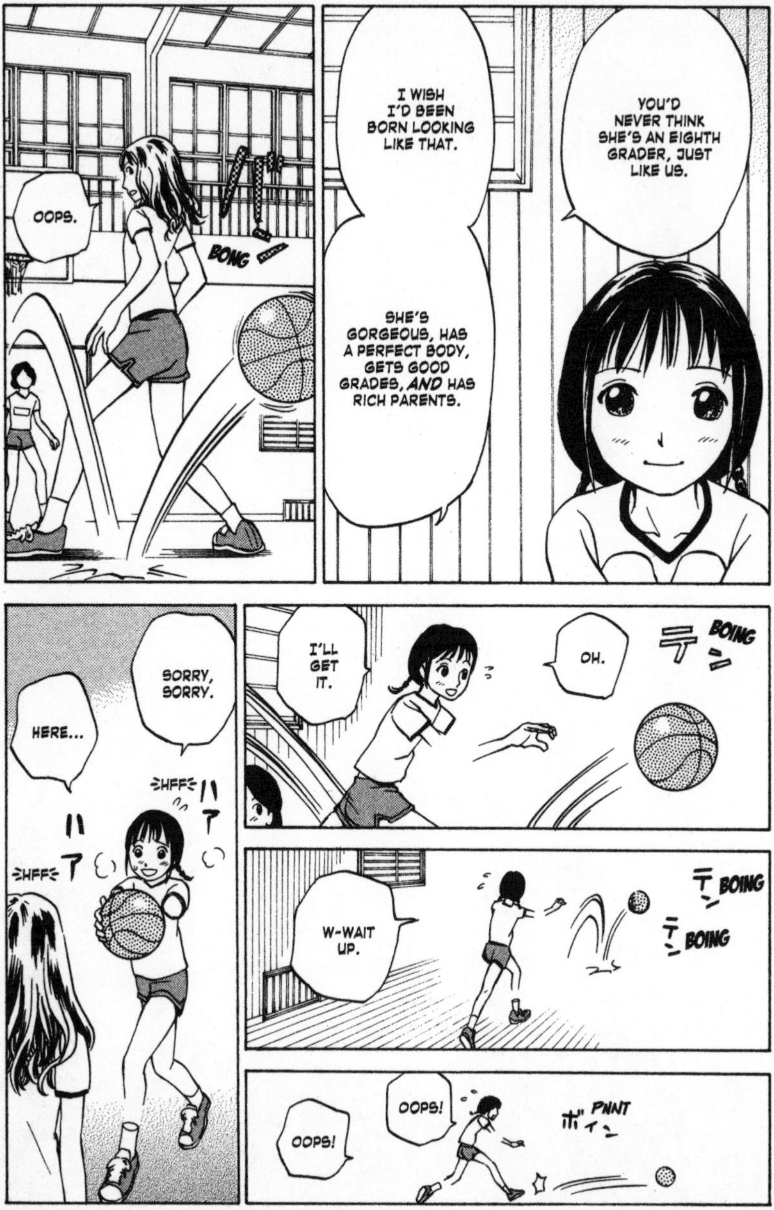
YOU'D NEVER THINK SHE'S AN EIGHTH GRADER, JUST LIKE US.
I WISH I'D BEEN BORN LOOKING LIKE THAT.
SHE'S GORGEOUS, HAS A PERFECT BODY, GETS GOOD GRADES, *AND* HAS RICH PARENTS.
OOPS.
BONG
BOING
OH.
I'LL GET IT.
BOING
BOING
W-WAIT UP.
PNNT
OOPS!
OOPS!
SORRY, SORRY.
HERE...
HFF
HFF

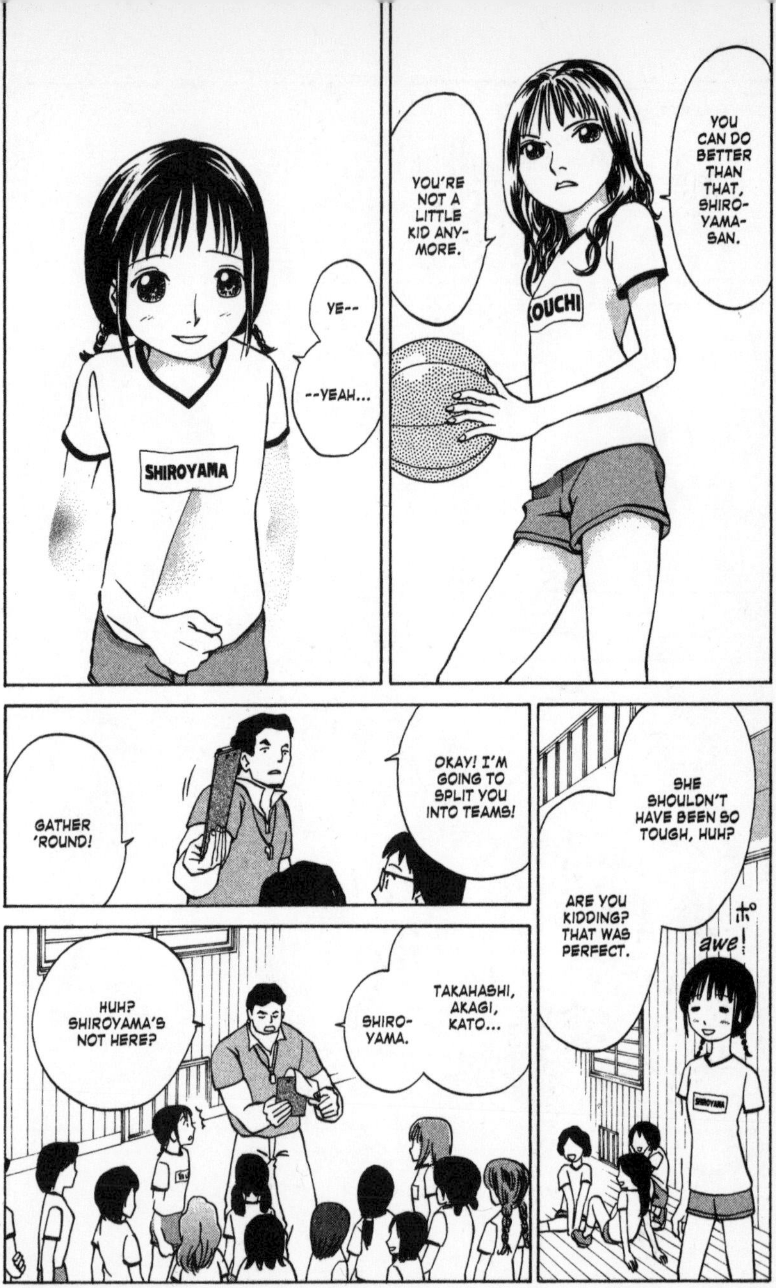
YOU CAN DO BETTER THAN THAT, SHIRO-YAMA-SAN.
YOU'RE NOT A LITTLE KID ANY-MORE.
KOUCHI
YE--
--YEAH...
SHIROYAMA
SHE SHOULDN'T HAVE BEEN SO TOUGH, HUH?
ARE YOU KIDDING? THAT WAS PERFECT.
awe!
OKAY! I'M GOING TO SPLIT YOU INTO TEAMS!
GATHER 'ROUND!
TAKAHASHI, AKAGI, KATO...
SHIRO-YAMA.
HUH? SHIROYAMA'S NOT HERE?

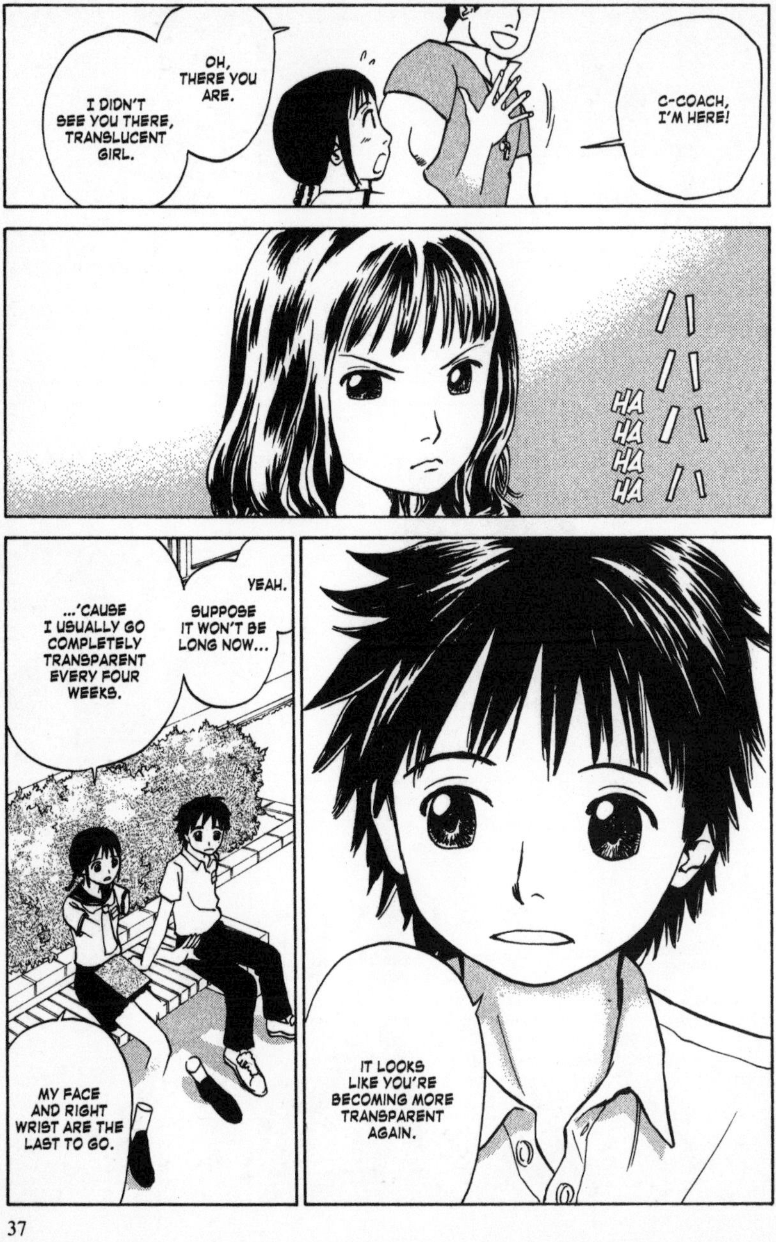
C-COACH, I'M HERE!
OH, THERE YOU ARE.
I DIDN'T SEE YOU THERE, TRANSLUCENT GIRL.
HA HA HA HA
IT LOOKS LIKE YOU'RE BECOMING MORE TRANSPARENT AGAIN.
YEAH.
SUPPOSE IT WON'T BE LONG NOW...
...'CAUSE I USUALLY GO COMPLETELY TRANSPARENT EVERY FOUR WEEKS.
MY FACE AND RIGHT WRIST ARE THE LAST TO GO.

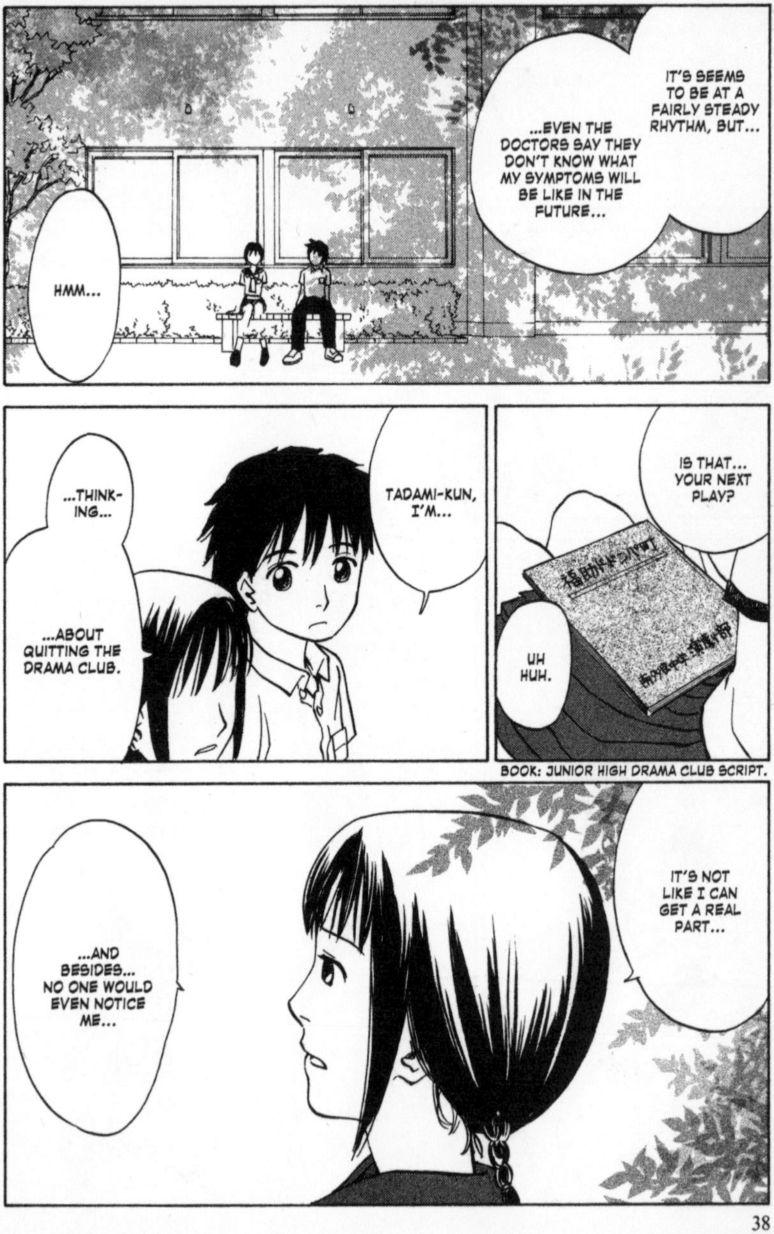
IT'S SEEMS TO BE AT A FAIRLY STEADY RHYTHM, BUT...
...EVEN THE DOCTORS SAY THEY DON'T KNOW WHAT MY SYMPTOMS WILL BE LIKE IN THE FUTURE...
HMM...
IS THAT... YOUR NEXT PLAY?
UH HUH.
BOOK: JUNIOR HIGH DRAMA CLUB SCRIPT.
TADAMI-KUN, I'M...
...THINKING...
...ABOUT QUITTING THE DRAMA CLUB.
IT'S NOT LIKE I CAN GET A REAL PART...
...AND BESIDES... NO ONE WOULD EVEN NOTICE ME...

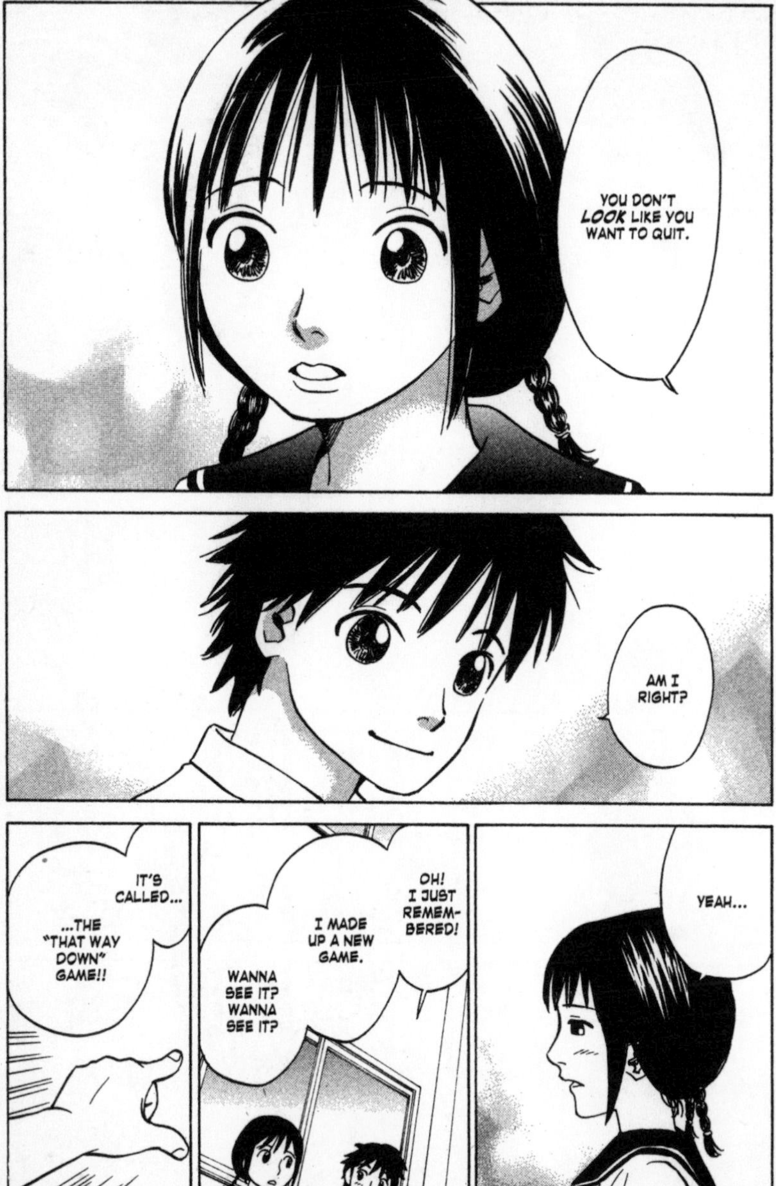
YOU DON'T *LOOK* LIKE YOU WANT TO QUIT.
AM I RIGHT?
YEAH...
OH! I JUST REMEM-BERED!
I MADE UP A NEW GAME.
WANNA SEE IT? WANNA SEE IT?
IT'S CALLED...
...THE "THAT WAY DOWN" GAME!!

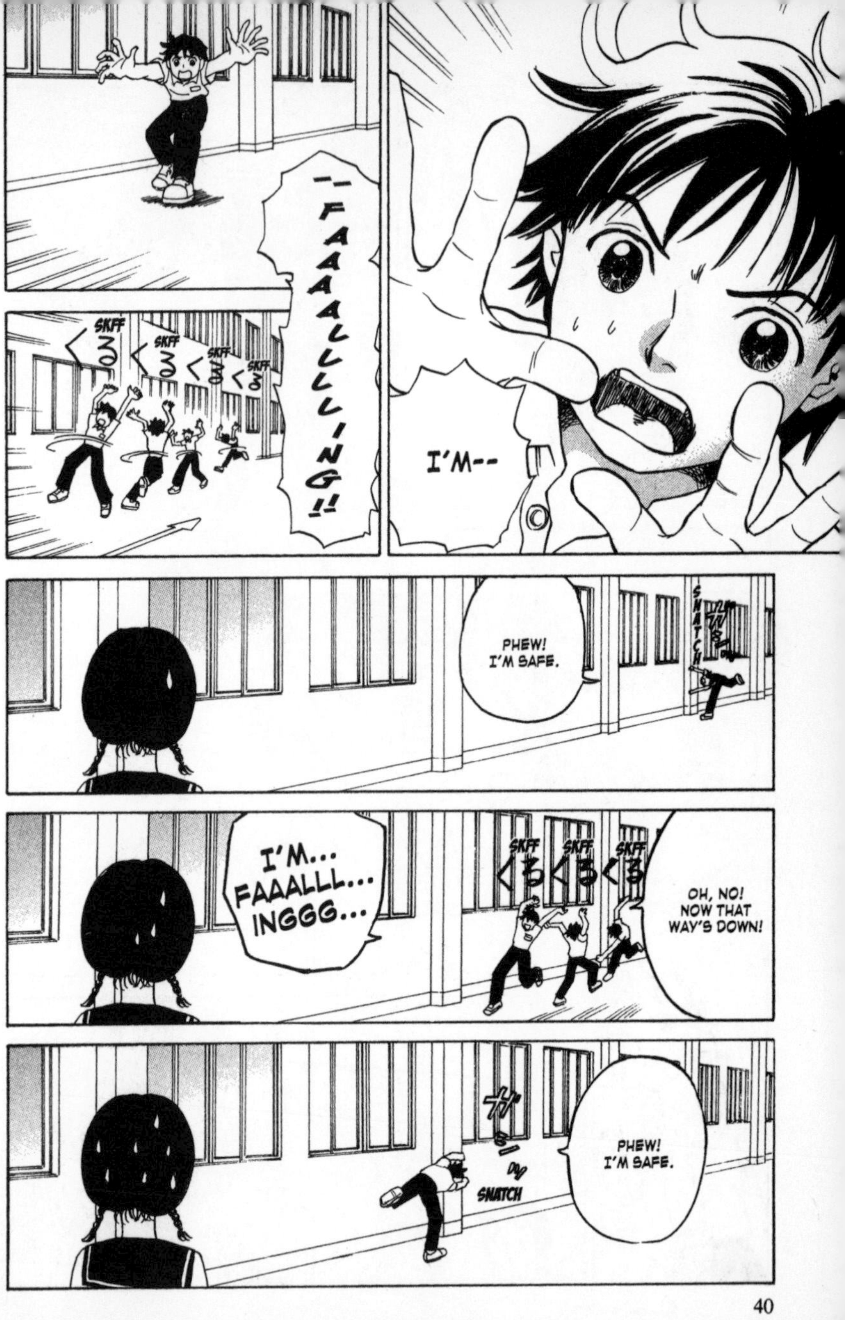
I'M--
--FAAAALLLLLING!!
SKFF
くる
SKFF
くる
SKFF
くる
SKFF
くる
SNATCH
PHEW! I'M SAFE.
OH, NO! NOW THAT WAY'S DOWN!
SKFF
くる
SKFF
くる
SKFF
くる
I'M... FAAALLL... INGGG...
PHEW! I'M SAFE.
SNATCH

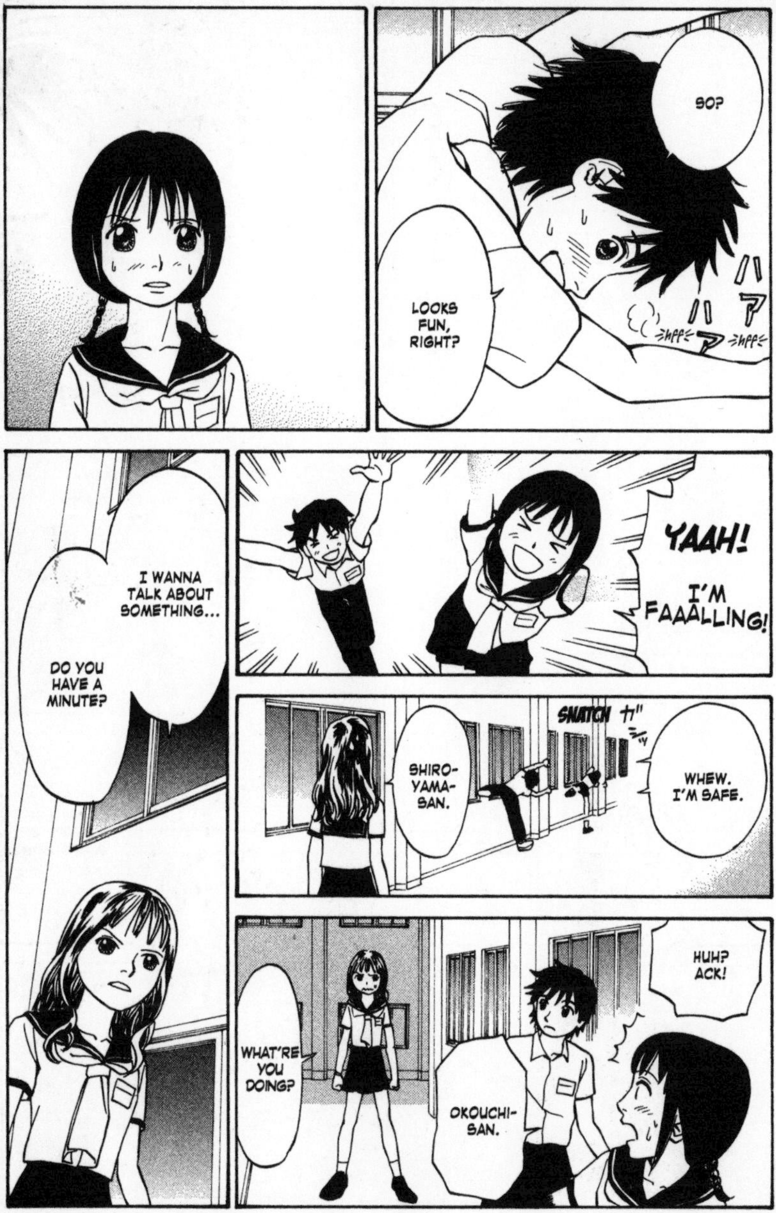
SO?
LOOKS FUN, RIGHT?
ハァ ハァ
hff hff
YAAH!
I'M FAAALLING!
SNATCH ガッ
WHEW. I'M SAFE.
SHIRO-YAMA-SAN.
HUH? ACK!
OKOUCHI-SAN.
WHAT'RE YOU DOING?
I WANNA TALK ABOUT SOMETHING...
DO YOU HAVE A MINUTE?

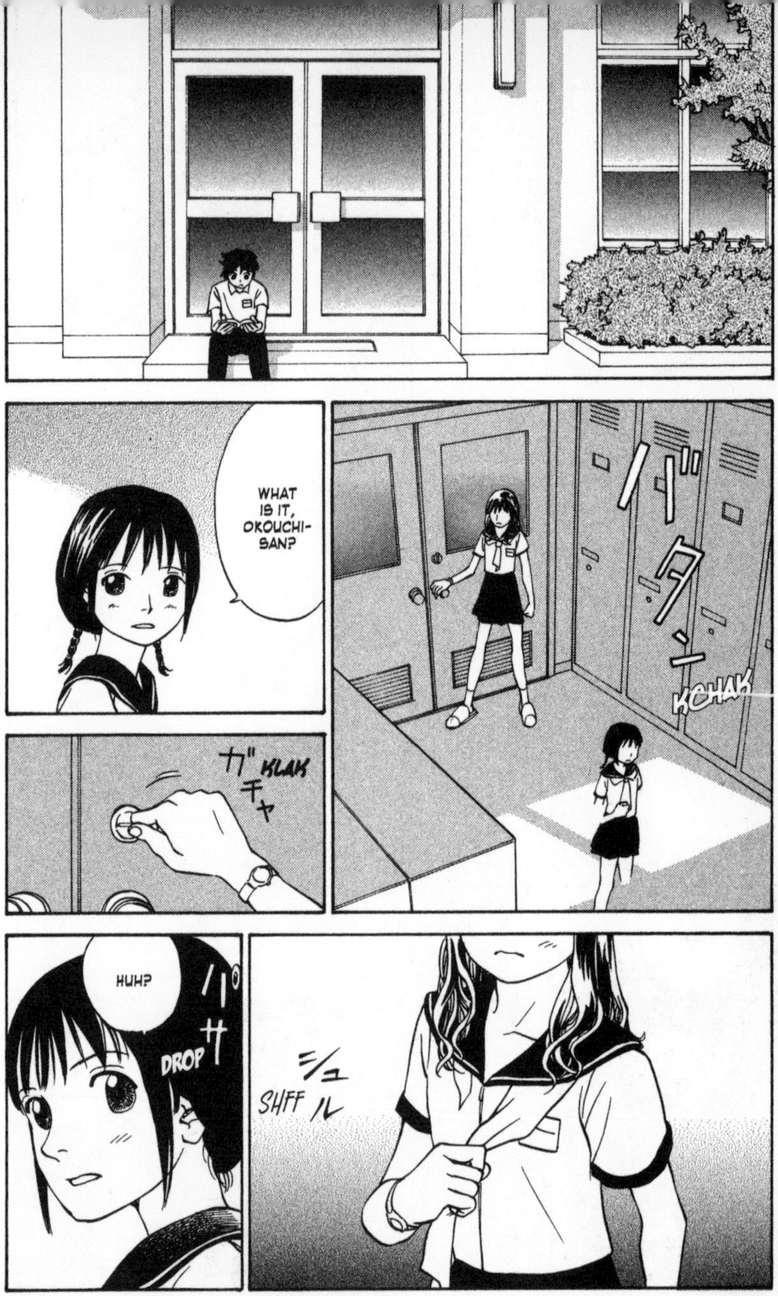
バダン
KCHAK
WHAT IS IT, OKOUCHI-SAN?
ガチャ
KLAK
シュル
SHFF
HUH?
パサ
DROP

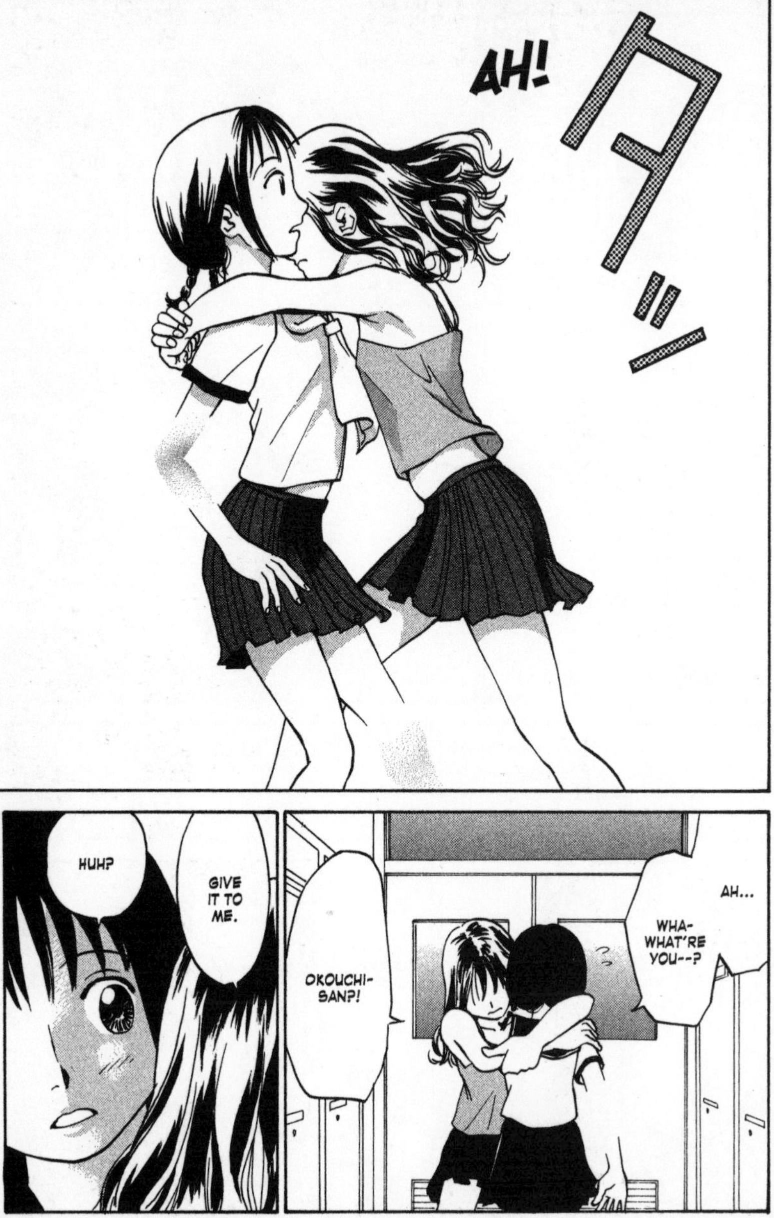
AH!
AH...
WHA-WHAT'RE YOU--?
OKOUCHI-SAN?!
GIVE IT TO ME.
HUH?

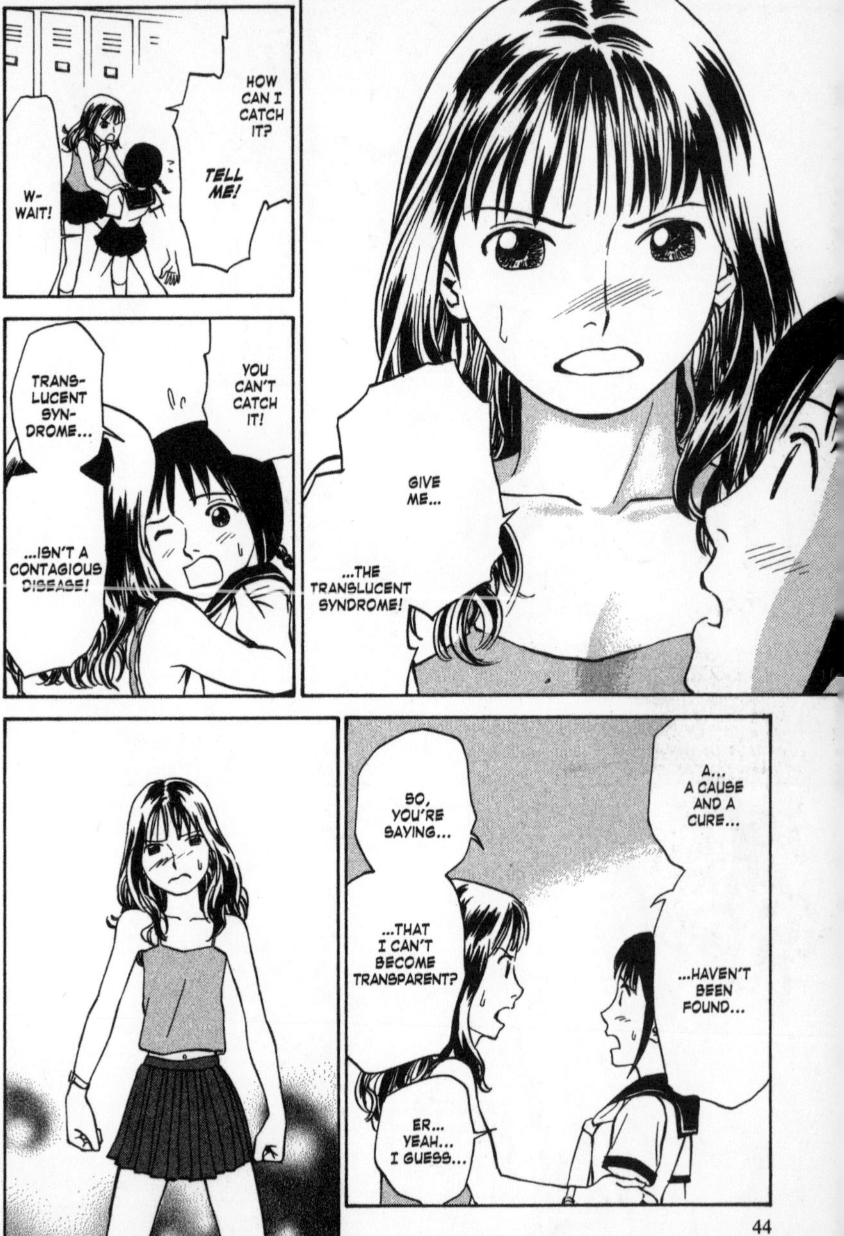
GIVE ME...
...THE TRANSLUCENT SYNDROME!
HOW CAN I CATCH IT?
TELL ME!
W-WAIT!
YOU CAN'T CATCH IT!
TRANS-LUCENT SYN-DROME...
...ISN'T A CONTAGIOUS DISEASE!
A... A CAUSE AND A CURE...
...HAVEN'T BEEN FOUND...
SO, YOU'RE SAYING...
...THAT I CAN'T BECOME TRANSPARENT?
ER... YEAH... I GUESS...

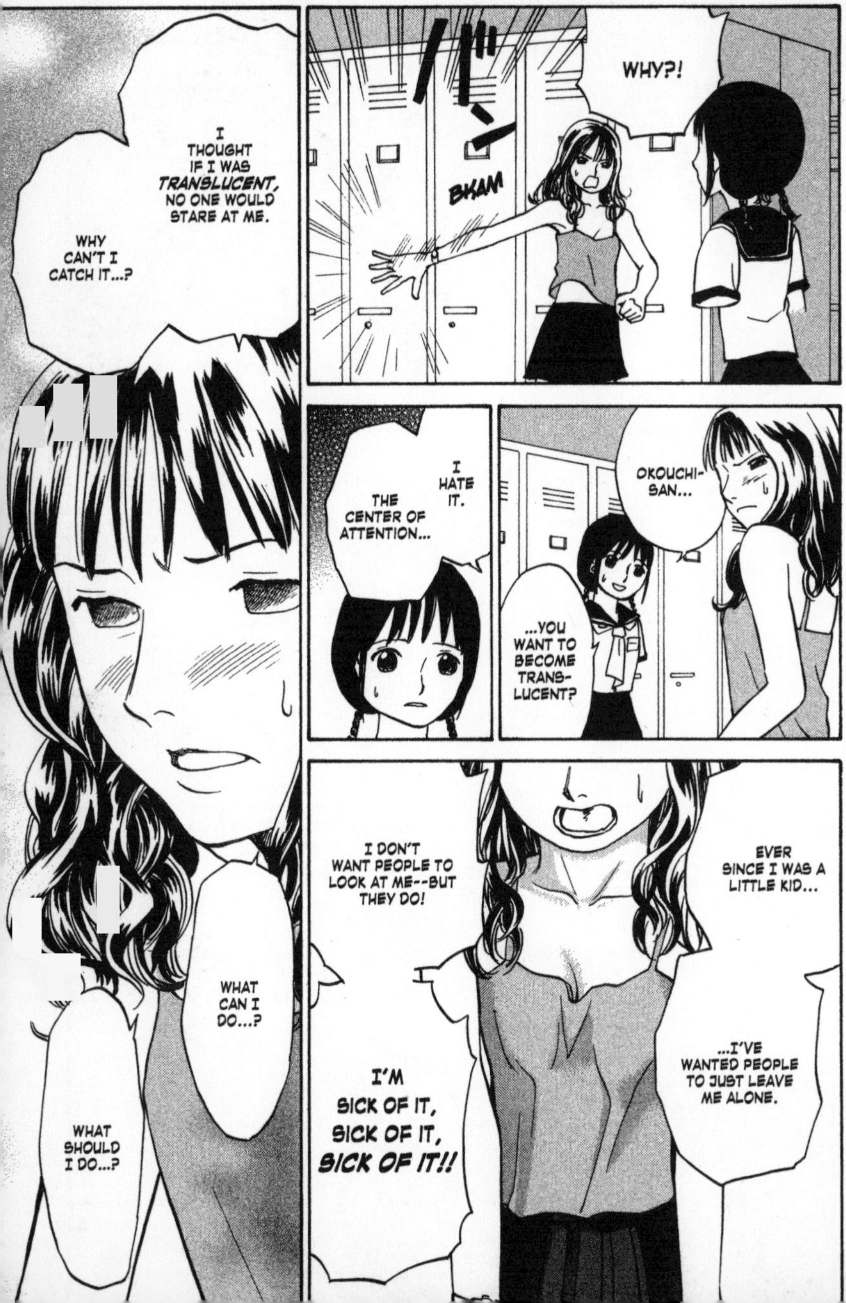
WHY?!
BKAM
OKOUCHI-SAN...
...YOU WANT TO BECOME TRANSLUCENT?
I HATE IT.
THE CENTER OF ATTENTION...
EVER SINCE I WAS A LITTLE KID...
...I'VE WANTED PEOPLE TO JUST LEAVE ME ALONE.
I DON'T WANT PEOPLE TO LOOK AT ME--BUT THEY DO!
I'M SICK OF IT, SICK OF IT, *SICK OF IT!!*
I THOUGHT IF I WAS *TRANSLUCENT,* NO ONE WOULD STARE AT ME.
WHY CAN'T I CATCH IT...?
WHAT CAN I DO...?
WHAT SHOULD I DO...?

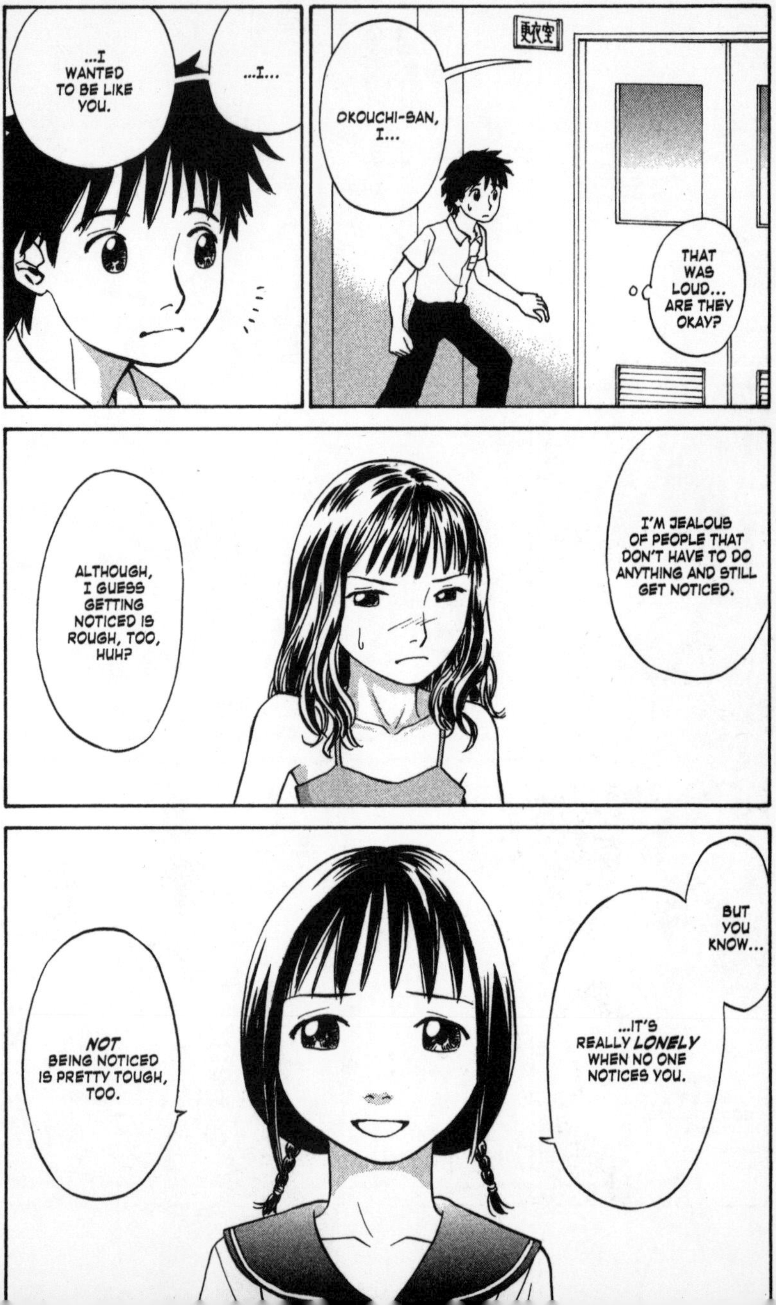
更衣室
THAT WAS LOUD... ARE THEY OKAY?
OKOUCHI-SAN, I...
...I...
...I WANTED TO BE LIKE YOU.
I'M JEALOUS OF PEOPLE THAT DON'T HAVE TO DO ANYTHING AND STILL GET NOTICED.
ALTHOUGH, I GUESS GETTING NOTICED IS ROUGH, TOO, HUH?
BUT YOU KNOW...
...IT'S REALLY *LONELY* WHEN NO ONE NOTICES YOU.
NOT BEING NOTICED IS PRETTY TOUGH, TOO.

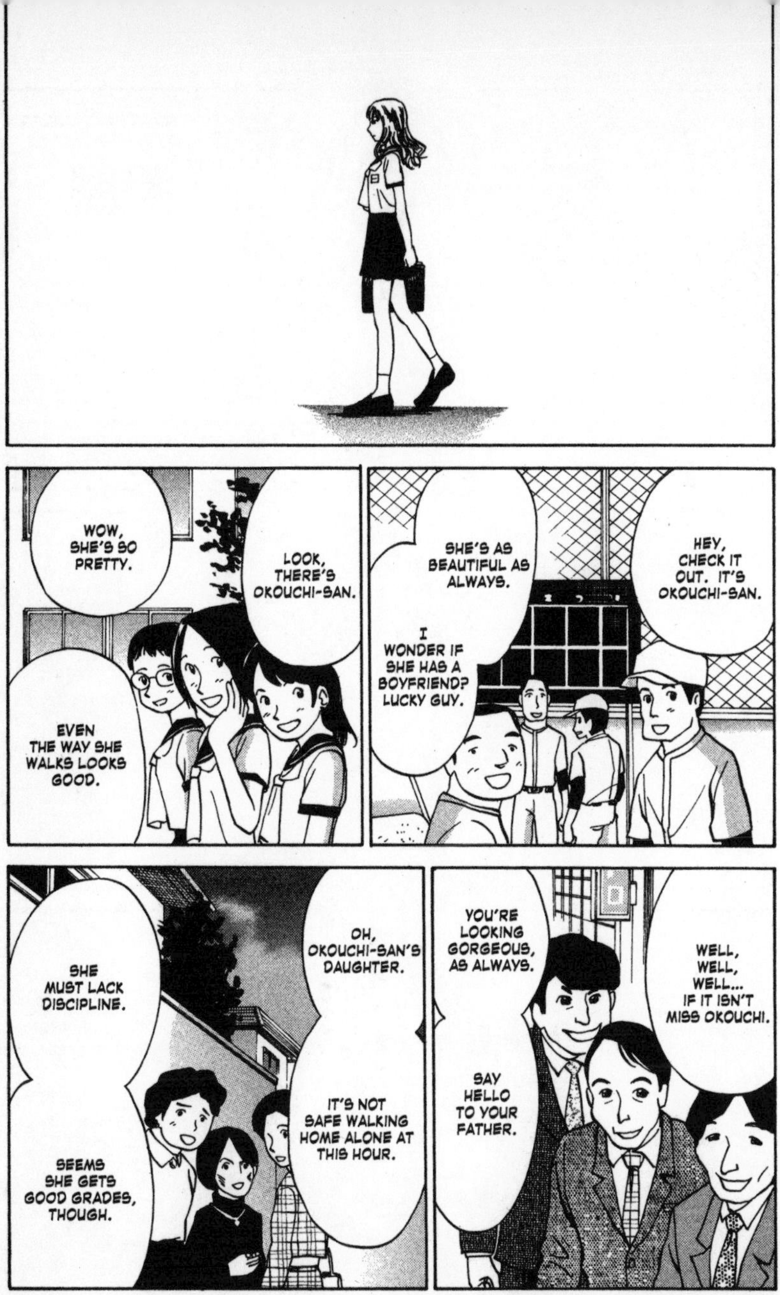
HEY, CHECK IT OUT. IT'S OKOUCHI-SAN.
SHE'S AS BEAUTIFUL AS ALWAYS.
I WONDER IF SHE HAS A BOYFRIEND? LUCKY GUY.
LOOK, THERE'S OKOUCHI-SAN.
WOW, SHE'S SO PRETTY.
EVEN THE WAY SHE WALKS LOOKS GOOD.
WELL, WELL, WELL... IF IT ISN'T MISS OKOUCHI.
YOU'RE LOOKING GORGEOUS, AS ALWAYS.
SAY HELLO TO YOUR FATHER.
OH, OKOUCHI-SAN'S DAUGHTER.
SHE MUST LACK DISCIPLINE.
IT'S NOT SAFE WALKING HOME ALONE AT THIS HOUR.
SEEMS SHE GETS GOOD GRADES, THOUGH.

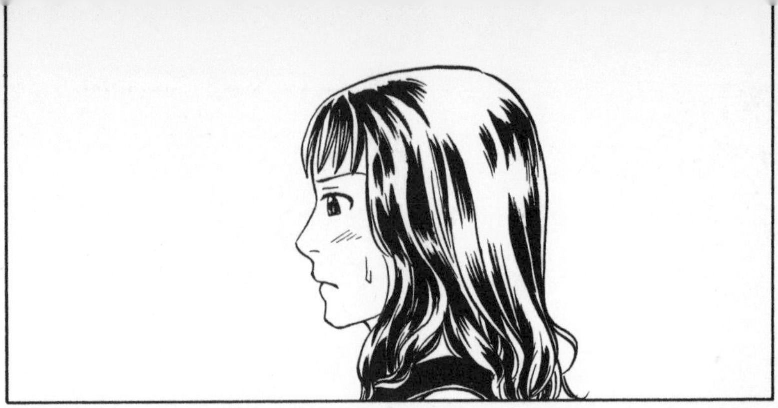

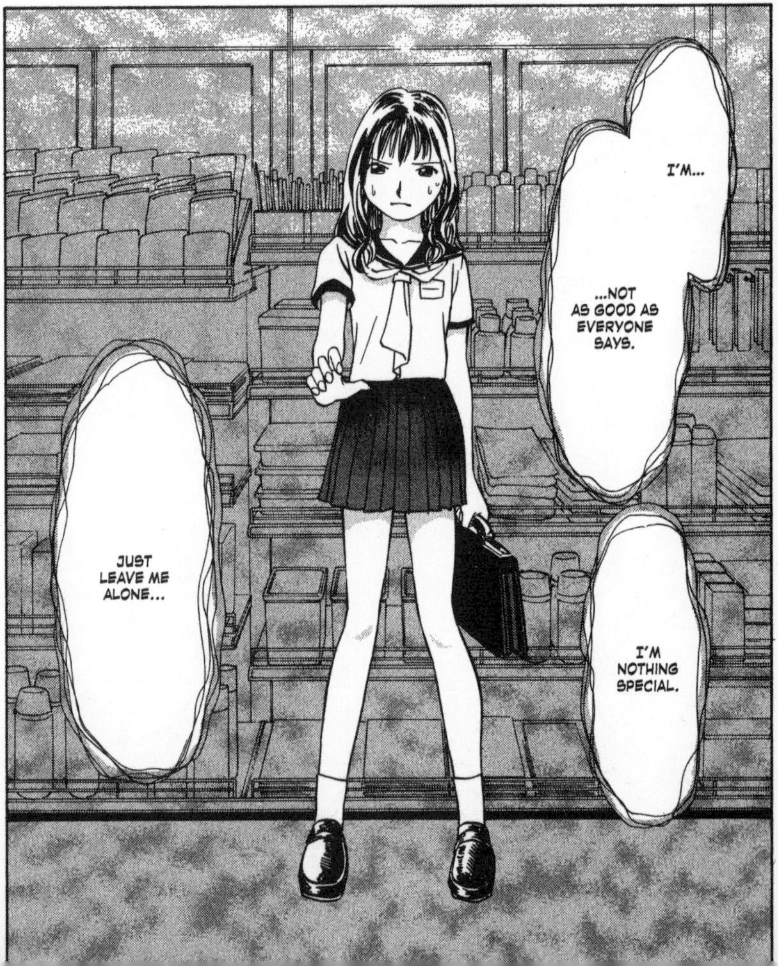
I'M...
...NOT AS GOOD AS EVERYONE SAYS.
I'M NOTHING SPECIAL.
JUST LEAVE ME ALONE...

HFF ハァ HFF ハァ
グッ FTCH
FWSH ダッ
STUDENT BODY PRESIDENT?
ME?

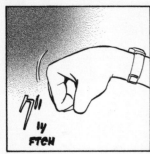

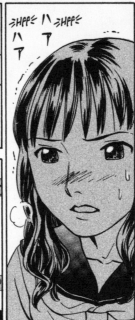

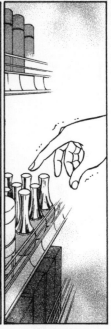

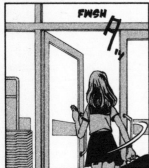

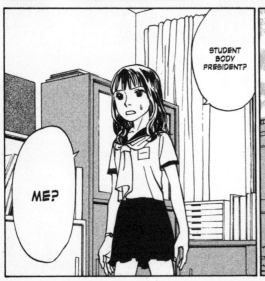

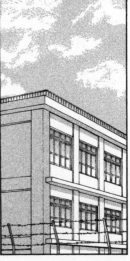

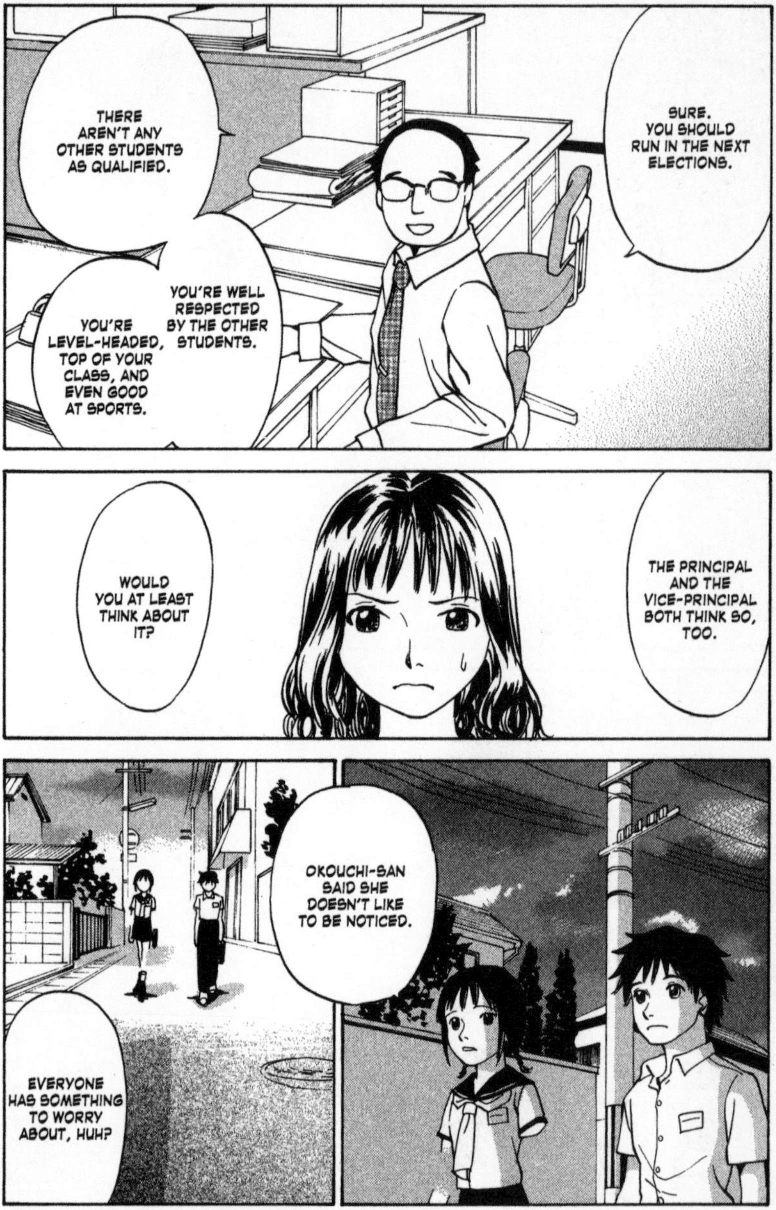
SURE. YOU SHOULD RUN IN THE NEXT ELECTIONS.
THERE AREN'T ANY OTHER STUDENTS AS QUALIFIED.
YOU'RE WELL RESPECTED BY THE OTHER STUDENTS.
YOU'RE LEVEL-HEADED, TOP OF YOUR CLASS, AND EVEN GOOD AT SPORTS.
THE PRINCIPAL AND THE VICE-PRINCIPAL BOTH THINK SO, TOO.
WOULD YOU AT LEAST THINK ABOUT IT?
OKOUCHI-SAN SAID SHE DOESN'T LIKE TO BE NOTICED.
EVERYONE HAS SOMETHING TO WORRY ABOUT, HUH?

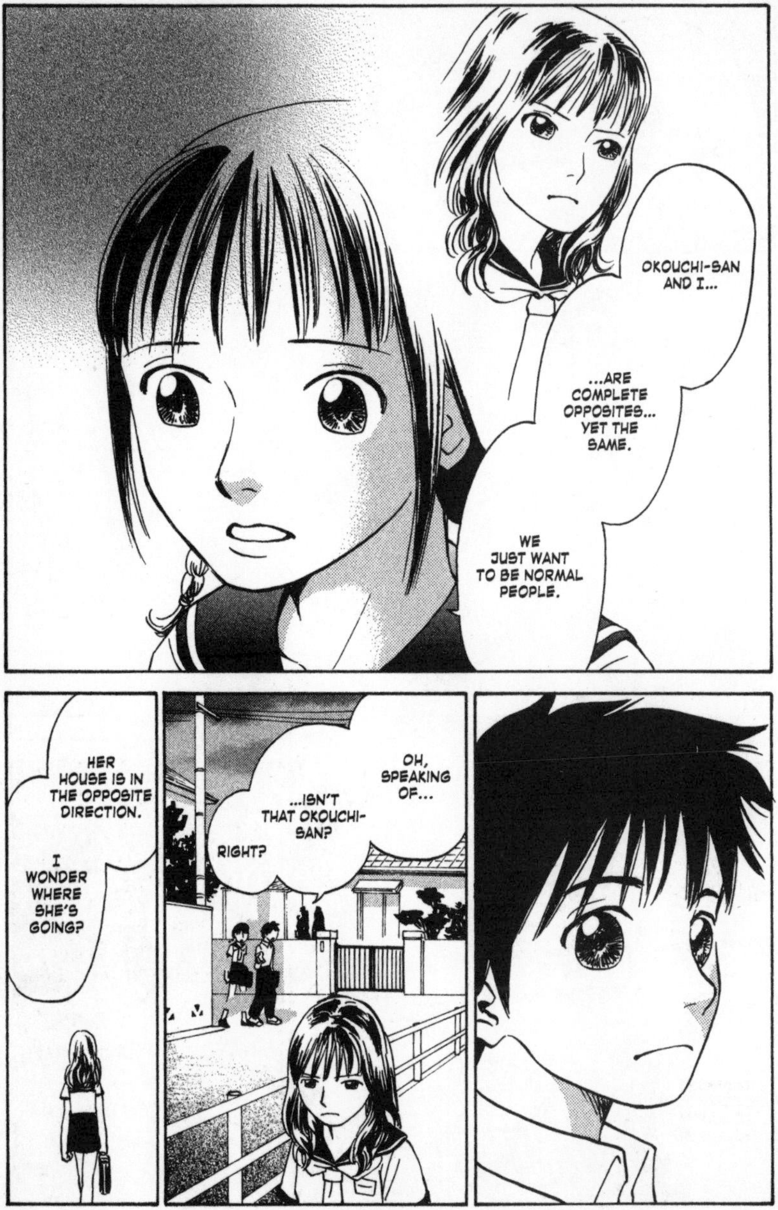
OKOUCHI-SAN AND I...
...ARE COMPLETE OPPOSITES... YET THE SAME.
WE JUST WANT TO BE NORMAL PEOPLE.
OH, SPEAKING OF...
...ISN'T THAT OKOUCHI-SAN?
RIGHT?
HER HOUSE IS IN THE OPPOSITE DIRECTION.
I WONDER WHERE SHE'S GOING?

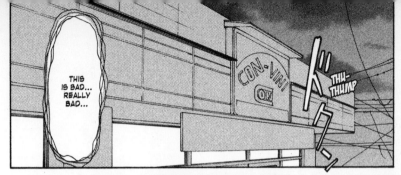

CON-VINI
CN
ドクン
THU-THUMP
THIS IS BAD... REALLY BAD...
IF I GO IN THERE TODAY...
ドクン
THU-THUMP
ドクン
THU-THUMP
...I'M DEFINITELY GONNA DO IT.
THE STORE CLERK WILL SEE ME...
HELLO, THERE.
ドクン
THU-THUMP
ドクン
THU-THUMP
...AND HE'LL CALL THE POLICE.
ドクン
THU-THUMP
I'LL BE A NUISANCE TO THE SCHOOL... AND MY DAD AND MY MOM.
ドクン
THU-THUMP
ドクン
THU-THUMP
MY FRIENDS AND EVERYONE WILL ALL LOOK DOWN ON ME.
ドクン
THU-THUMP
EVEN STILL...

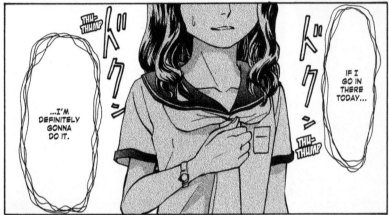

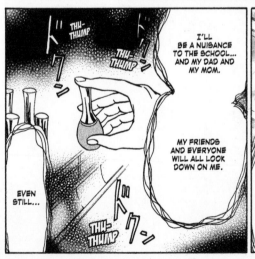

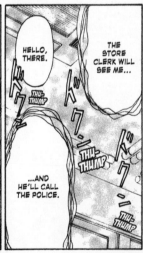

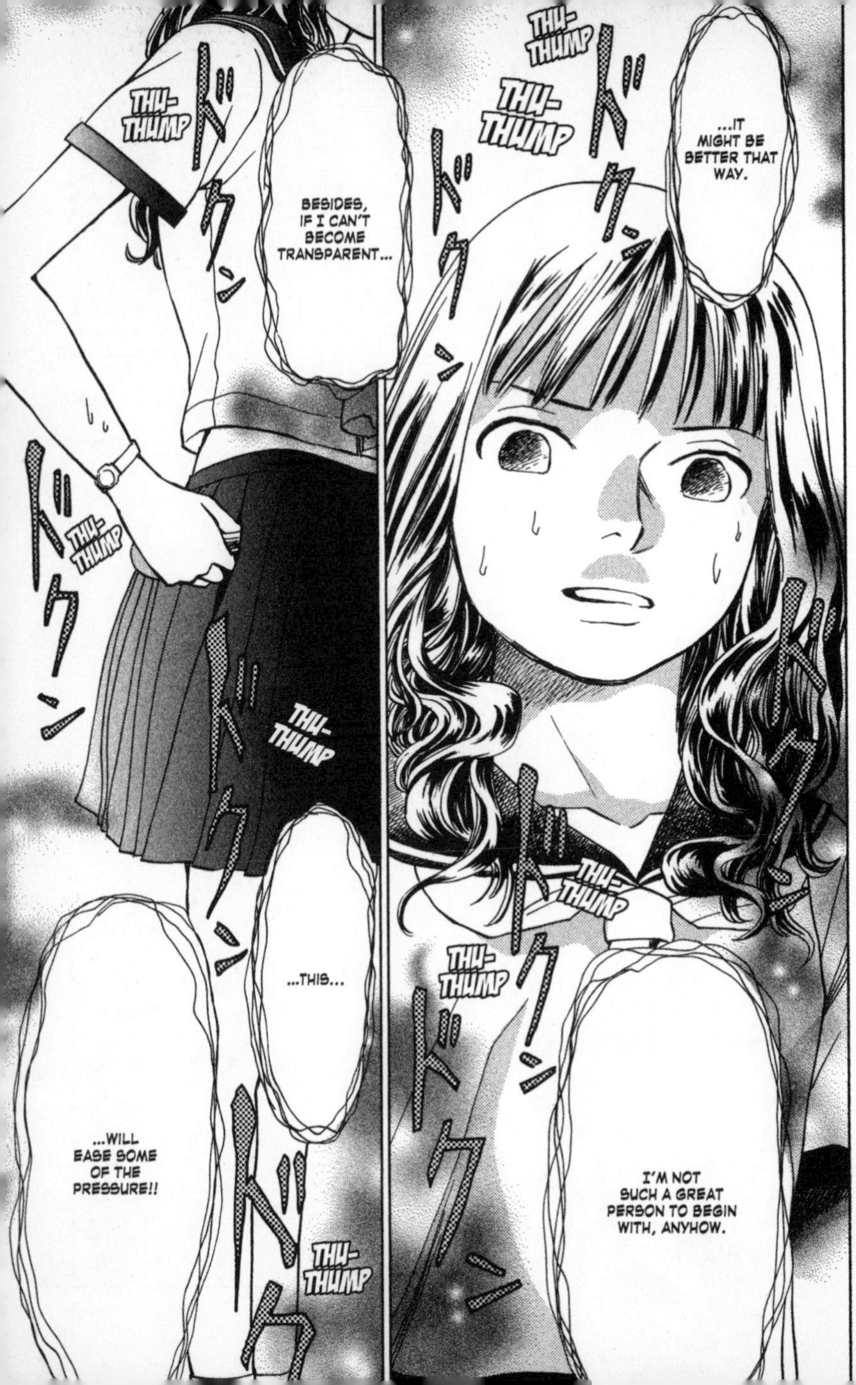

THU-THUMP
THU-THUMP
...IT MIGHT BE BETTER THAT WAY.
THU-THUMP
THU-THUMP
I'M NOT SUCH A GREAT PERSON TO BEGIN WITH, ANYHOW.
THU-THUMP
BESIDES, IF I CAN'T BECOME TRANSPARENT...
THU-THUMP
THU-THUMP
...THIS...
...WILL EASE SOME OF THE PRESSURE!!
THU-THUMP

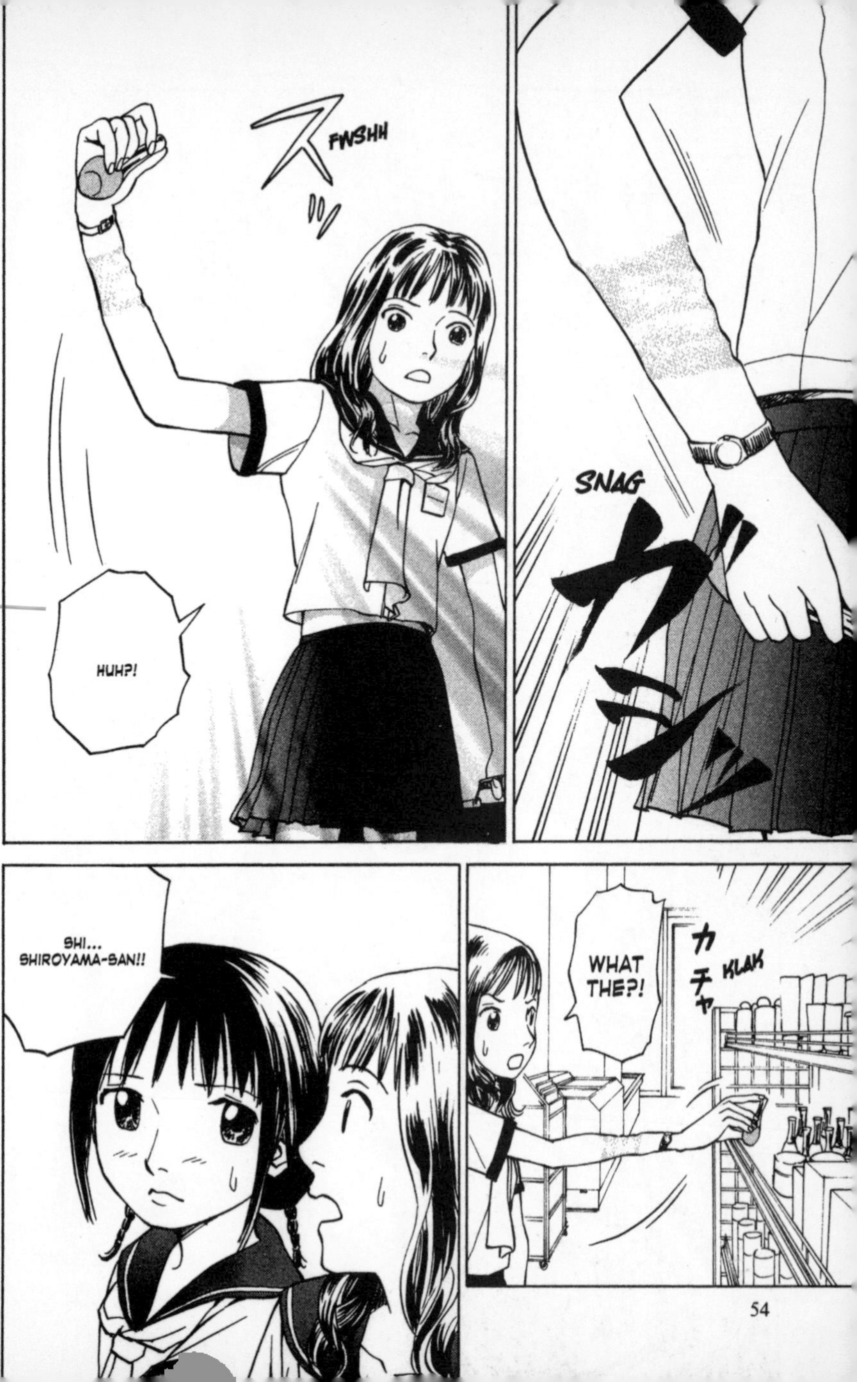
SNAG
ス
FWSHH
HUH?!
WHAT THE?!
カチャ
KLAK
SHI... SHIROYAMA-SAN!!

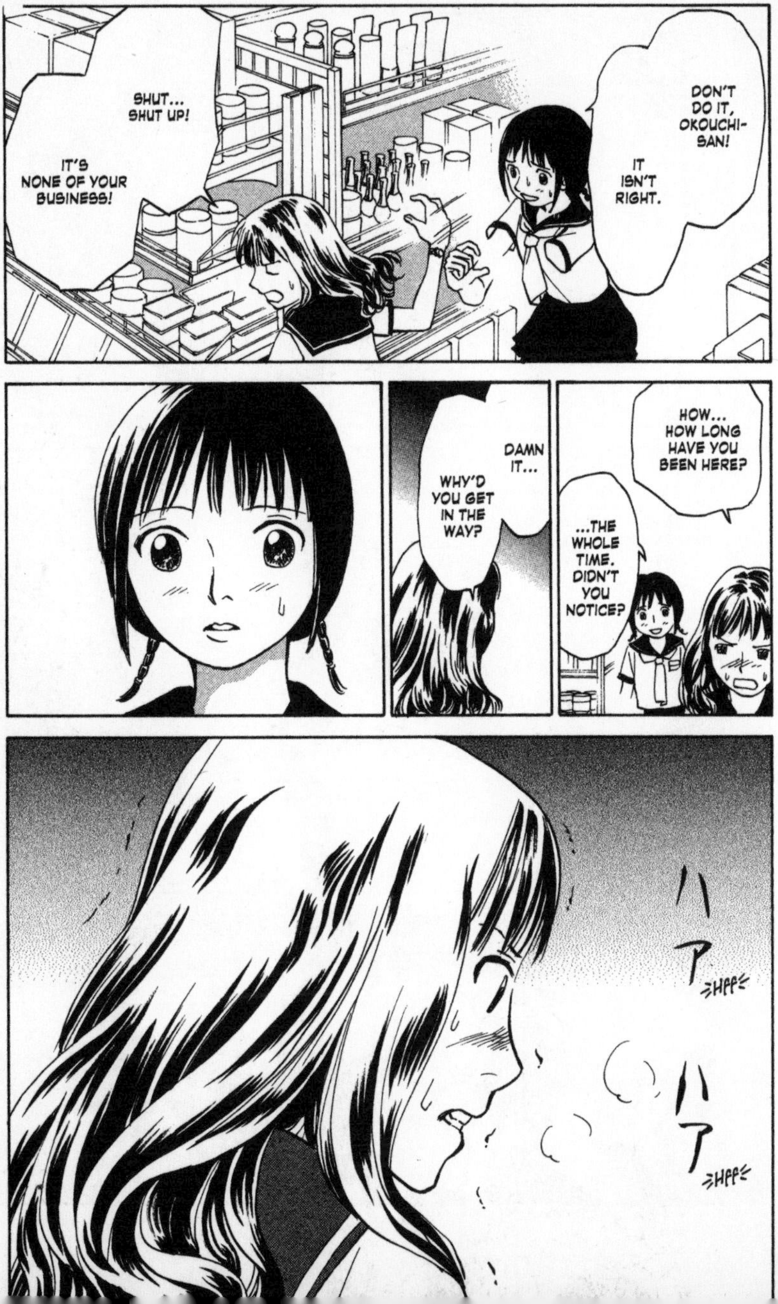
DON'T DO IT, OKOUCHI-SAN!
IT ISN'T RIGHT.
SHUT... SHUT UP!
IT'S NONE OF YOUR BUSINESS!
HOW... HOW LONG HAVE YOU BEEN HERE?
...THE WHOLE TIME. DIDN'T YOU NOTICE?
DAMN IT...
WHY'D YOU GET IN THE WAY?
ハア
HFF
ハア
HFF

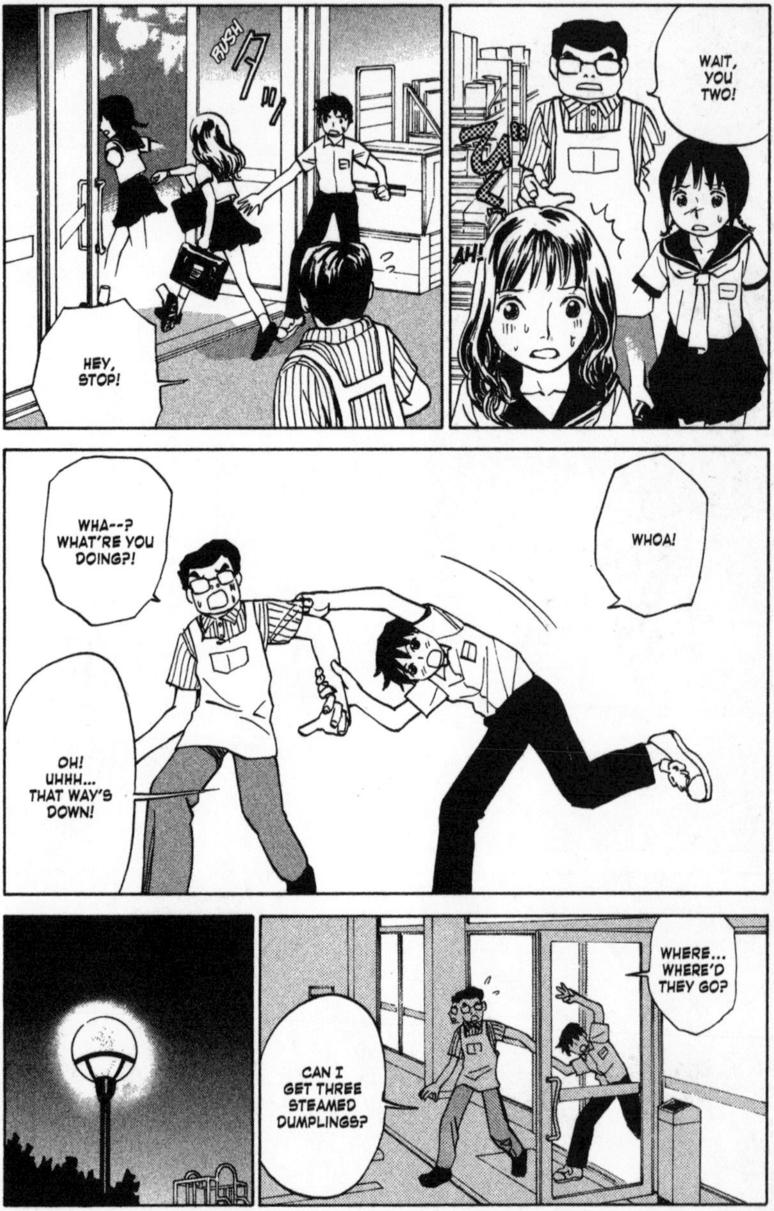
WAIT, YOU TWO!
AH!
RUSH
HEY, STOP!
WHOA!
WHA--? WHAT'RE YOU DOING?!
OH! UHHH... THAT WAY'S DOWN!
WHERE... WHERE'D THEY GO?
CAN I GET THREE STEAMED DUMPLINGS?

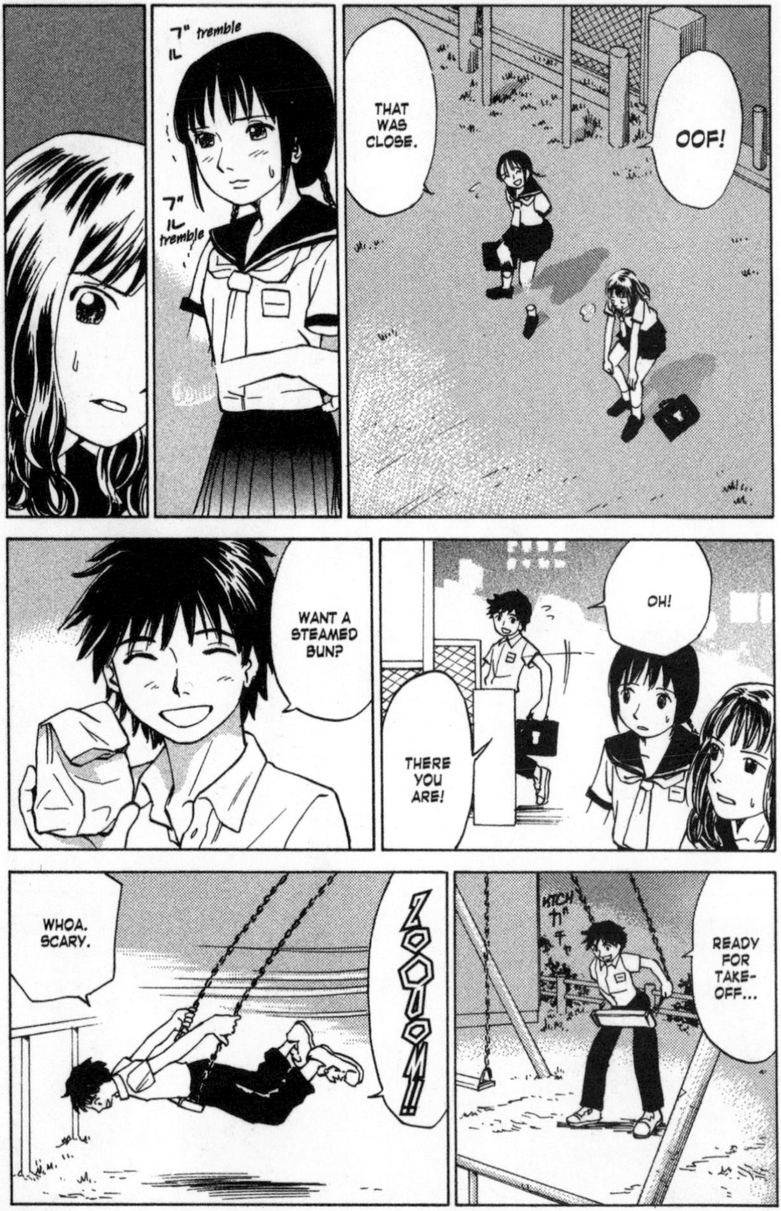
OOF!
THAT WAS CLOSE.
ブル tremble
ブル tremble
OH!
THERE YOU ARE!
WANT A STEAMED BUN?
KTCH ガチャ
READY FOR TAKE-OFF...
ZOOOOM!!
WHOA. SCARY.

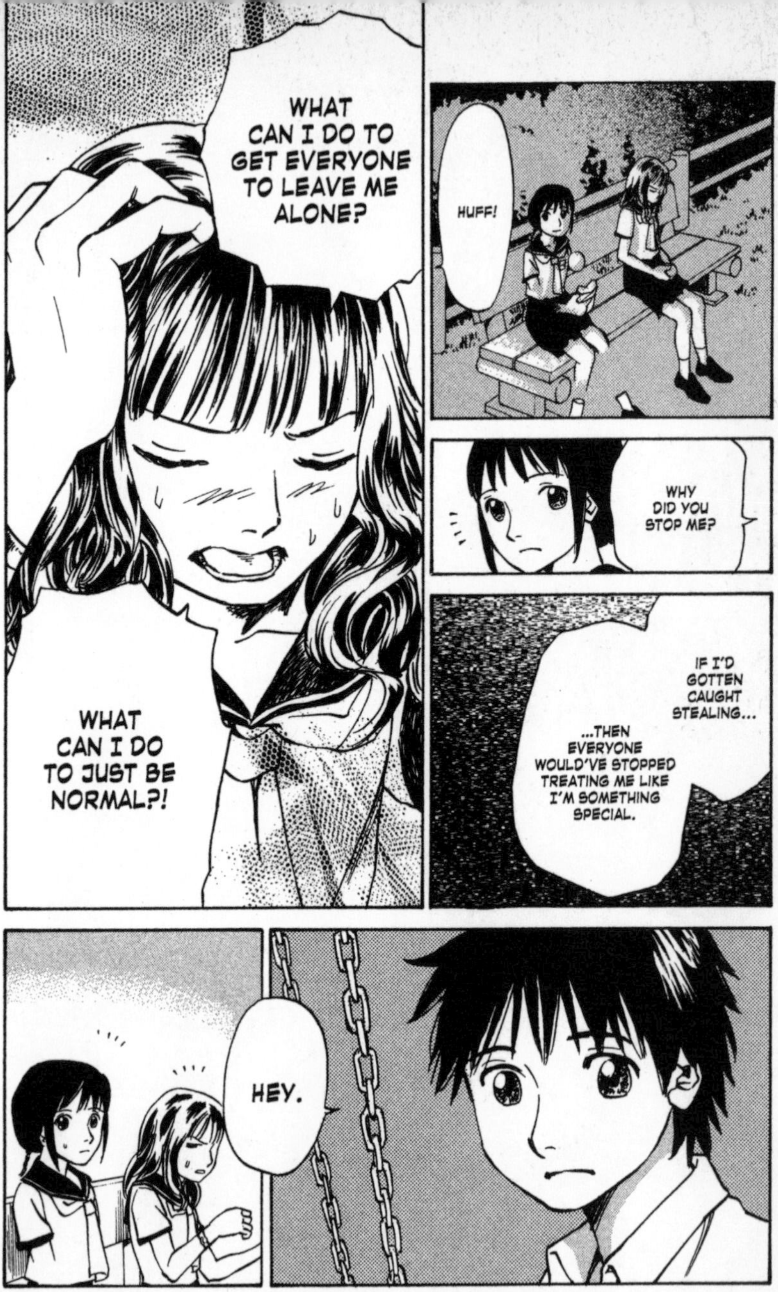
HUFF!
WHY DID YOU STOP ME?
IF I'D GOTTEN CAUGHT STEALING...
...THEN EVERYONE WOULD'VE STOPPED TREATING ME LIKE I'M SOMETHING SPECIAL.
WHAT CAN I DO TO GET EVERYONE TO LEAVE ME ALONE?
WHAT CAN I DO TO JUST BE NORMAL?!
HEY.

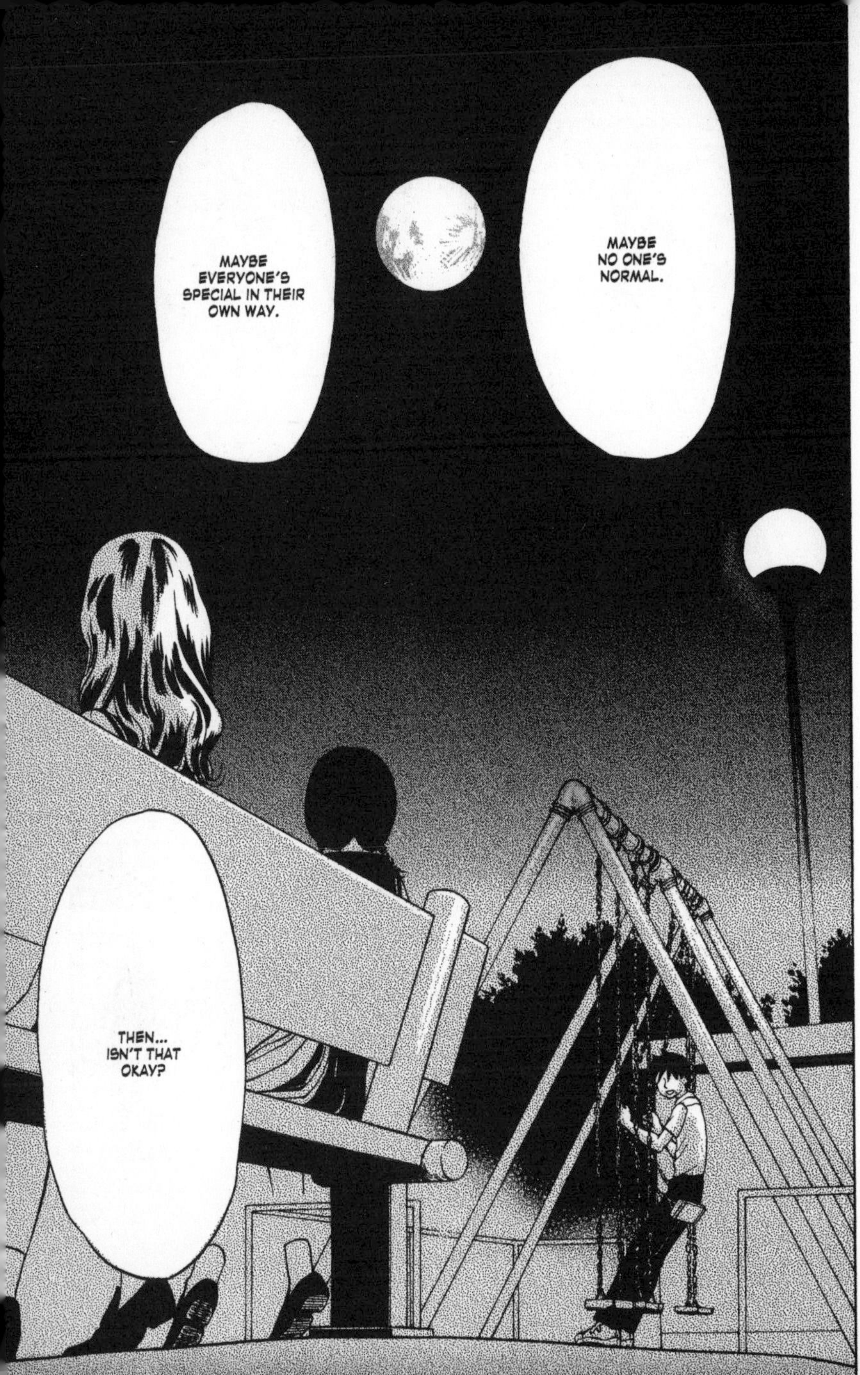
MAYBE NO ONE'S NORMAL.
MAYBE EVERYONE'S SPECIAL IN THEIR OWN WAY.
THEN... ISN'T THAT OKAY?

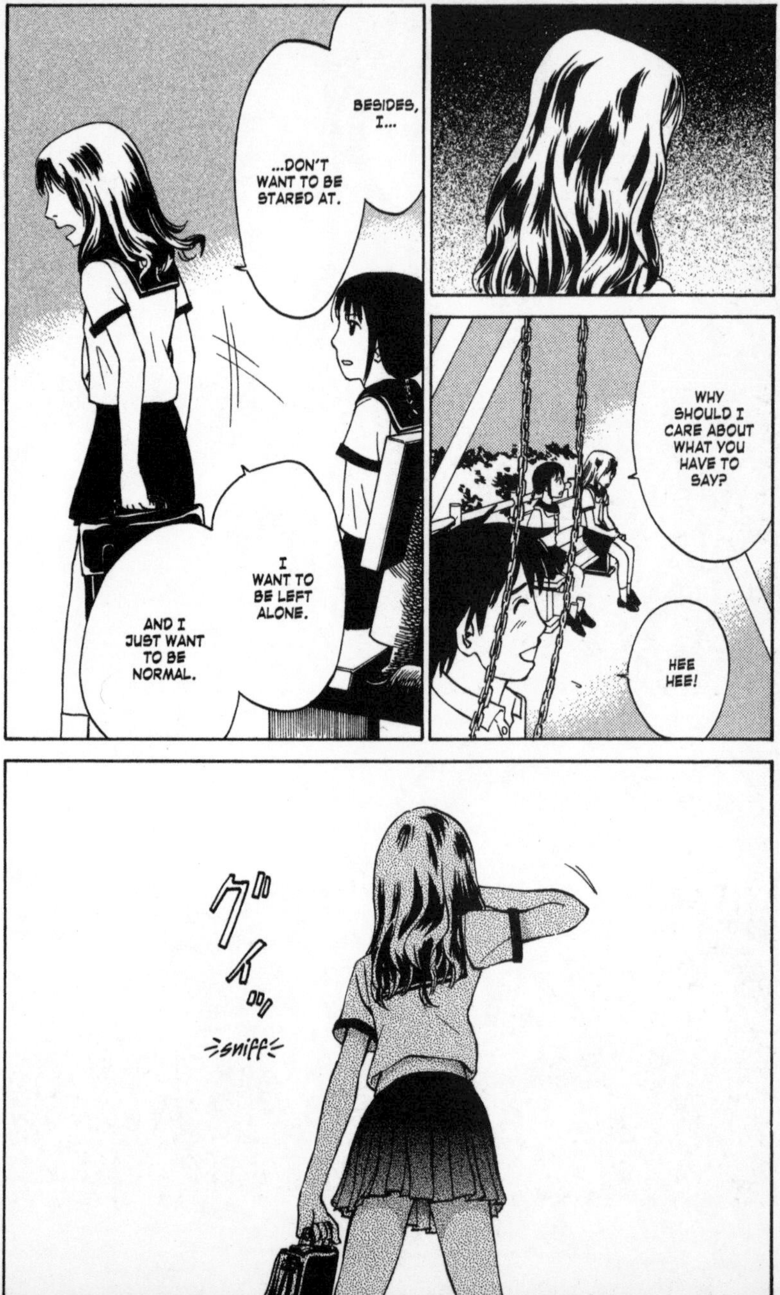
WHY SHOULD I CARE ABOUT WHAT YOU HAVE TO SAY?
HEE HEE!
BESIDES, I...
...DON'T WANT TO BE STARED AT.
I WANT TO BE LEFT ALONE.
AND I JUST WANT TO BE NORMAL.
sniff

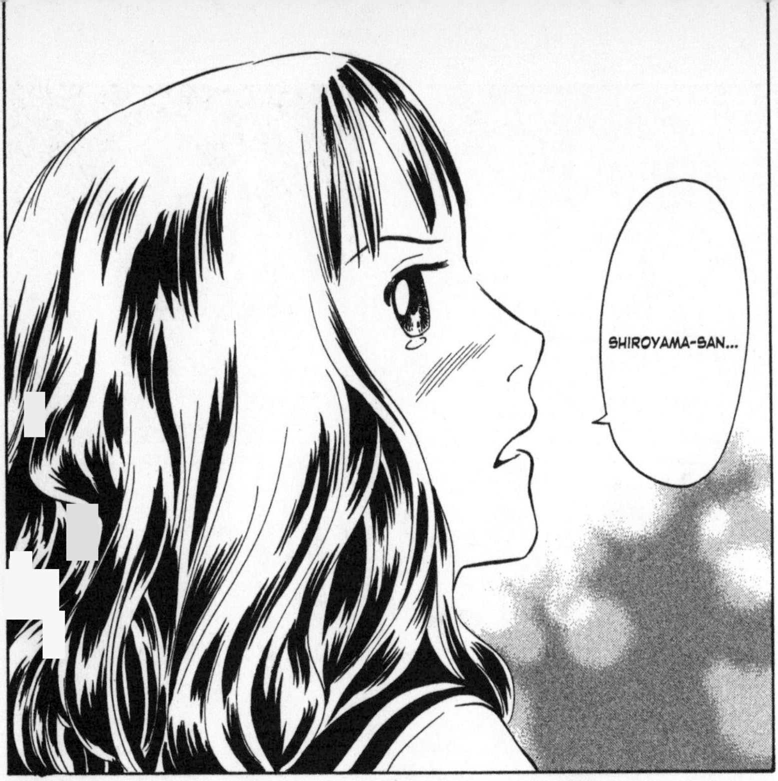
SHIROYAMA-SAN...
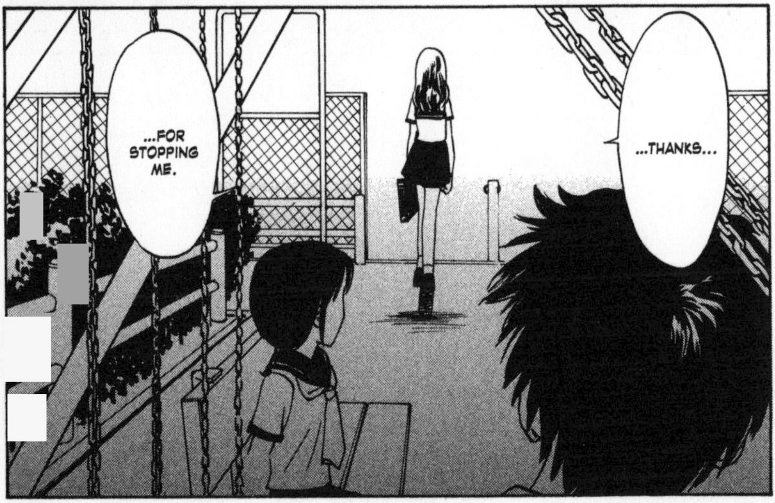
...THANKS...
...FOR STOPPING ME.

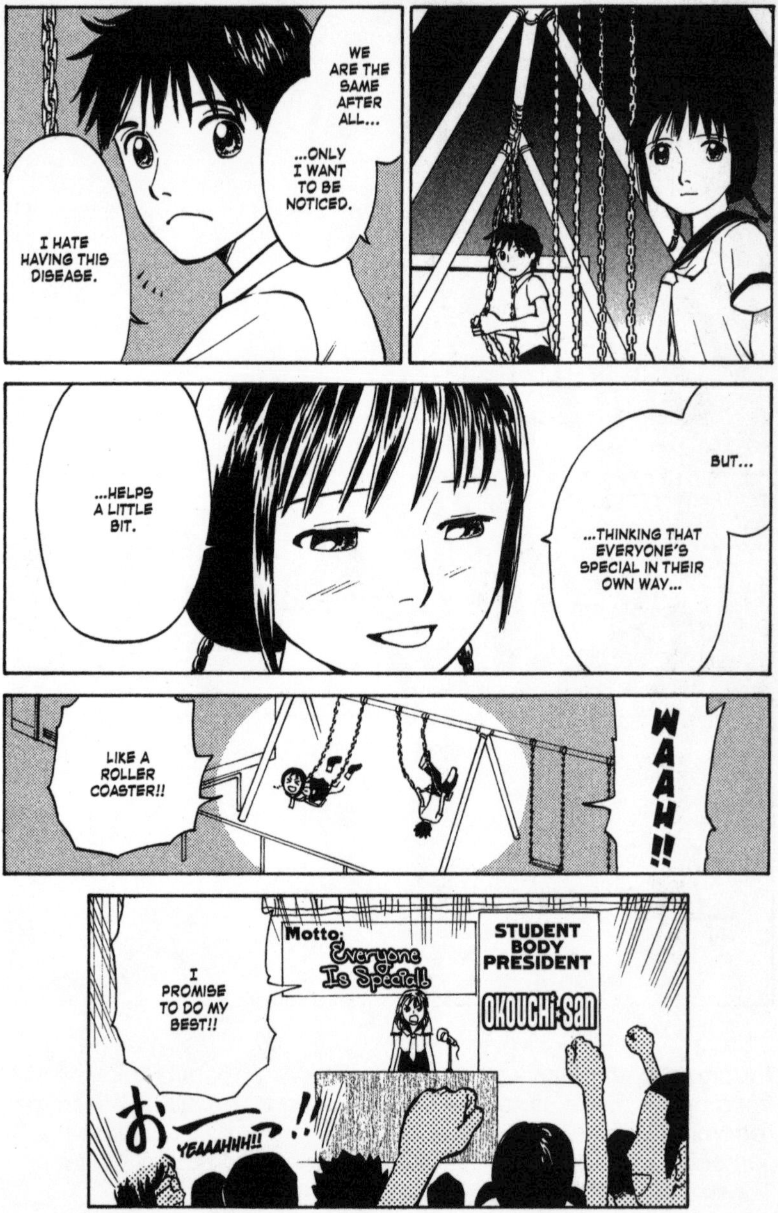
WE ARE THE SAME AFTER ALL...
...ONLY I WANT TO BE NOTICED.
I HATE HAVING THIS DISEASE.
BUT...
...THINKING THAT EVERYONE'S SPECIAL IN THEIR OWN WAY...
...HELPS A LITTLE BIT.
WAAAH!!
LIKE A ROLLER COASTER!!
STUDENT BODY PRESIDENT
OKOUCHI-SAN
Motto: Everyone Is Special!
I PROMISE TO DO MY BEST!!
お──っ!!
YEAAAHHH!!

OMAKE

ONE-PAGE BONUS MANGA #1

1

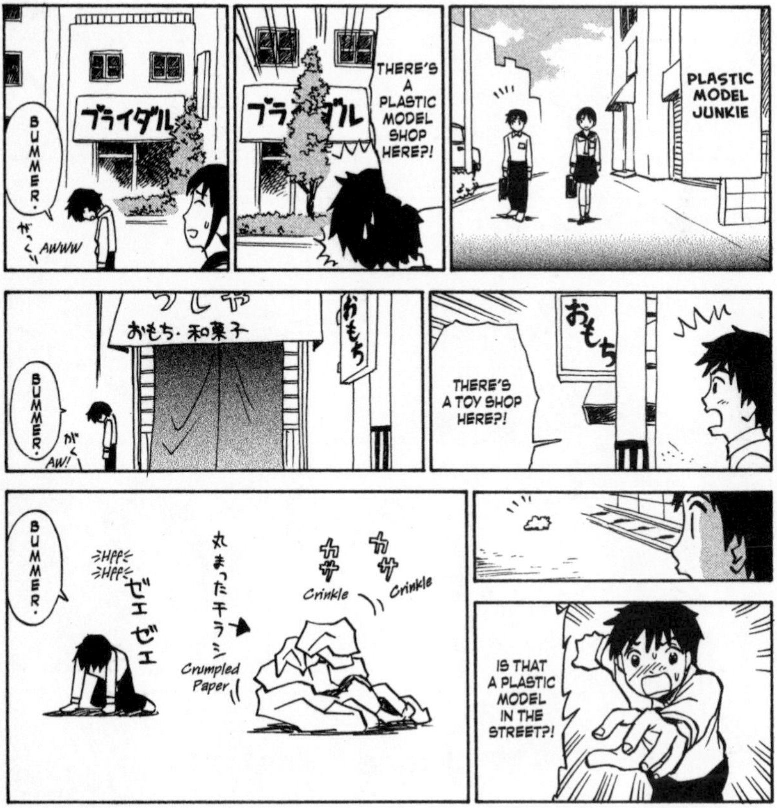
PLASTIC MODEL JUNKIE
THERE'S A PLASTIC MODEL SHOP HERE?!
ブライダル
BUMMER.
がっくり
AWWW
おもち
THERE'S A TOY SHOP HERE?!
おもち・和菓子
おもち
BUMMER.
がく
AW!
IS THAT A PLASTIC MODEL IN THE STREET?!
BUMMER.
HFF
HFF
ゼエゼエ
丸まったチラシ
Crumpled Paper
カサ
Crinkle
カサ
Crinkle

Tadami thinks that the sign in panel two is going to read "playmodel" (for a plastic model store), but it actually reads "bridal." A little further, Tadami thinks that the sign in panel four reads "toys," but it reads "*omochi*" for a Japanese candy. The bigger sign in panel five reads "*Tsushiya, omochi,* Japanese sweets."

OMAKE

ONE-PAGE BONUS MANGA #2

2

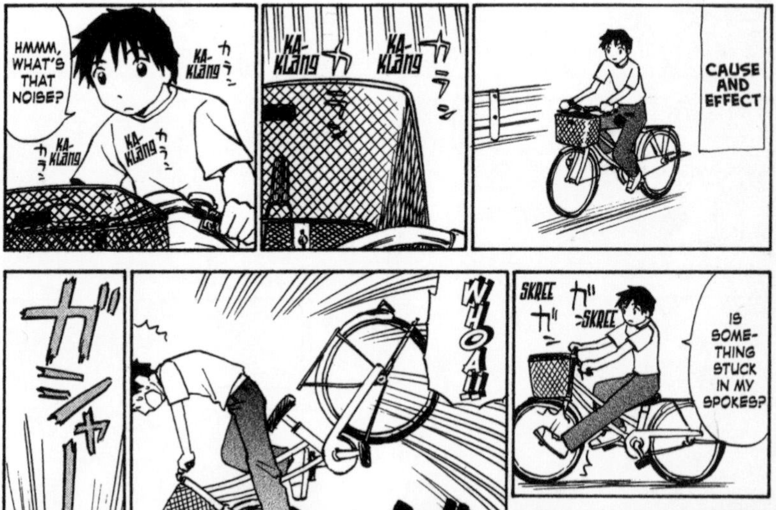

CAUSE AND EFFECT
KA-KLANG
KA-KLANG
KA-KLANG
HMMM, WHAT'S THAT NOISE?
KA-KLANG
KA-KLANG
SKREE
SKREE
IS SOMETHING STUCK IN MY SPOKES?
KICK
WHOA!!
FLIP
SKASH
KA-KLAK
HOW--
--HOW'D THAT HAPPEN?

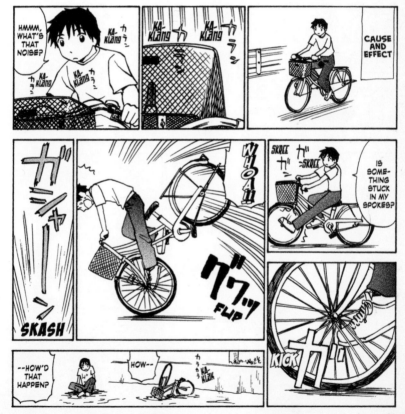

PART 3 Fully Transparent Keiko-san

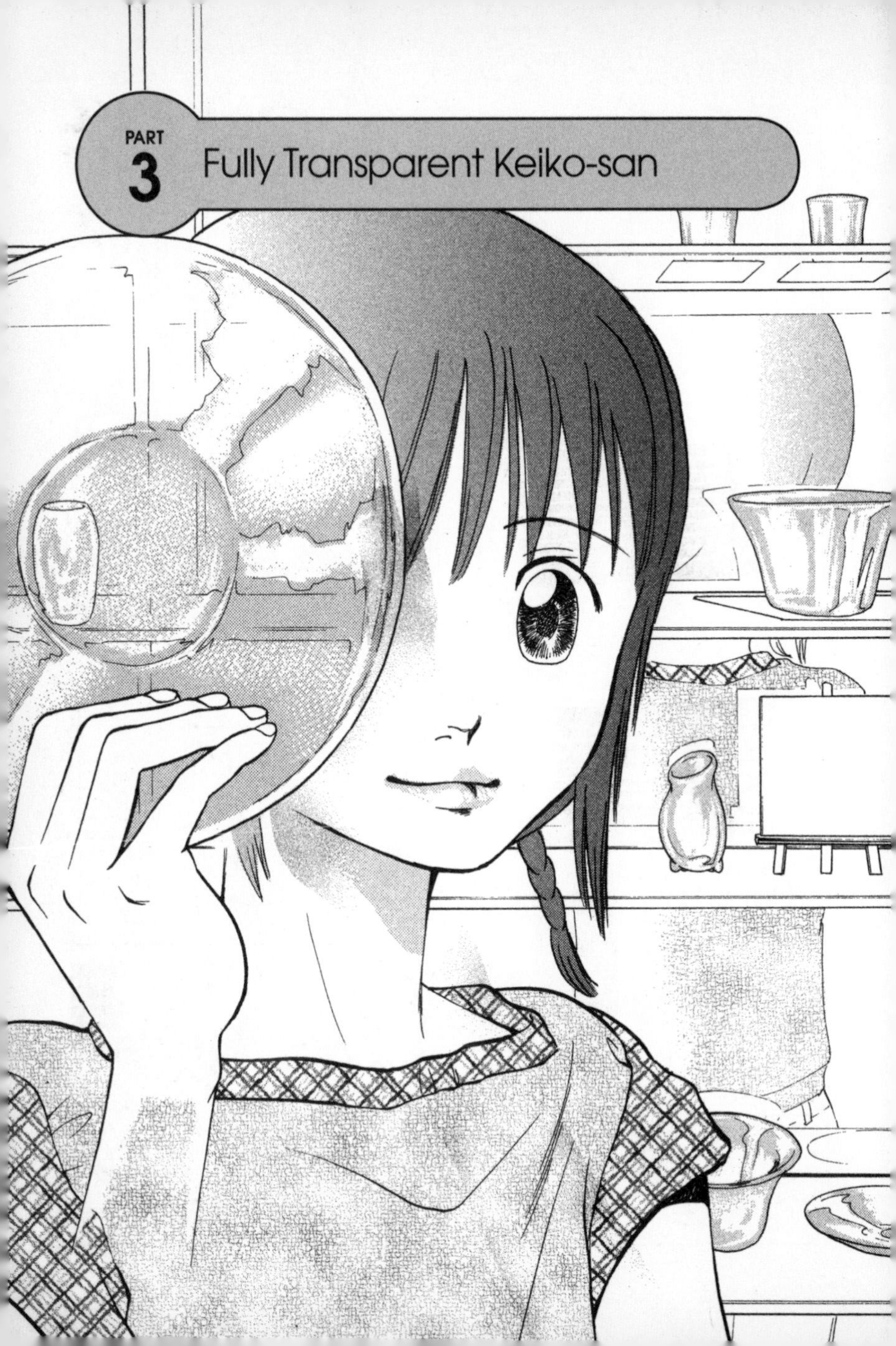

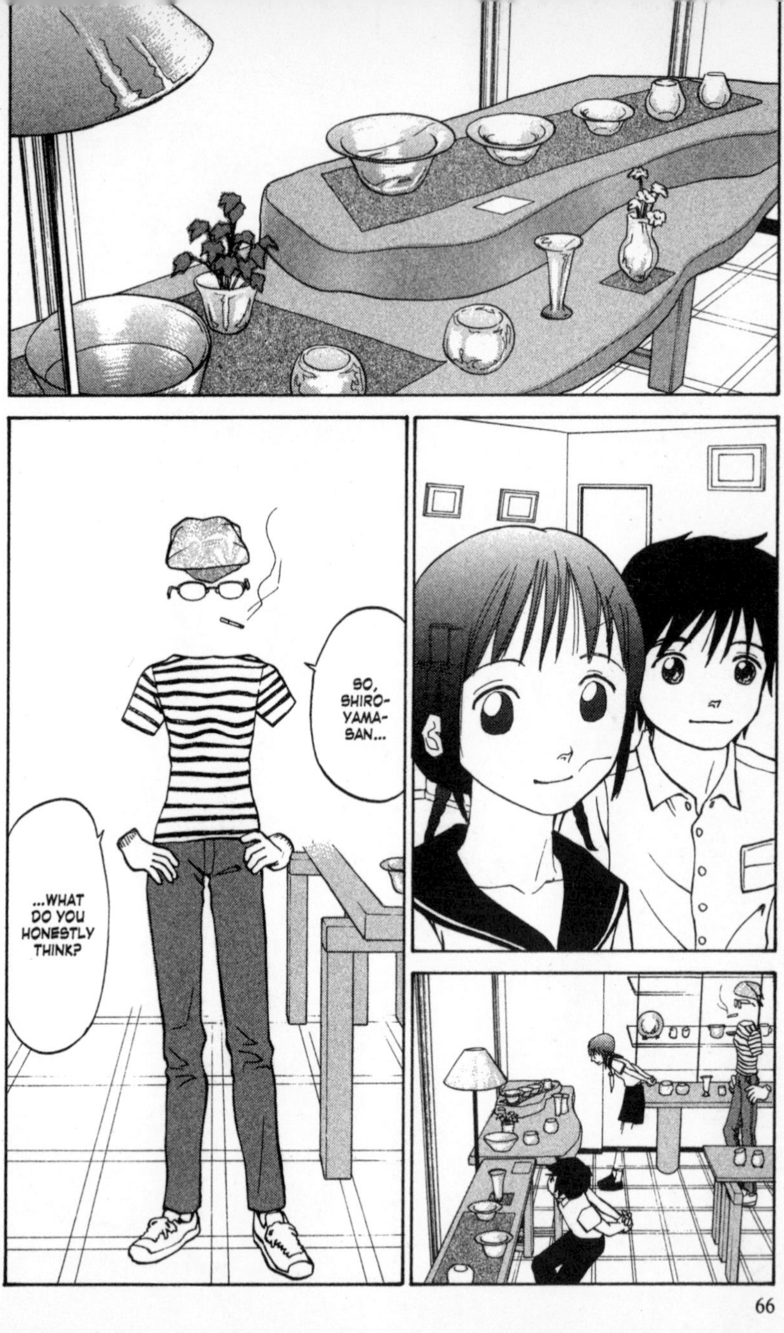
SO, SHIRO-YAMA-SAN...
...WHAT DO YOU HONESTLY THINK?

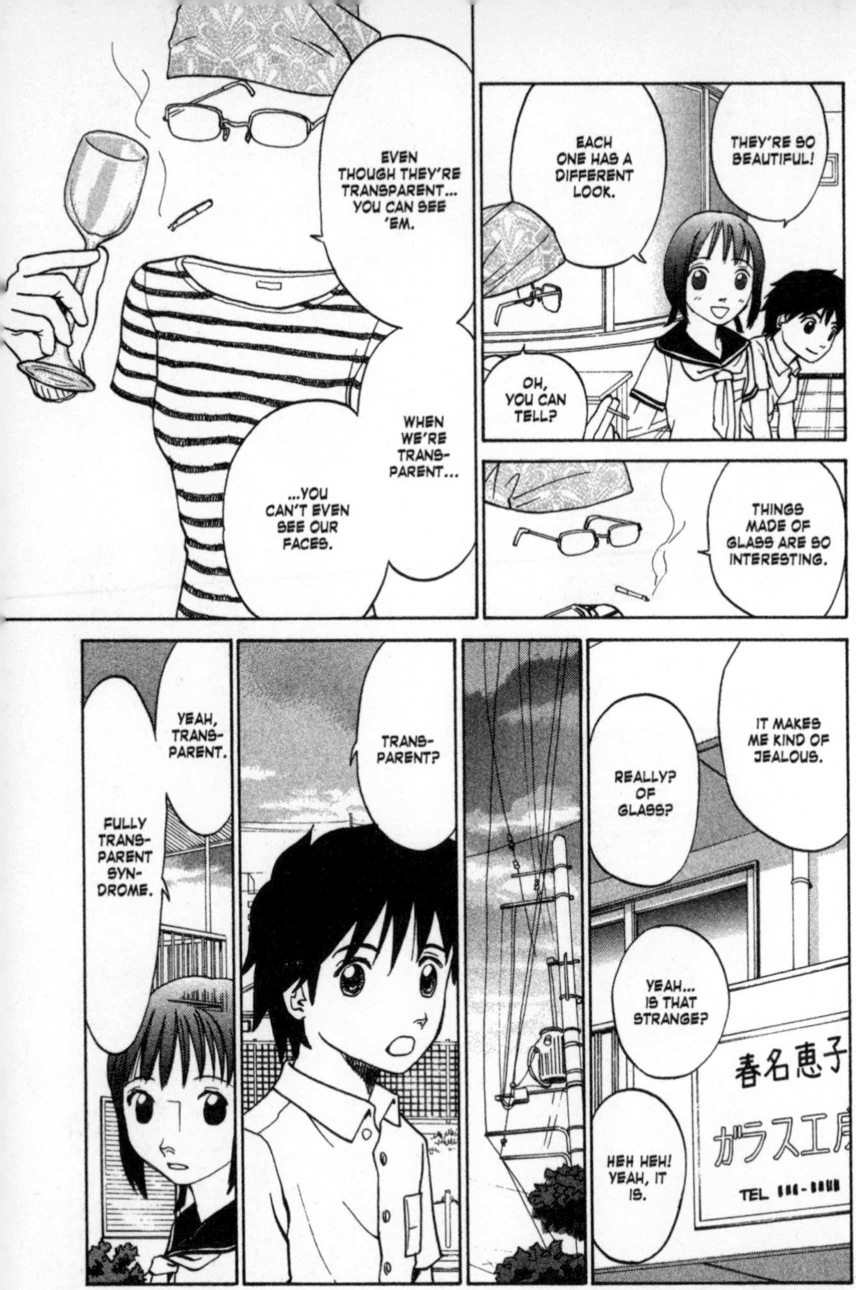
THEY'RE SO BEAUTIFUL!
EACH ONE HAS A DIFFERENT LOOK.
OH, YOU CAN TELL?
THINGS MADE OF GLASS ARE SO INTERESTING.
EVEN THOUGH THEY'RE TRANSPARENT... YOU CAN SEE 'EM.
WHEN WE'RE TRANS-PARENT...
...YOU CAN'T EVEN SEE OUR FACES.
IT MAKES ME KIND OF JEALOUS.
REALLY? OF GLASS?
YEAH... IS THAT STRANGE?
HEH HEH! YEAH, IT IS.
春名恵子
ガラス工
TEL
TRANS-PARENT?
YEAH, TRANS-PARENT.
FULLY TRANS-PARENT SYN-DROME.

SIGN: KEIKO HARUNA / GLASS STUDIO

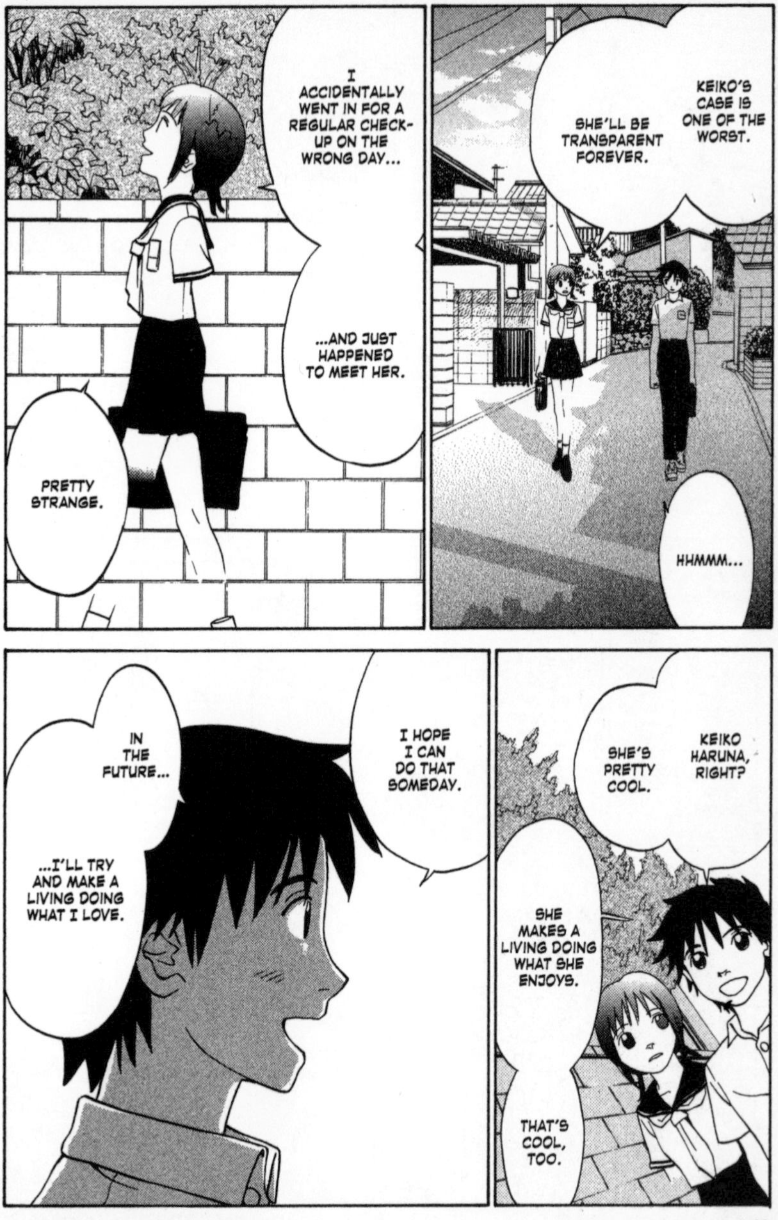
KEIKO'S CASE IS ONE OF THE WORST.
SHE'LL BE TRANSPARENT FOREVER.
HHMMM...
I ACCIDENTALLY WENT IN FOR A REGULAR CHECK-UP ON THE WRONG DAY...
...AND JUST HAPPENED TO MEET HER.
PRETTY STRANGE.
KEIKO HARUNA, RIGHT?
SHE'S PRETTY COOL.
SHE MAKES A LIVING DOING WHAT SHE ENJOYS.
THAT'S COOL, TOO.
I HOPE I CAN DO THAT SOMEDAY.
IN THE FUTURE...
...I'LL TRY AND MAKE A LIVING DOING WHAT I LOVE.

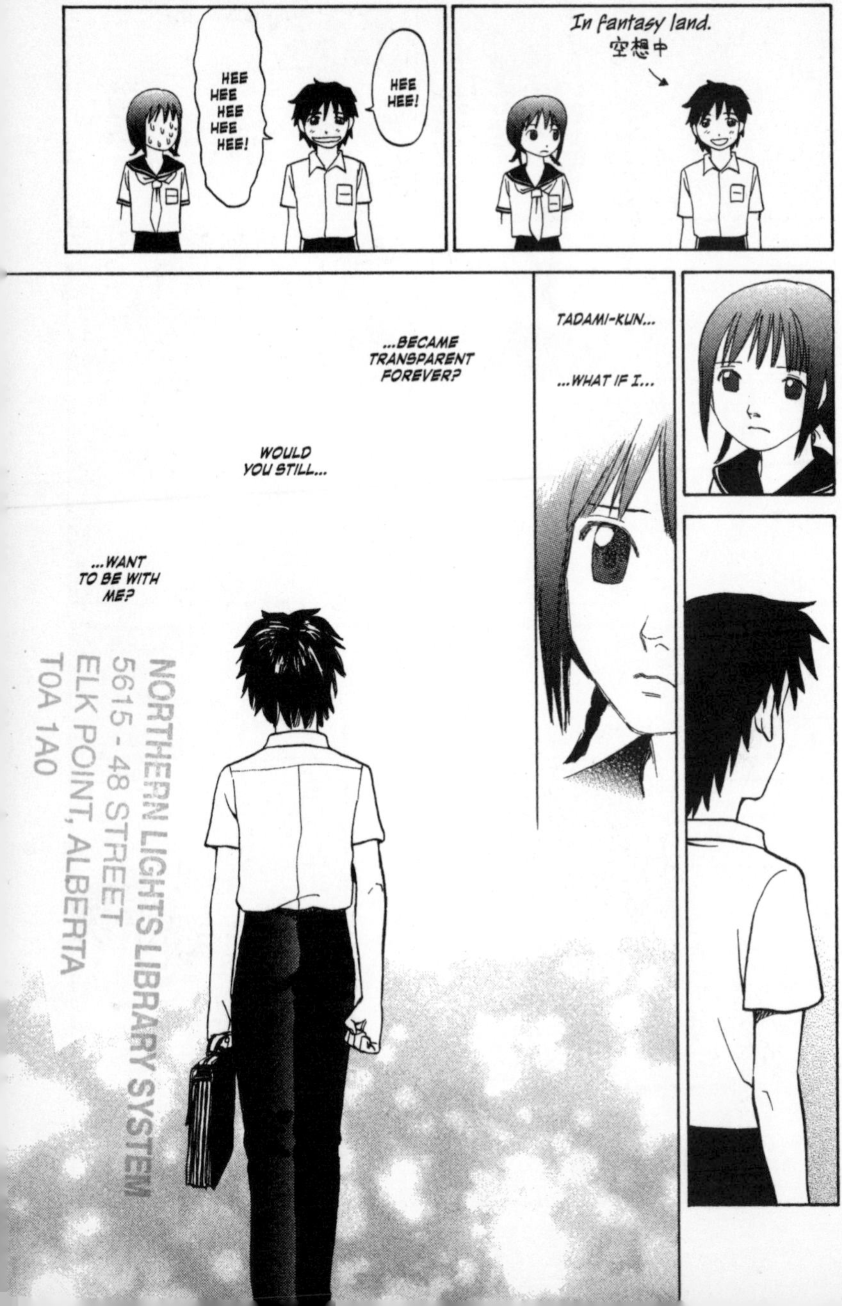
In fantasy land.
空想中
HEE HEE!
HEE HEE HEE HEE HEE!
TADAMI-KUN...
...WHAT IF I...
...BECAME TRANSPARENT FOREVER?
WOULD YOU STILL...
...WANT TO BE WITH ME?

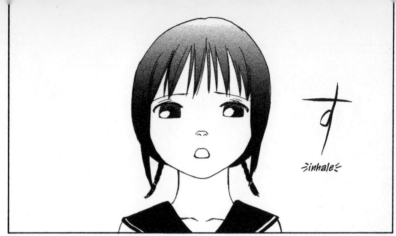

す
inhale
I ALMOST...
ふう
sigh
...SAID THAT...
...OUT LOUD.
SHIZUKA-CHAN, JUST YOU TODAY?
春名
ガラス工房
TEL
SO...
...THIS IS WHAT YOU'RE PROGRESSION IS LIKE.
YOU'RE LOOKING MORE LIKE ME NOW.
YEAH... IT'S BASICALLY A MONTHLY PROGRESSION.
ABOUT THE SAME CYCLE AS MY PERIOD.
INTERESTING...

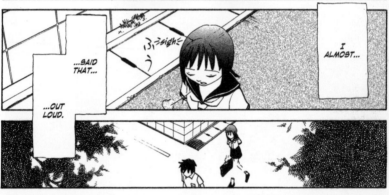

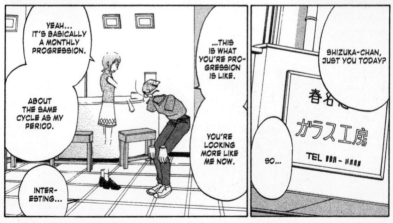

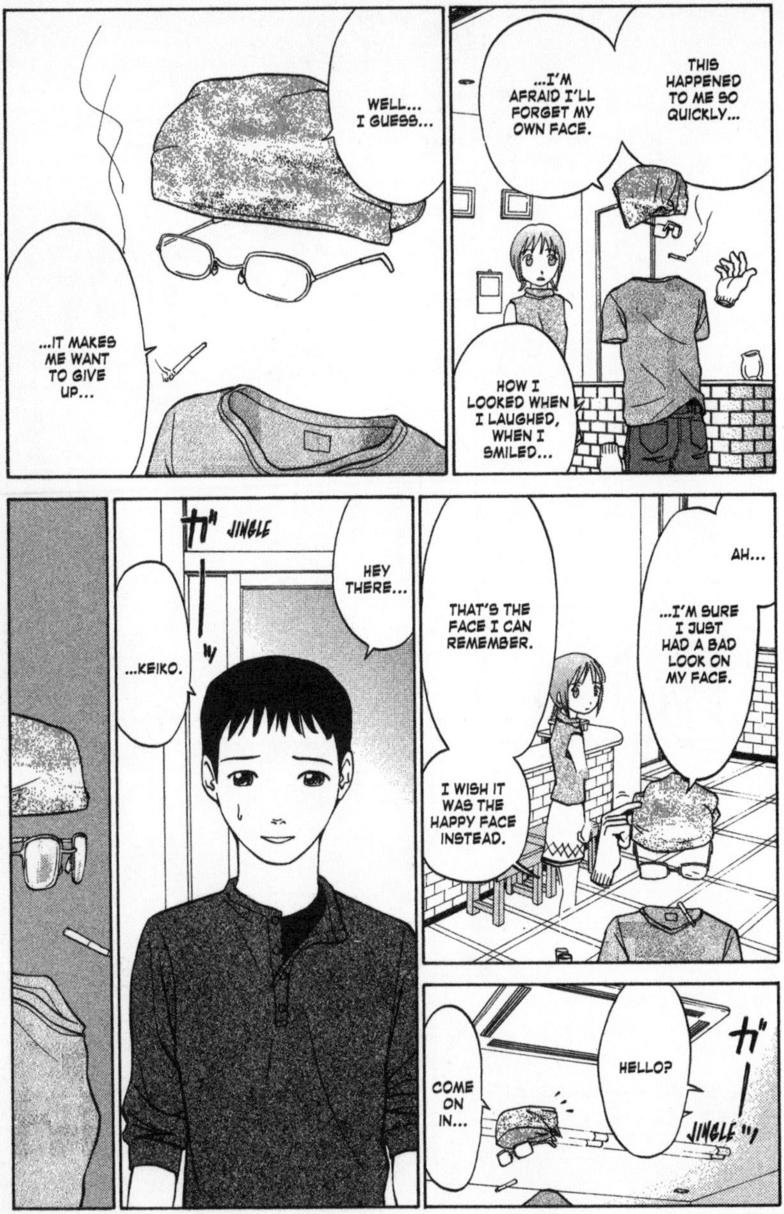
THIS HAPPENED TO ME SO QUICKLY...
...I'M AFRAID I'LL FORGET MY OWN FACE.
HOW I LOOKED WHEN I LAUGHED, WHEN I SMILED...
WELL... I GUESS...
...IT MAKES ME WANT TO GIVE UP...
AH... ...I'M SURE I JUST HAD A BAD LOOK ON MY FACE.
THAT'S THE FACE I CAN REMEMBER.
I WISH IT WAS THE HAPPY FACE INSTEAD.
ガー
JINGLE
HELLO?
COME ON IN...
ガー
JINGLE
HEY THERE...
...KEIKO.

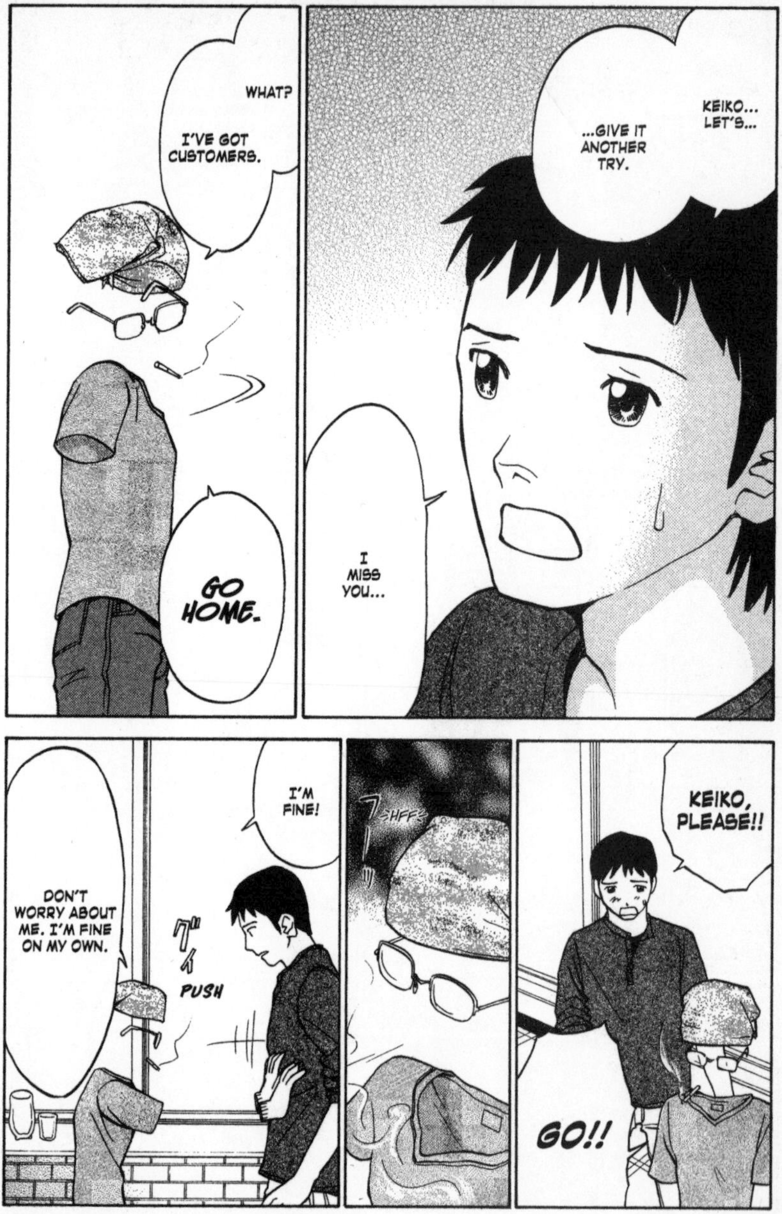
KEIKO... LET'S...
...GIVE IT ANOTHER TRY.
I MISS YOU...
WHAT?
I'VE GOT CUSTOMERS.
GO HOME.
KEIKO, PLEASE!!
GO!!
SHFF
I'M FINE!
DON'T WORRY ABOUT ME. I'M FINE ON MY OWN.
PUSH

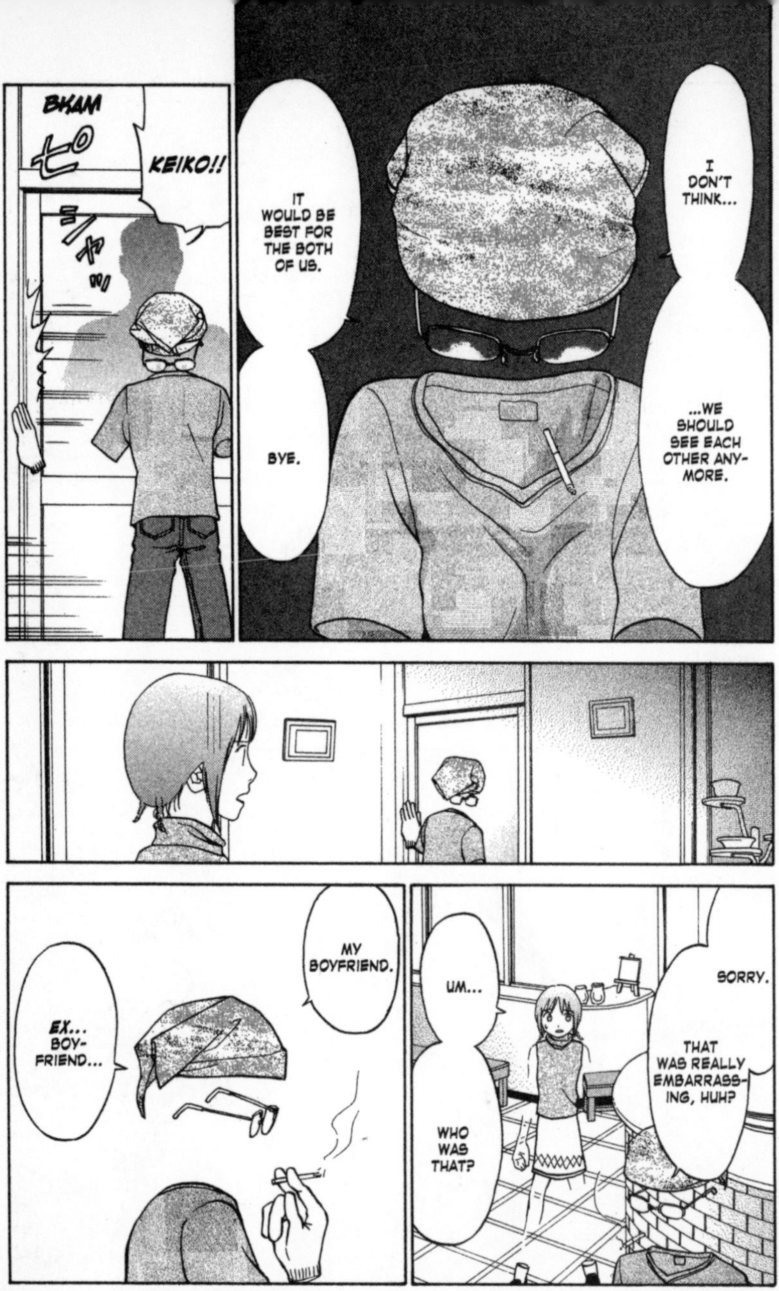
I DON'T THINK...
...WE SHOULD SEE EACH OTHER ANYMORE.
IT WOULD BE BEST FOR THE BOTH OF US.
BYE.
KEIKO!!
BKAM
SORRY.
THAT WAS REALLY EMBARRASSING, HUH?
UM...
WHO WAS THAT?
MY BOYFRIEND.
EX... BOYFRIEND...

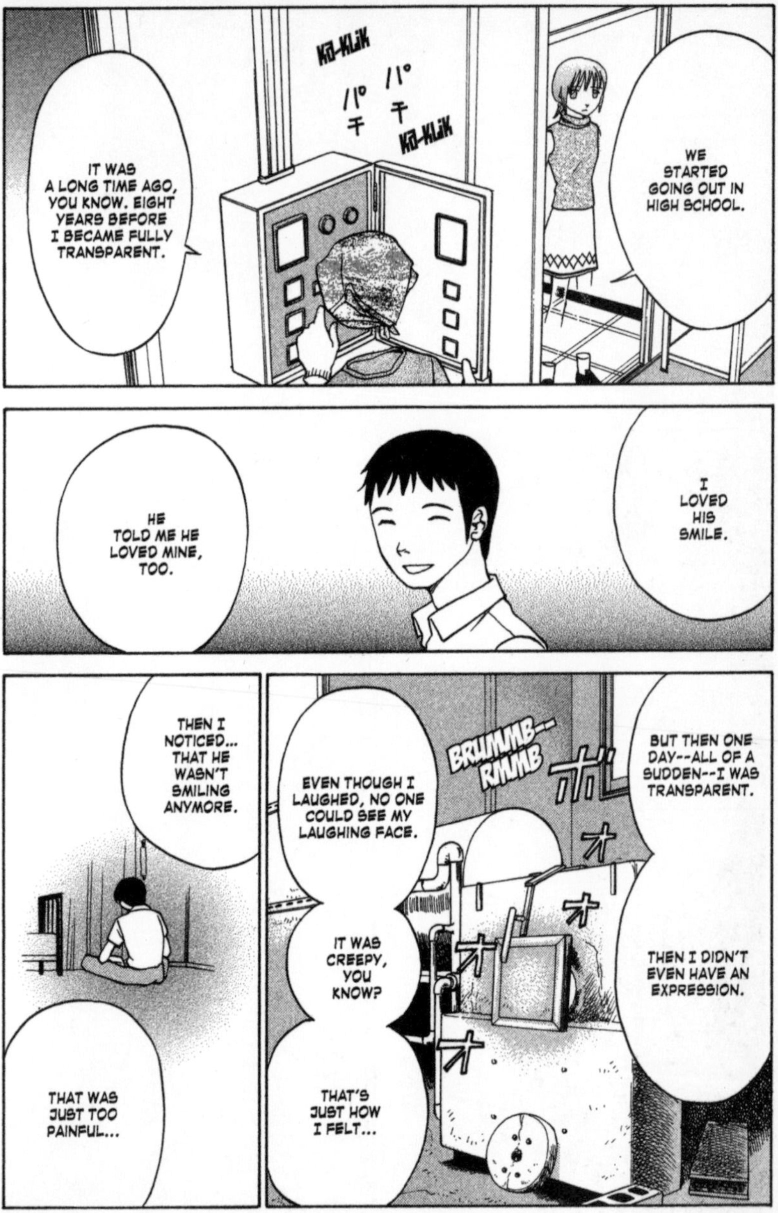
WE STARTED GOING OUT IN HIGH SCHOOL.
KA-KLIK
パチ パチ
KA-KLIK
IT WAS A LONG TIME AGO, YOU KNOW. EIGHT YEARS BEFORE I BECAME FULLY TRANSPARENT.
I LOVED HIS SMILE.
HE TOLD ME HE LOVED MINE, TOO.
BUT THEN ONE DAY--ALL OF A SUDDEN--I WAS TRANSPARENT.
THEN I DIDN'T EVEN HAVE AN EXPRESSION.
BRUMMB--RMMB
ボオオオオ
EVEN THOUGH I LAUGHED, NO ONE COULD SEE MY LAUGHING FACE.
IT WAS CREEPY, YOU KNOW?
THAT'S JUST HOW I FELT...
THEN I NOTICED... THAT HE WASN'T SMILING ANYMORE.
THAT WAS JUST TOO PAINFUL...

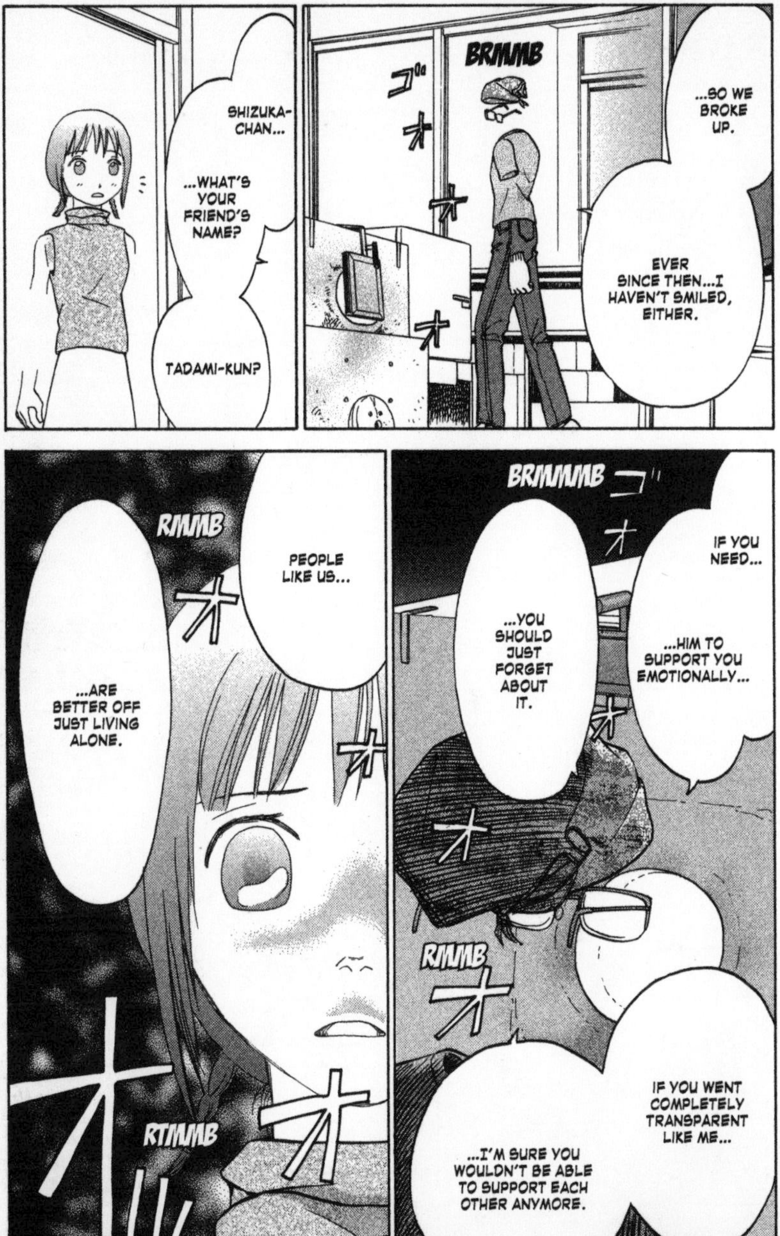
BRMMB
...SO WE BROKE UP.
EVER SINCE THEN...I HAVEN'T SMILED, EITHER.
SHIZUKA-CHAN...
...WHAT'S YOUR FRIEND'S NAME?
TADAMI-KUN?
BRMMMB
IF YOU NEED...
...HIM TO SUPPORT YOU EMOTIONALLY...
...YOU SHOULD JUST FORGET ABOUT IT.
RMMB
IF YOU WENT COMPLETELY TRANSPARENT LIKE ME...
...I'M SURE YOU WOULDN'T BE ABLE TO SUPPORT EACH OTHER ANYMORE.
RMMB
PEOPLE LIKE US...
...ARE BETTER OFF JUST LIVING ALONE.
RTMMB

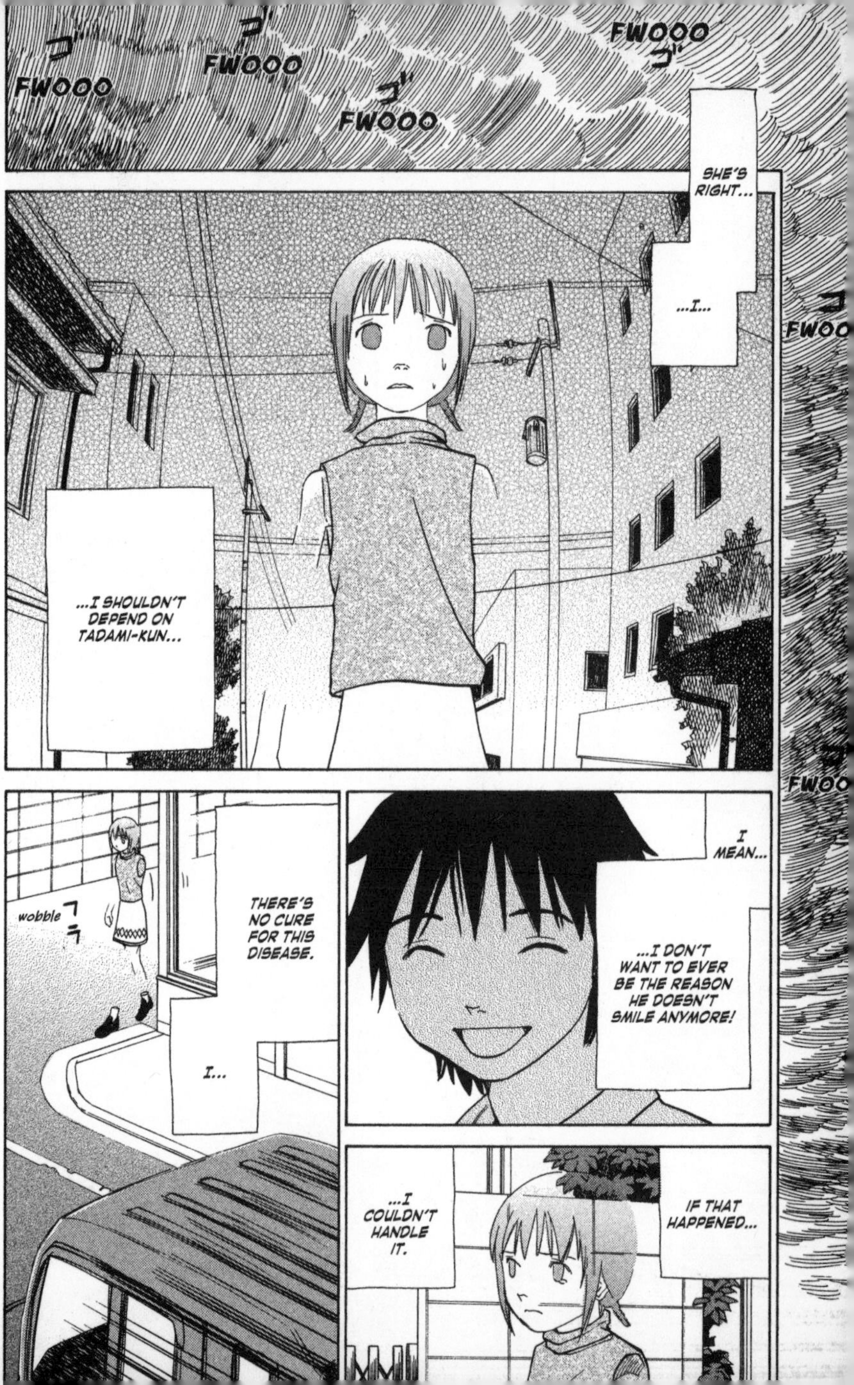
FWOOO
FWOOO
FWOOO
FWOOO
SHE'S RIGHT...
...I...
FWOO
...I SHOULDN'T DEPEND ON TADAMI-KUN...
FWOO
I MEAN...
...I DON'T WANT TO EVER BE THE REASON HE DOESN'T SMILE ANYMORE!
IF THAT HAPPENED...
...I COULDN'T HANDLE IT.
THERE'S NO CURE FOR THIS DISEASE.
I...
wobble

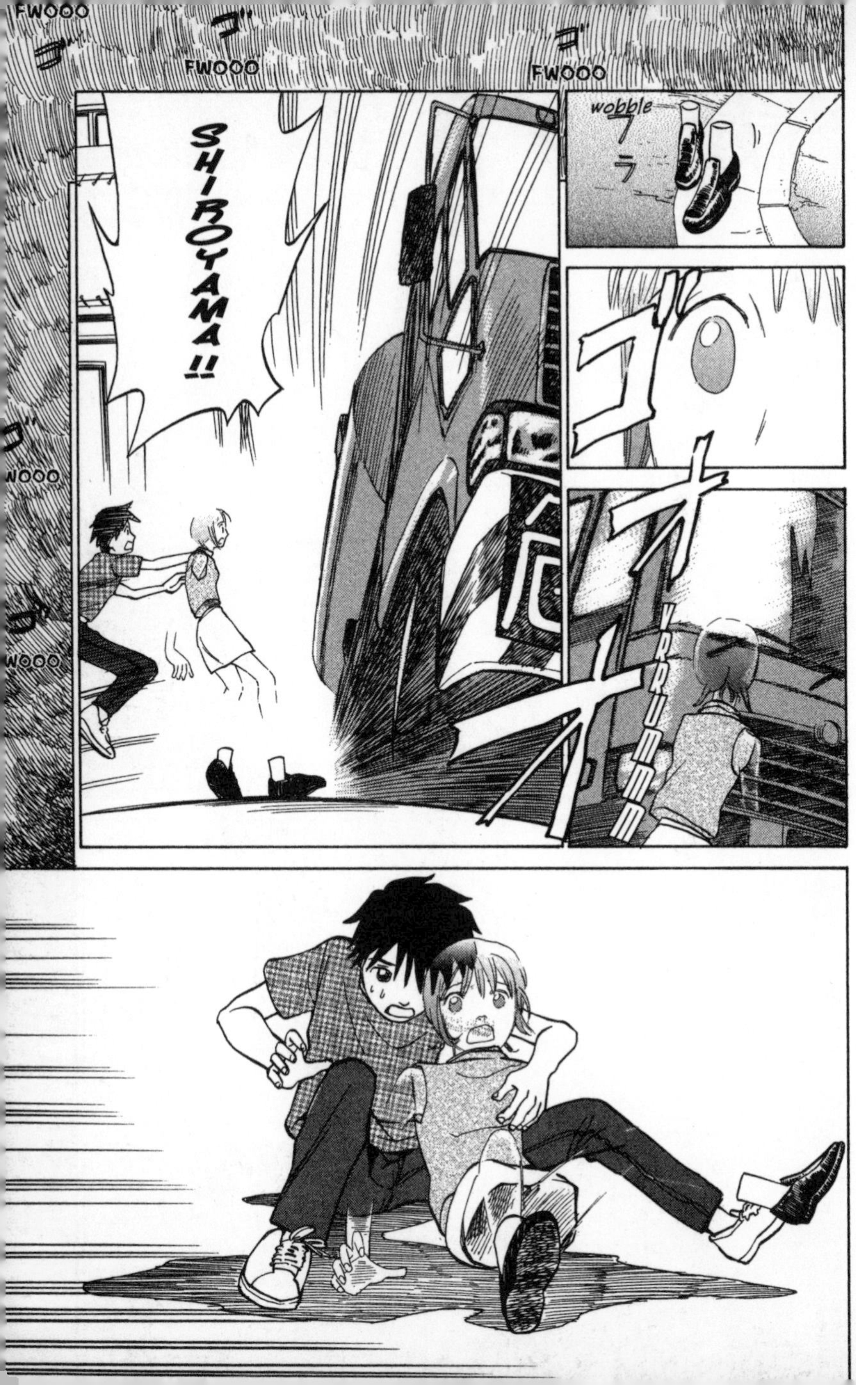
FWOOO
FWOOO
FWOOO
wobble
フラ
ゴオオ
VRRUMMM
SHIROYAMA!!
WOOO
WOOO

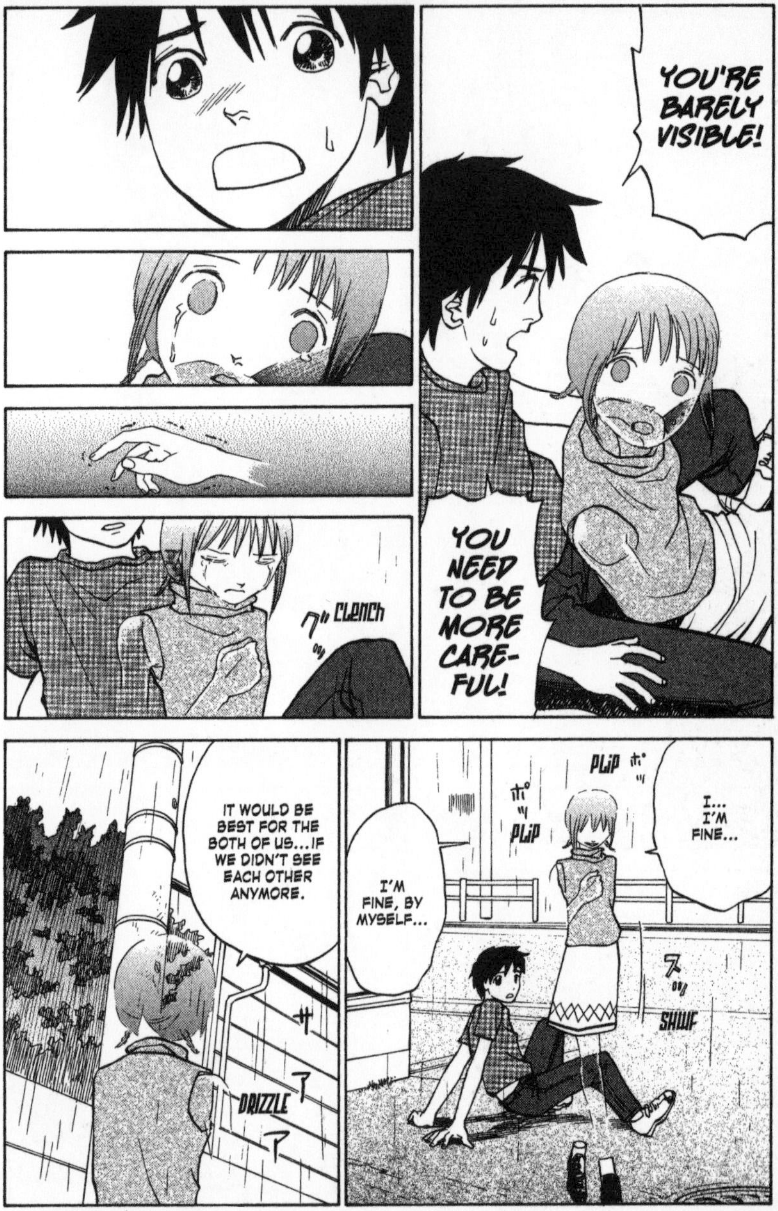

YOU'RE BARELY VISIBLE!
YOU NEED TO BE MORE CARE-FUL!
グッ CLENCH
PLiP ポッ
ポッ PLiP
I... I'M FINE...
I'M FINE, BY MYSELF...
ス SHUF
IT WOULD BE BEST FOR THE BOTH OF US...IF WE DIDN'T SEE EACH OTHER ANYMORE.
サ DRIZZLE ア ア

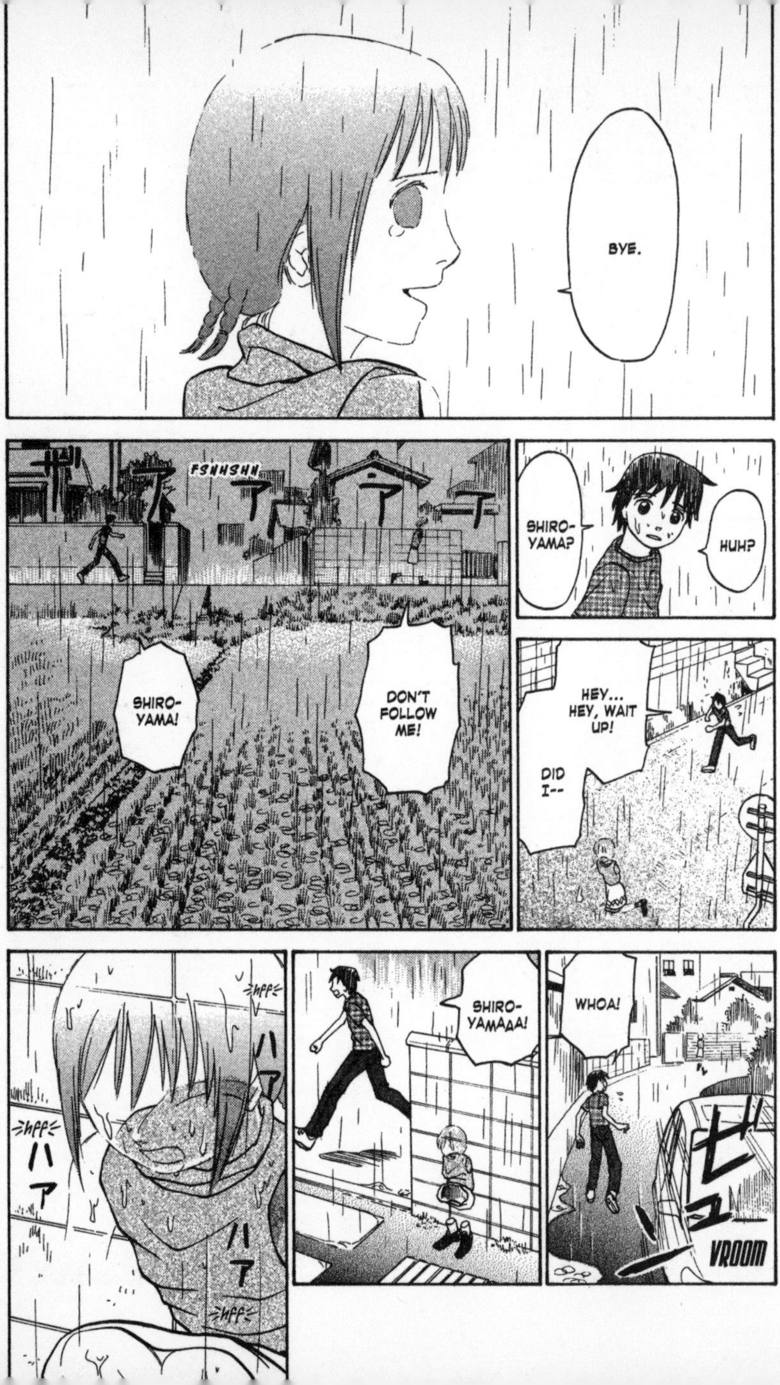
BYE.
HUH?
SHIRO-YAMA?
HEY... HEY, WAIT UP!
DID I--
FSNHSHN
DON'T FOLLOW ME!
SHIRO-YAMA!
WHOA!
VROOM
SHIRO-YAMAAA!
hff
hff
hff

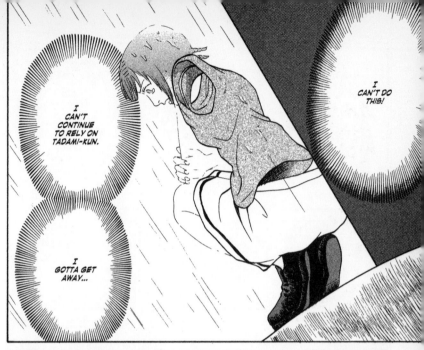

I CAN'T
CONTINUE
TO RELY ON
TADAMI-KUN.

I CAN'T DO
THIS!

I GOTTA GET
AWAY...

WHERE
...?

WHERE
ARE--

HUH?

SPLISH

...FOR
HIS SAKE.

...FROM
HIM!

I GOTTA GET
AWAY...

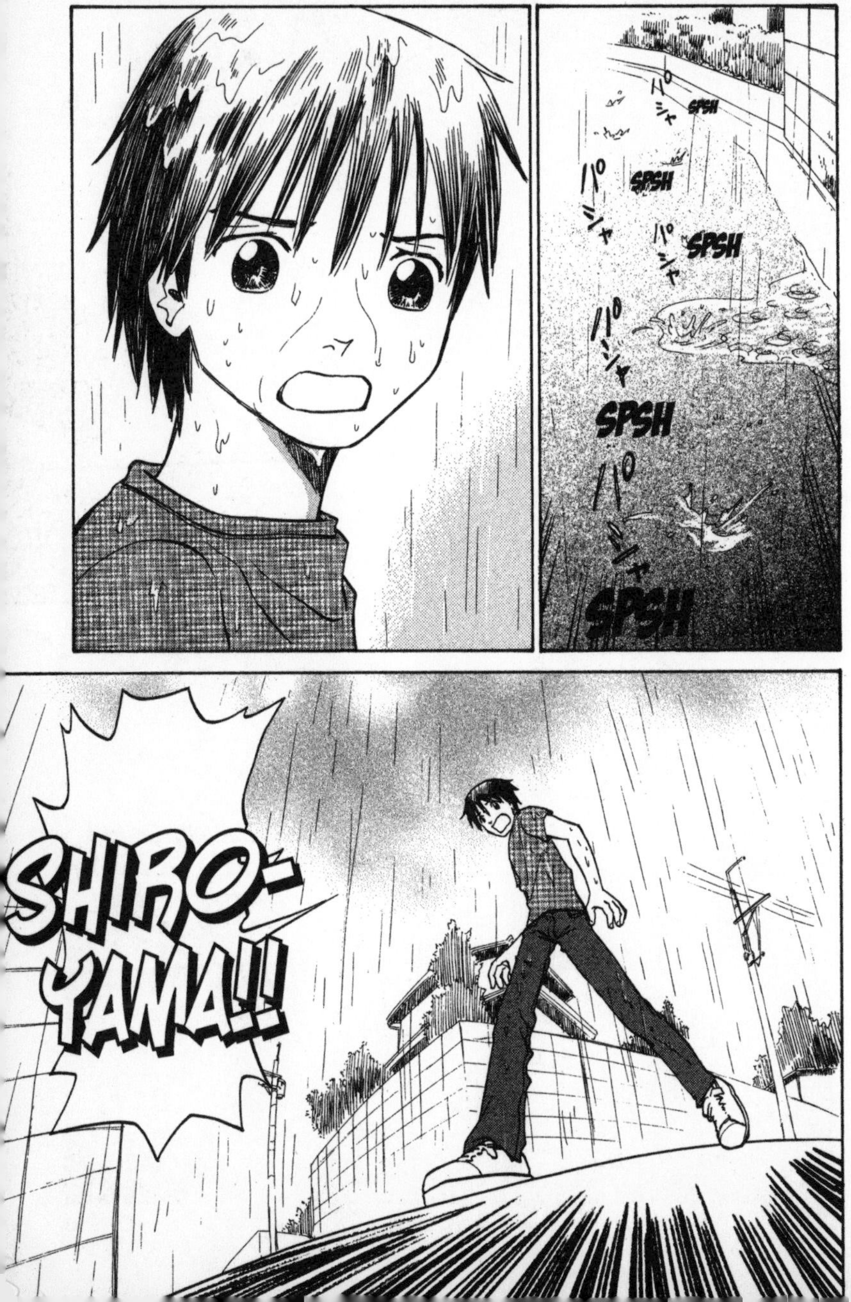

パシャ
SPSH
パシャ
SPSH
パシャ
SPSH
パシャ
SPSH
パシャ
SPSH
SHIRO-YAMA!!

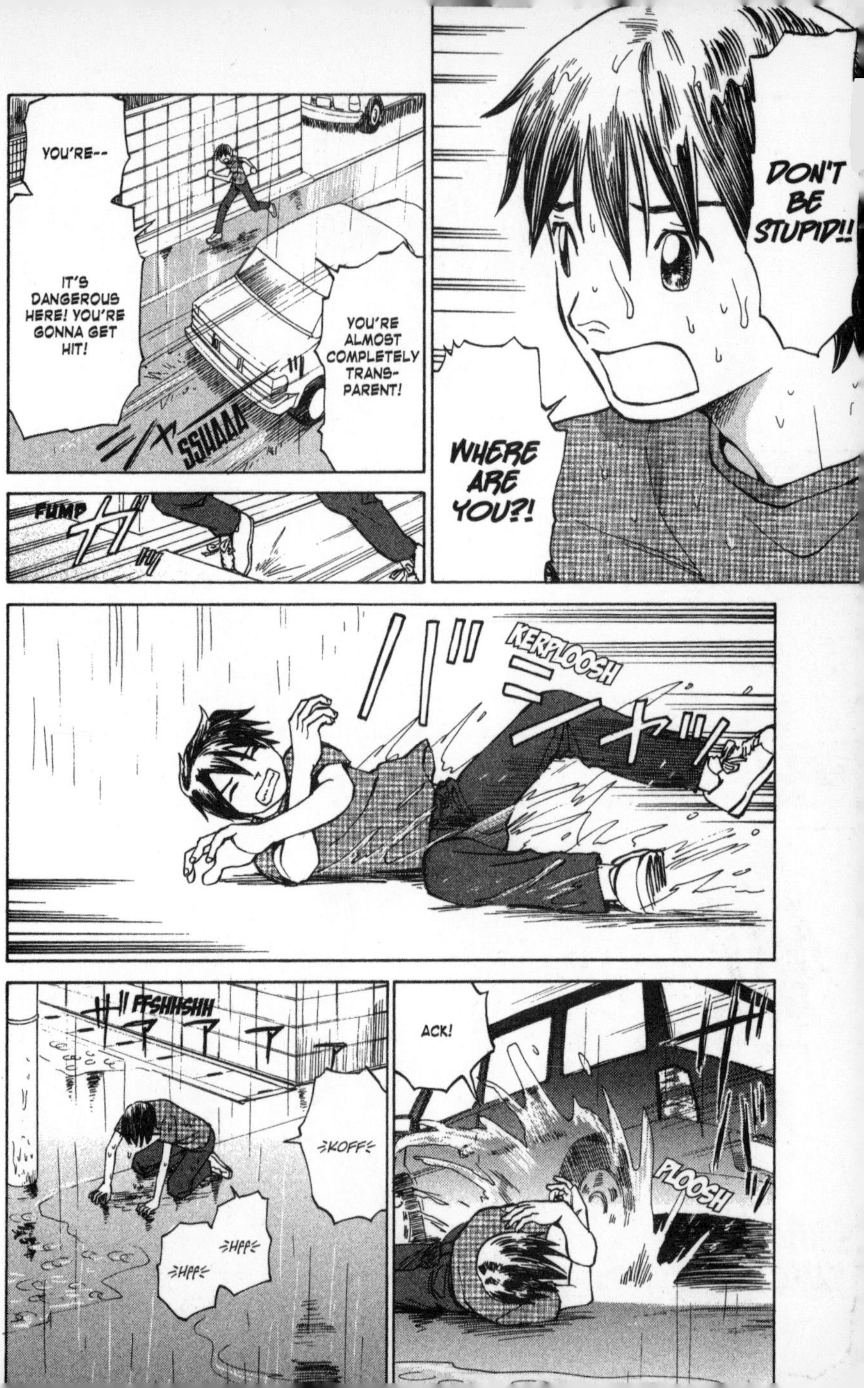

DON'T BE STUPID!!
WHERE ARE YOU?!
YOU'RE--
YOU'RE ALMOST COMPLETELY TRANS-PARENT!
IT'S DANGEROUS HERE! YOU'RE GONNA GET HIT!
SSHAAA
FUMP
KERPLOOSH
ACK!
PLOOSH
FFSHHSHH
≈KOFF≈
≈HFF≈
≈HFF≈

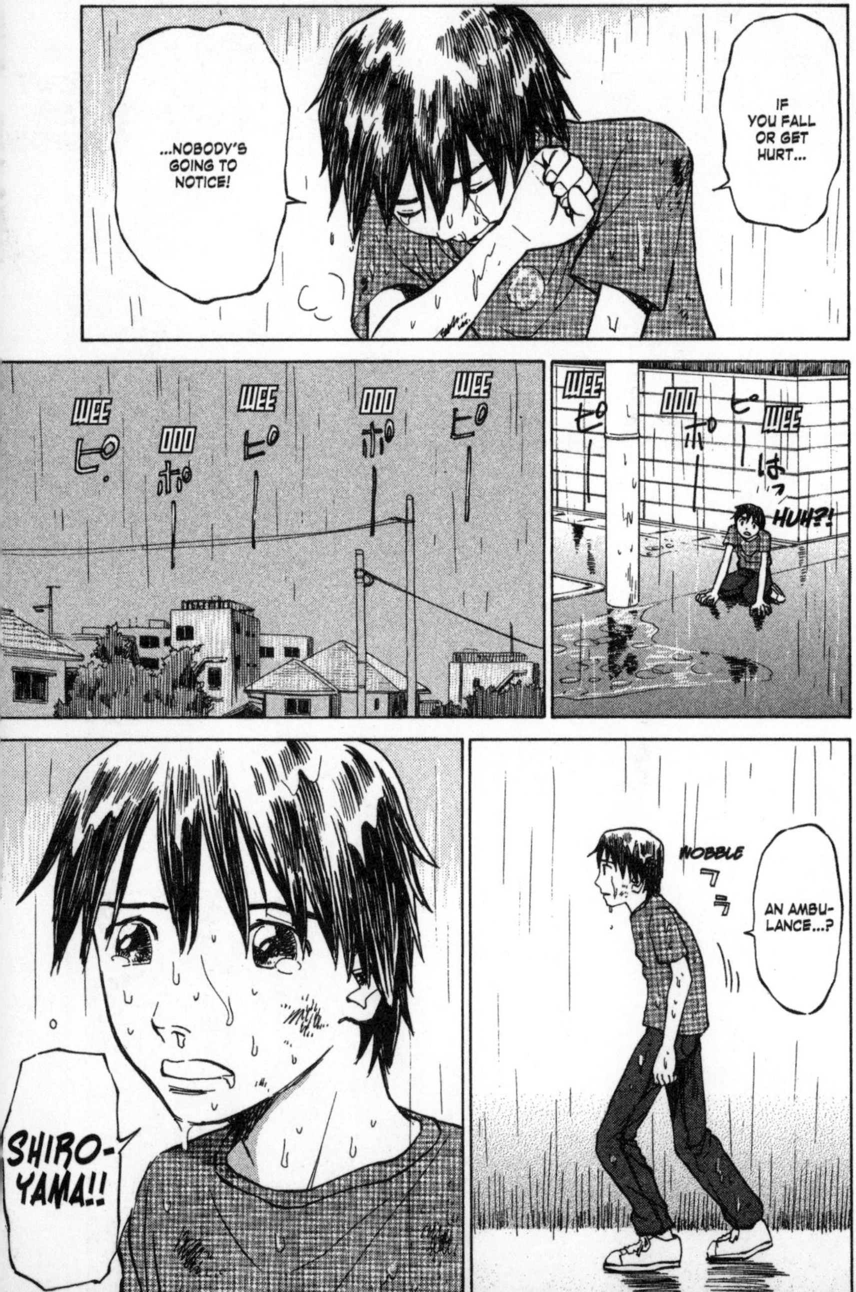
IF YOU FALL OR GET HURT...
...NOBODY'S GOING TO NOTICE!
WEE ピー
OOO ポー
WEE ピー
はっ
HUH?!
WEE ピー
OOO ポー
WEE ピー
OOO ポー
WEE ピ
WOBBLE フラ
AN AMBU-LANCE...?
SHIRO-YAMA!!

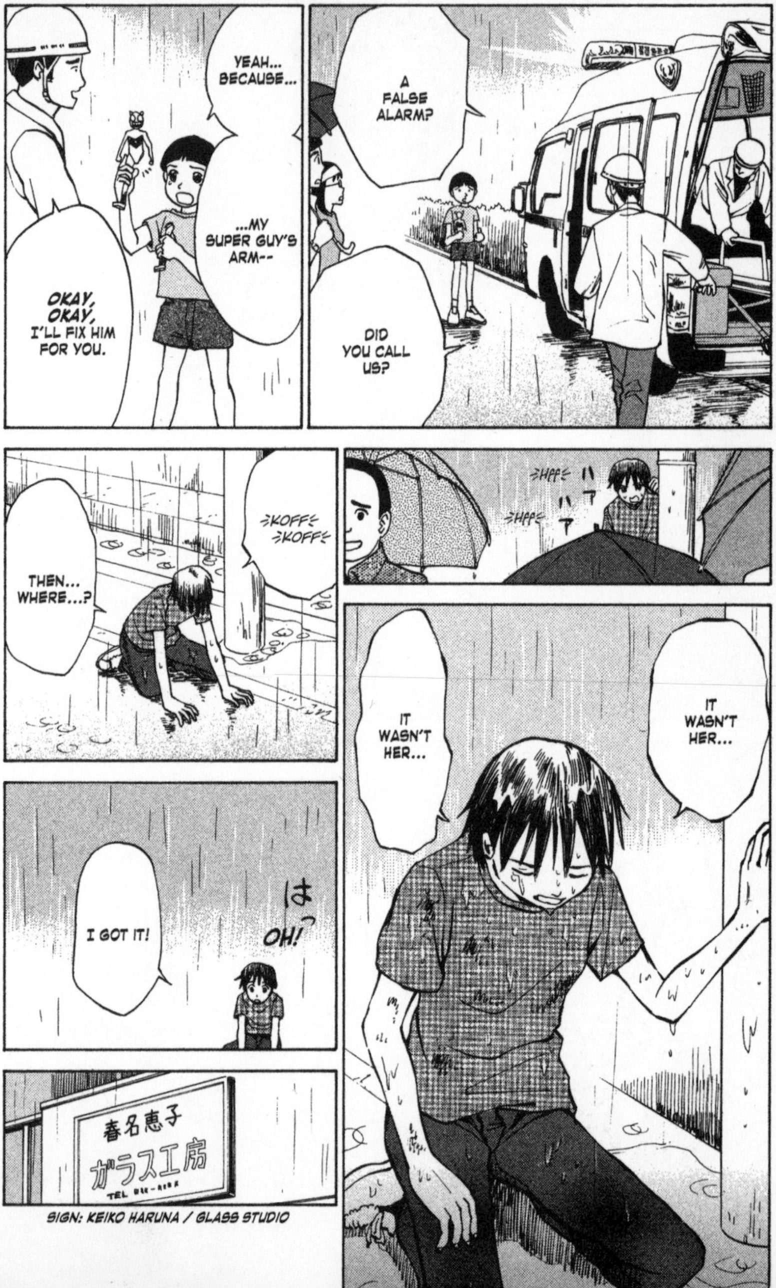
A FALSE ALARM?
DID YOU CALL US?
YEAH... BECAUSE...
...MY SUPER GUY'S ARM--
OKAY, OKAY, I'LL FIX HIM FOR YOU.
HFF HFF
ハァ ハァ
IT WASN'T HER...
...
IT WASN'T HER...
KOFF KOFF
THEN... WHERE...?
はっ
OH!
I GOT IT!
春名恵子
ガラス工房
SIGN: KEIKO HARUNA / GLASS STUDIO

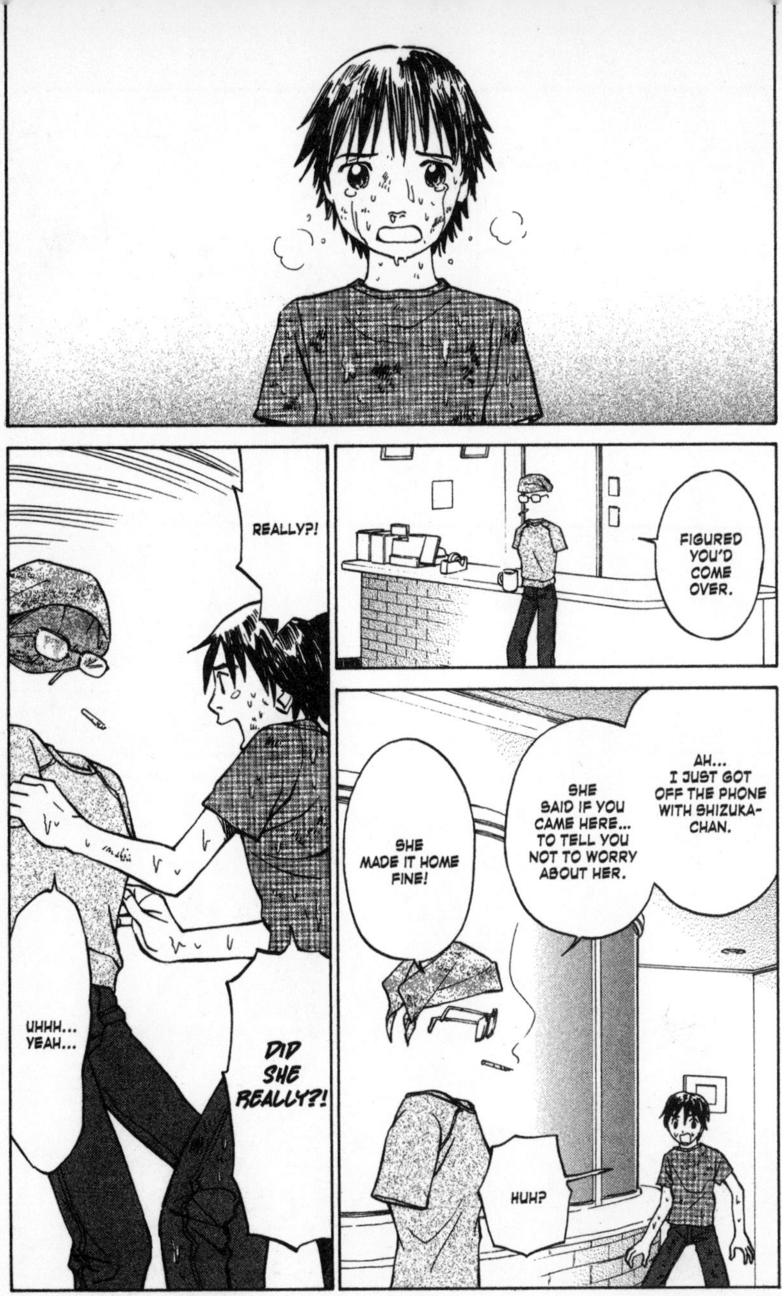
FIGURED YOU'D COME OVER.
AH... I JUST GOT OFF THE PHONE WITH SHIZUKA-CHAN.
SHE SAID IF YOU CAME HERE... TO TELL YOU NOT TO WORRY ABOUT HER.
SHE MADE IT HOME FINE!
HUH?
REALLY?!
DID SHE REALLY?!
UHHH... YEAH...

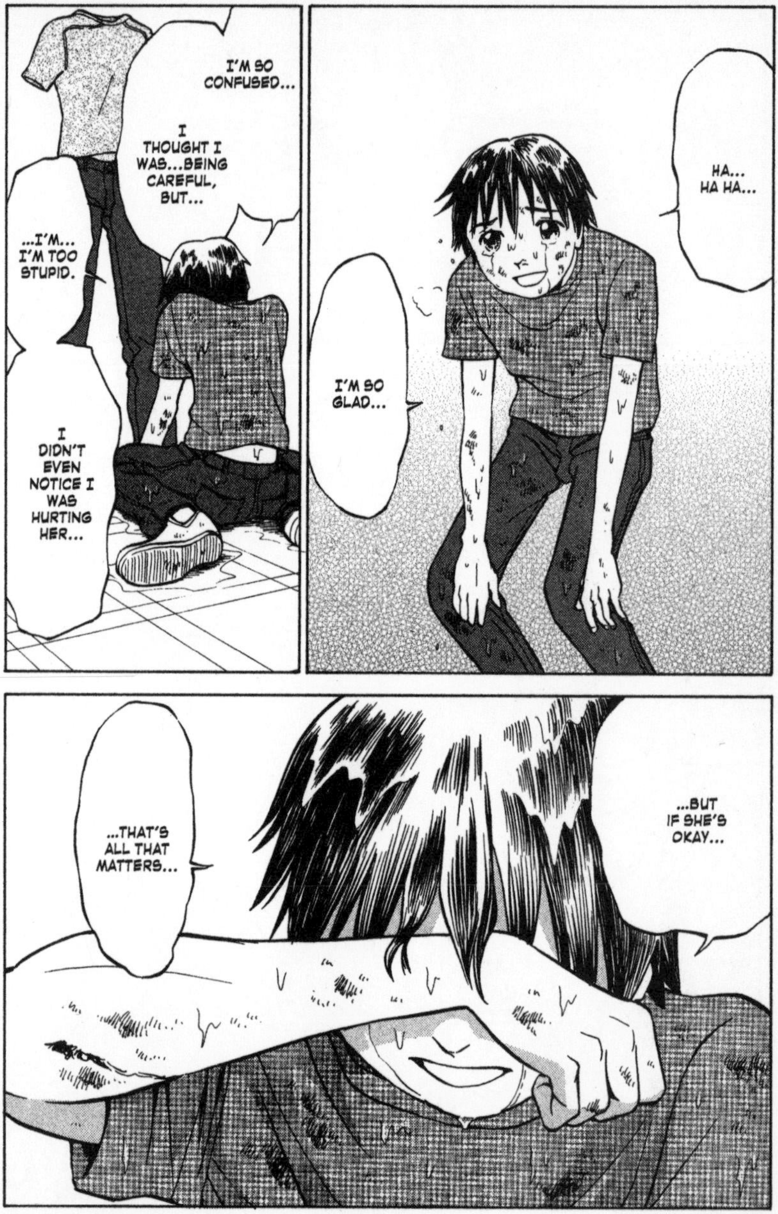
HA... HA HA...
I'M SO GLAD...
I'M SO CONFUSED...
I THOUGHT I WAS...BEING CAREFUL, BUT...
...I'M... I'M TOO STUPID.
I DIDN'T EVEN NOTICE I WAS HURTING HER...
...BUT IF SHE'S OKAY...
...THAT'S ALL THAT MATTERS...

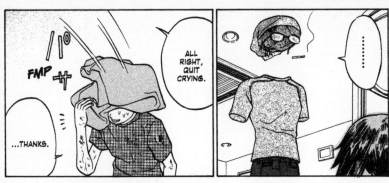

......
ALL RIGHT, QUIT CRYING.
FMP
...THANKS.
HEY, TADAMI-KUN...
...IF SHIZUKA-CHAN BECAME TRANSPARENT *FOREVER...*
...WHAT WOULD YOU DO?
WHAT DO YOU MEAN?
IF SHE BECAME TRANSPARENT AND STAYED THAT WAY...
...WOULD YOU STILL WANT TO BE WITH HER?

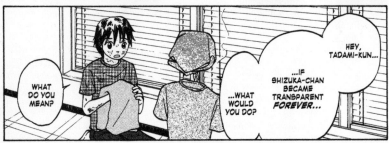

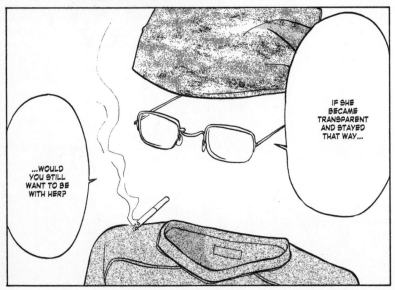

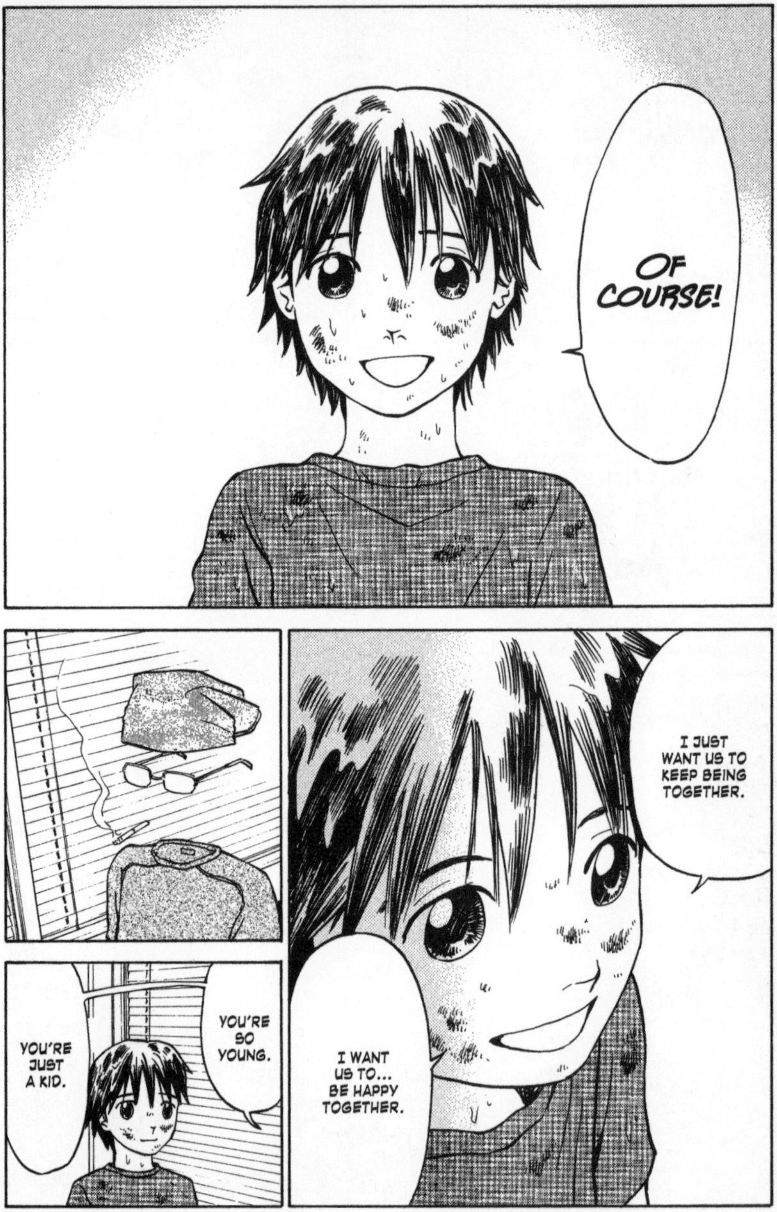
OF COURSE!
I JUST WANT US TO KEEP BEING TOGETHER.
I WANT US TO... BE HAPPY TOGETHER.
YOU'RE SO YOUNG.
YOU'RE JUST A KID.

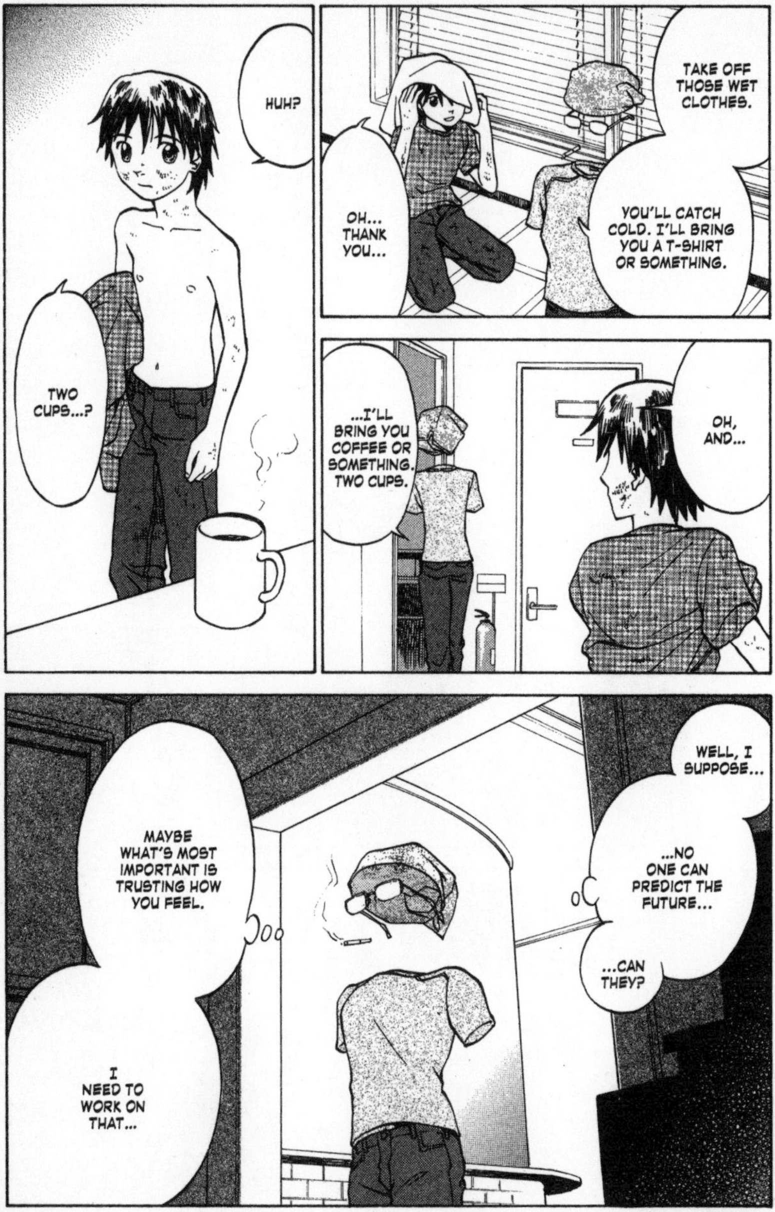
TAKE OFF THOSE WET CLOTHES.
YOU'LL CATCH COLD. I'LL BRING YOU A T-SHIRT OR SOMETHING.
OH... THANK YOU...
OH, AND...
...I'LL BRING YOU COFFEE OR SOMETHING. TWO CUPS.
HUH?
TWO CUPS...?
WELL, I SUPPOSE...
...NO ONE CAN PREDICT THE FUTURE...
...CAN THEY?
MAYBE WHAT'S MOST IMPORTANT IS TRUSTING HOW YOU FEEL.
I NEED TO WORK ON THAT...

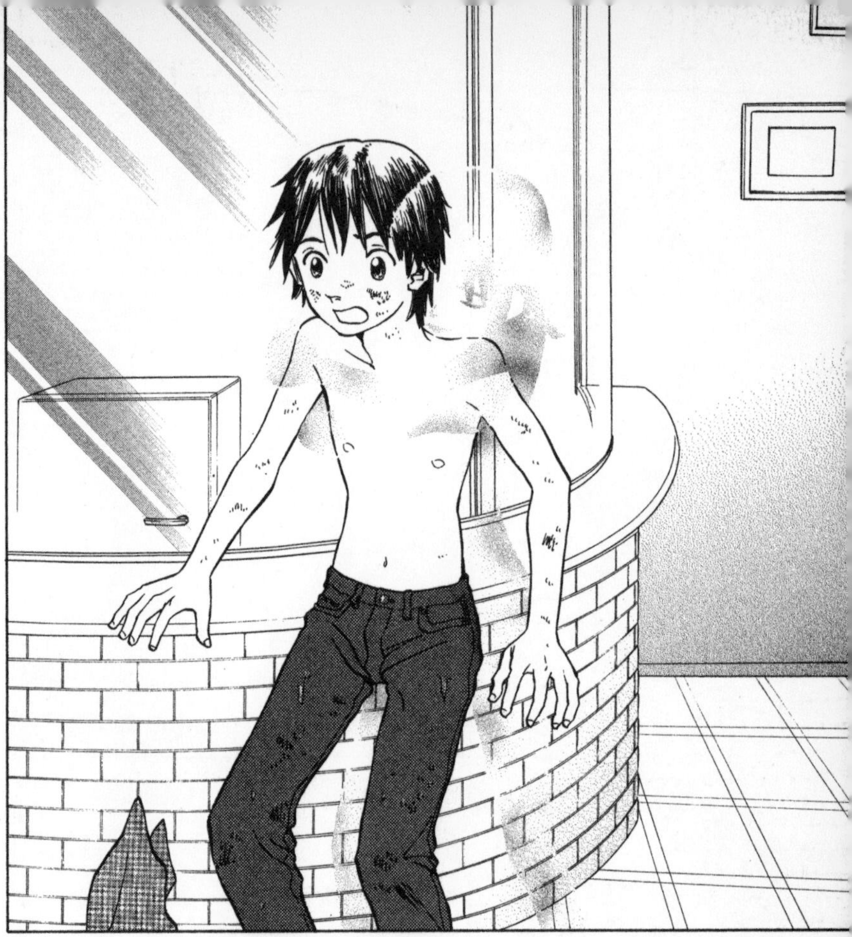

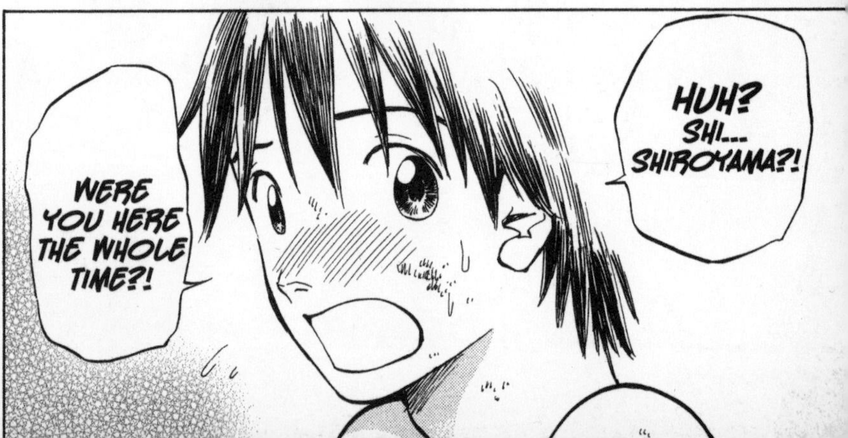
HUH?
SHI... SHIROYAMA?!
WERE YOU HERE THE WHOLE TIME?!

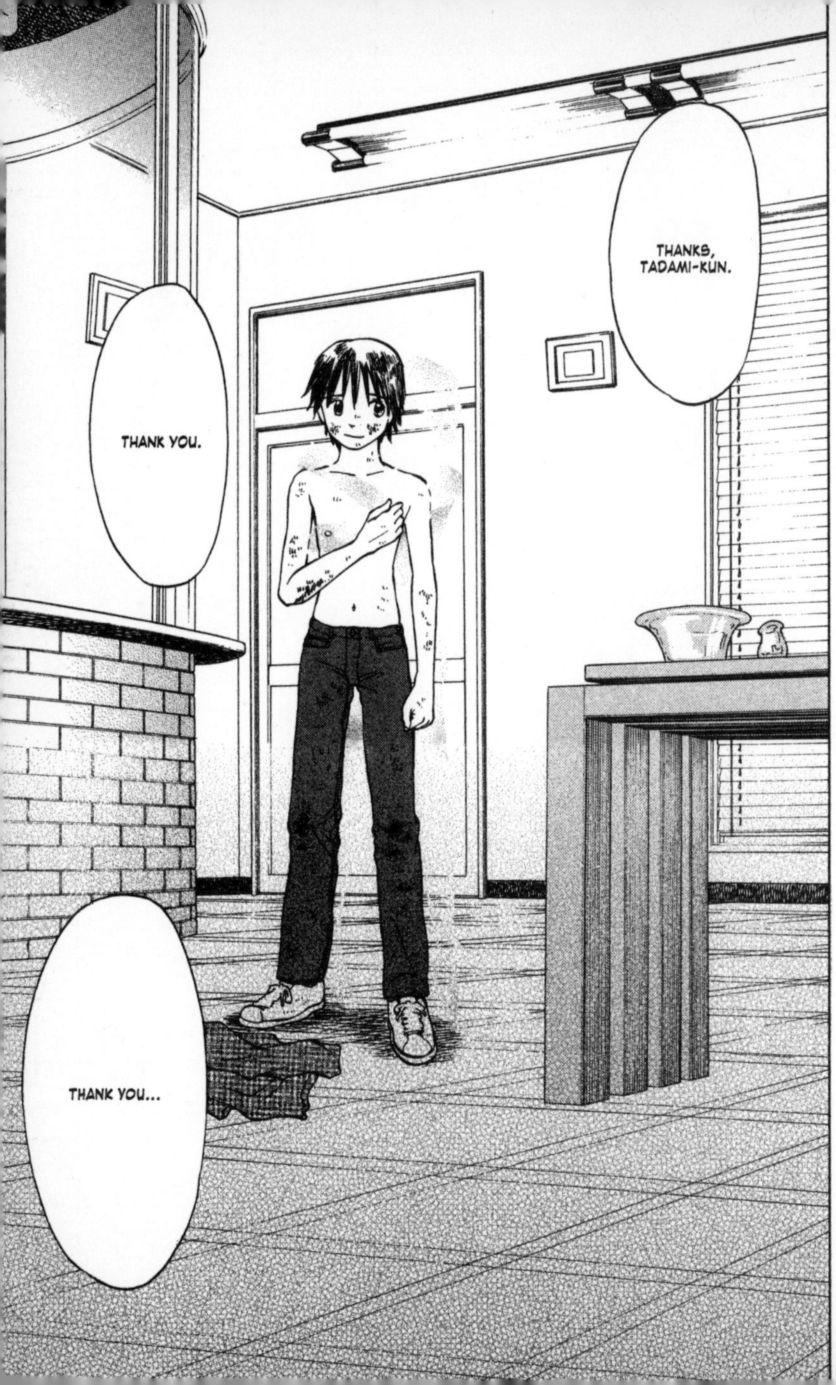
THANKS, TADAMI-KUN.
THANK YOU.
THANK YOU...

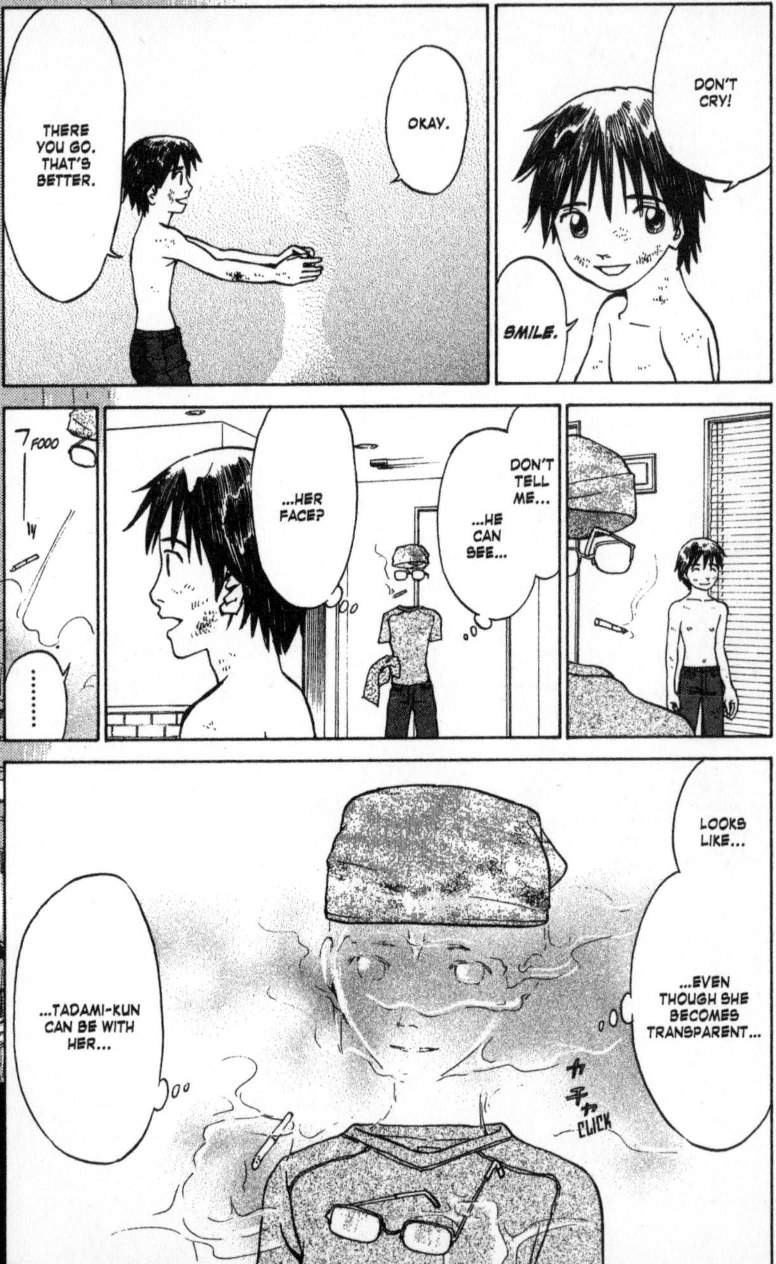
DON'T CRY!
SMILE.
OKAY.
THERE YOU GO. THAT'S BETTER.
DON'T TELL ME...
...HE CAN SEE...
...HER FACE?
FOOO
....
LOOKS LIKE...
...EVEN THOUGH SHE BECOMES TRANSPARENT...
CLICK
...TADAMI-KUN CAN BE WITH HER...

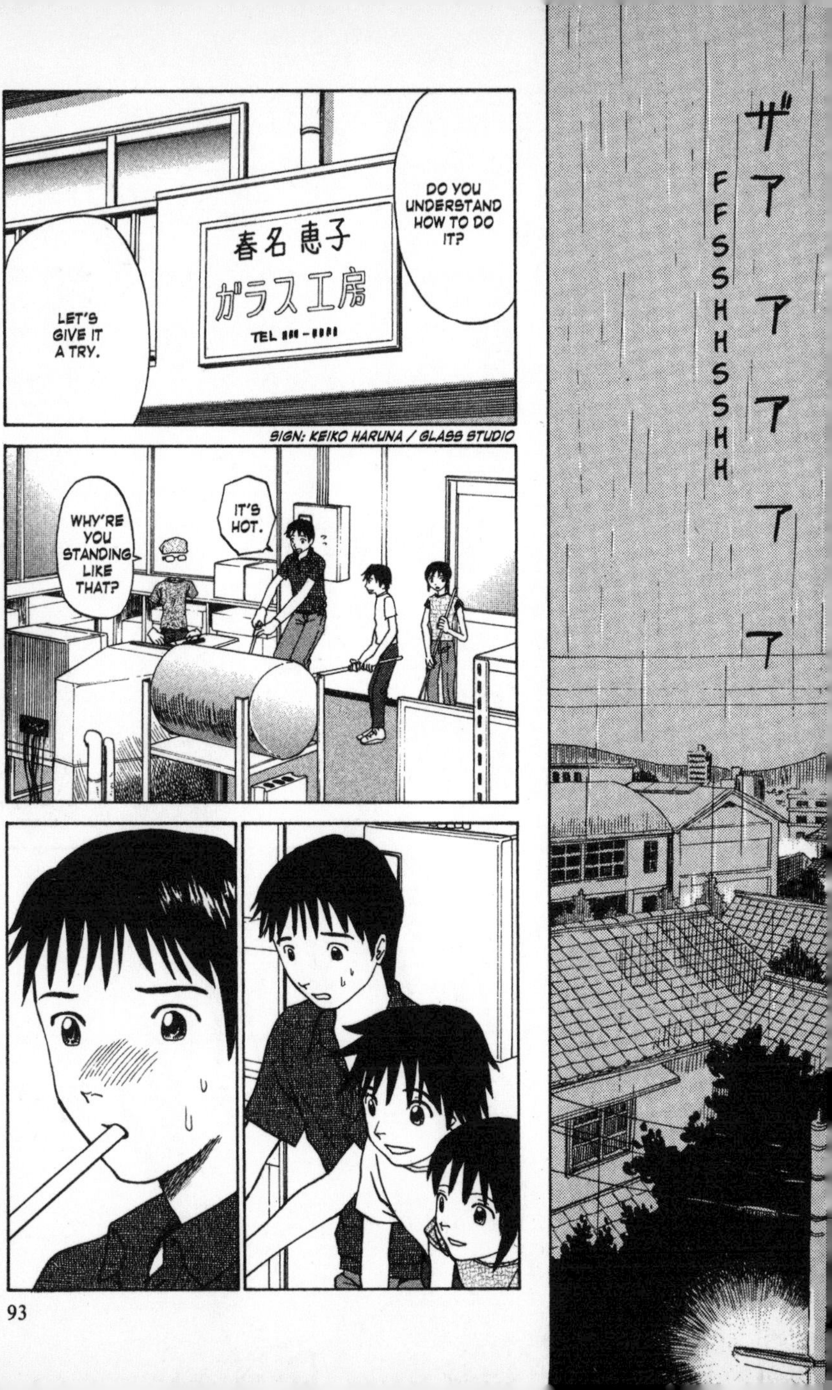
ザァァァァ
FFSSHHSSHH
DO YOU UNDERSTAND HOW TO DO IT?
LET'S GIVE IT A TRY.
春名恵子
ガラス工房
SIGN: KEIKO HARUNA / GLASS STUDIO
IT'S HOT.
WHY'RE YOU STANDING LIKE THAT?

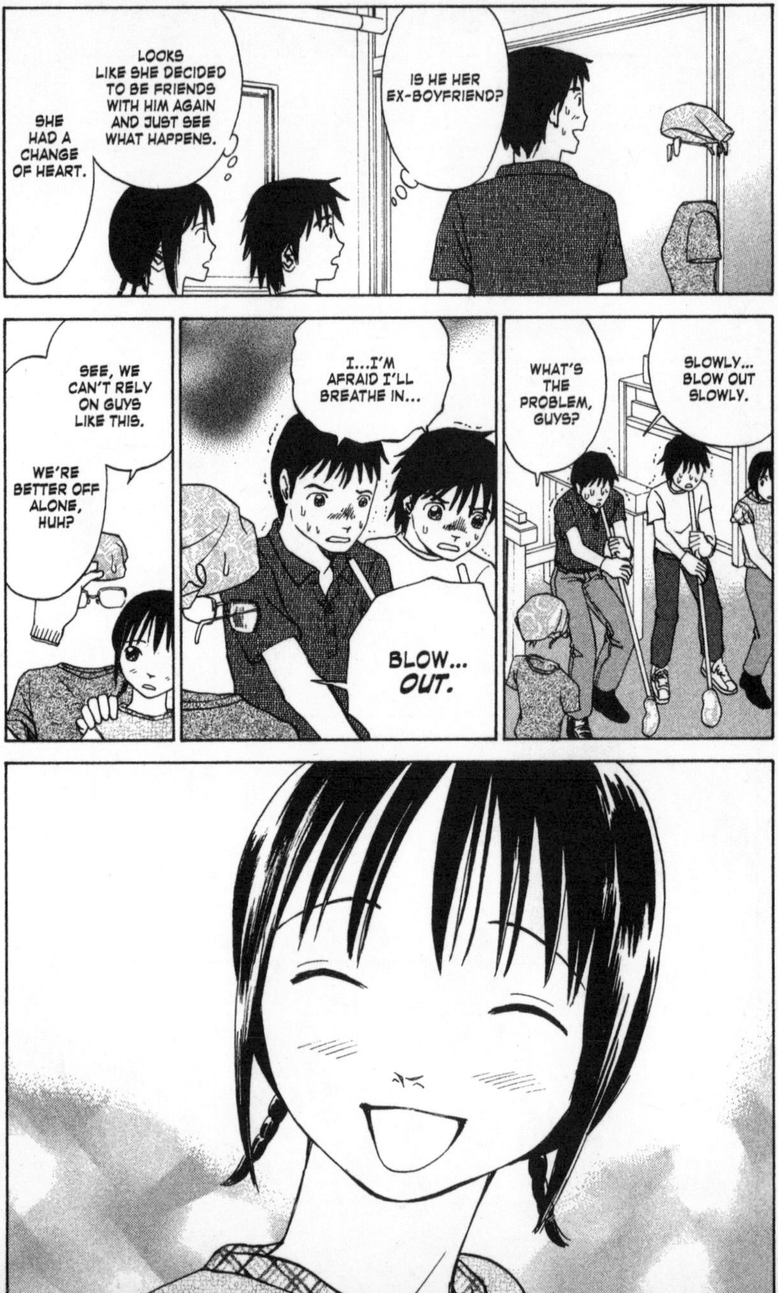
IS HE HER EX-BOYFRIEND?
LOOKS LIKE SHE DECIDED TO BE FRIENDS WITH HIM AGAIN AND JUST SEE WHAT HAPPENS.
SHE HAD A CHANGE OF HEART.
SLOWLY... BLOW OUT SLOWLY.
WHAT'S THE PROBLEM, GUYS?
I...I'M AFRAID I'LL BREATHE IN...
BLOW... OUT.
SEE, WE CAN'T RELY ON GUYS LIKE THIS.
WE'RE BETTER OFF ALONE, HUH?

PART 4 Shizuka Transfers Schools?!

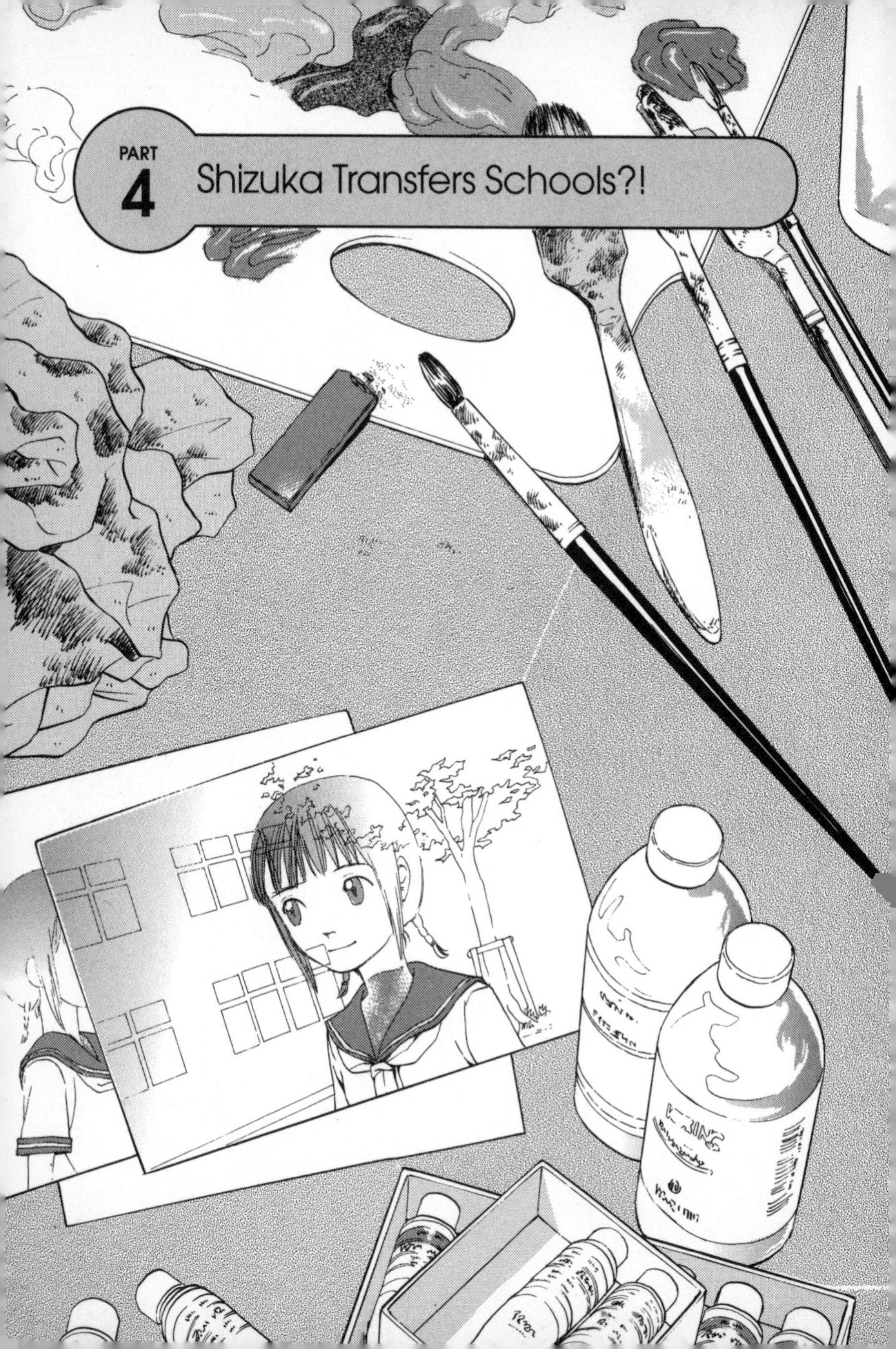

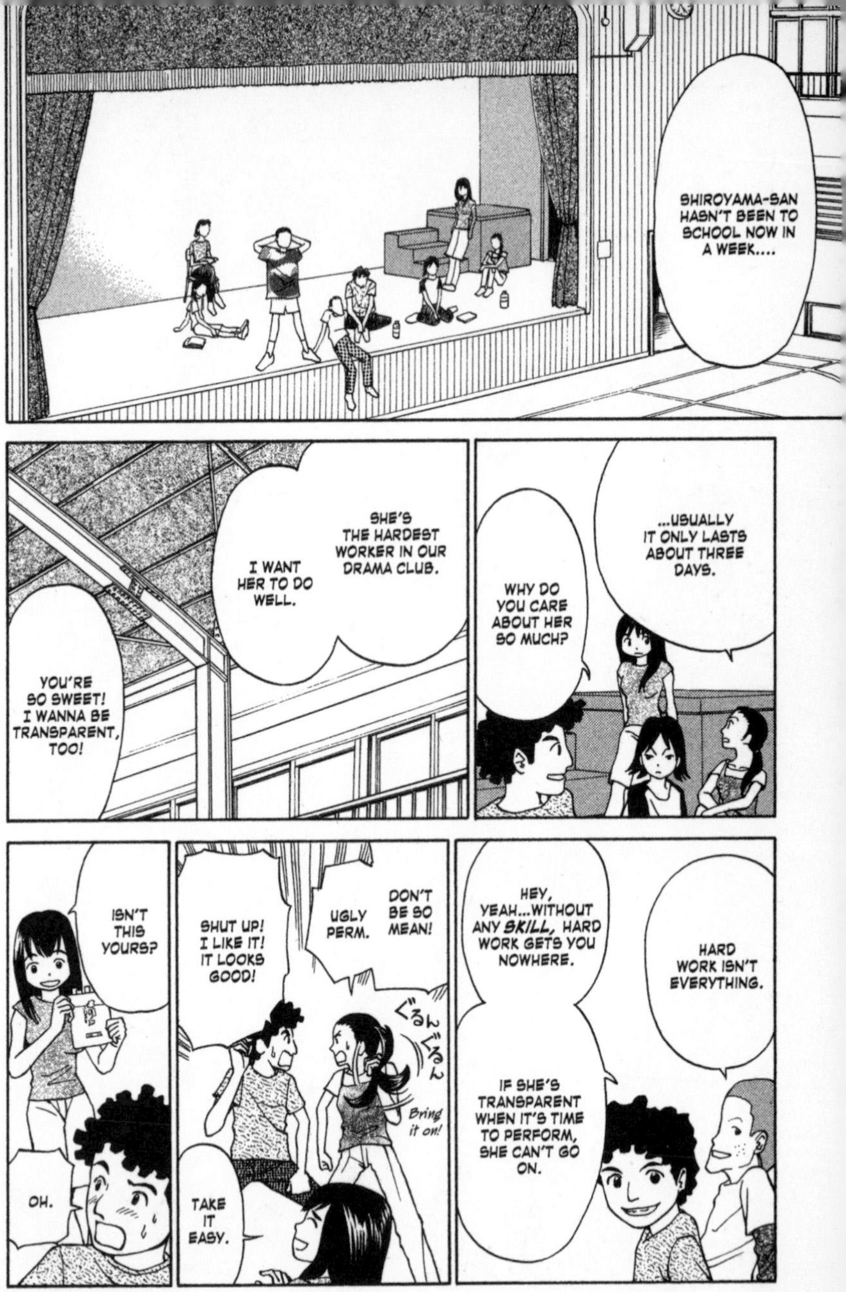
SHIROYAMA-SAN HASN'T BEEN TO SCHOOL NOW IN A WEEK....
...USUALLY IT ONLY LASTS ABOUT THREE DAYS.
WHY DO YOU CARE ABOUT HER SO MUCH?
SHE'S THE HARDEST WORKER IN OUR DRAMA CLUB.
I WANT HER TO DO WELL.
YOU'RE SO SWEET! I WANNA BE TRANSPARENT, TOO!
HARD WORK ISN'T EVERYTHING.
HEY, YEAH...WITHOUT ANY SKILL, HARD WORK GETS YOU NOWHERE.
IF SHE'S TRANSPARENT WHEN IT'S TIME TO PERFORM, SHE CAN'T GO ON.
DON'T BE SO MEAN!
UGLY PERM.
SHUT UP! I LIKE IT! IT LOOKS GOOD!
ぐるんぐるん
Bring it on!
TAKE IT EASY.
ISN'T THIS YOURS?
OH.

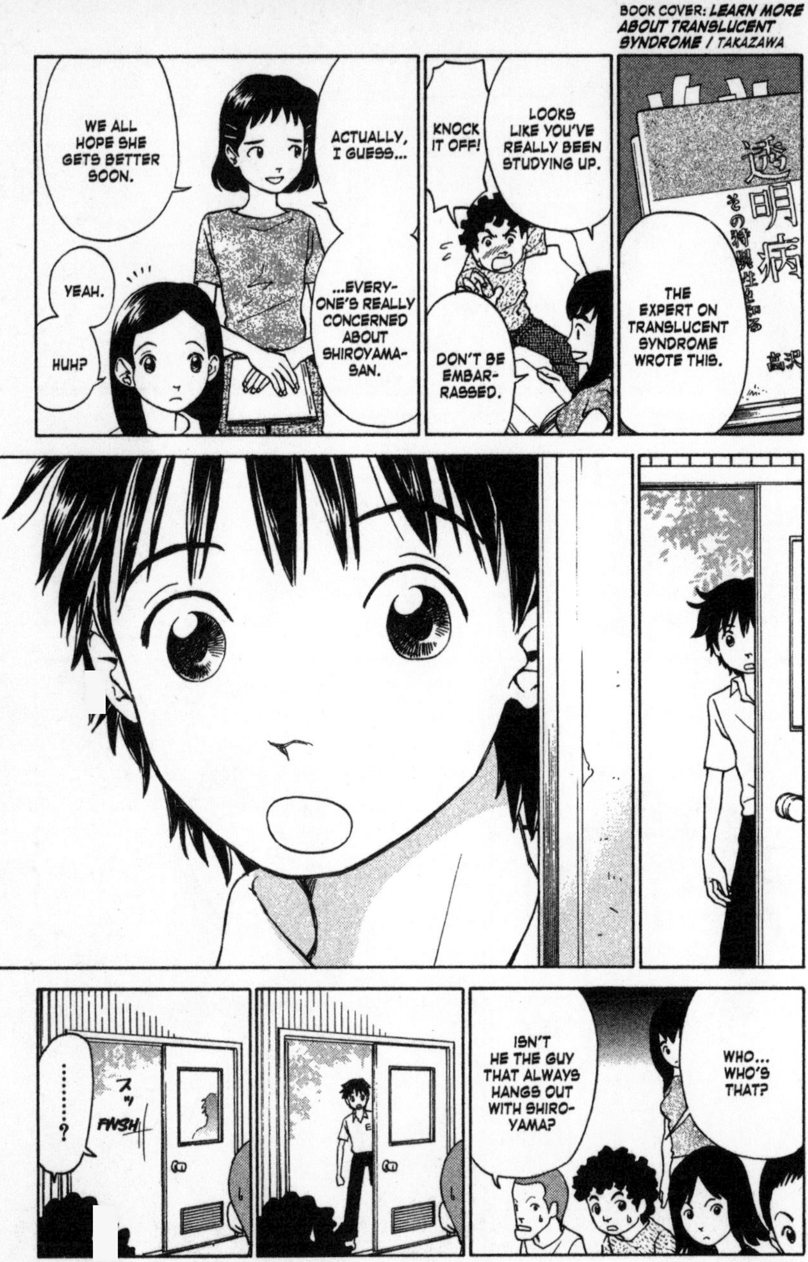
BOOK COVER: LEARN MORE ABOUT TRANSLUCENT SYNDROME / TAKAZAWA
透明病
高沢
THE EXPERT ON TRANSLUCENT SYNDROME WROTE THIS.
LOOKS LIKE YOU'VE REALLY BEEN STUDYING UP.
KNOCK IT OFF!
DON'T BE EMBARRASSED.
ACTUALLY, I GUESS...
...EVERY-ONE'S REALLY CONCERNED ABOUT SHIROYAMA-SAN.
WE ALL HOPE SHE GETS BETTER SOON.
YEAH.
HUH?
WHO... WHO'S THAT?
ISN'T HE THE GUY THAT ALWAYS HANGS OUT WITH SHIRO-YAMA?
スッ
FWSH
.........?

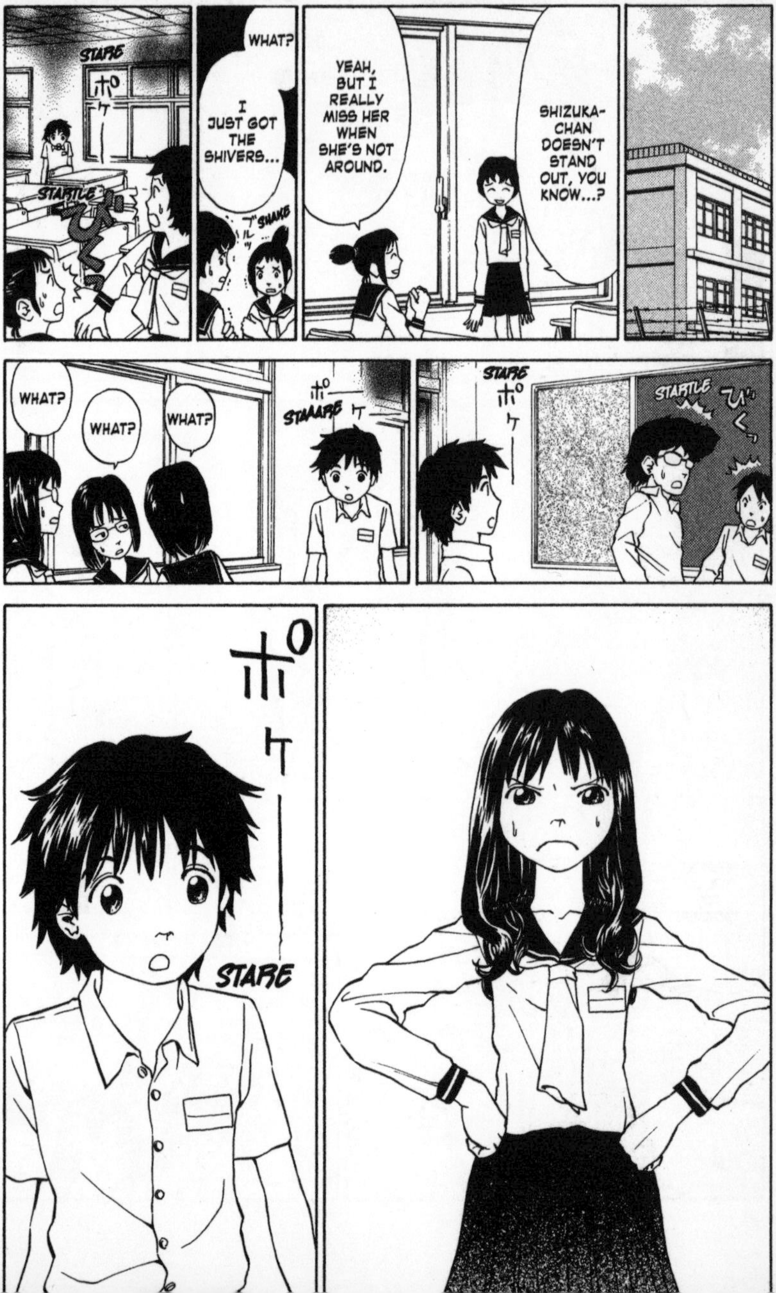
SHIZUKA-CHAN DOESN'T STAND OUT, YOU KNOW...?
YEAH, BUT I REALLY MISS HER WHEN SHE'S NOT AROUND.
WHAT?
I JUST GOT THE SHIVERS...
SHAKE
ブルッ
STARE
ポケ
STARTLE
びくっ
STARE
ポケー
STARTLE
びくっ
ポケ
STAAARE
WHAT?
WHAT?
WHAT?
ポケー
STARE

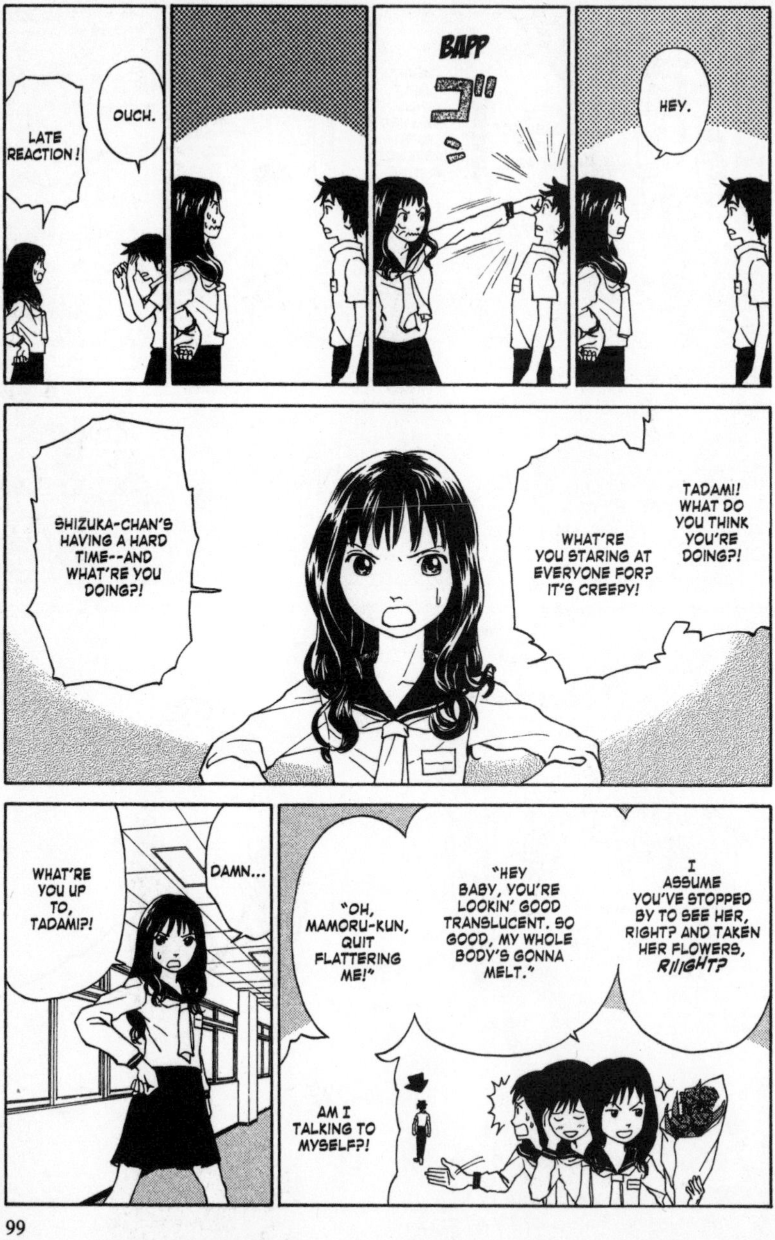
HEY.
BAPP
ゴ
OUCH.
LATE REACTION!
TADAMI! WHAT DO YOU THINK YOU'RE DOING?!
WHAT'RE YOU STARING AT EVERYONE FOR? IT'S CREEPY!
SHIZUKA-CHAN'S HAVING A HARD TIME--AND WHAT'RE YOU DOING?!
I ASSUME YOU'VE STOPPED BY TO SEE HER, RIGHT? AND TAKEN HER FLOWERS, RIIGHT?
"HEY BABY, YOU'RE LOOKIN' GOOD TRANSLUCENT. SO GOOD, MY WHOLE BODY'S GONNA MELT."
"OH, MAMORU-KUN, QUIT FLATTERING ME!"
AM I TALKING TO MYSELF?!
DAMN...
WHAT'RE YOU UP TO, TADAMI?!

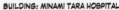

BUILDING: MINAMI TARA HOSPITAL

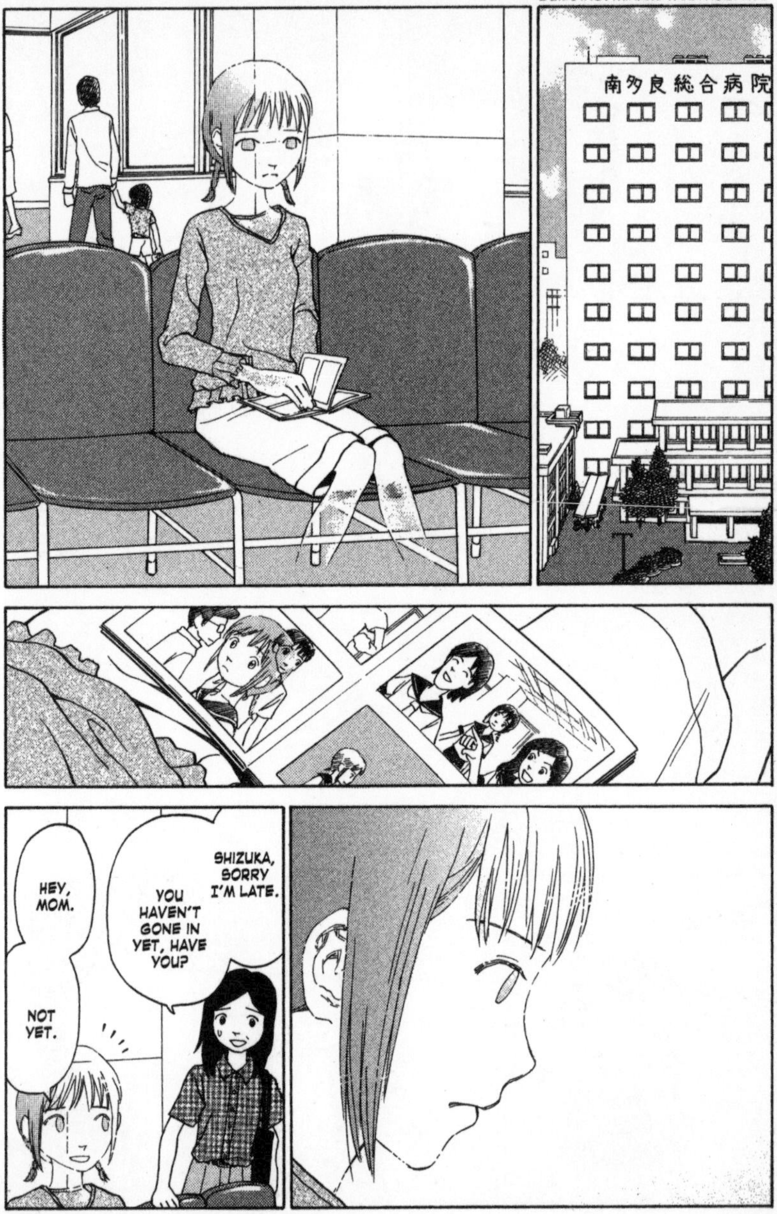

南多良総合病院
SHIZUKA, SORRY I'M LATE.
YOU HAVEN'T GONE IN YET, HAVE YOU?
HEY, MOM.
NOT YET.

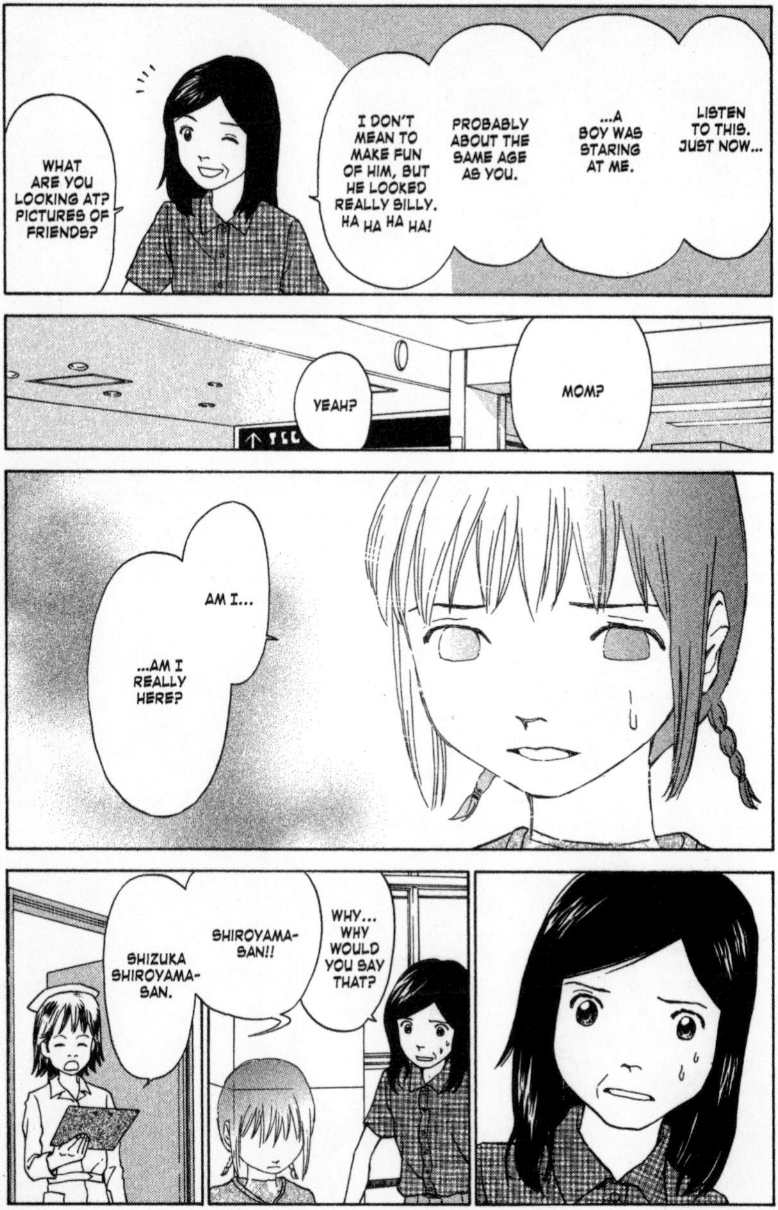
LISTEN TO THIS. JUST NOW...
...A BOY WAS STARING AT ME.
PROBABLY ABOUT THE SAME AGE AS YOU.
I DON'T MEAN TO MAKE FUN OF HIM, BUT HE LOOKED REALLY SILLY. HA HA HA HA!
WHAT ARE YOU LOOKING AT? PICTURES OF FRIENDS?
MOM?
YEAH?
AM I...
...AM I REALLY HERE?
WHY... WHY WOULD YOU SAY THAT?
SHIROYAMA-SAN!!
SHIZUKA SHIROYAMA-SAN.

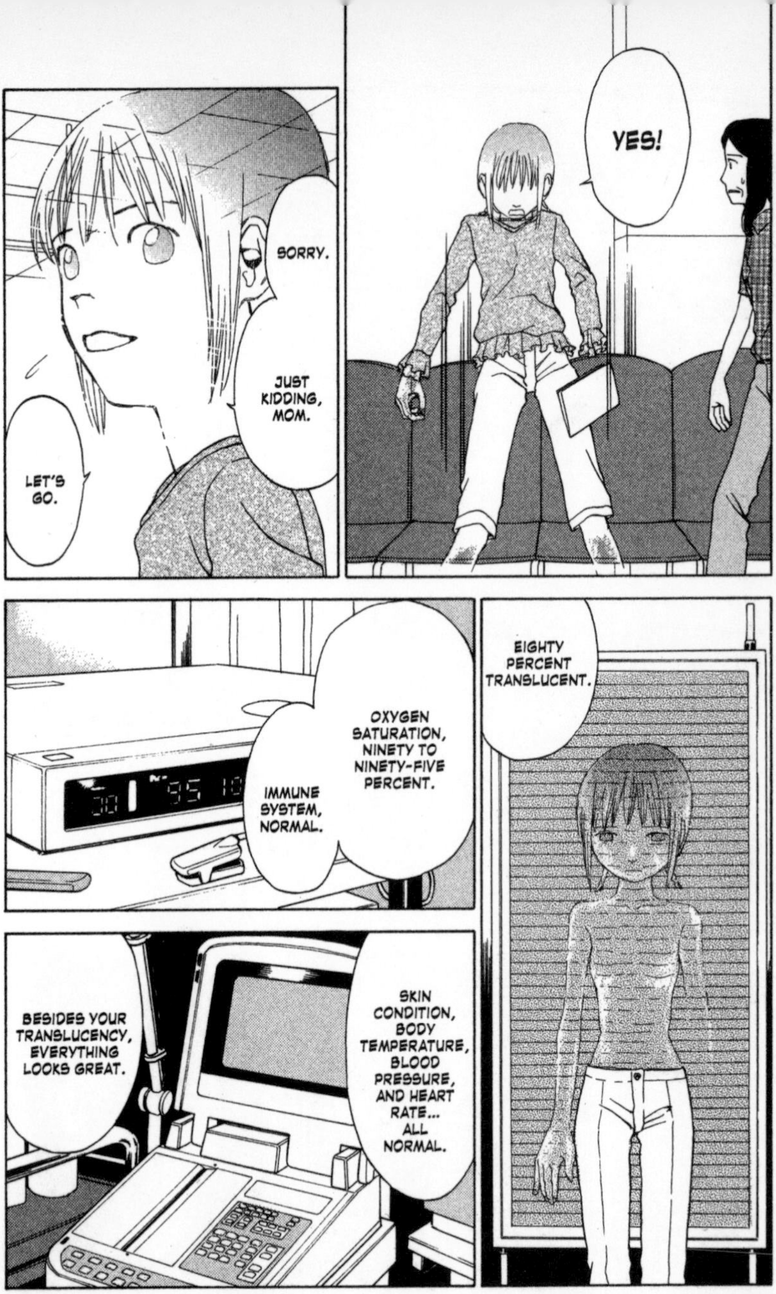
YES!
SORRY.
JUST KIDDING, MOM.
LET'S GO.
EIGHTY PERCENT TRANSLUCENT.
OXYGEN SATURATION, NINETY TO NINETY-FIVE PERCENT.
IMMUNE SYSTEM, NORMAL.
SKIN CONDITION, BODY TEMPERATURE, BLOOD PRESSURE, AND HEART RATE... ALL NORMAL.
BESIDES YOUR TRANSLUCENCY, EVERYTHING LOOKS GREAT.

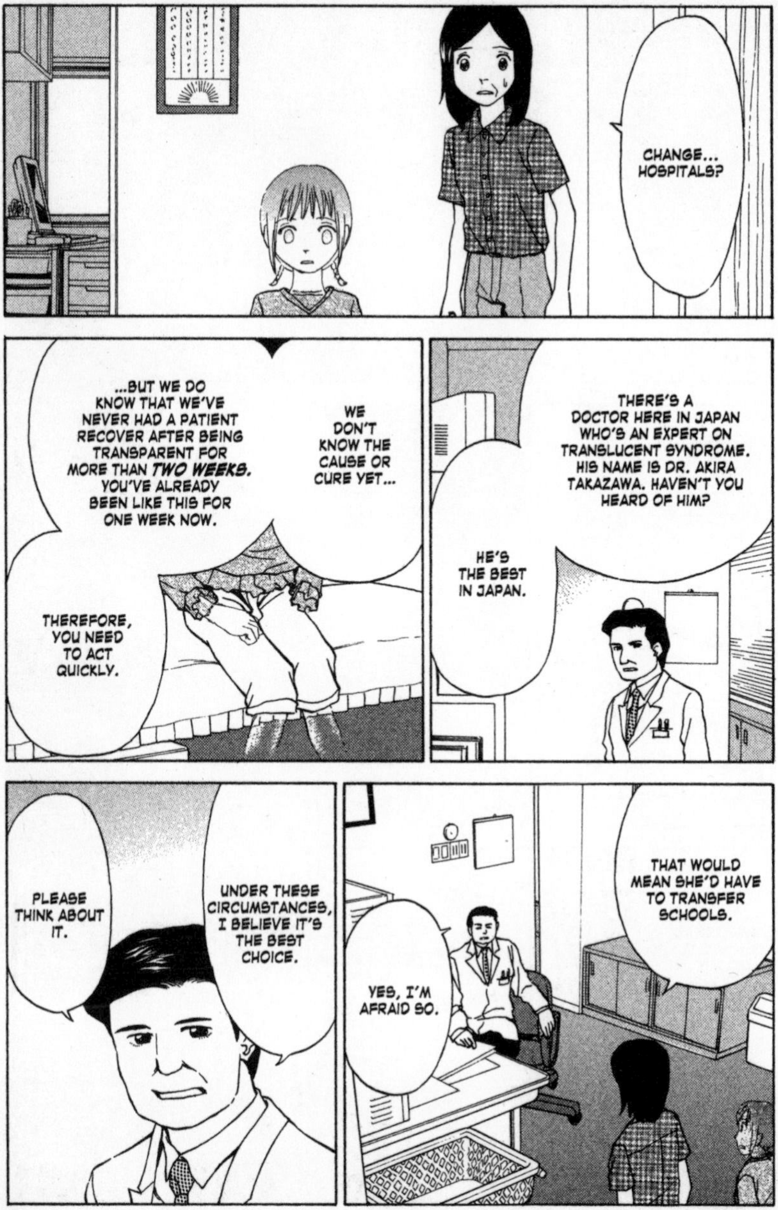
CHANGE... HOSPITALS?
THERE'S A DOCTOR HERE IN JAPAN WHO'S AN EXPERT ON TRANSLUCENT SYNDROME. HIS NAME IS DR. AKIRA TAKAZAWA. HAVEN'T YOU HEARD OF HIM?
HE'S THE BEST IN JAPAN.
WE DON'T KNOW THE CAUSE OR CURE YET...
...BUT WE DO KNOW THAT WE'VE NEVER HAD A PATIENT RECOVER AFTER BEING TRANSPARENT FOR MORE THAN *TWO WEEKS.* YOU'VE ALREADY BEEN LIKE THIS FOR ONE WEEK NOW.
THEREFORE, YOU NEED TO ACT QUICKLY.
THAT WOULD MEAN SHE'D HAVE TO TRANSFER SCHOOLS.
YES, I'M AFRAID SO.
UNDER THESE CIRCUMSTANCES, I BELIEVE IT'S THE BEST CHOICE.
PLEASE THINK ABOUT IT.

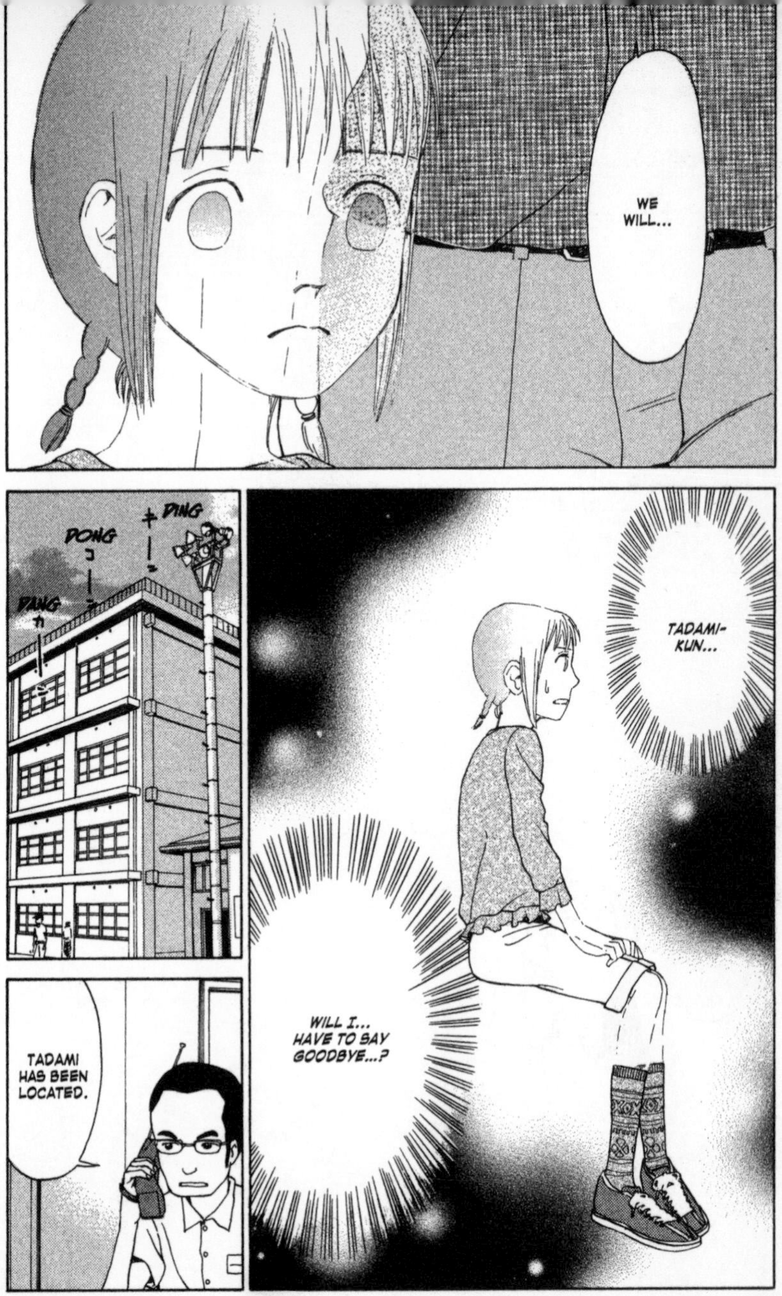
WE WILL...
TADAMI-KUN...
WILL I... HAVE TO SAY GOODBYE...?
DING
DONG
DANG
TADAMI HAS BEEN LOCATED.

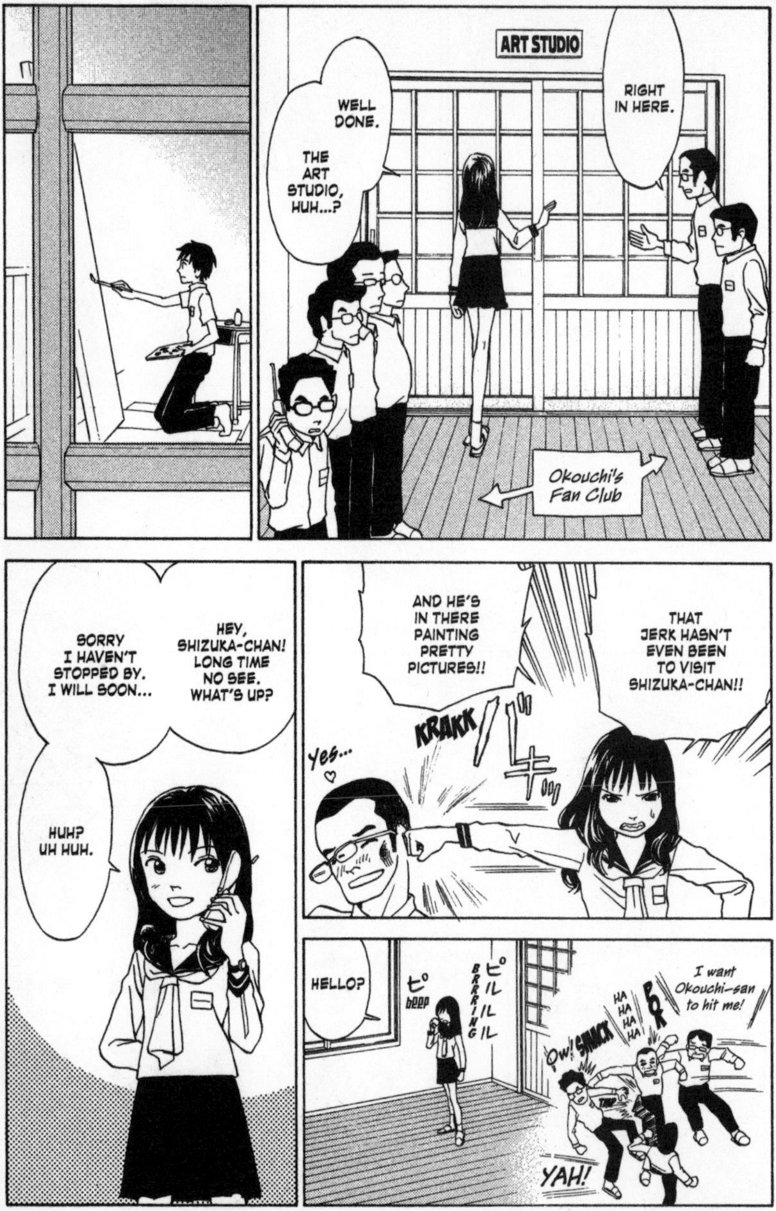
ART STUDIO
RIGHT IN HERE.
WELL DONE.
THE ART STUDIO, HUH...?
Okouchi's Fan Club
THAT JERK HASN'T EVEN BEEN TO VISIT SHIZUKA-CHAN!!
AND HE'S IN THERE PAINTING PRETTY PICTURES!!
KRAKK
Yes...
I want Okouchi-san to hit me!
HA HA HA HA
POK
Ow!
SMACK
YAH!
BRRRING
beep
HELLO?
HEY, SHIZUKA-CHAN! LONG TIME NO SEE. WHAT'S UP?
SORRY I HAVEN'T STOPPED BY. I WILL SOON...
HUH? UH HUH.

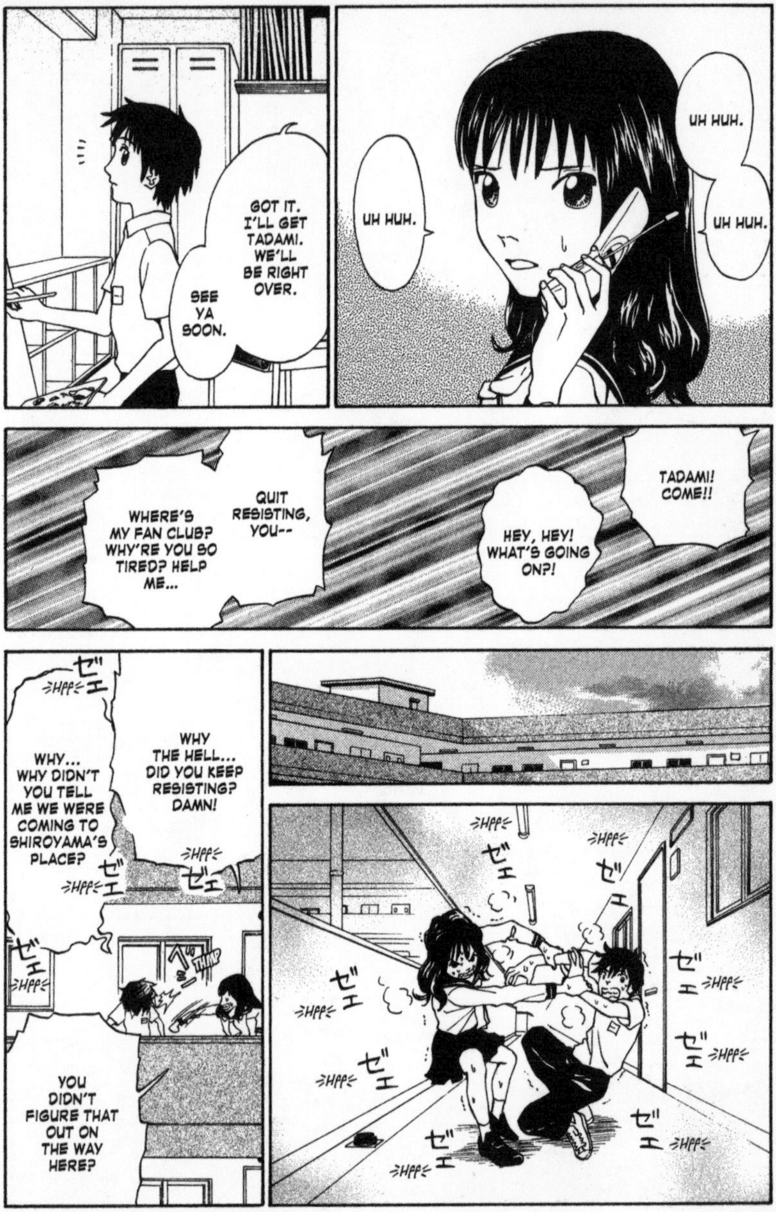
UH HUH.
UH HUH.
UH HUH.
GOT IT. I'LL GET TADAMI. WE'LL BE RIGHT OVER.
SEE YA SOON.
TADAMI! COME!!
HEY, HEY! WHAT'S GOING ON?!
QUIT RESISTING, YOU--
WHERE'S MY FAN CLUB? WHY'RE YOU SO TIRED? HELP ME...
HFF ゼェ
WHY THE HELL... DID YOU KEEP RESISTING? DAMN!
WHY... WHY DIDN'T YOU TELL ME WE WERE COMING TO SHIROYAMA'S PLACE?
HFF ゼェ
THMP
YOU DIDN'T FIGURE THAT OUT ON THE WAY HERE?

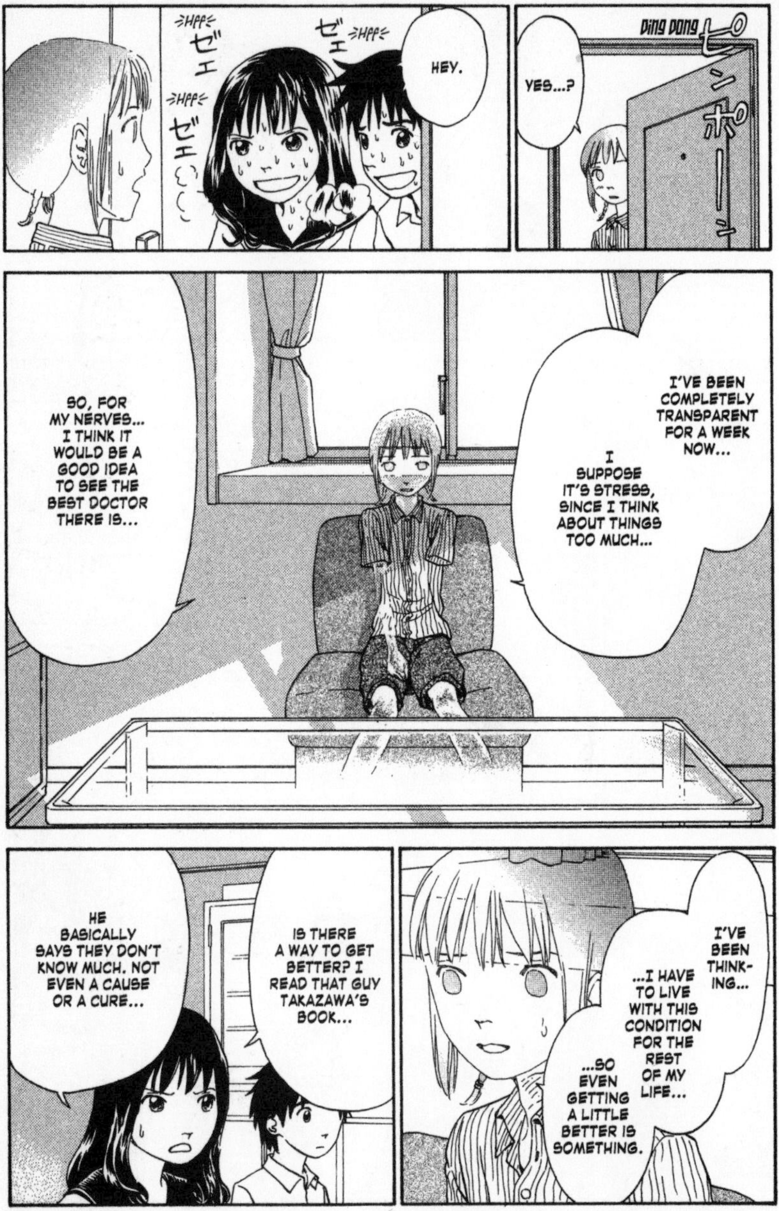
Ding Dong
ピンポーン
YES...?
HEY.
HFF
ゼェ
HFF
HFF
ゼェ
I'VE BEEN COMPLETELY TRANSPARENT FOR A WEEK NOW...
I SUPPOSE IT'S STRESS, SINCE I THINK ABOUT THINGS TOO MUCH...
SO, FOR MY NERVES... I THINK IT WOULD BE A GOOD IDEA TO SEE THE BEST DOCTOR THERE IS...
I'VE BEEN THINKING...
...I HAVE TO LIVE WITH THIS CONDITION FOR THE REST OF MY LIFE...
...SO EVEN GETTING A LITTLE BETTER IS SOMETHING.
IS THERE A WAY TO GET BETTER? I READ THAT GUY TAKAZAWA'S BOOK...
HE BASICALLY SAYS THEY DON'T KNOW MUCH. NOT EVEN A CAUSE OR A CURE...

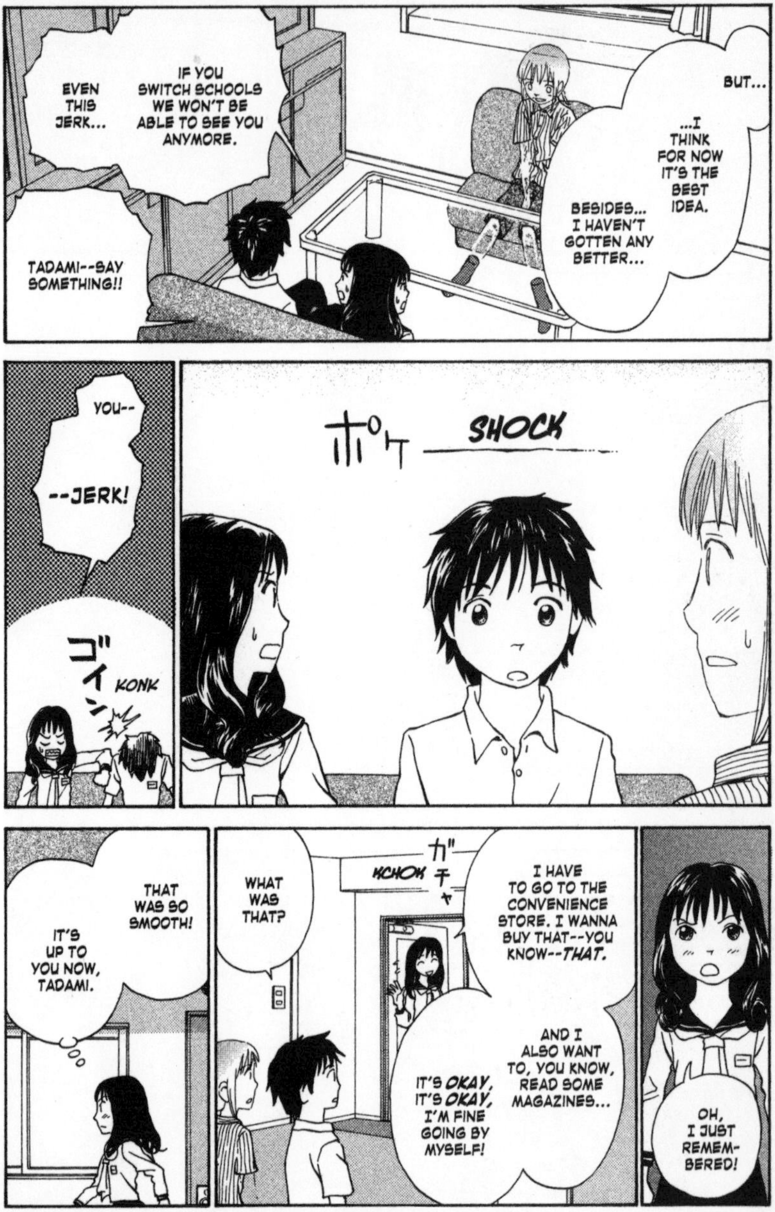
BUT...
...I THINK FOR NOW IT'S THE BEST IDEA.
BESIDES... I HAVEN'T GOTTEN ANY BETTER...
IF YOU SWITCH SCHOOLS WE WON'T BE ABLE TO SEE YOU ANYMORE.
EVEN THIS JERK...
TADAMI--SAY SOMETHING!!
ポケ
SHOCK
YOU--
--JERK!
ゴイン
KONK
OH, I JUST REMEM-BERED!
ガチャ
KCHOK
I HAVE TO GO TO THE CONVENIENCE STORE. I WANNA BUY THAT--YOU KNOW--*THAT.*
AND I ALSO WANT TO, YOU KNOW, READ SOME MAGAZINES...
IT'S *OKAY,* IT'S *OKAY,* I'M FINE GOING BY MYSELF!
WHAT WAS THAT?
THAT WAS SO SMOOTH!
IT'S UP TO YOU NOW, TADAMI.

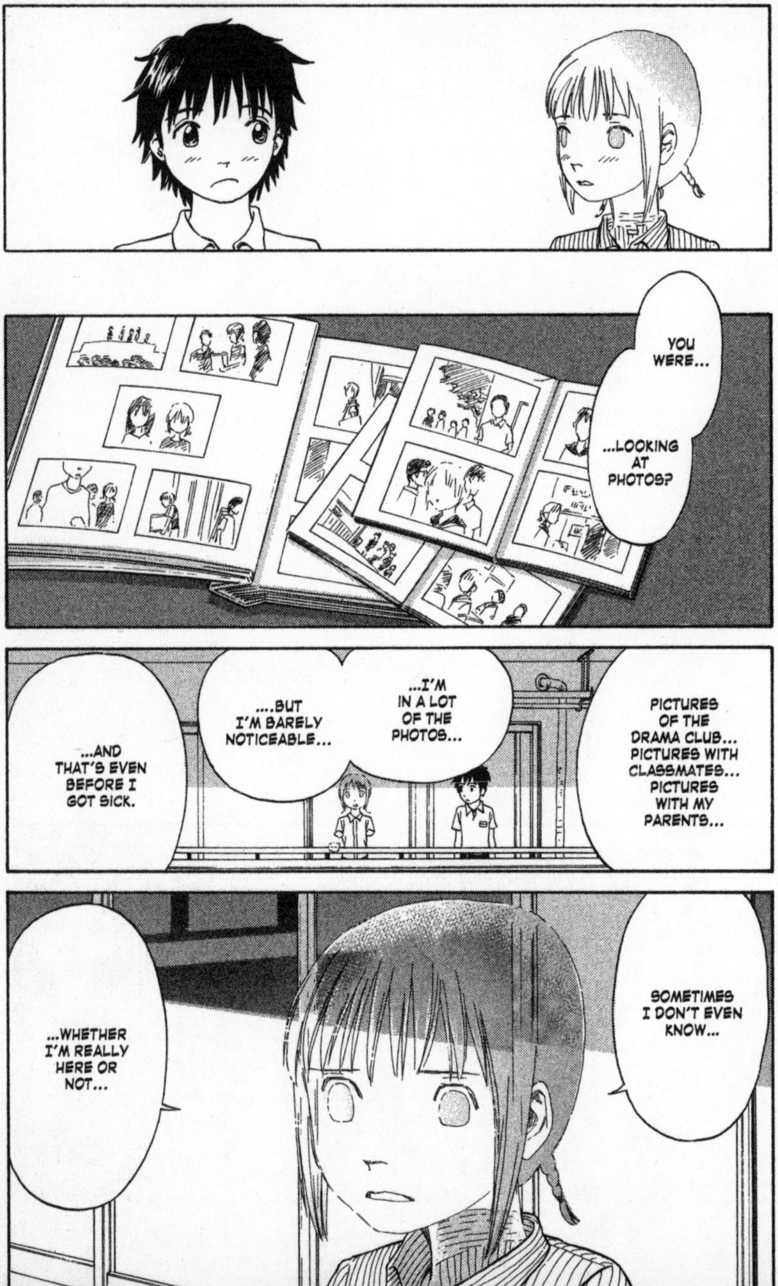
YOU WERE...
...LOOKING AT PHOTOS?
PICTURES OF THE DRAMA CLUB... PICTURES WITH CLASSMATES... PICTURES WITH MY PARENTS...
...I'M IN A LOT OF THE PHOTOS...
....BUT I'M BARELY NOTICEABLE...
...AND THAT'S EVEN BEFORE I GOT SICK.
SOMETIMES I DON'T EVEN KNOW...
...WHETHER I'M REALLY HERE OR NOT...

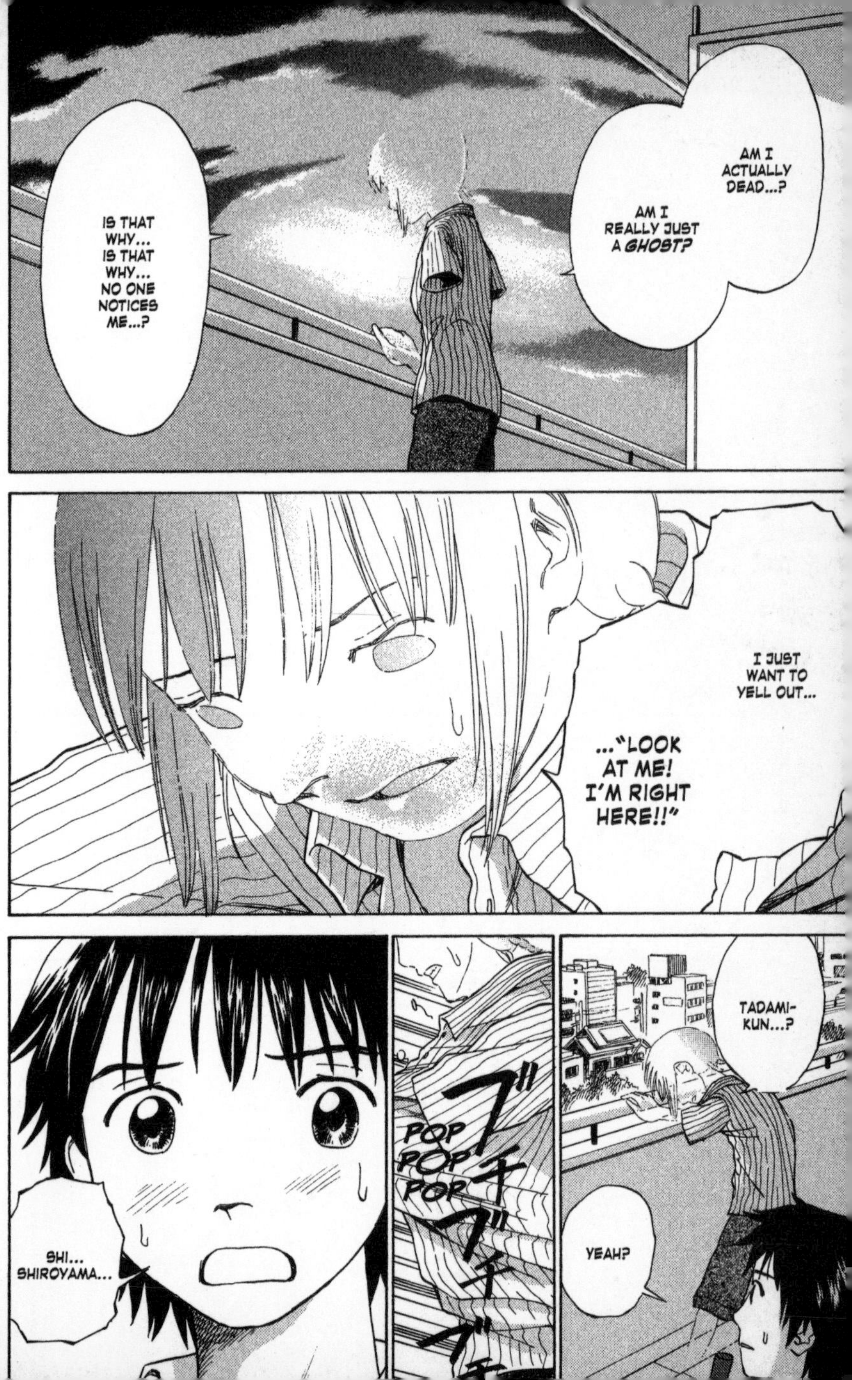
AM I ACTUALLY DEAD...?
AM I REALLY JUST A *GHOST?*
IS THAT WHY... IS THAT WHY... NO ONE NOTICES ME...?
I JUST WANT TO YELL OUT...
..."LOOK AT ME! I'M RIGHT HERE!!"
TADAMI-KUN...?
YEAH?
POP POP POP
SHI... SHIROYAMA...

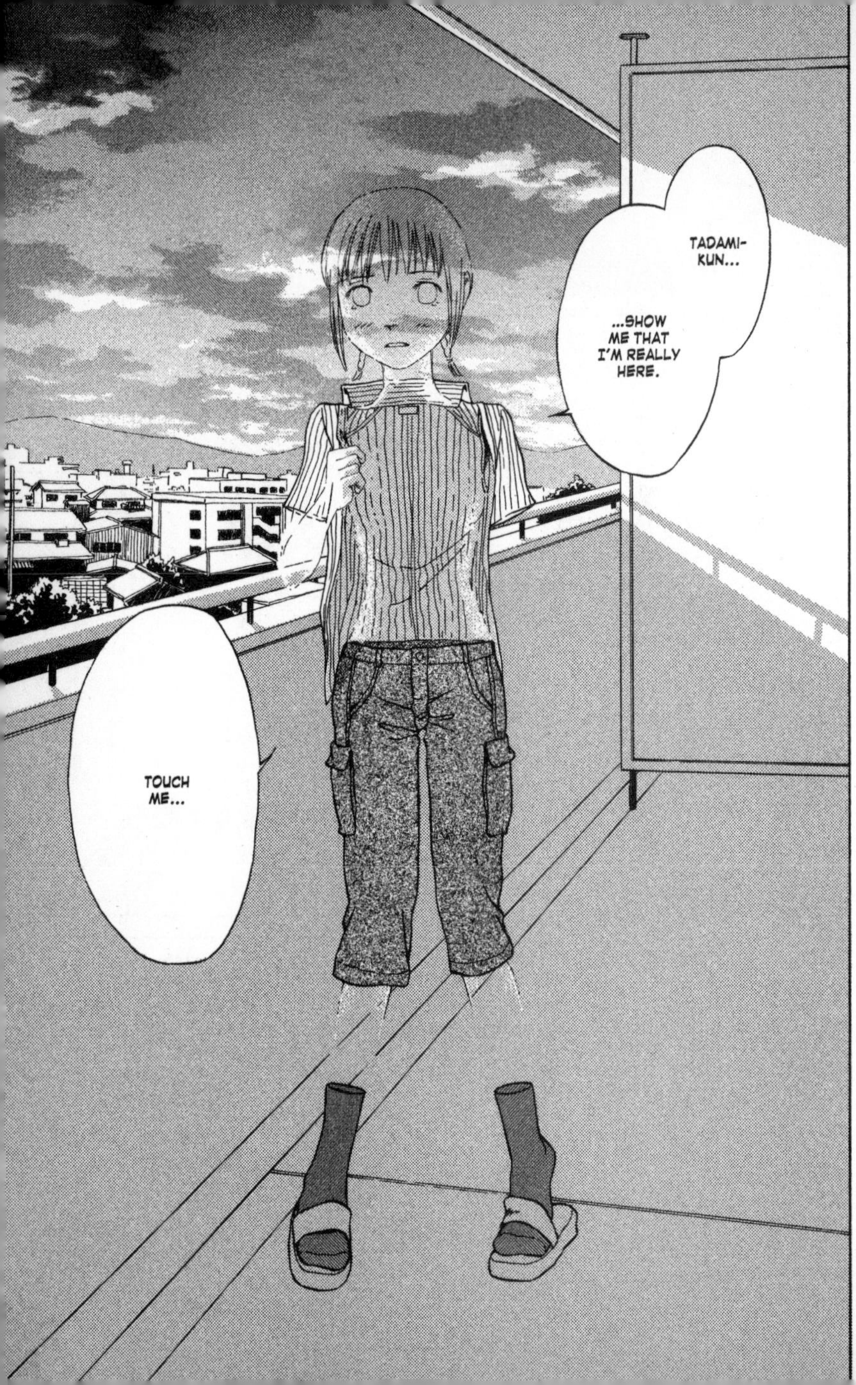
TADAMI-KUN...
...SHOW ME THAT I'M REALLY HERE.
TOUCH ME...

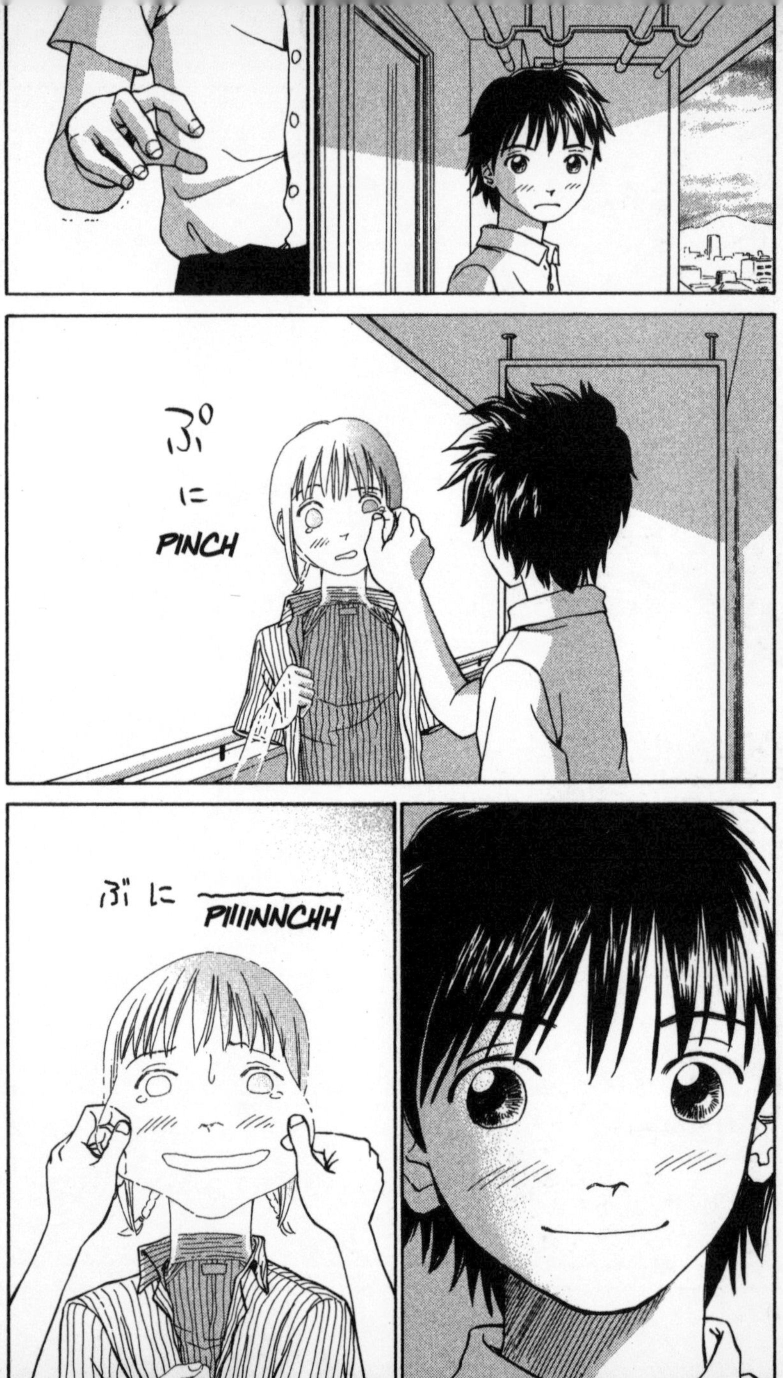
ぷに
PINCH
ぷに
PIIIINNCHH

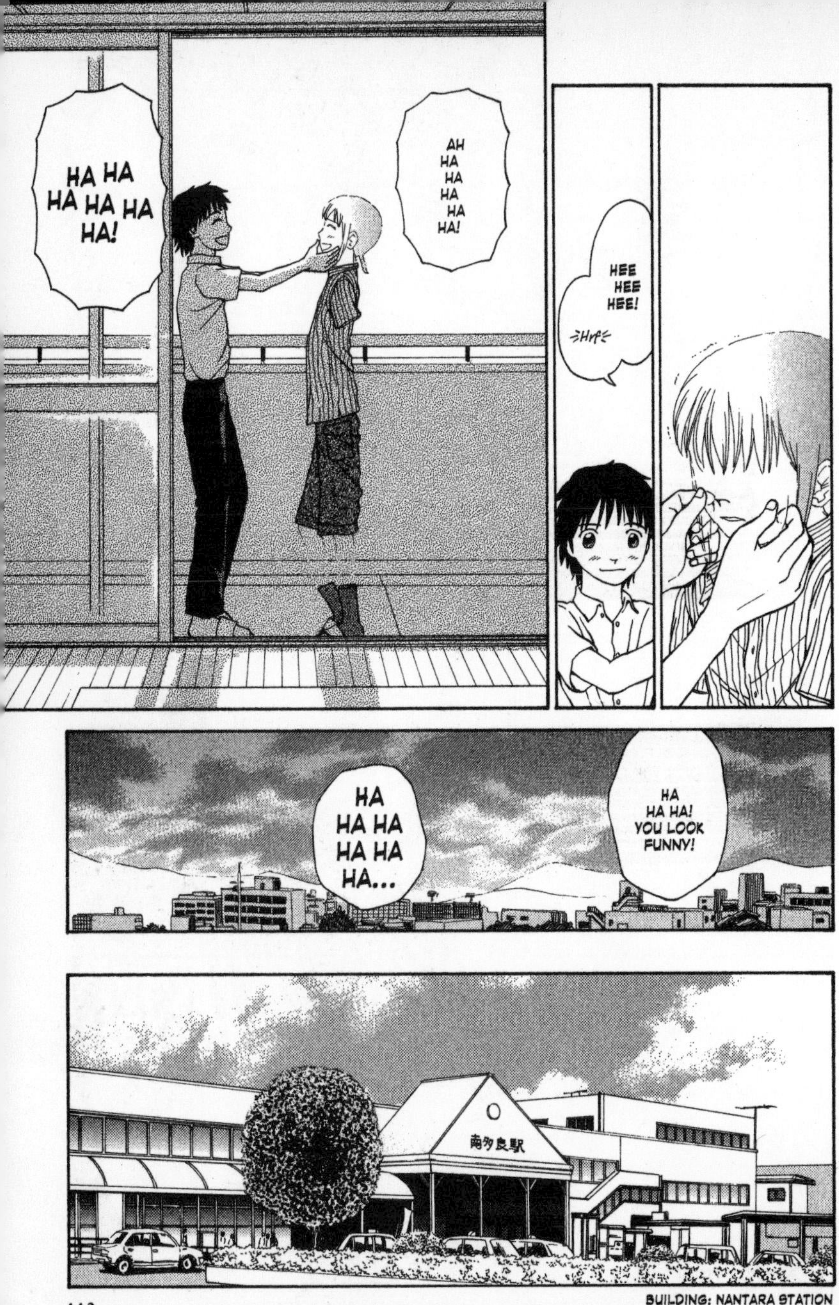
HEE HEE HEE!
Hrf
AH HA HA HA HA HA!
HA HA HA HA HA HA!
HA HA HA! YOU LOOK FUNNY!
HA HA HA HA HA HA...
南多良駅

BUILDING: NANTARA STATION

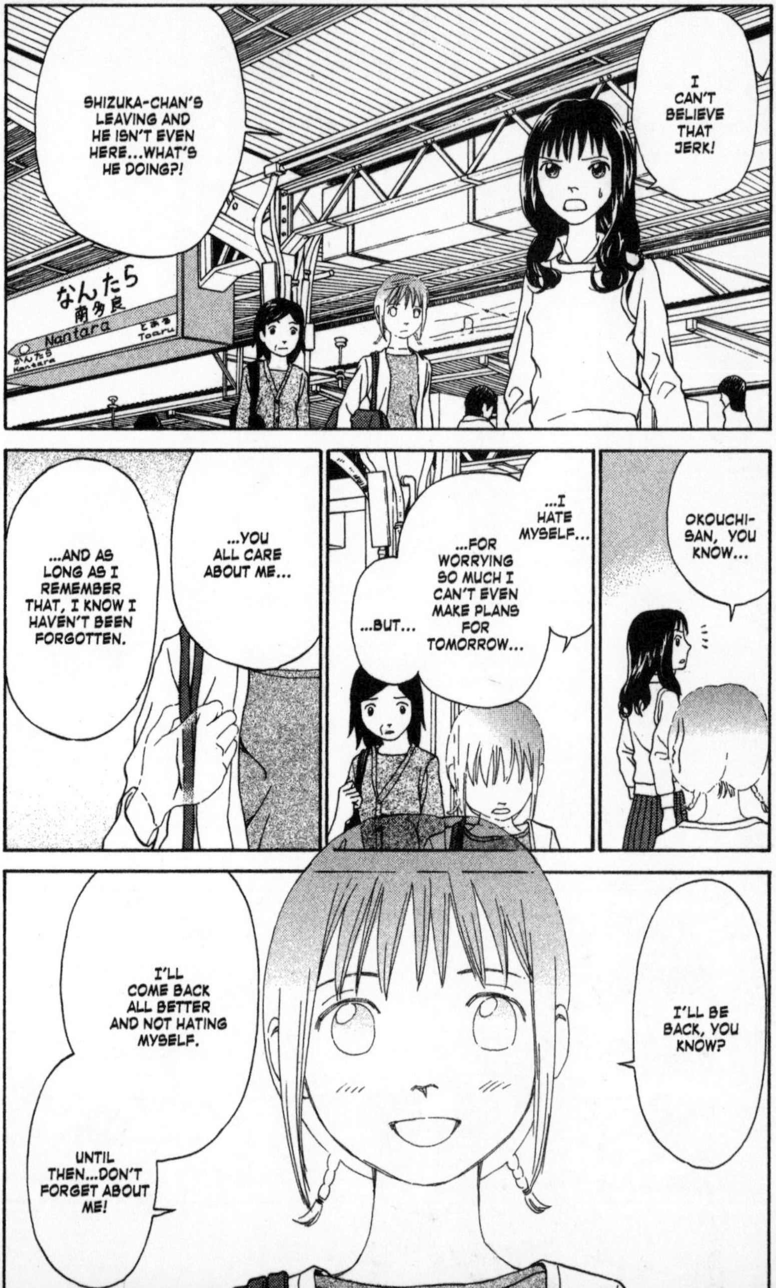
I CAN'T BELIEVE THAT JERK!
SHIZUKA-CHAN'S LEAVING AND HE ISN'T EVEN HERE...WHAT'S HE DOING?!
なんたら
南多良
Nantara
とおる
Toaru
なんたら
Nantara
OKOUCHI-SAN, YOU KNOW...
...I HATE MYSELF...
...FOR WORRYING SO MUCH I CAN'T EVEN MAKE PLANS FOR TOMORROW...
...BUT...
...YOU ALL CARE ABOUT ME...
...AND AS LONG AS I REMEMBER THAT, I KNOW I HAVEN'T BEEN FORGOTTEN.
I'LL BE BACK, YOU KNOW?
I'LL COME BACK ALL BETTER AND NOT HATING MYSELF.
UNTIL THEN...DON'T FORGET ABOUT ME!

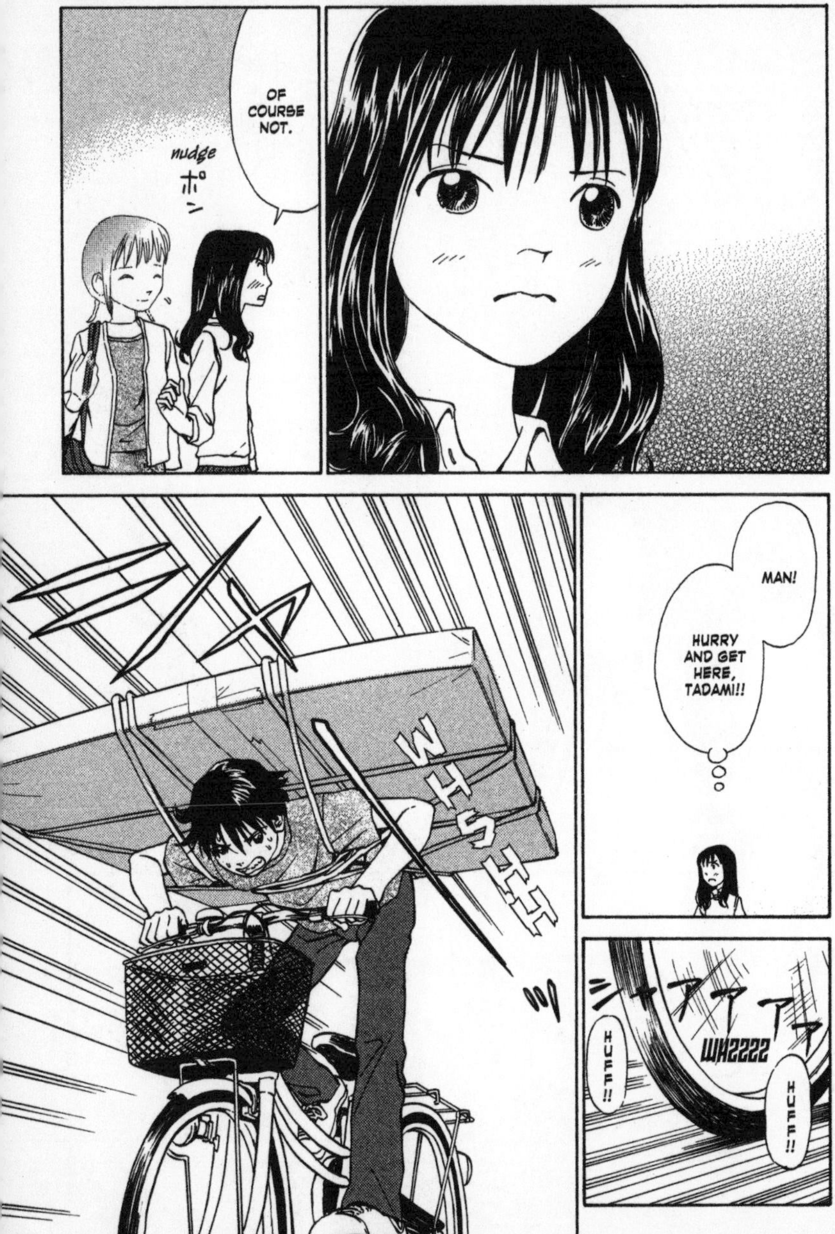
OF COURSE NOT.
nudge
ポン
MAN!
HURRY AND GET HERE, TADAMI!!
シャアアア
WHZZZZ
HUFF!!
HUFF!!
WHISH

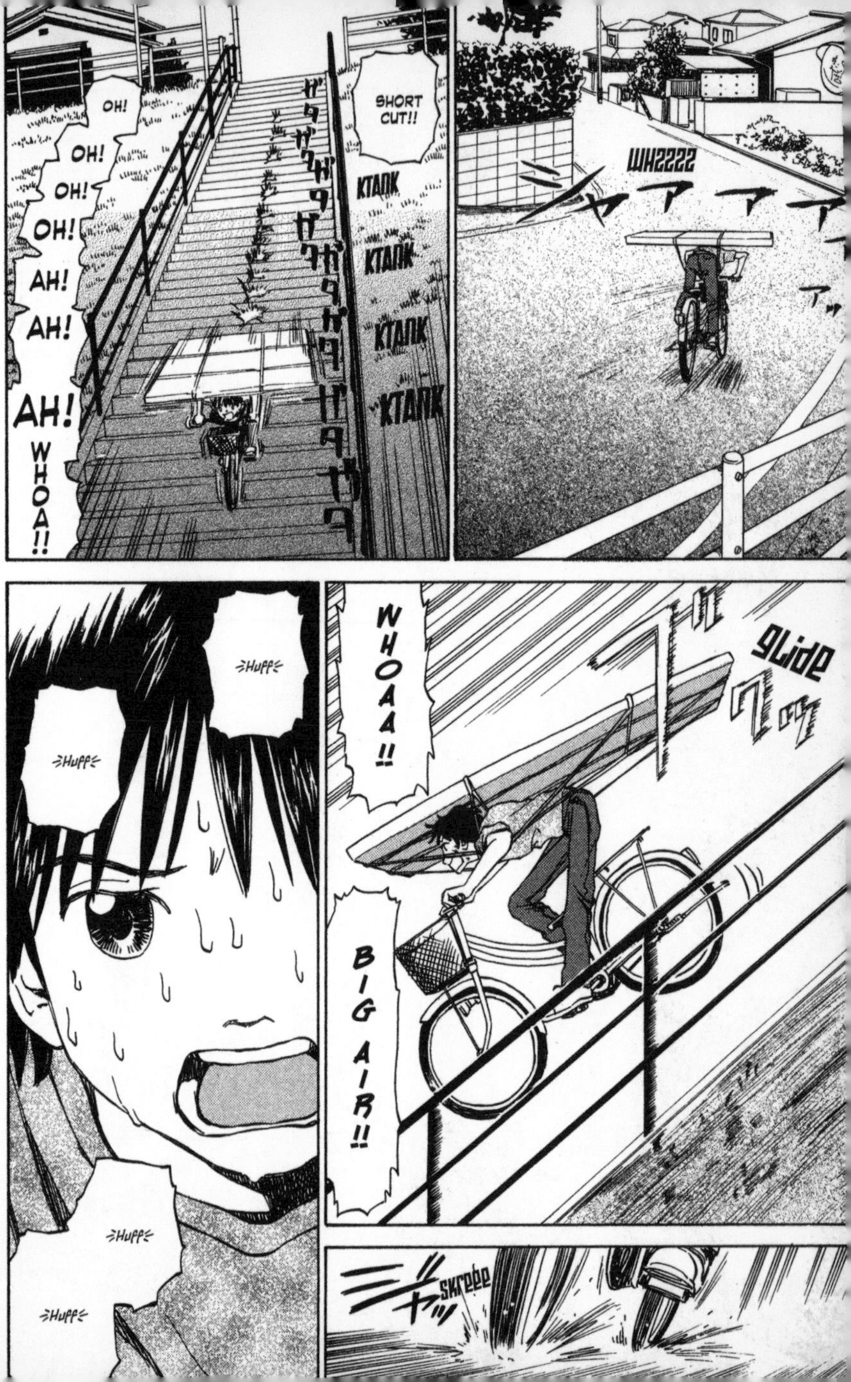
WHZZZZ
SHORT CUT!!
KTANK
KTANK
KTANK
KTANK
OH!
OH!
OH!
OH!
AH!
AH!
AH!
WHOA!!
glide
WHOAA!!
BIG AIR!!
Skreee
Huff
Huff
Huff
Huff

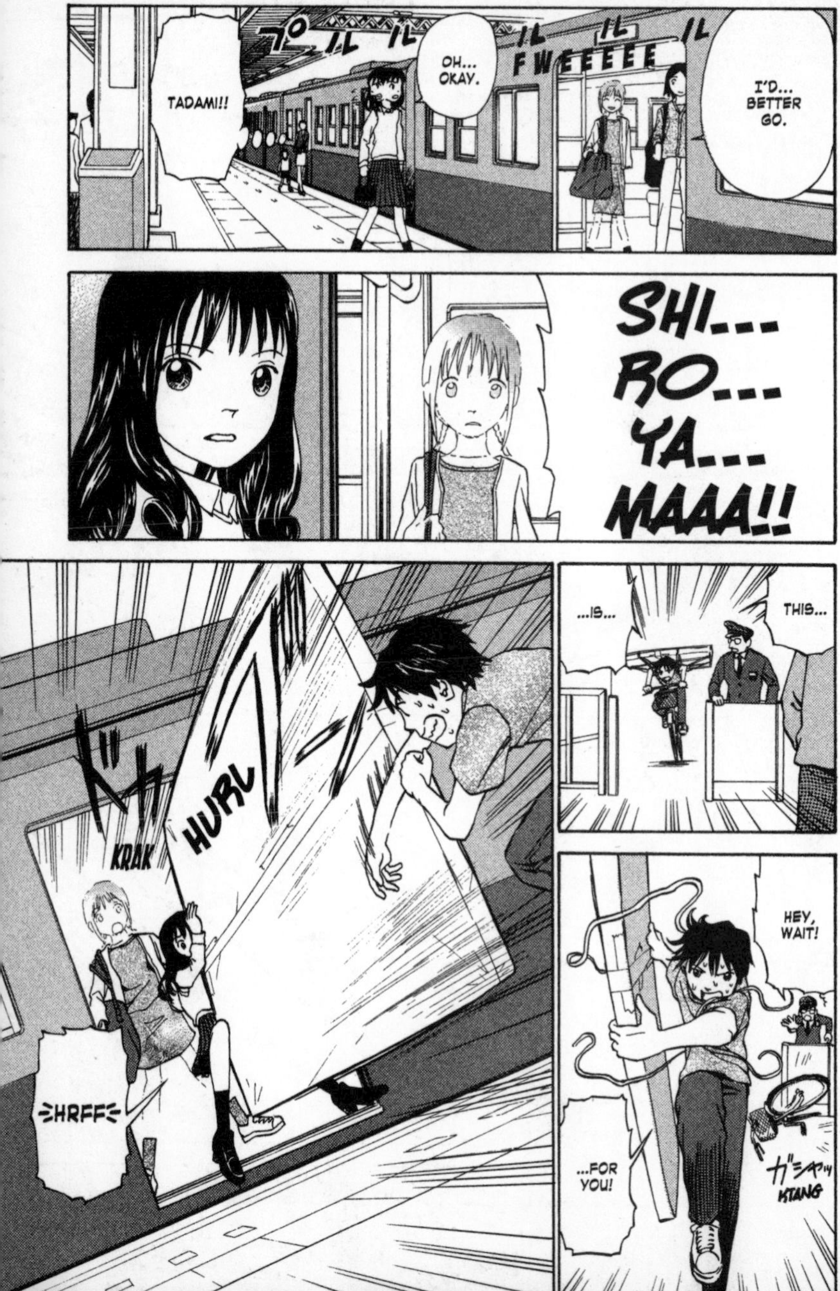
I'D... BETTER GO.
プルルルルル
FWEEEEE
OH... OKAY.
TADAMI!!
SHI... RO... YA... MAAA!!
THIS...
...IS...
HEY, WAIT!
ガシャッ
KTANG
...FOR YOU!
HURL
ドカ
KRAK
HRFF

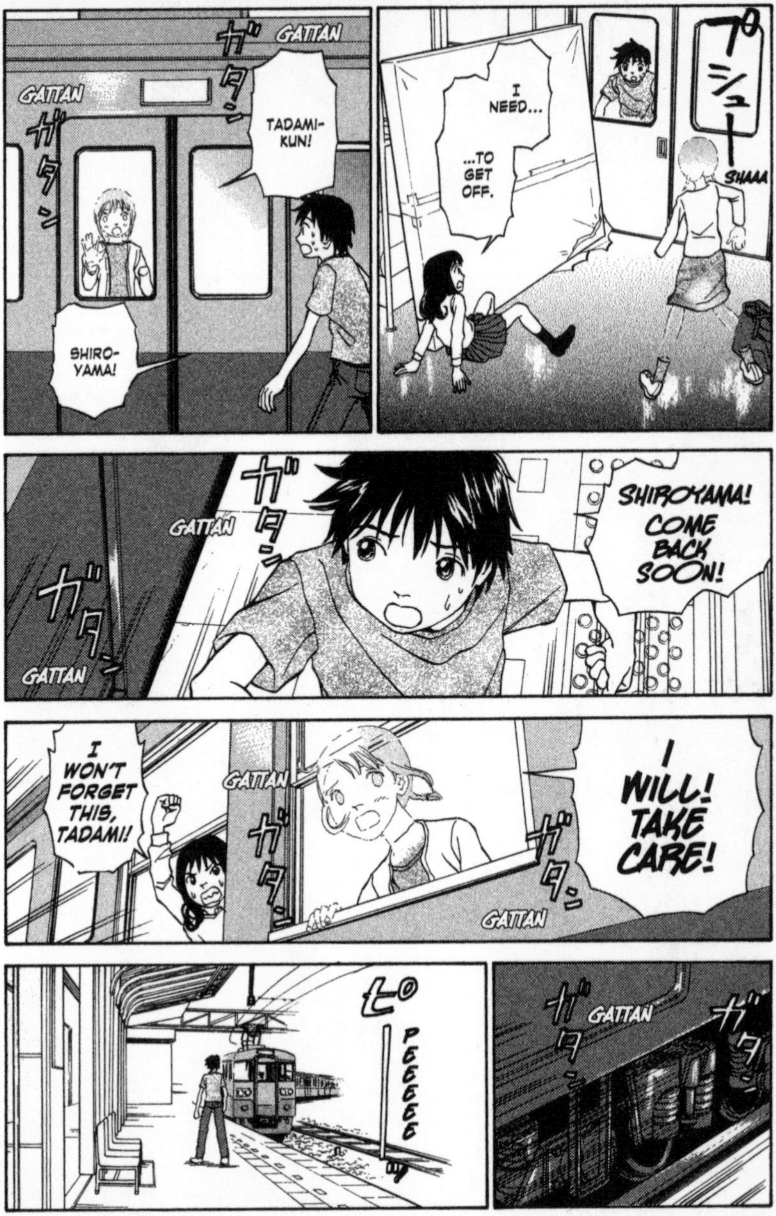

プシュー
SHAAA
I NEED...
...TO GET OFF.
ガタン
GATTAN
TADAMI-KUN!
ガタン
GATTAN
SHIROYAMA!
SHIROYAMA! COME BACK SOON!
ガタン
GATTAN
ガタン
GATTAN
I WILL! TAKE CARE!
ガタン
GATTAN
ガタン
GATTAN
I WON'T FORGET THIS, TADAMI!
ガタン
GATTAN
ガタ
ピー
PEEEEEE

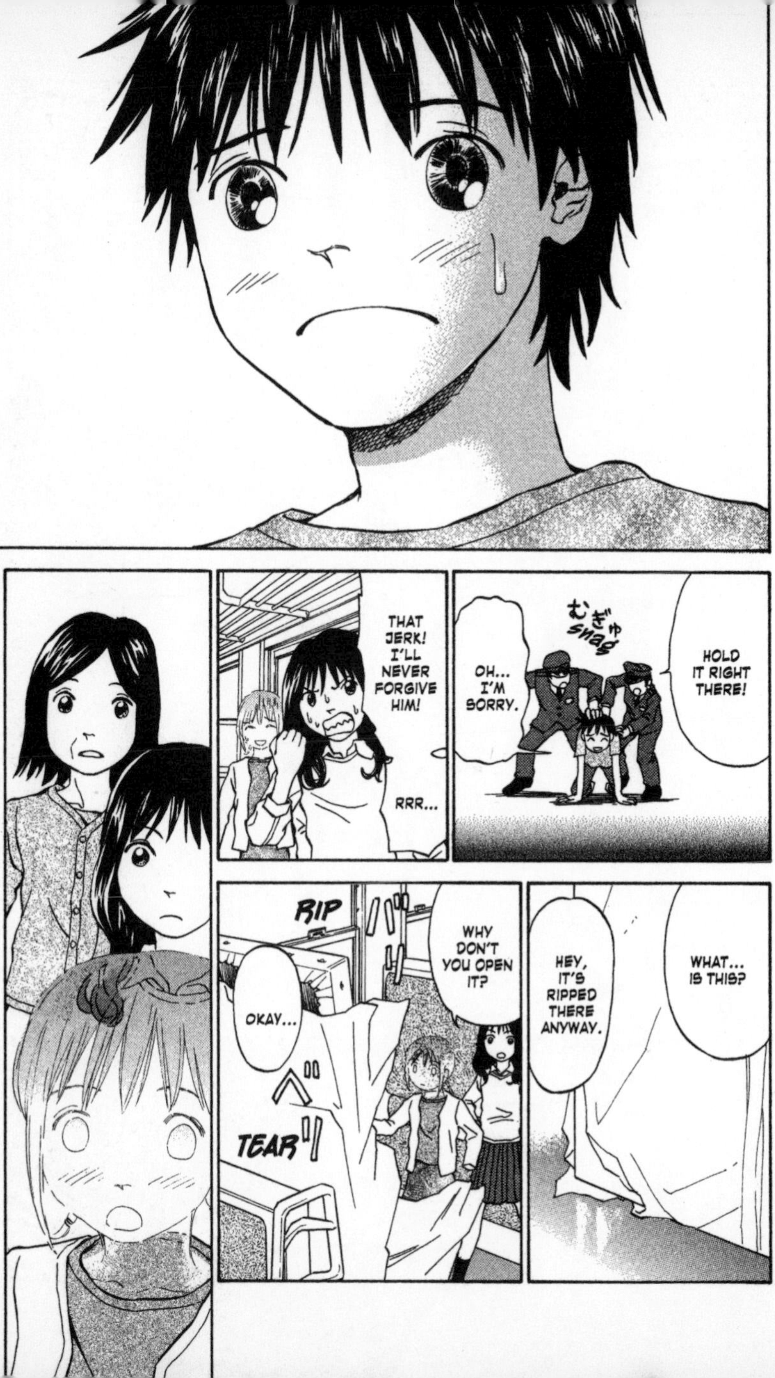
HOLD IT RIGHT THERE!
むぎゅ
snag
OH... I'M SORRY.
THAT JERK! I'LL NEVER FORGIVE HIM!
RRR...
WHAT... IS THIS?
HEY, IT'S RIPPED THERE ANYWAY.
WHY DON'T YOU OPEN IT?
RIP
OKAY...
TEAR

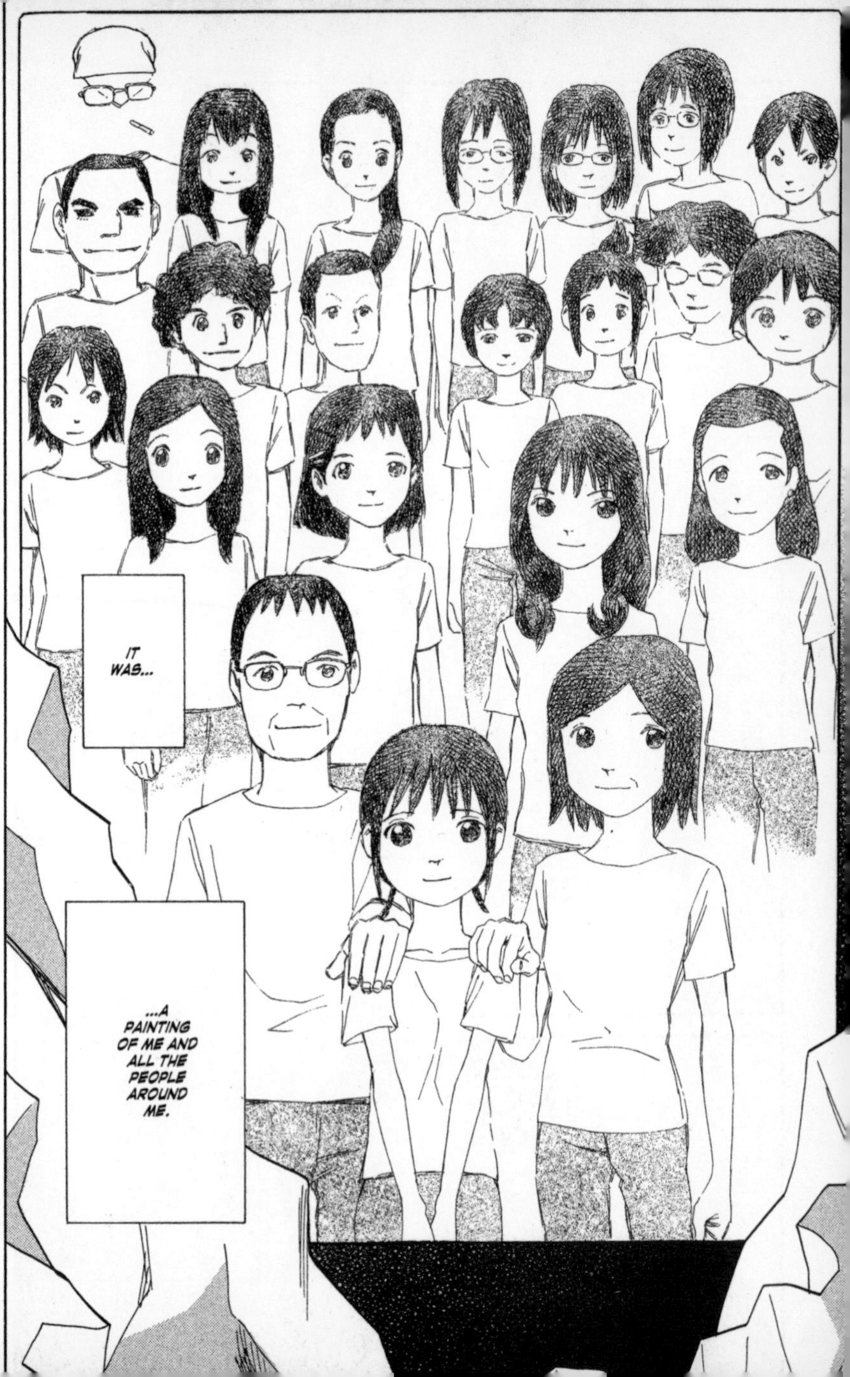
IT WAS...
...A PAINTING OF ME AND ALL THE PEOPLE AROUND ME.

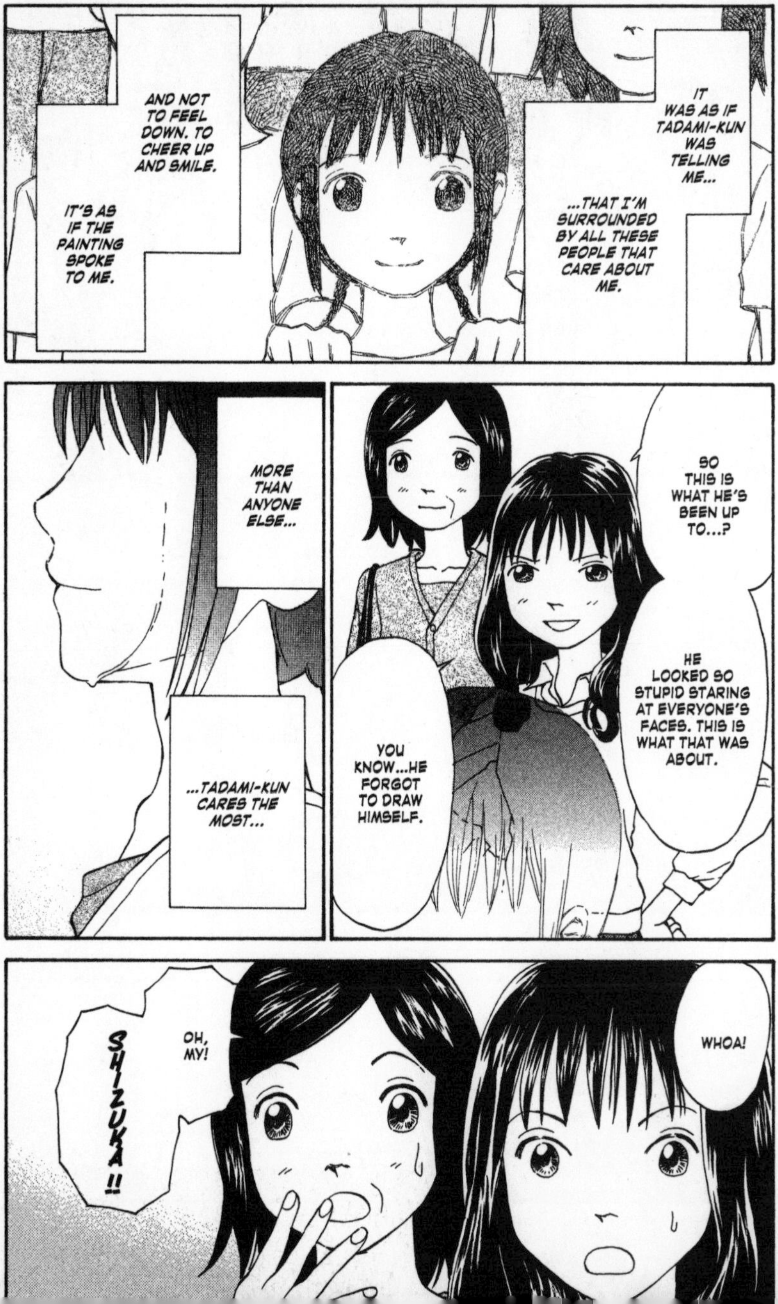
IT WAS AS IF TADAMI-KUN WAS TELLING ME...
...THAT I'M SURROUNDED BY ALL THESE PEOPLE THAT CARE ABOUT ME.
AND NOT TO FEEL DOWN. TO CHEER UP AND SMILE.
IT'S AS IF THE PAINTING SPOKE TO ME.
SO THIS IS WHAT HE'S BEEN UP TO...?
HE LOOKED SO STUPID STARING AT EVERYONE'S FACES. THIS IS WHAT THAT WAS ABOUT.
YOU KNOW...HE FORGOT TO DRAW HIMSELF.
MORE THAN ANYONE ELSE...
...TADAMI-KUN CARES THE MOST...
WHOA!
OH, MY!
SHIZUKA!!

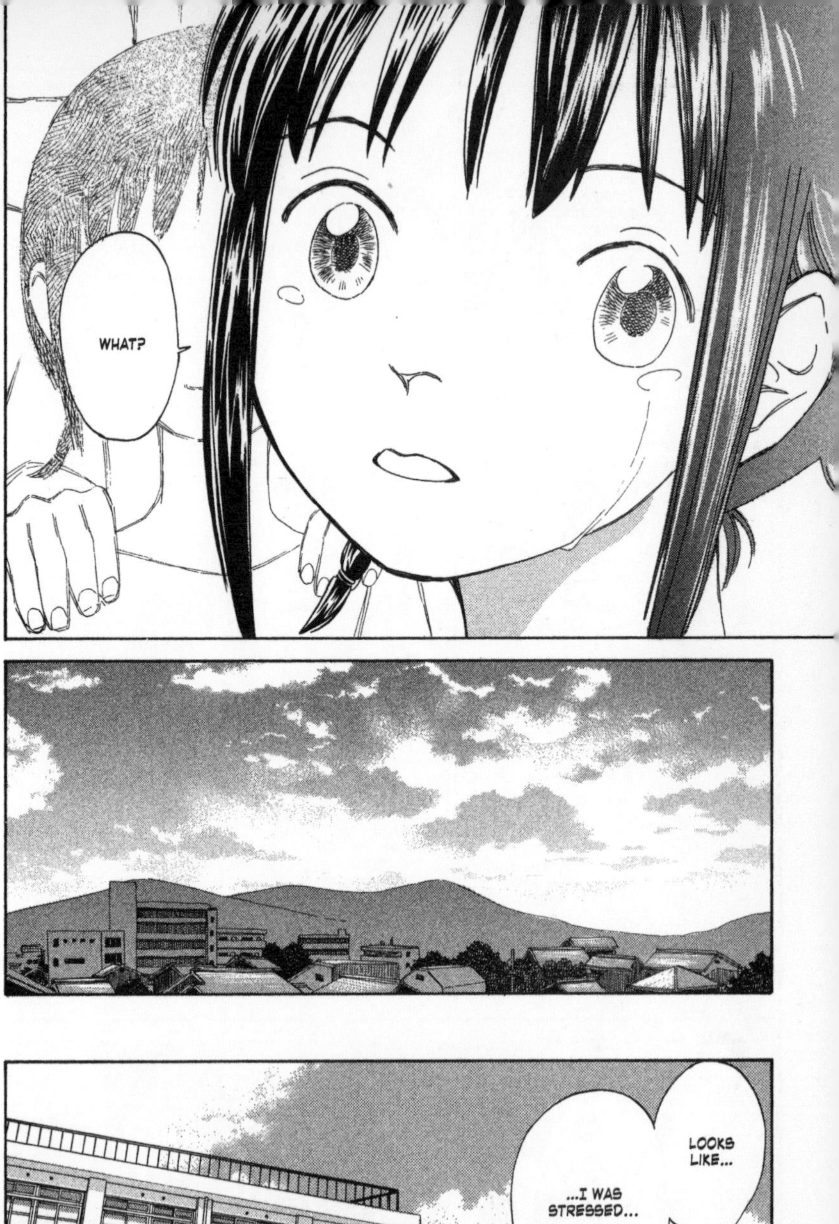
WHAT?
LOOKS LIKE...
...I WAS STRESSED...

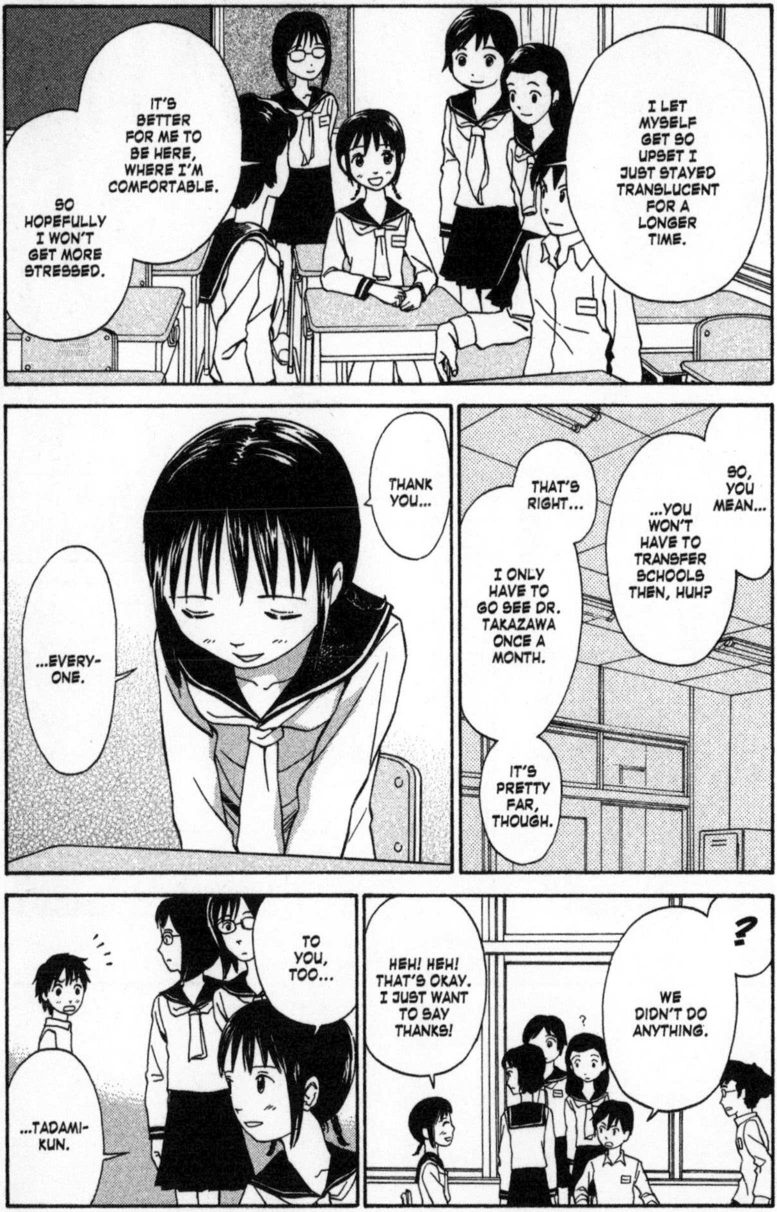
I LET MYSELF GET SO UPSET I JUST STAYED TRANSLUCENT FOR A LONGER TIME.
IT'S BETTER FOR ME TO BE HERE, WHERE I'M COMFORTABLE.
SO HOPEFULLY I WON'T GET MORE STRESSED.
SO, YOU MEAN...
...YOU WON'T HAVE TO TRANSFER SCHOOLS THEN, HUH?
THAT'S RIGHT...
I ONLY HAVE TO GO SEE DR. TAKAZAWA ONCE A MONTH.
IT'S PRETTY FAR, THOUGH.
THANK YOU...
...EVERY-ONE.
?
WE DIDN'T DO ANYTHING.
HEH! HEH! THAT'S OKAY. I JUST WANT TO SAY THANKS!
TO YOU, TOO...
...TADAMI-KUN.

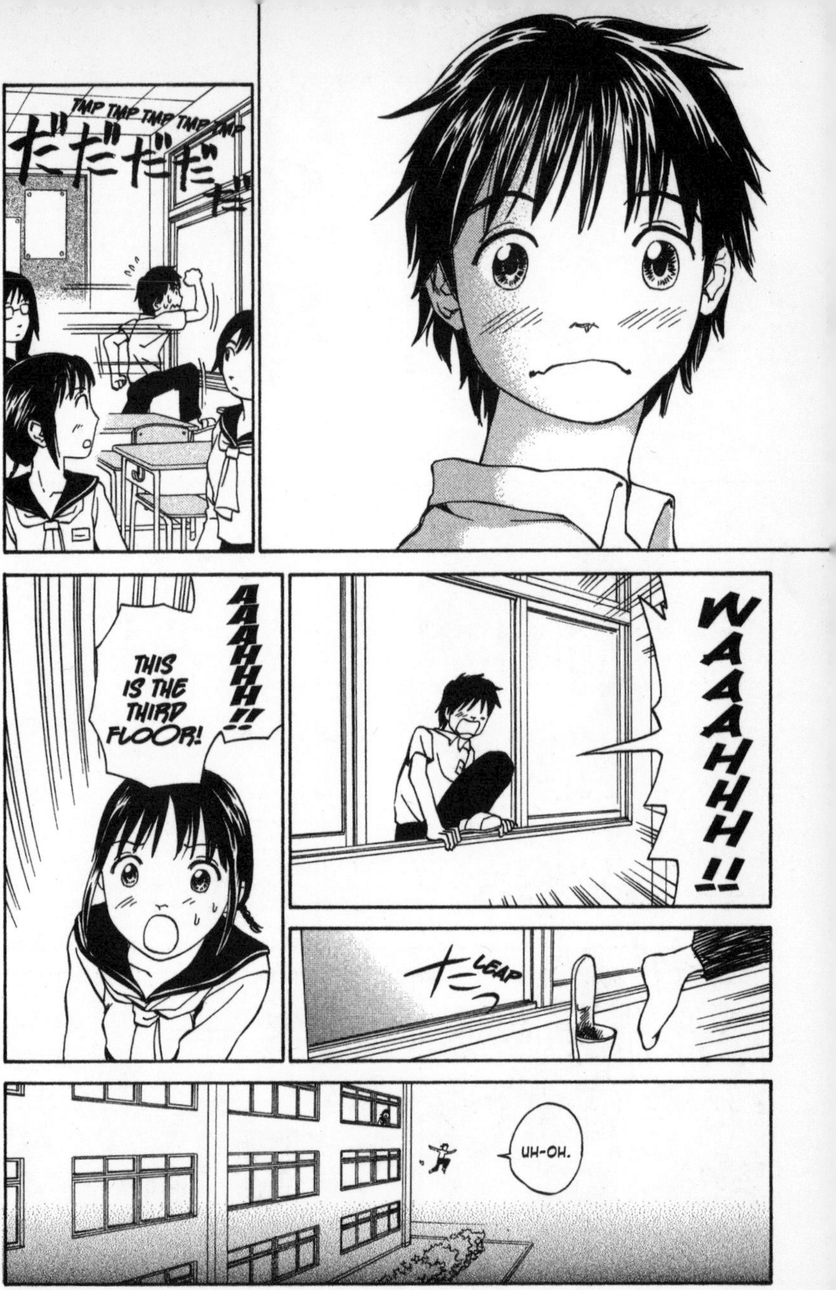
だだだだだ
TMP TMP TMP TMP TMP
WAAAHHH!!
たっ
LEAP
AAAHHH!!
THIS IS THE THIRD FLOOR!
UH-OH.

OMAKE

ONE-PAGE BONUS MANGA #3

3

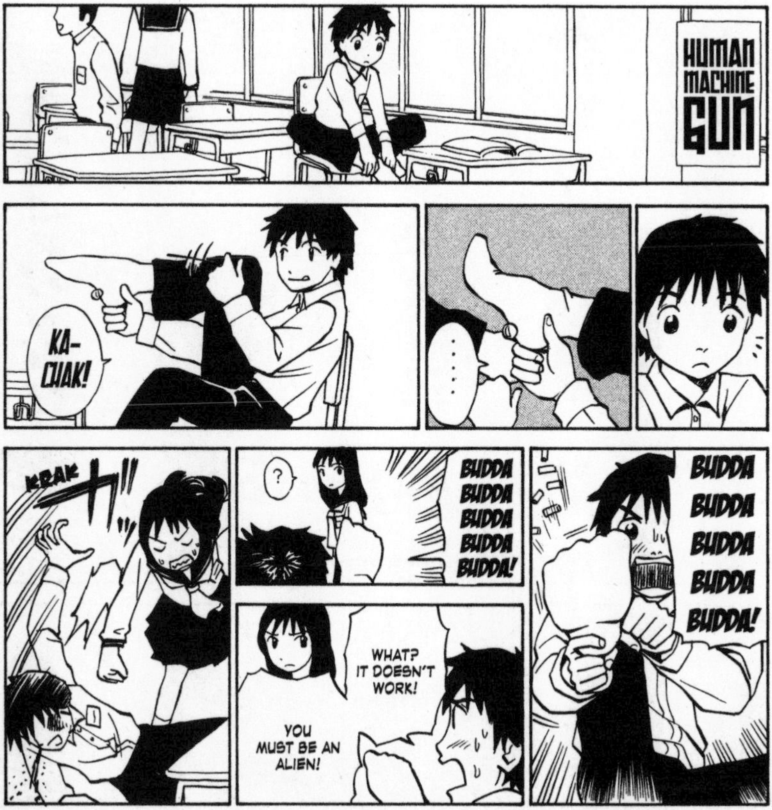
HUMAN MACHINE GUN
......
KA-CHAK!
BUDDA BUDDA BUDDA BUDDA BUDDA!
BUDDA BUDDA BUDDA BUDDA BUDDA!
?
WHAT? IT DOESN'T WORK!
YOU MUST BE AN ALIEN!
KRAK

OMAKE

ONE-PAGE BONUS MANGA #4

4

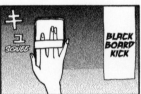

BLACK BOARD KICK
キュ
SQUEE
キュ
SQUEEEEEE
DAB
DAB
PER-FECT.
ALL DONE!
SO, LET ME TELL YOU HOW YOU CAN ACTUALLY POOP LIKE THIS...
FITCH
FITCH
FUSH
BEAUTIFUL!
PUNT
OKOUCHI'S FAN CLUB

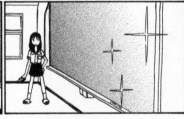

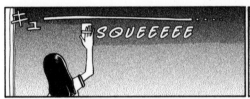

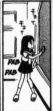

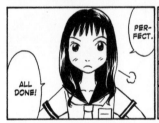

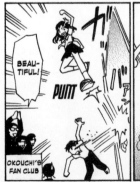

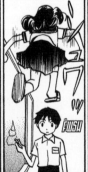

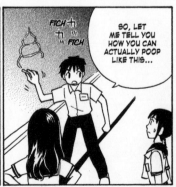

PART 5 The Disappearing Roxane

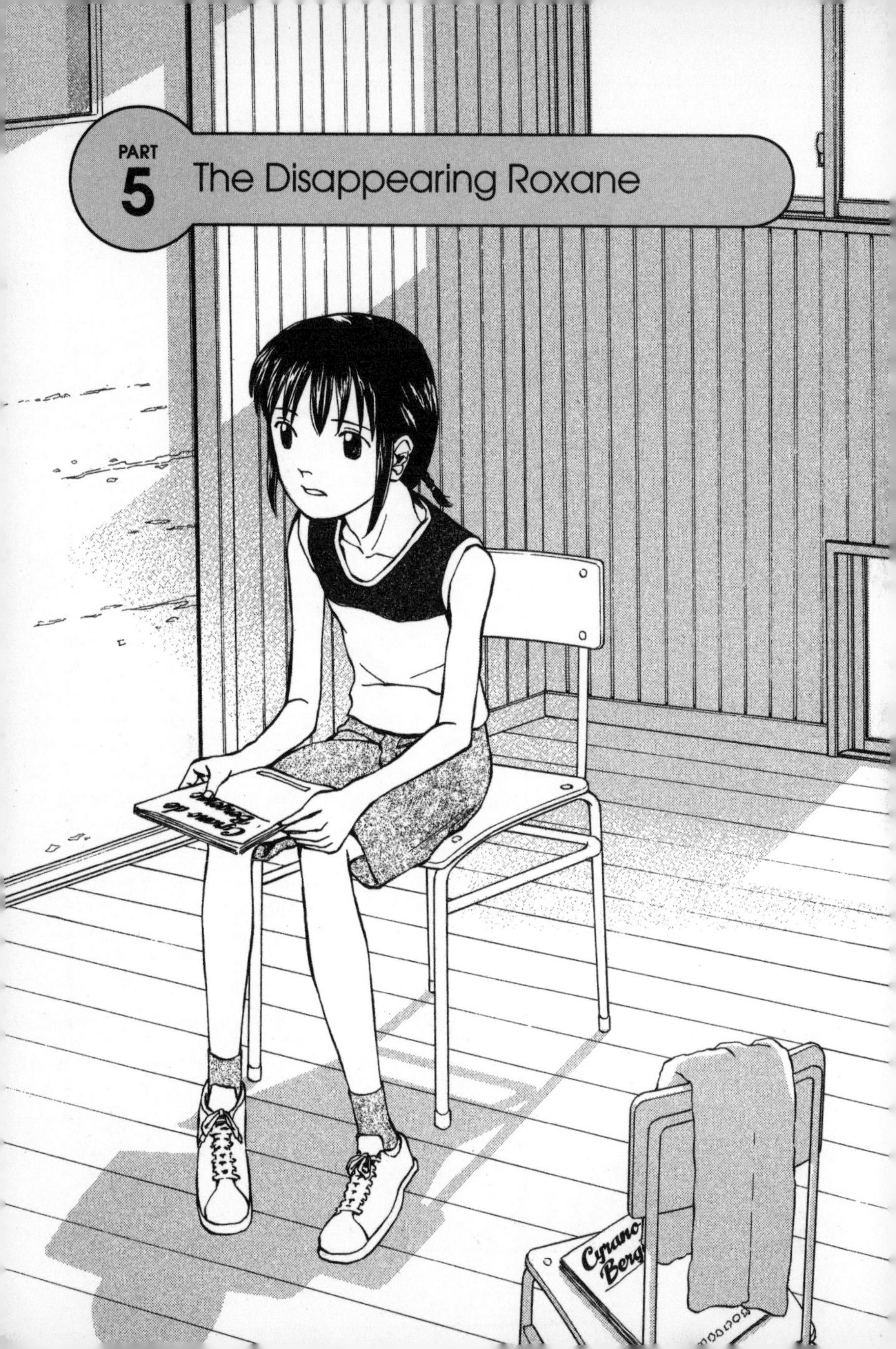
Cyrano

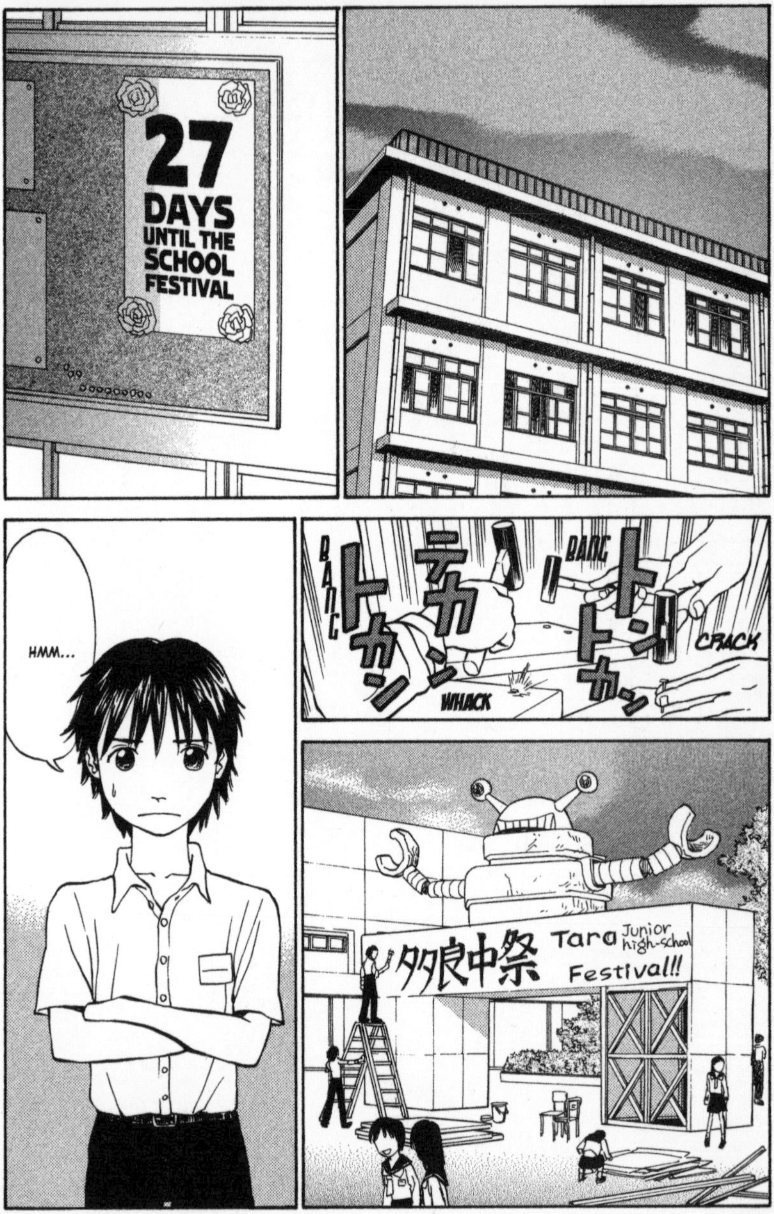
27
DAYS
UNTIL THE
SCHOOL
FESTIVAL
BANG
BANG
CRACK
WHACK
タタ良中祭
Tara Junior high-school Festival!!
HMM...

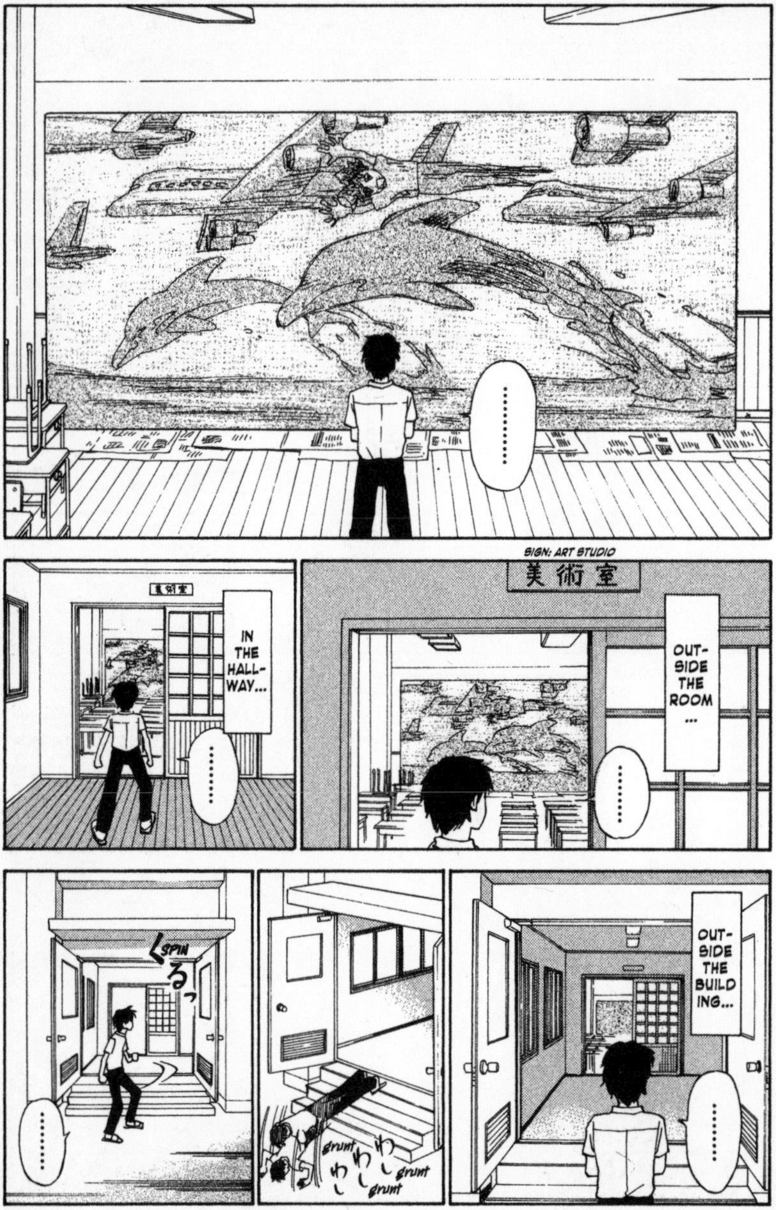
……
SIGN: ART STUDIO
美術室
OUT-SIDE THE ROOM ...
……
IN THE HALL-WAY...
……
OUT-SIDE THE BUILD ING...
……
わし grunt
わし grunt
わし grunt
くるっ SPIN
……

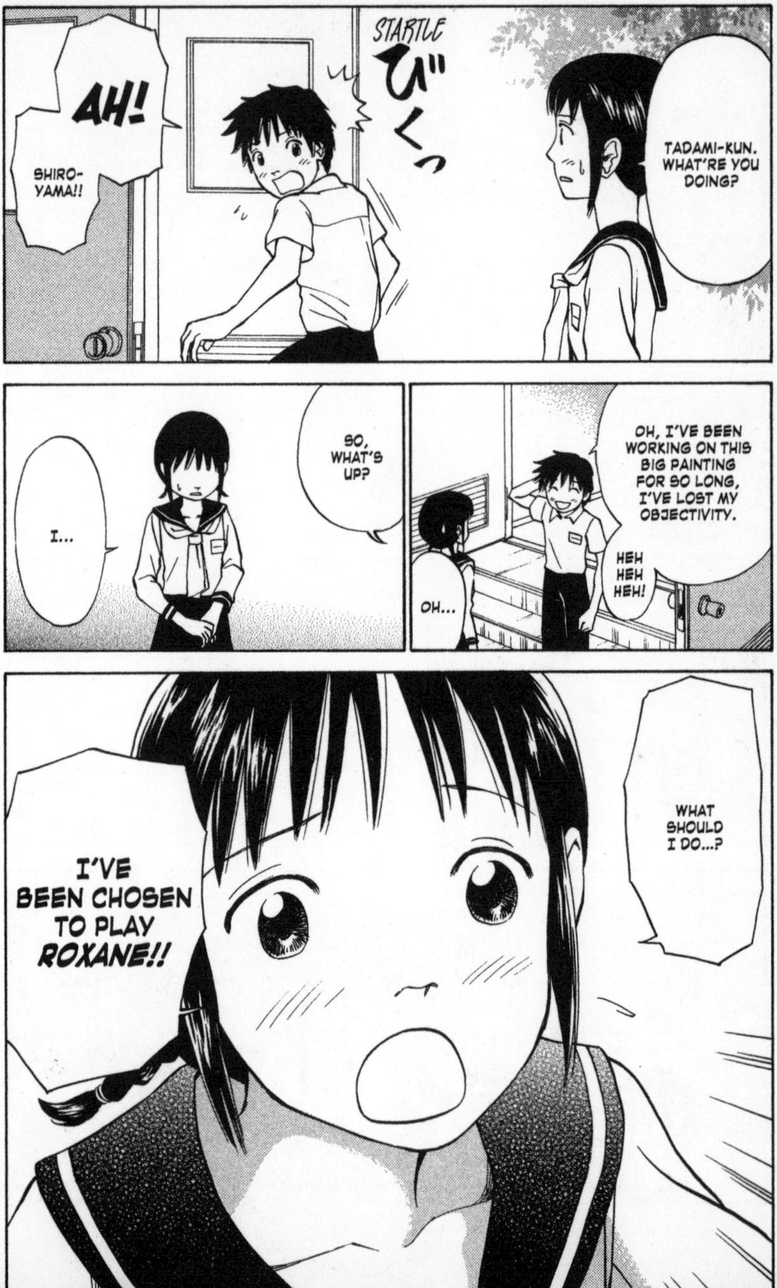
TADAMI-KUN. WHAT'RE YOU DOING?
STARTLE
びくっ
AH!
SHIRO-YAMA!!
OH, I'VE BEEN WORKING ON THIS BIG PAINTING FOR SO LONG, I'VE LOST MY OBJECTIVITY.
HEH HEH HEH!
OH...
SO, WHAT'S UP?
I...
WHAT SHOULD I DO...?
I'VE BEEN CHOSEN TO PLAY *ROXANE!!*

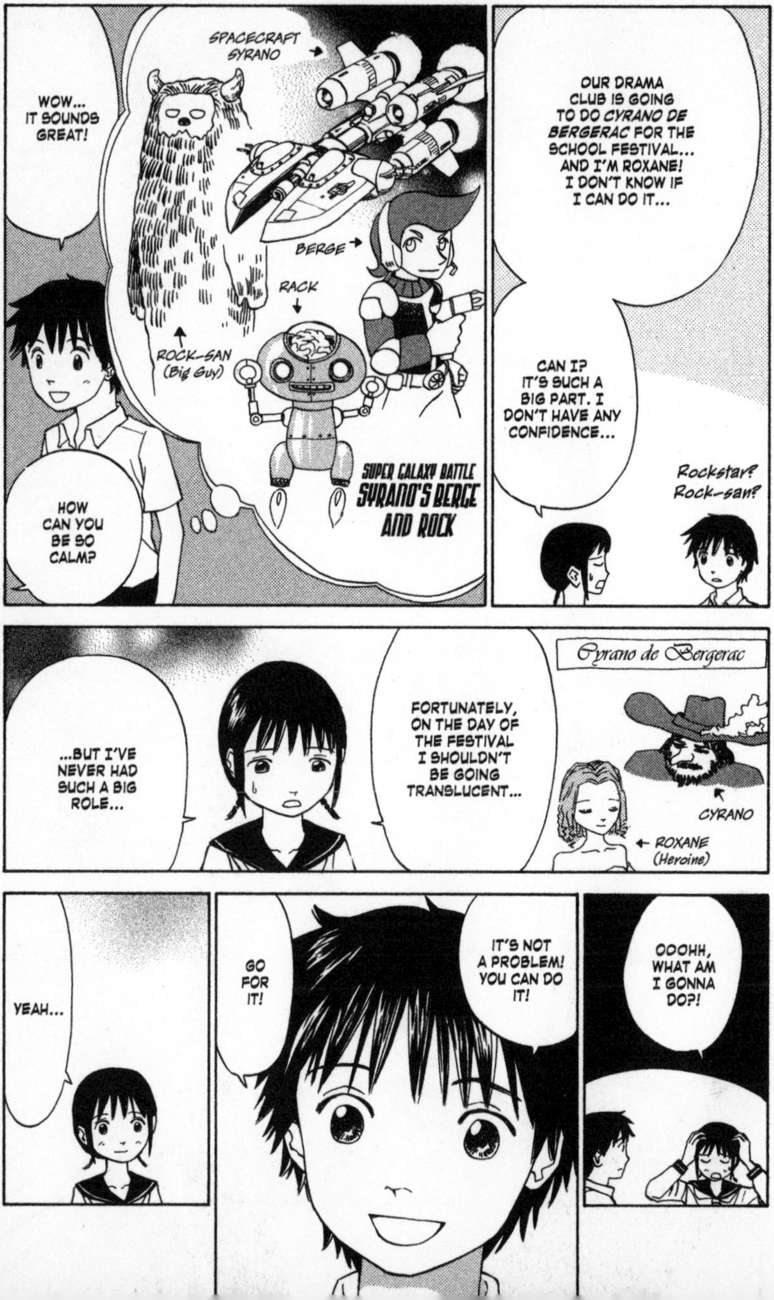
OUR DRAMA CLUB IS GOING TO DO *CYRANO DE BERGERAC* FOR THE SCHOOL FESTIVAL... AND I'M ROXANE! I DON'T KNOW IF I CAN DO IT...
CAN I? IT'S SUCH A BIG PART. I DON'T HAVE ANY CONFIDENCE...
Rockstar? Rock-san?
SPACECRAFT SYRANO
BERGE
RACK
ROCK-SAN (Big Guy)
SUPER GALAXY BATTLE SYRANO'S BERGE AND ROCK
WOW... IT SOUNDS GREAT!
HOW CAN YOU BE SO CALM?
Cyrano de Bergerac
CYRANO
ROXANE (Heroine)
FORTUNATELY, ON THE DAY OF THE FESTIVAL I SHOULDN'T BE GOING TRANSLUCENT...
...BUT I'VE NEVER HAD SUCH A BIG ROLE...
OOOHH, WHAT AM I GONNA DO?!
IT'S NOT A PROBLEM! YOU CAN DO IT!
GO FOR IT!
YEAH...

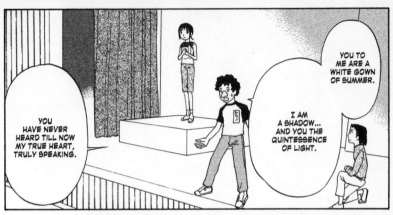

YOU TO ME ARE A WHITE GOWN OF SUMMER.
I AM A SHADOW... AND YOU THE QUINTESSENCE OF LIGHT.
YOU HAVE NEVER HEARD TILL NOW MY TRUE HEART, TRULY SPEAKING.
...UUUMM...
HIS SHIRT READS "CYRANO"
HER SHIRT READS "CHRISTIAN"
"THERE..."
THE... THERE...
クリスチャン
"...WAS A CERTAIN OBLIQUITY, A SORT OF HAZE CAUSED BY THIS VERTIGO."
YOU'VE GOT TO REMEMBER YOUR LINES.
DO YOU SENSE MY HEART RISING TOWARD YOU IN THIS INTENSE STILLNESS? MY WORDS MAKE YOU TREMBLE IN THE BLUE SHADOWS OF THE TREES.
I SAID IT!
YES, I DO TREMBLE.
AND I LOVE YOU, YOU HAVE MADE ME LOVE YOU.
SHIZUKA'S SHIRT READS "ROXANE"
ロクサー

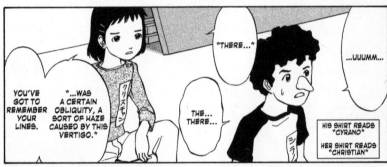

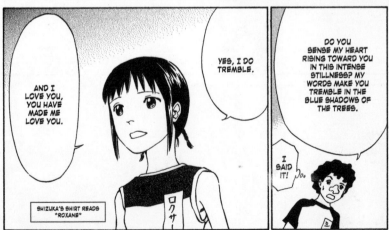

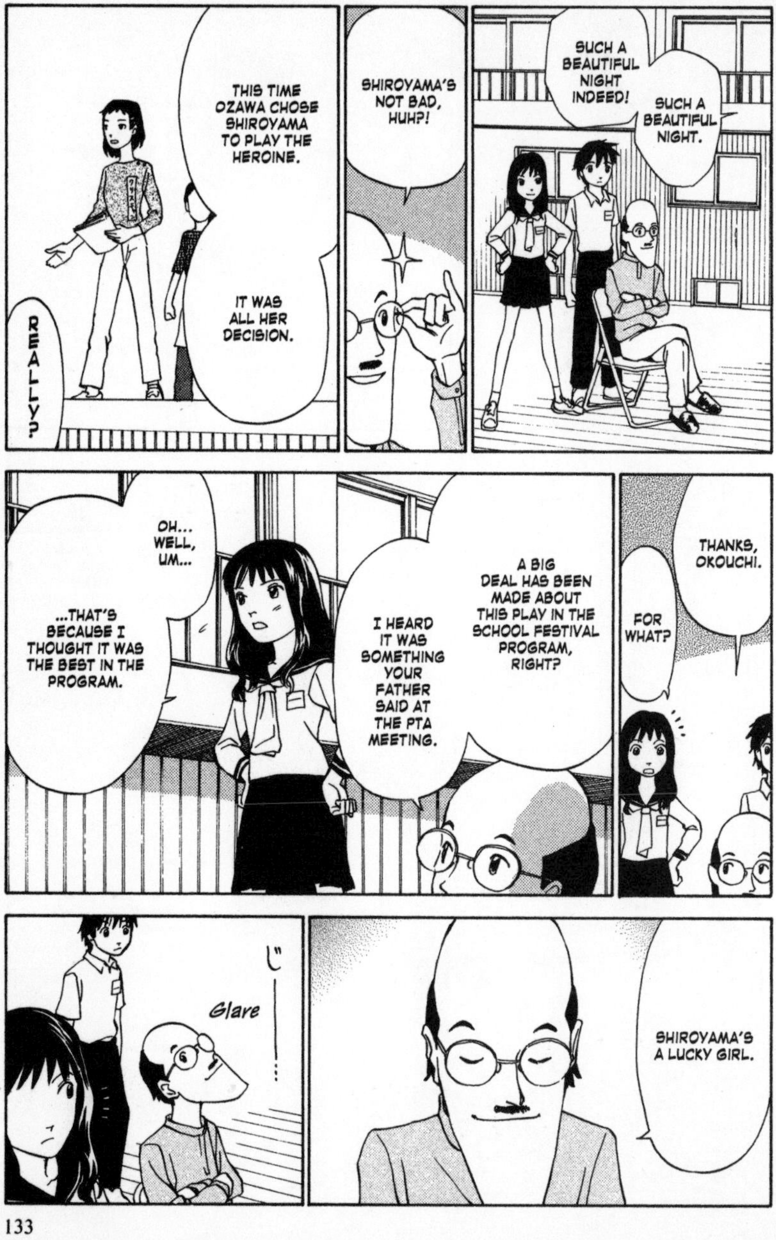
SUCH A BEAUTIFUL NIGHT INDEED!
SUCH A BEAUTIFUL NIGHT.
SHIROYAMA'S NOT BAD, HUH?!
THIS TIME OZAWA CHOSE SHIROYAMA TO PLAY THE HEROINE.
IT WAS ALL HER DECISION.
REALLY?
THANKS, OKOUCHI.
FOR WHAT?
A BIG DEAL HAS BEEN MADE ABOUT THIS PLAY IN THE SCHOOL FESTIVAL PROGRAM, RIGHT?
I HEARD IT WAS SOMETHING YOUR FATHER SAID AT THE PTA MEETING.
OH... WELL, UM...
...THAT'S BECAUSE I THOUGHT IT WAS THE BEST IN THE PROGRAM.
SHIROYAMA'S A LUCKY GIRL.
じー……
Glare

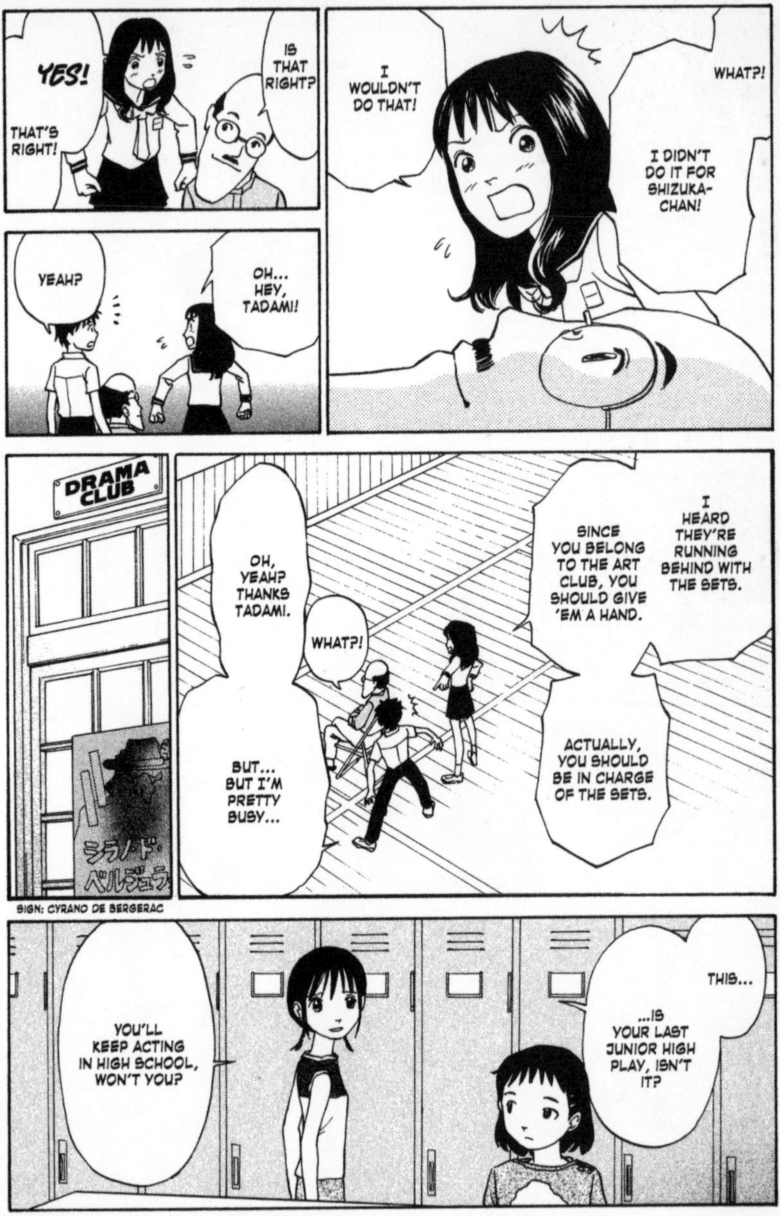
WHAT?!
I DIDN'T DO IT FOR SHIZUKA-CHAN!
I WOULDN'T DO THAT!
IS THAT RIGHT?
YES!
THAT'S RIGHT!
OH... HEY, TADAMI!
YEAH?
I HEARD THEY'RE RUNNING BEHIND WITH THE SETS.
SINCE YOU BELONG TO THE ART CLUB, YOU SHOULD GIVE 'EM A HAND.
ACTUALLY, YOU SHOULD BE IN CHARGE OF THE SETS.
WHAT?!
OH, YEAH? THANKS TADAMI.
BUT... BUT I'M PRETTY BUSY...
DRAMA CLUB
シラノ・ド・ベルジュラ
SIGN: CYRANO DE BERGERAC
THIS...
...IS YOUR LAST JUNIOR HIGH PLAY, ISN'T IT?
YOU'LL KEEP ACTING IN HIGH SCHOOL, WON'T YOU?

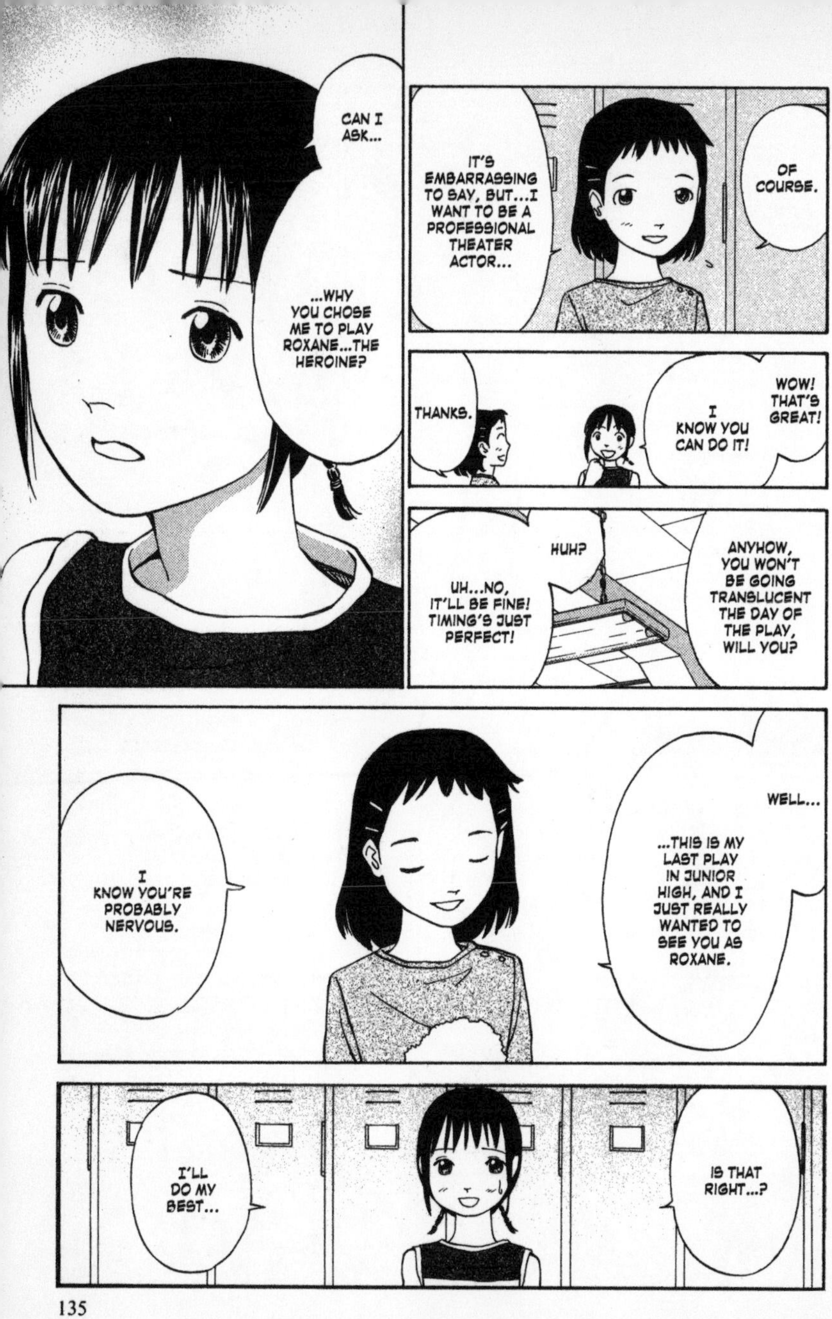

OF COURSE.
IT'S EMBARRASSING TO SAY, BUT...I WANT TO BE A PROFESSIONAL THEATER ACTOR...
WOW! THAT'S GREAT!
I KNOW YOU CAN DO IT!
THANKS.
ANYHOW, YOU WON'T BE GOING TRANSLUCENT THE DAY OF THE PLAY, WILL YOU?
HUH?
UH...NO, IT'LL BE FINE! TIMING'S JUST PERFECT!
CAN I ASK...
...WHY YOU CHOSE ME TO PLAY ROXANE...THE HEROINE?
WELL...
...THIS IS MY LAST PLAY IN JUNIOR HIGH, AND I JUST REALLY WANTED TO SEE YOU AS ROXANE.
I KNOW YOU'RE PROBABLY NERVOUS.
IS THAT RIGHT...?
I'LL DO MY BEST...

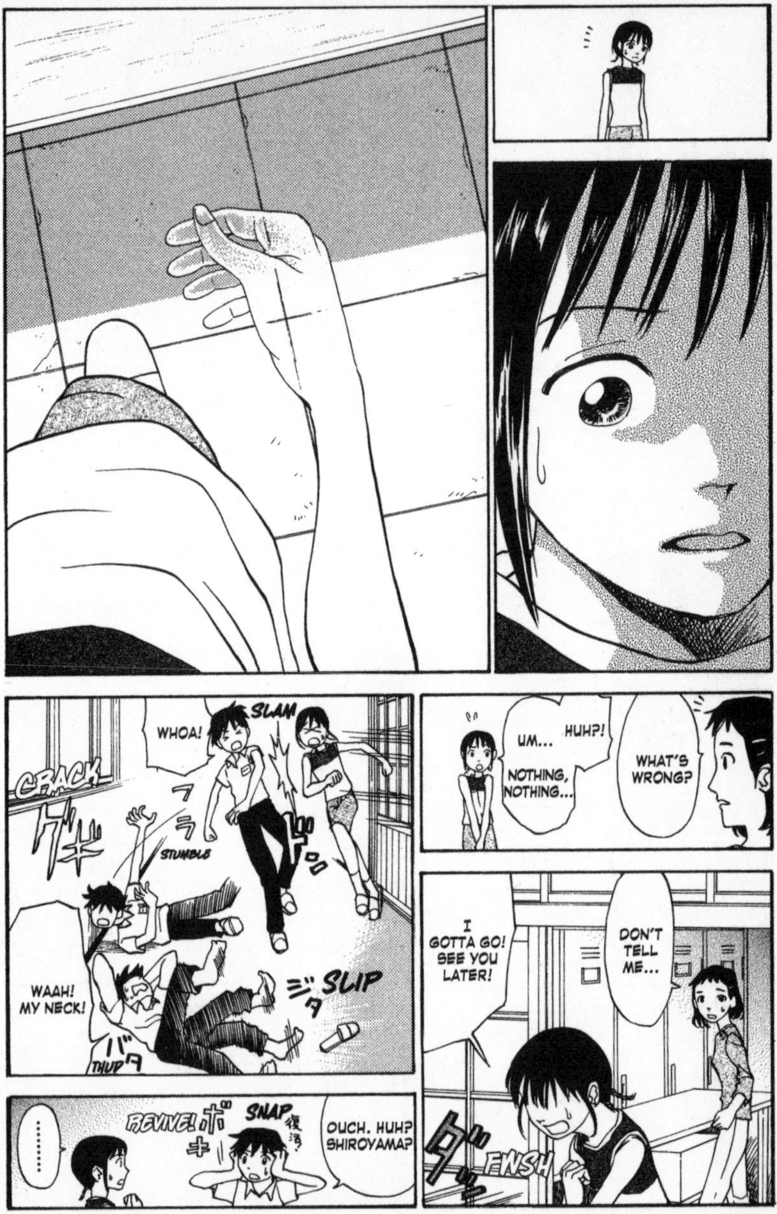
WHAT'S WRONG?
HUH?!
UM... NOTHING, NOTHING...
SLAM
WHOA!
CRACK
STUMBLE
SLIP
WAAH! MY NECK!
THUD
DON'T TELL ME...
I GOTTA GO! SEE YOU LATER!
FWSH
OUCH. HUH? SHIROYAMA?
SNAP
REVIVE!
....

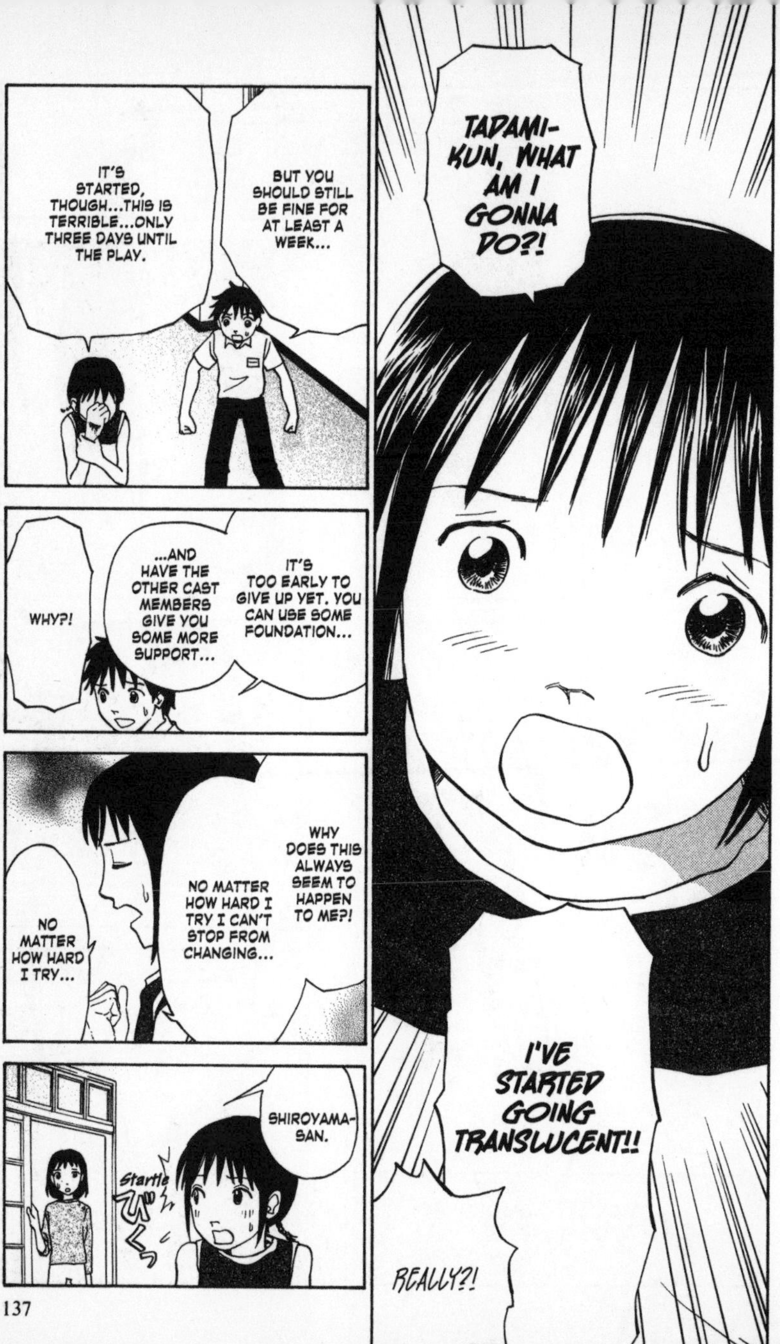
TADAMI-KUN, WHAT AM I GONNA DO?!
I'VE STARTED GOING TRANSLUCENT!!
REALLY?!
BUT YOU SHOULD STILL BE FINE FOR AT LEAST A WEEK...
IT'S STARTED, THOUGH...THIS IS TERRIBLE...ONLY THREE DAYS UNTIL THE PLAY.
IT'S TOO EARLY TO GIVE UP YET. YOU CAN USE SOME FOUNDATION...
...AND HAVE THE OTHER CAST MEMBERS GIVE YOU SOME MORE SUPPORT...
WHY?!
WHY DOES THIS ALWAYS SEEM TO HAPPEN TO ME?!
NO MATTER HOW HARD I TRY I CAN'T STOP FROM CHANGING...
NO MATTER HOW HARD I TRY...
SHIROYAMA-SAN.
Startle

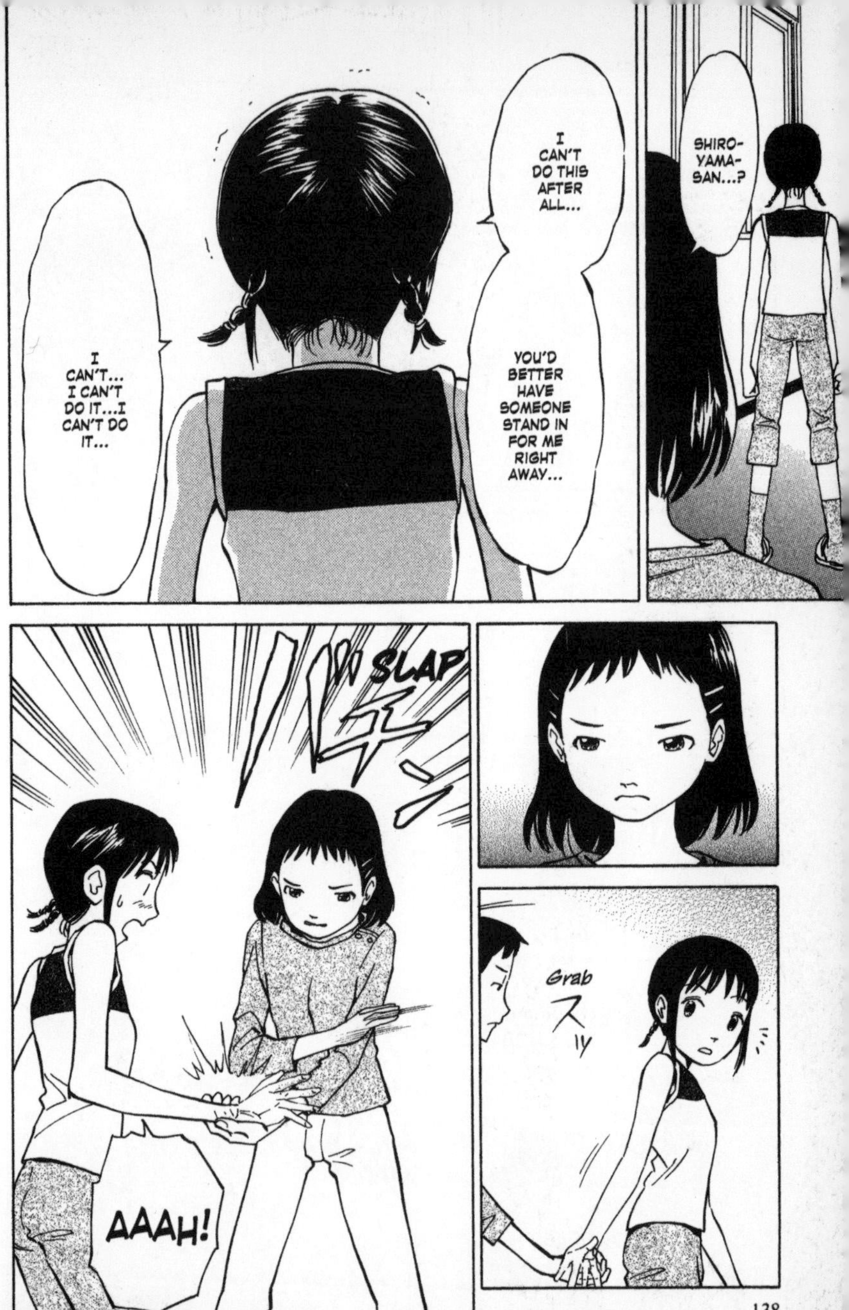
SHIRO-YAMA-SAN...?
...
I CAN'T DO THIS AFTER ALL...
YOU'D BETTER HAVE SOMEONE STAND IN FOR ME RIGHT AWAY...
I CAN'T... I CAN'T DO IT...I CAN'T DO IT...
Grab
SLAP
AAAH!

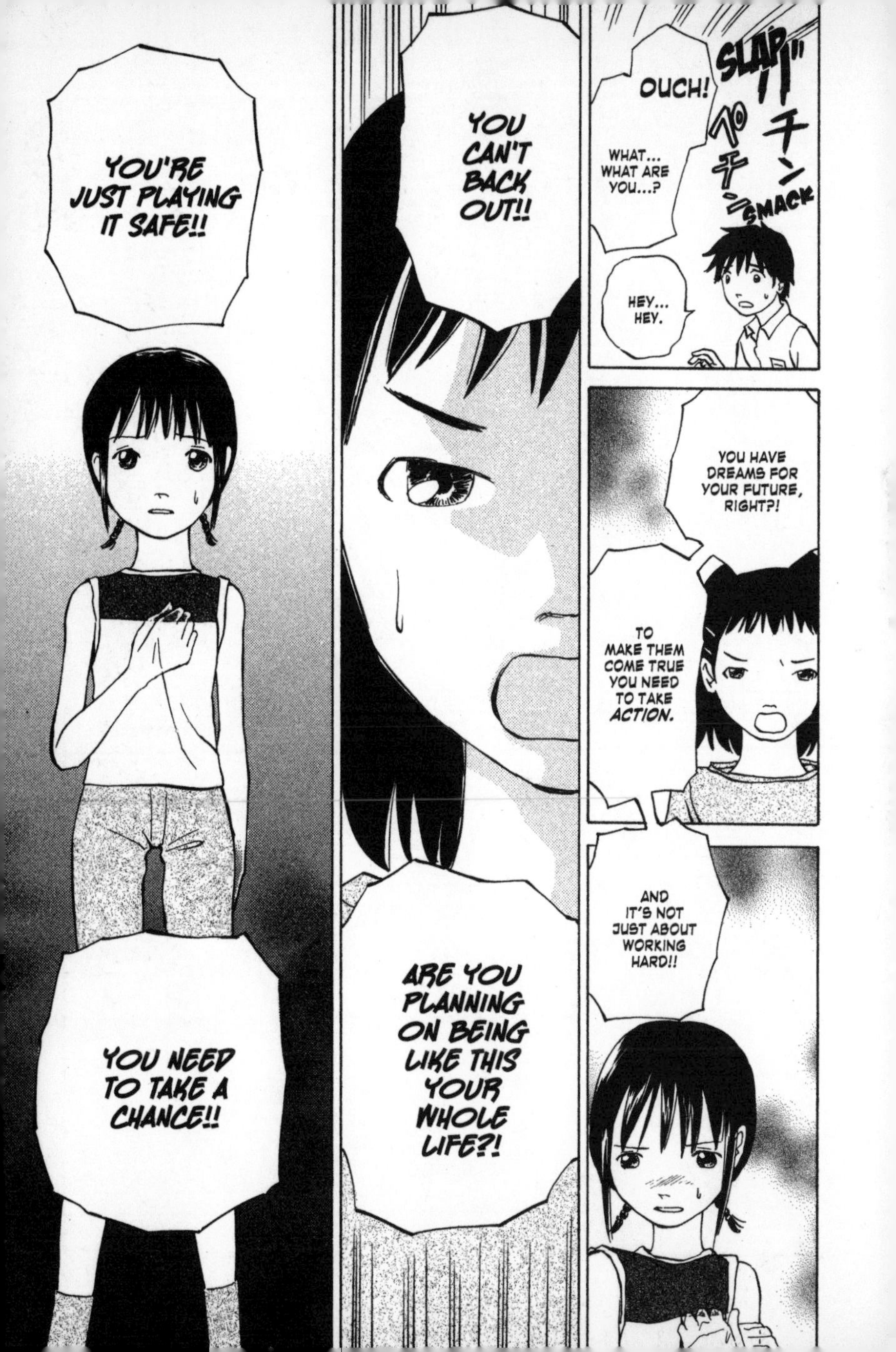
SLAP
パチン
OUCH!
ペチ
SMACK
WHAT... WHAT ARE YOU...?
HEY... HEY.
YOU HAVE DREAMS FOR YOUR FUTURE, RIGHT?!
TO MAKE THEM COME TRUE YOU NEED TO TAKE *ACTION*.
AND IT'S NOT JUST ABOUT WORKING HARD!!
YOU CAN'T BACK OUT!!
ARE YOU PLANNING ON BEING LIKE THIS YOUR WHOLE LIFE?!
YOU'RE JUST PLAYING IT SAFE!!
YOU NEED TO TAKE A CHANCE!!

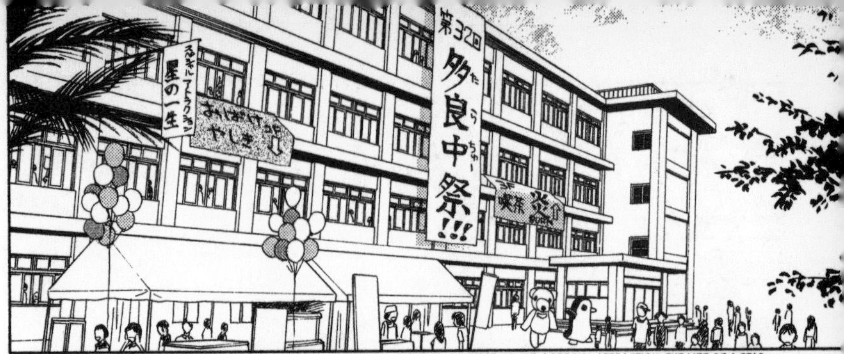
第32回 多良中祭!!!

PANEL ONE SIGNS: 3RD FL. CAFÉ BURN / 32ND TARA SCHOOL FESTIVAL / 2ND FL. HAUNTED HOUSE / SPECIAL ATTRACTION: THE LIFE OF A STAR

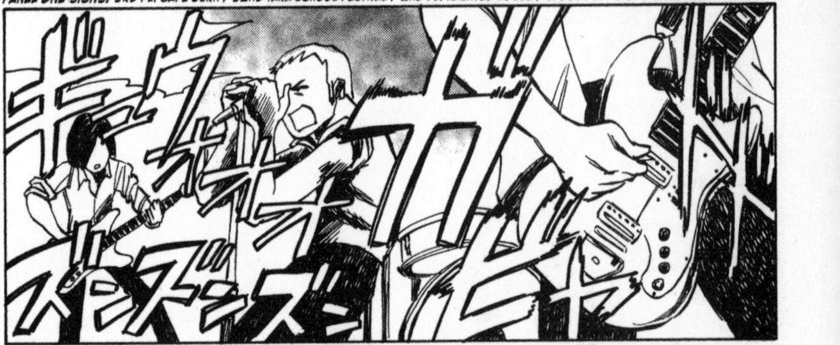

PANEL TWO BAND SOUNDS: DRUM'S RATTA TATTA, GUITAR'S TWANG, SINGER'S "YEEAH!," GUITAR'S CHANNGG, BASS GUITAR'S BOOM

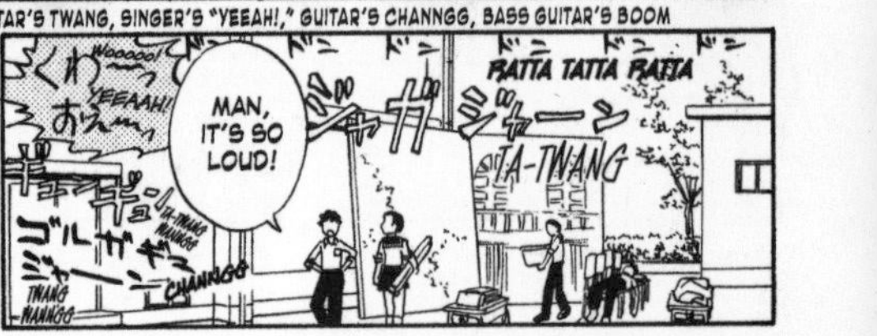
くわ～～～ Wooooo!
おぇ～～ YEEAAH!
MAN, IT'S SO LOUD!
RATTA TATTA RATTA
ジャガジャーン
TA-TWANG
CHANNGG

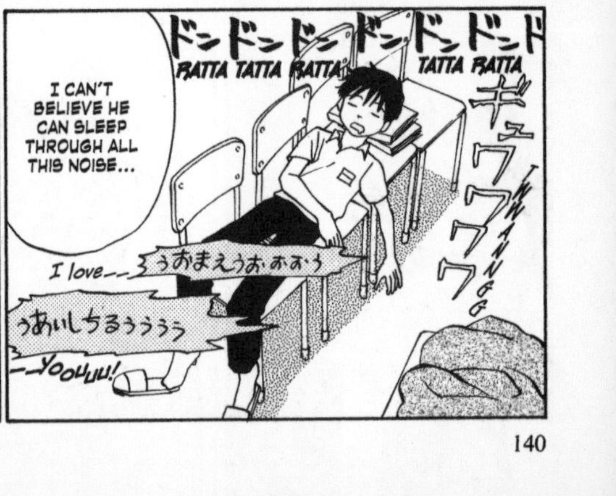
ドンドンドンドンドンドンドンド
RATTA TATTA RATTA
TATTA RATTA
I CAN'T BELIEVE HE CAN SLEEP THROUGH ALL THIS NOISE...
ギュウワワワワ
TWWANNGG
I love--- うおまえうおおおう
うあいしちるうううう
---YOOUUU!

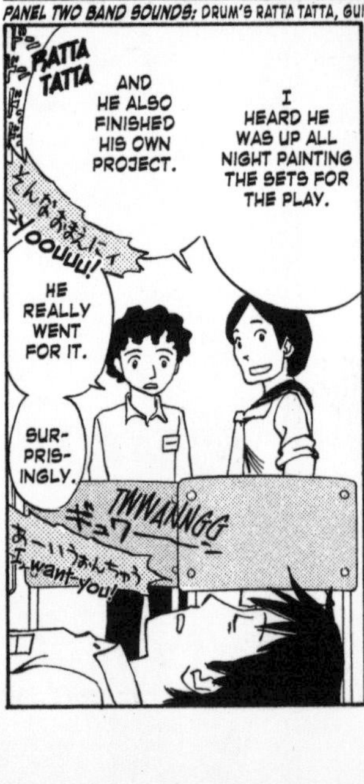
RATTA TATTA
I HEARD HE WAS UP ALL NIGHT PAINTING THE SETS FOR THE PLAY.
AND HE ALSO FINISHED HIS OWN PROJECT.
そんなおまんにィ YOOUUU!
HE REALLY WENT FOR IT.
SURPRISINGLY.
TWWANNGG
ギュワー
あーいうぉんちゅう I want you!

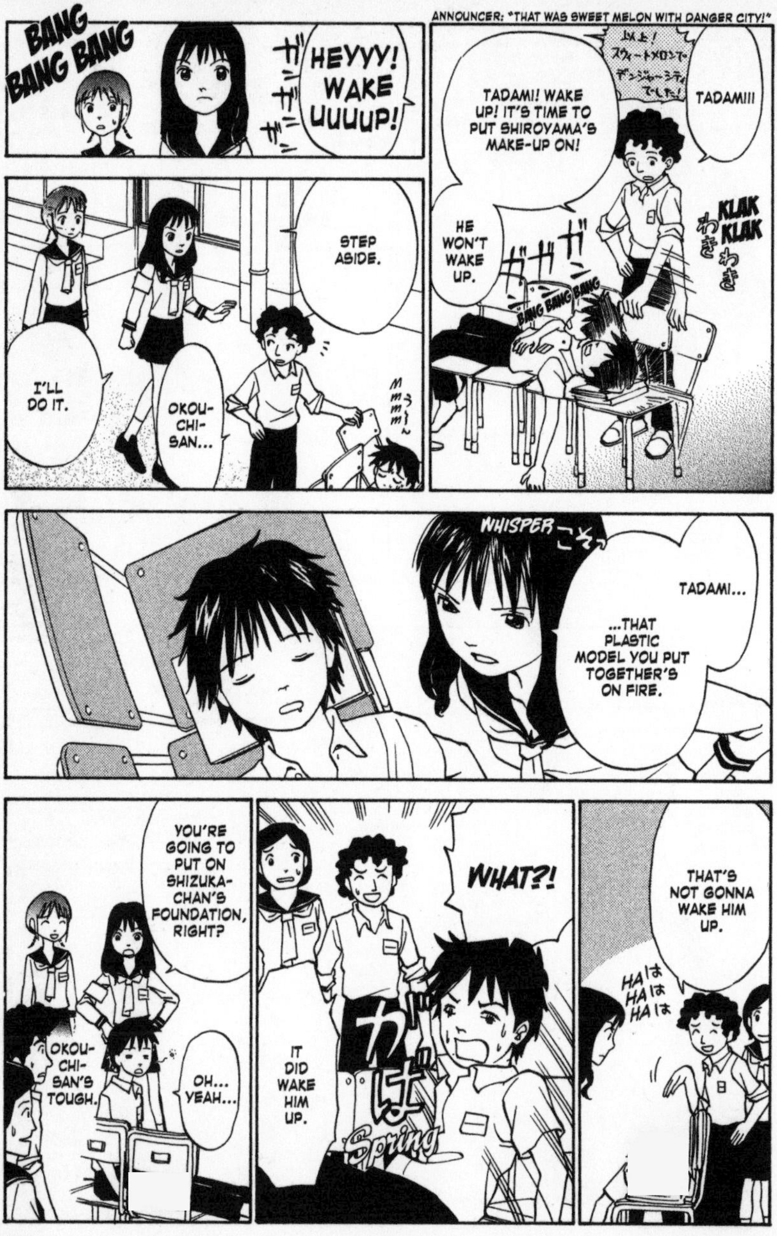
ANNOUNCER: "THAT WAS SWEET MELON WITH DANGER CITY!"
以上！スウィートメロンでデンジャーシティでした！
TADAMI!!!
TADAMI! WAKE UP! IT'S TIME TO PUT SHIROYAMA'S MAKE-UP ON!
KLAK KLAK
わきわき
HE WON'T WAKE UP.
ガガガン
BANG BANG BANG
HEYYY! WAKE UUUUP!
ガンガンガン
BANG BANG BANG
STEP ASIDE.
OKOUCHI-SAN...
I'LL DO IT.
Mmmm
うーん
WHISPER
こそっ
TADAMI...
...THAT PLASTIC MODEL YOU PUT TOGETHER'S ON FIRE.
THAT'S NOT GONNA WAKE HIM UP.
HA HA HA
ははは
WHAT?!
IT DID WAKE HIM UP.
がばっ
Spring
YOU'RE GOING TO PUT ON SHIZUKA-CHAN'S FOUNDATION, RIGHT?
OH... YEAH...
OKOUCHI-SAN'S TOUGH.

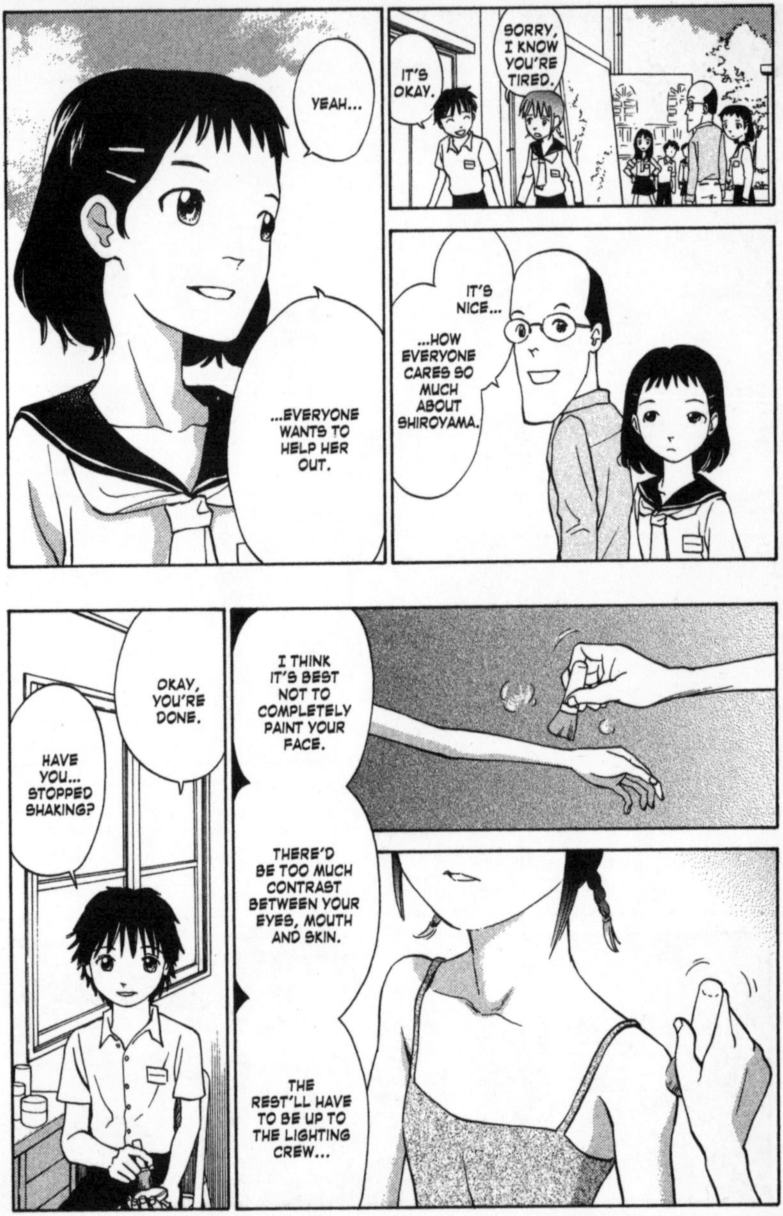
SORRY, I KNOW YOU'RE TIRED.
IT'S OKAY.
IT'S NICE...
...HOW EVERYONE CARES SO MUCH ABOUT SHIROYAMA.
YEAH...
...EVERYONE WANTS TO HELP HER OUT.
I THINK IT'S BEST NOT TO COMPLETELY PAINT YOUR FACE.
THERE'D BE TOO MUCH CONTRAST BETWEEN YOUR EYES, MOUTH AND SKIN.
THE REST'LL HAVE TO BE UP TO THE LIGHTING CREW...
OKAY, YOU'RE DONE.
HAVE YOU... STOPPED SHAKING?

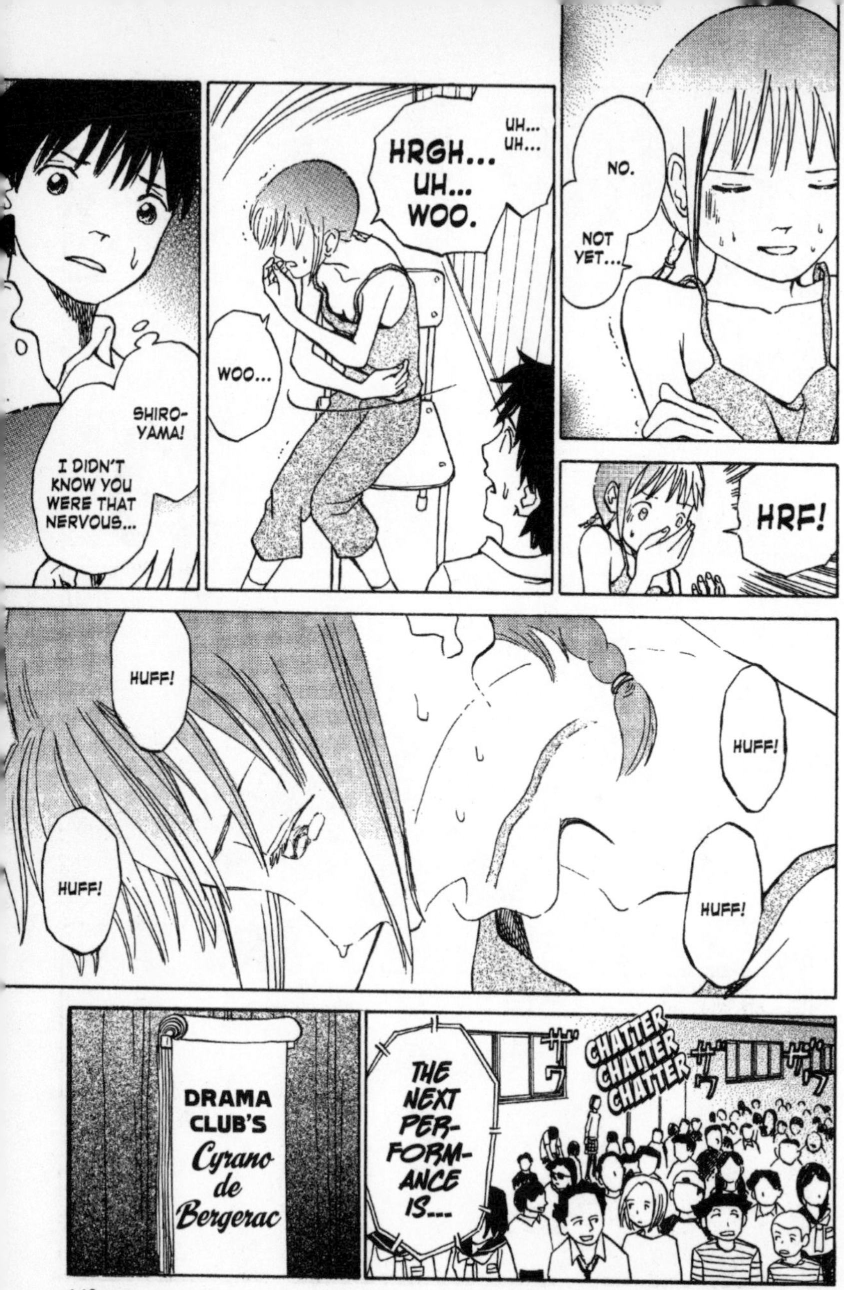
NO.
NOT YET...
HRF!
UH... UH...
HRGH... UH... WOO.
WOO...
SHIRO-YAMA!
I DIDN'T KNOW YOU WERE THAT NERVOUS...
HUFF!
HUFF!
HUFF!
HUFF!
CHATTER CHATTER CHATTER
THE NEXT PERFORMANCE IS...
DRAMA CLUB'S Cyrano de Bergerac

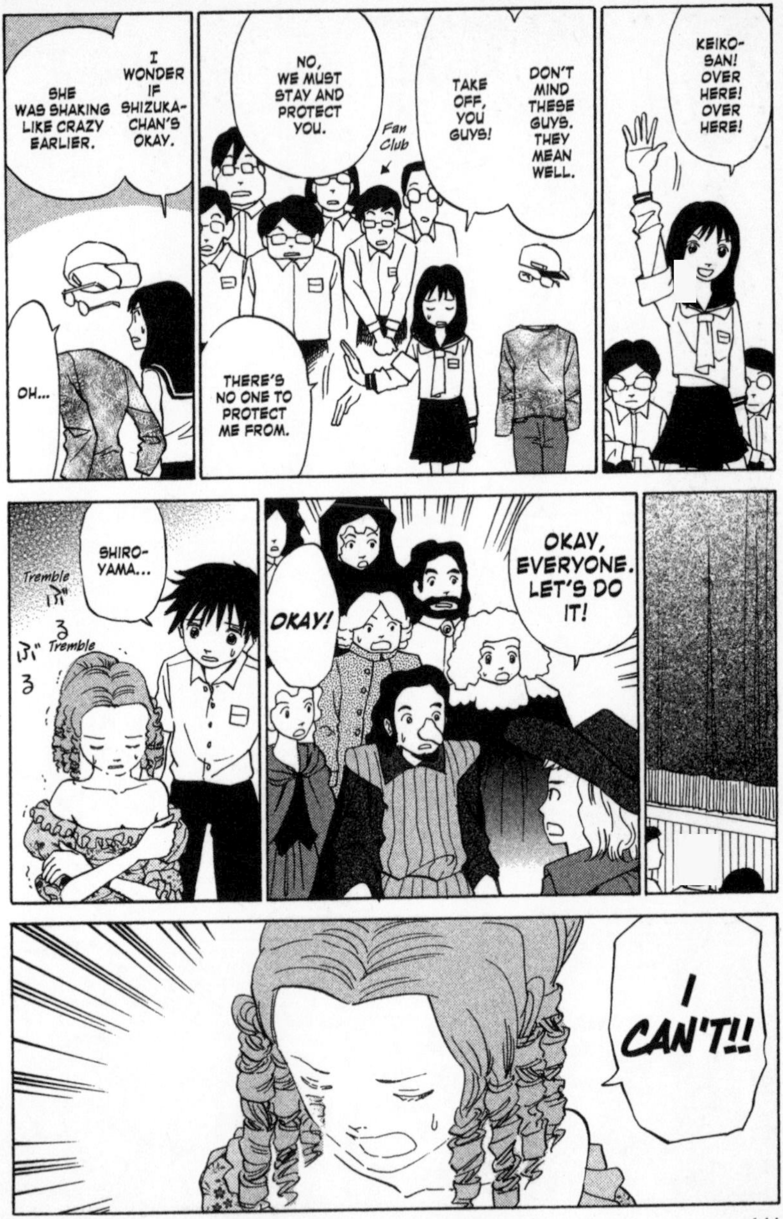
KEIKO-SAN! OVER HERE! OVER HERE!
DON'T MIND THESE GUYS. THEY MEAN WELL.
TAKE OFF, YOU GUYS!
NO, WE MUST STAY AND PROTECT YOU.
Fan Club
THERE'S NO ONE TO PROTECT ME FROM.
I WONDER IF SHIZUKA-CHAN'S OKAY.
SHE WAS SHAKING LIKE CRAZY EARLIER.
OH...
OKAY, EVERYONE. LET'S DO IT!
OKAY!
SHIRO-YAMA...
Tremble
ぶる
Tremble
ぶる
I CAN'T!!

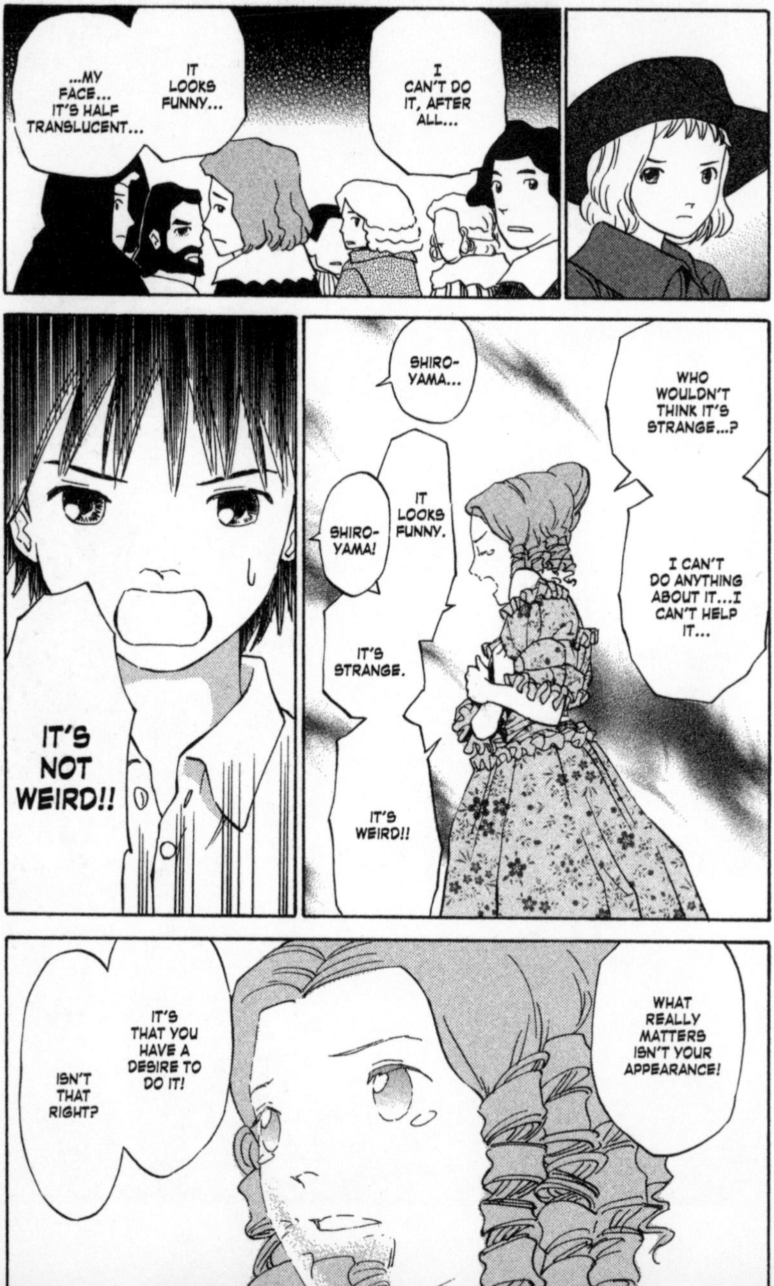
I CAN'T DO IT, AFTER ALL...
IT LOOKS FUNNY...
...MY FACE... IT'S HALF TRANSLUCENT...
WHO WOULDN'T THINK IT'S STRANGE...?
SHIRO-YAMA...
IT LOOKS FUNNY.
SHIRO-YAMA!
I CAN'T DO ANYTHING ABOUT IT...I CAN'T HELP IT...
IT'S STRANGE.
IT'S WEIRD!!
IT'S NOT WEIRD!!
WHAT REALLY MATTERS ISN'T YOUR APPEARANCE!
IT'S THAT YOU HAVE A DESIRE TO DO IT!
ISN'T THAT RIGHT?

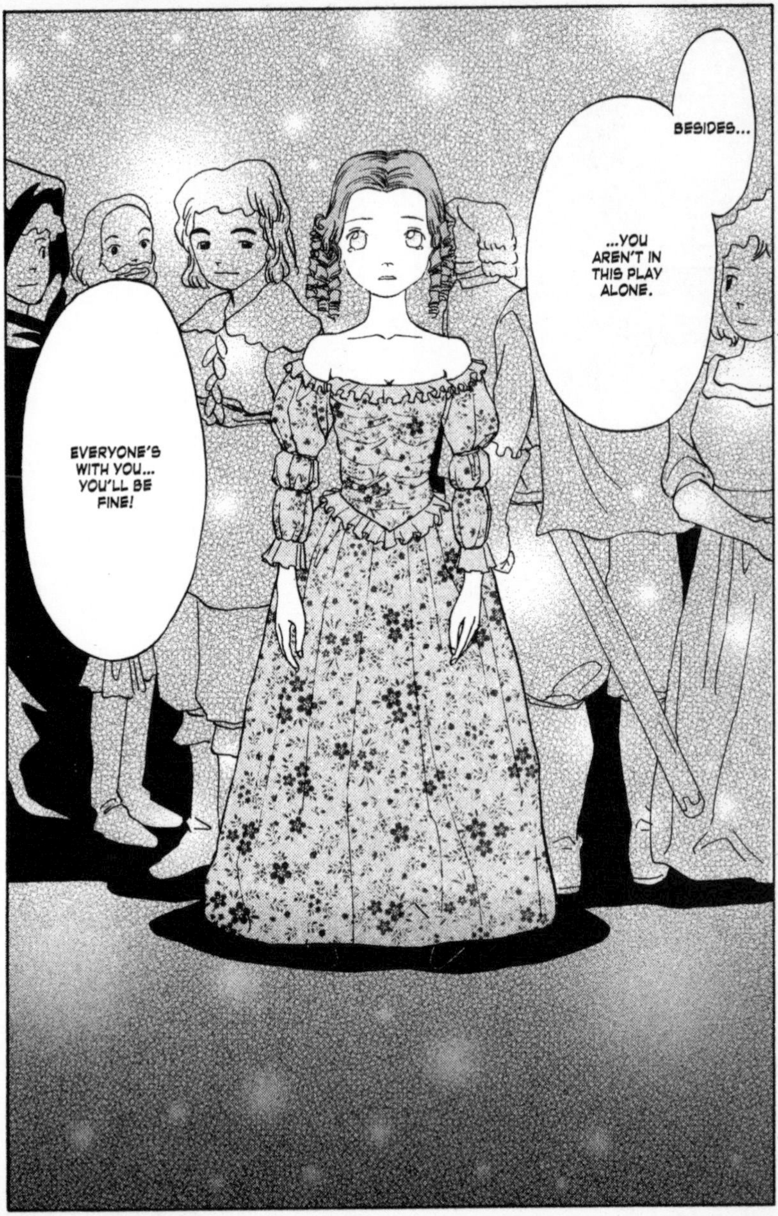
BESIDES...
...YOU AREN'T IN THIS PLAY ALONE.
EVERYONE'S WITH YOU... YOU'LL BE FINE!

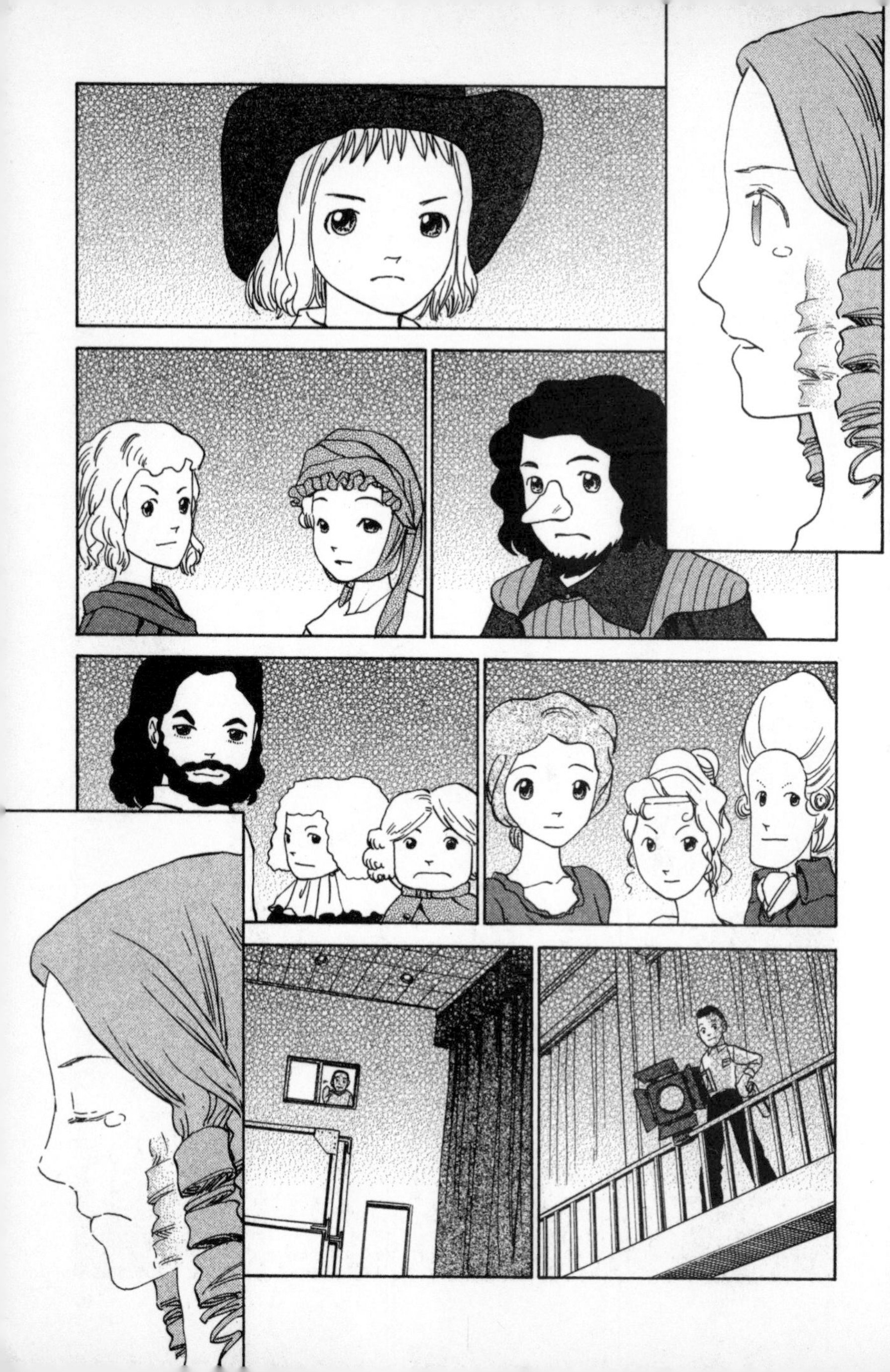

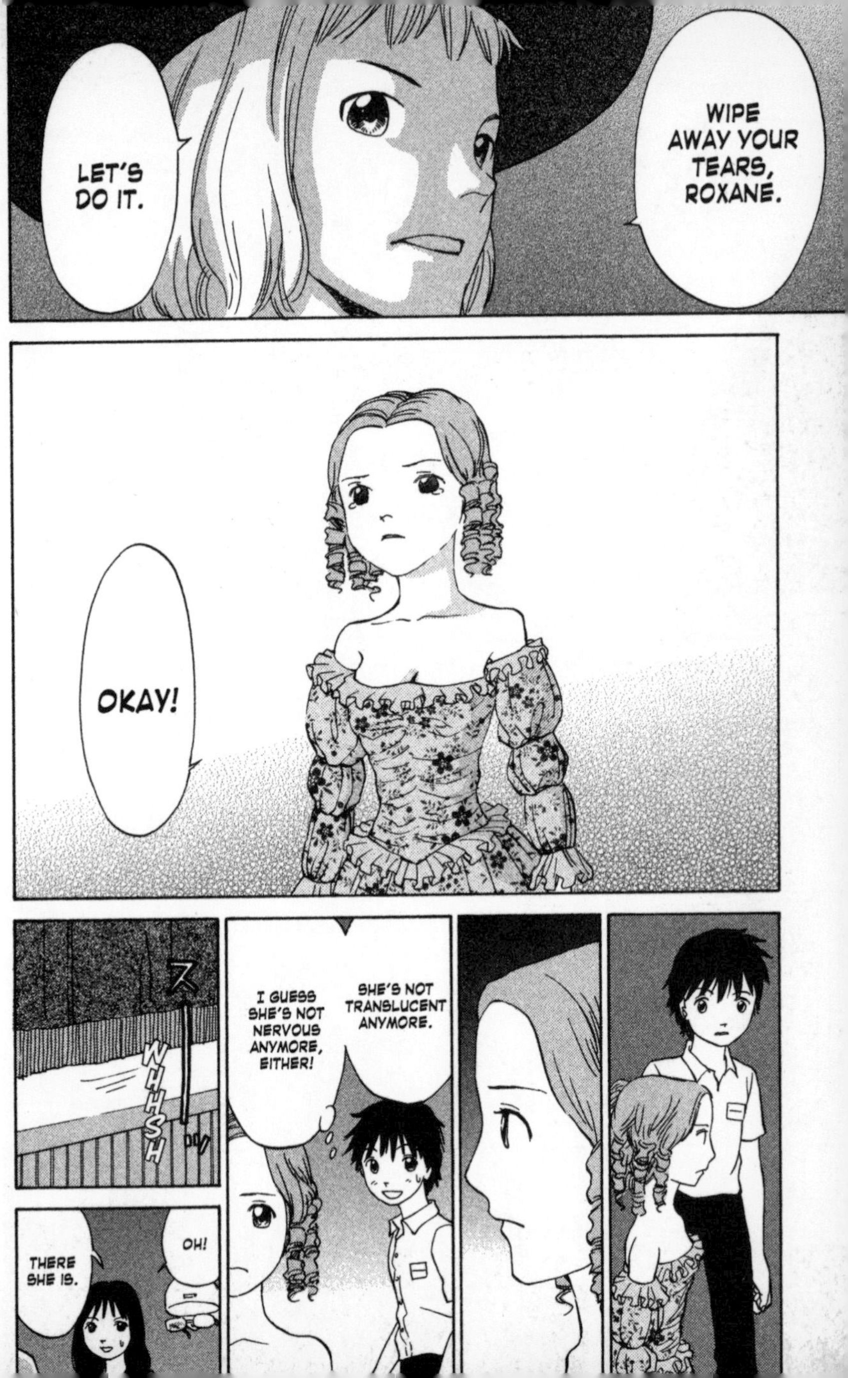
WIPE AWAY YOUR TEARS, ROXANE.
LET'S DO IT.
OKAY!
SHE'S NOT TRANSLUCENT ANYMORE.
I GUESS SHE'S NOT NERVOUS ANYMORE, EITHER!
ス
WHHSH
OH!
THERE SHE IS.

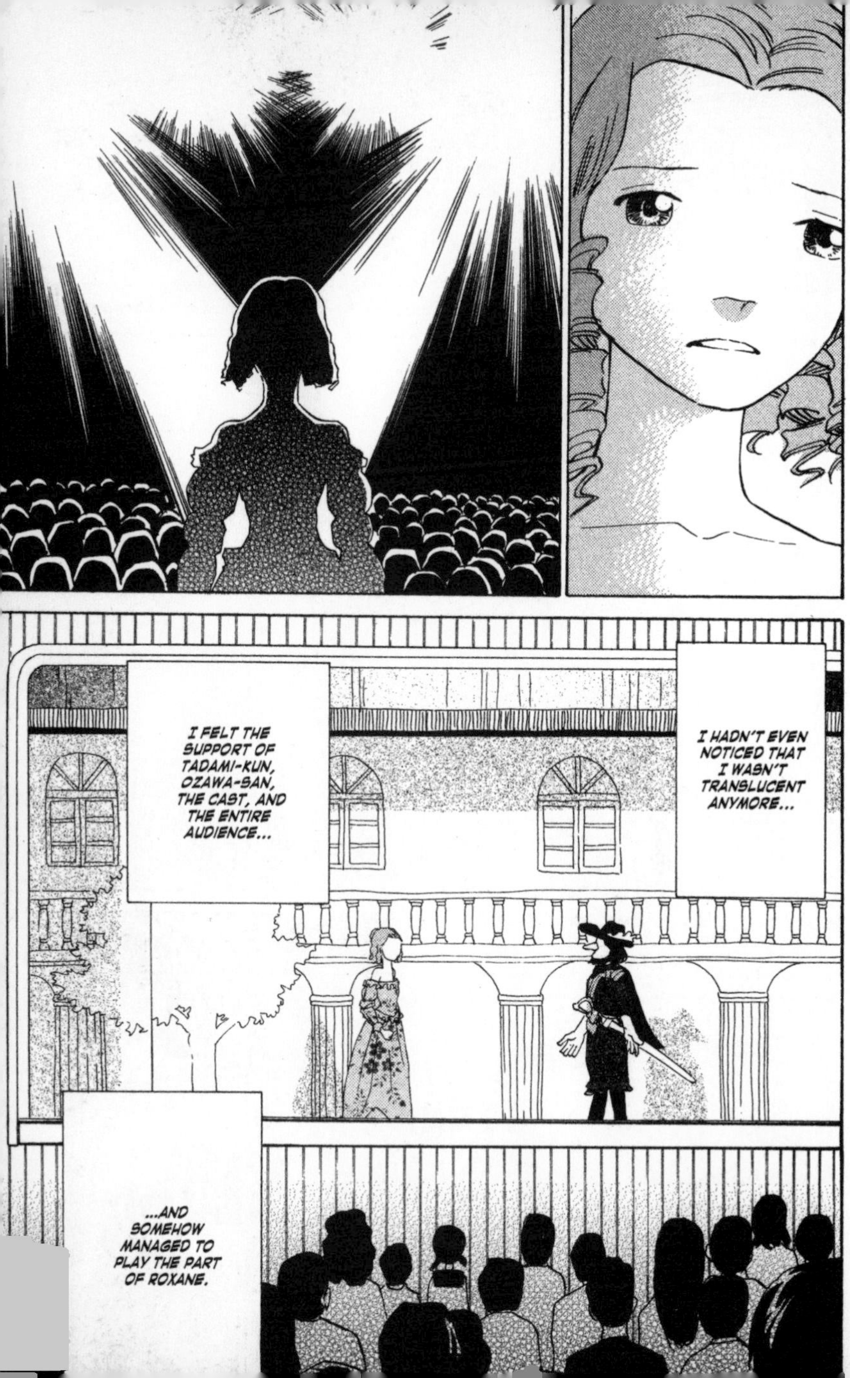
I HADN'T EVEN NOTICED THAT I WASN'T TRANSLUCENT ANYMORE...
I FELT THE SUPPORT OF TADAMI-KUN, OZAWA-SAN, THE CAST, AND THE ENTIRE AUDIENCE...
...AND SOMEHOW MANAGED TO PLAY THE PART OF ROXANE.

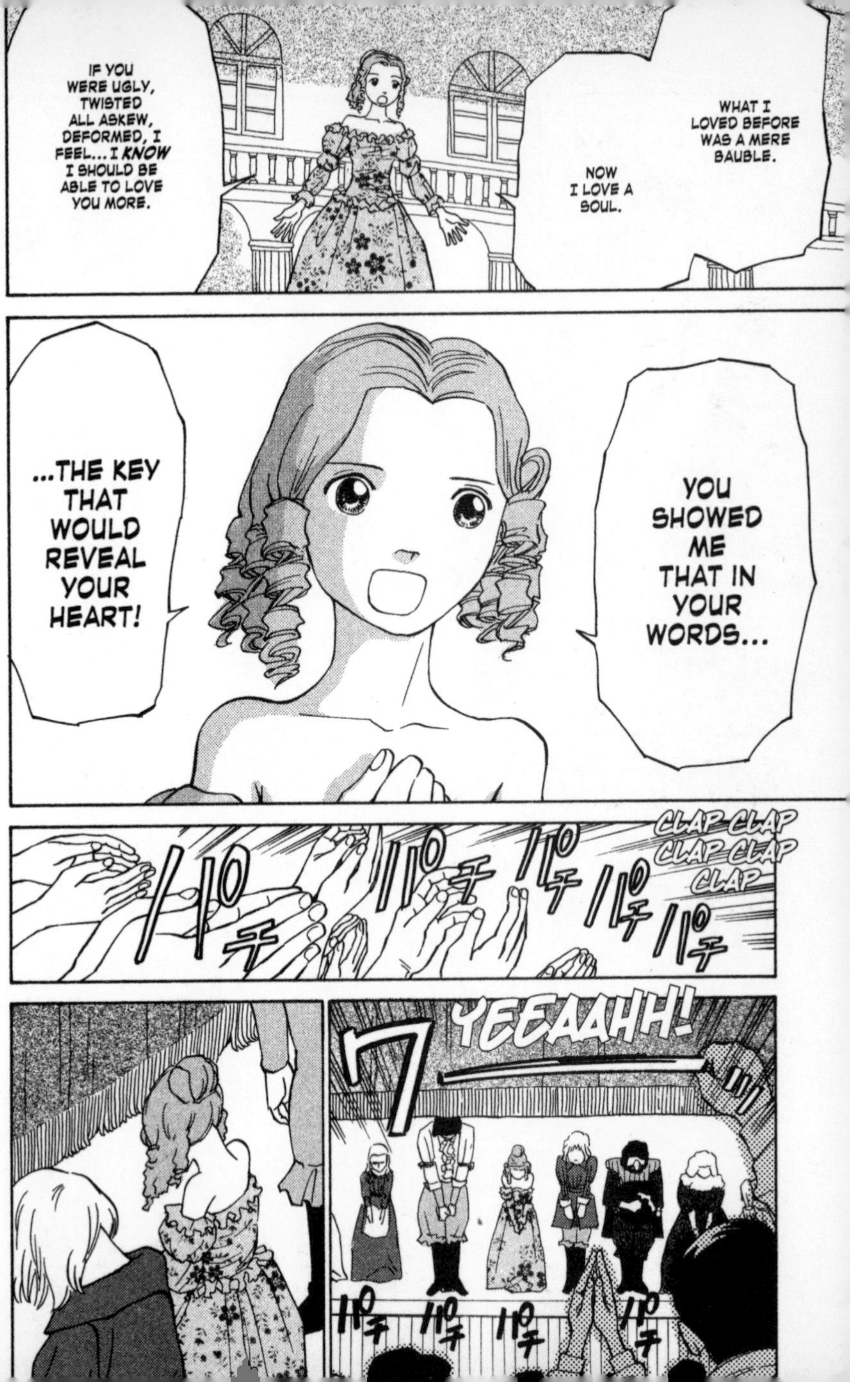
WHAT I LOVED BEFORE WAS A MERE BAUBLE.
NOW I LOVE A SOUL.
IF YOU WERE UGLY, TWISTED ALL ASKEW, DEFORMED, I FEEL... I *KNOW* I SHOULD BE ABLE TO LOVE YOU MORE.
YOU SHOWED ME THAT IN YOUR WORDS...
...THE KEY THAT WOULD REVEAL YOUR HEART!
CLAP CLAP CLAP CLAP CLAP
YEEAAHH!

SHIRO-YAMA! WHAT'S WRONG?

ARE YOU HURT?

HUH?

FUMP

HEY!

I...

TADAMI-KUN.

TADAMI-KUN.

YEAH?

SOMEONE BRING A BLANKET!

ARE YOU COLD?

OH... OKAY.

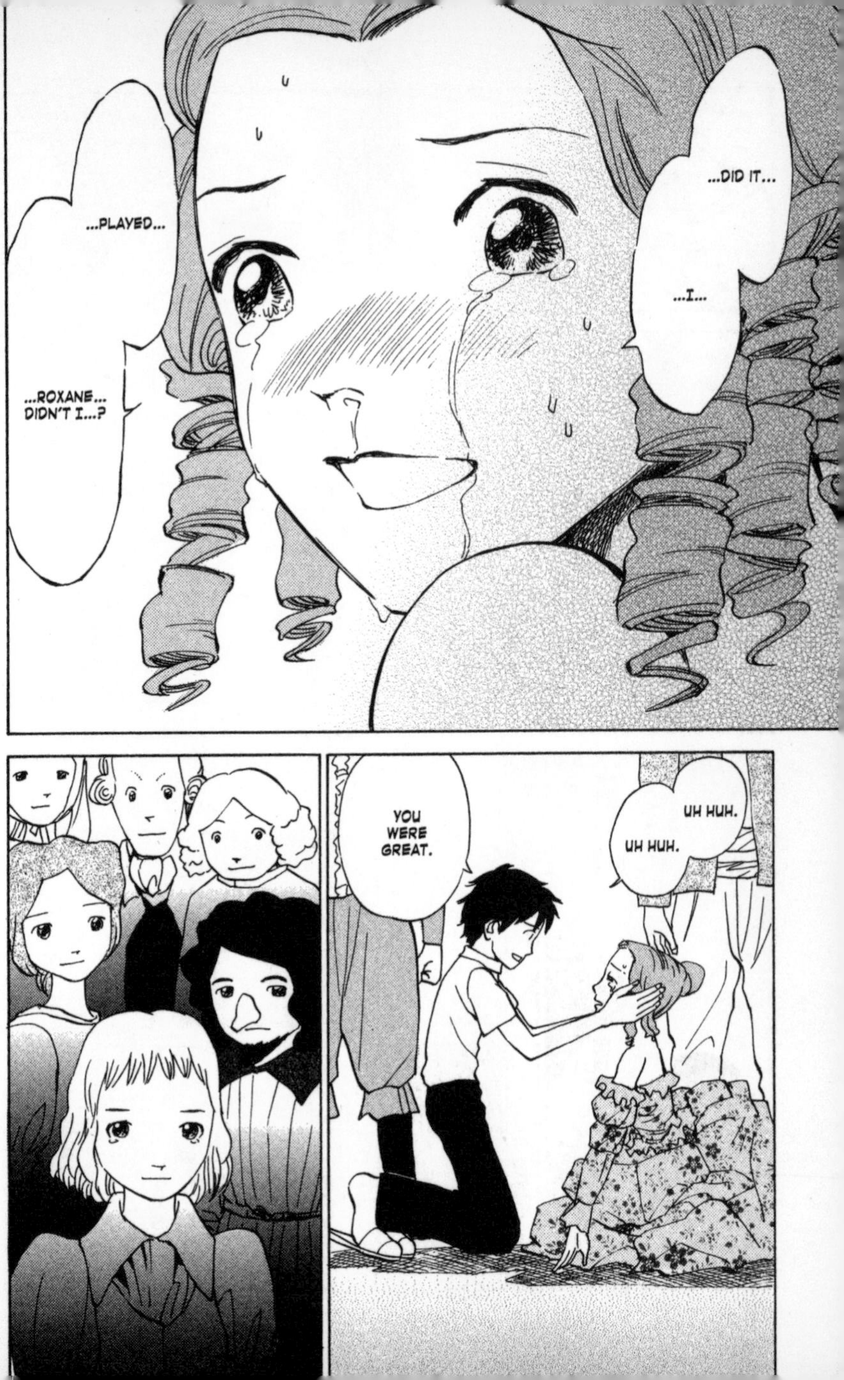
...DID IT...
...I...
...PLAYED...
...ROXANE... DIDN'T I...?
UH HUH.
UH HUH.
YOU WERE GREAT.

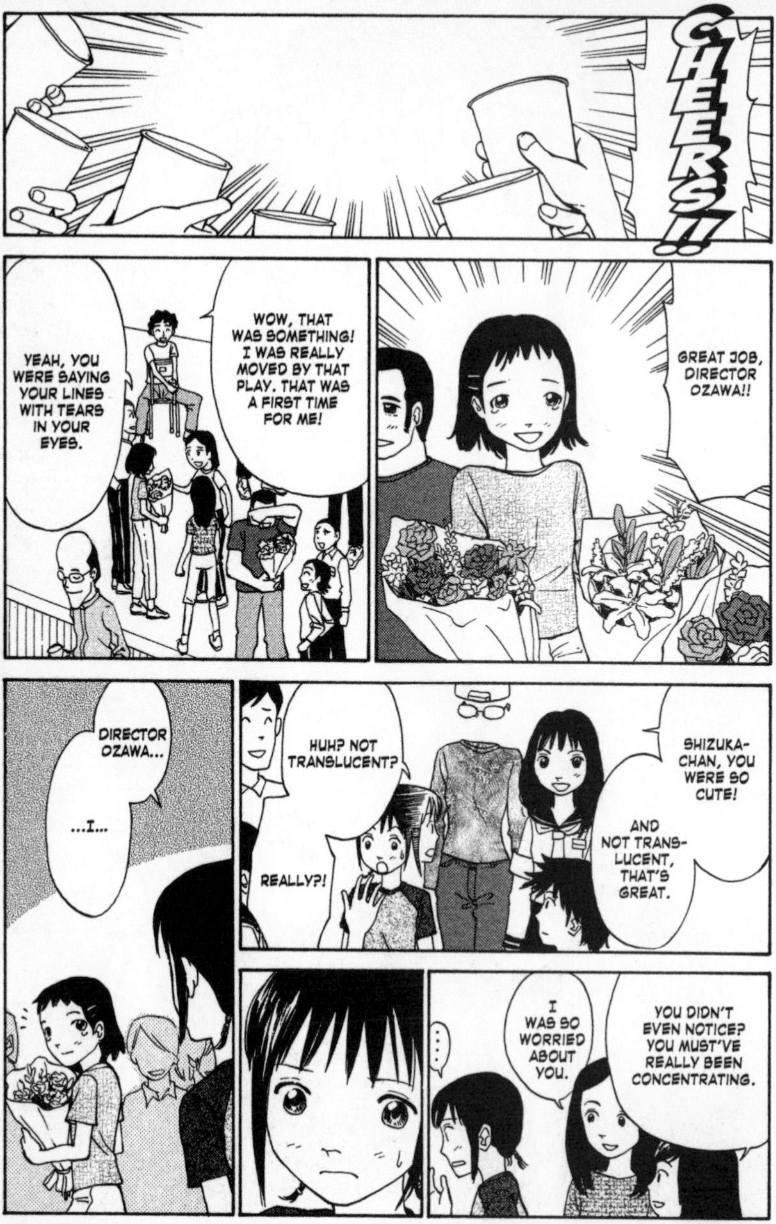
CHEERS!!
GREAT JOB, DIRECTOR OZAWA!!
WOW, THAT WAS SOMETHING! I WAS REALLY MOVED BY THAT PLAY. THAT WAS A FIRST TIME FOR ME!
YEAH, YOU WERE SAYING YOUR LINES WITH TEARS IN YOUR EYES.
SHIZUKA-CHAN, YOU WERE SO CUTE!
AND NOT TRANS-LUCENT, THAT'S GREAT.
HUH? NOT TRANSLUCENT?
REALLY?!
YOU DIDN'T EVEN NOTICE? YOU MUST'VE REALLY BEEN CONCENTRATING.
I WAS SO WORRIED ABOUT YOU.
....
DIRECTOR OZAWA...
...I...

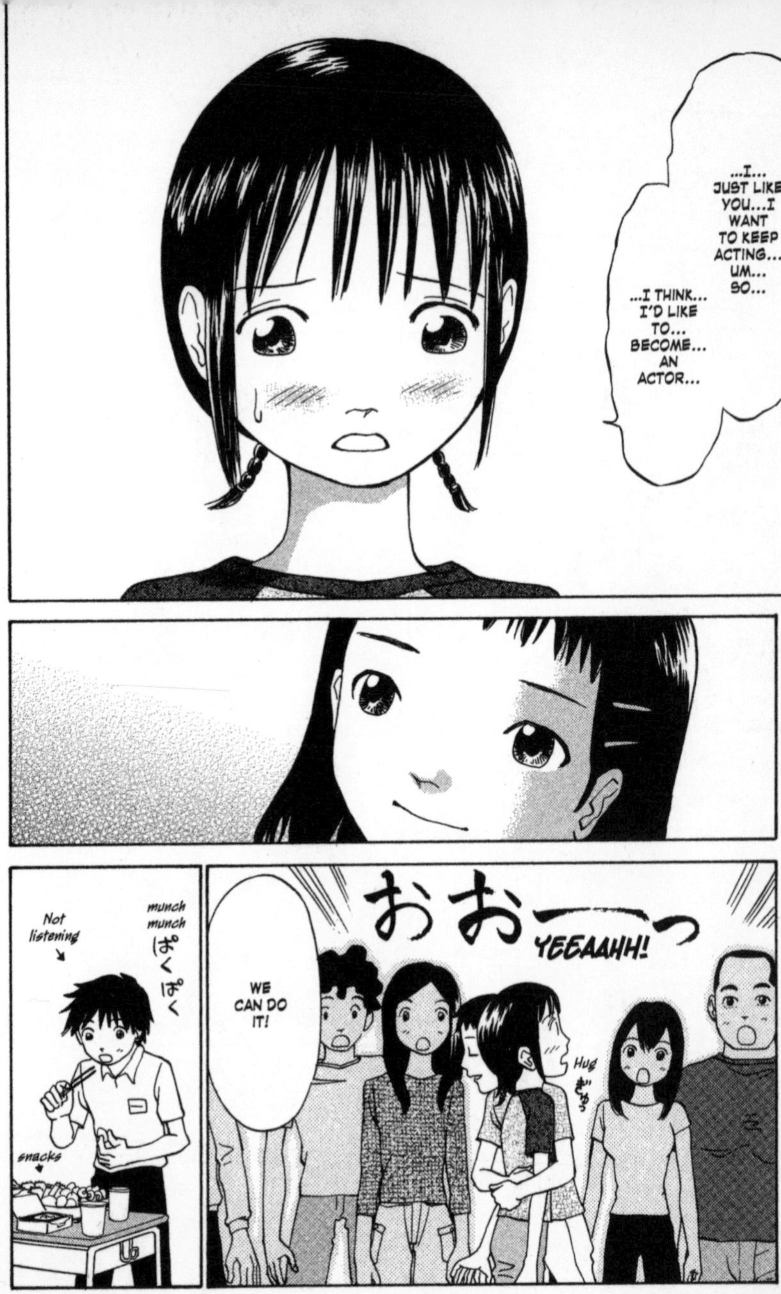
...I... JUST LIKE YOU...I WANT TO KEEP ACTING... UM... SO...
...I THINK... I'D LIKE TO... BECOME... AN ACTOR...
おおーーっ
YEEAAHH!
WE CAN DO IT!
Hug
ぎゅっ
munch munch
ぱくぱく
Not listening
snacks

PART 6 Translucent Father and Daughter

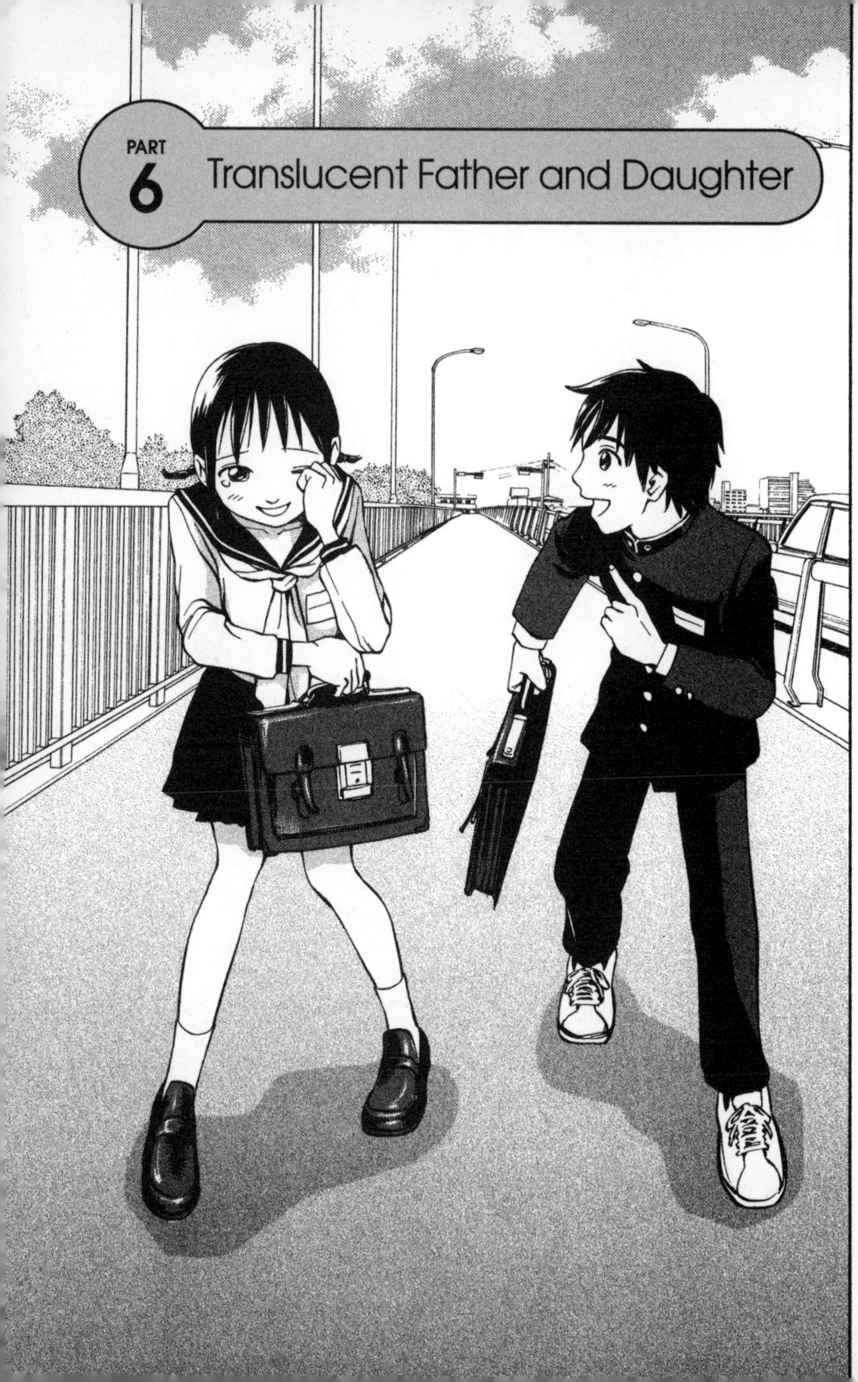

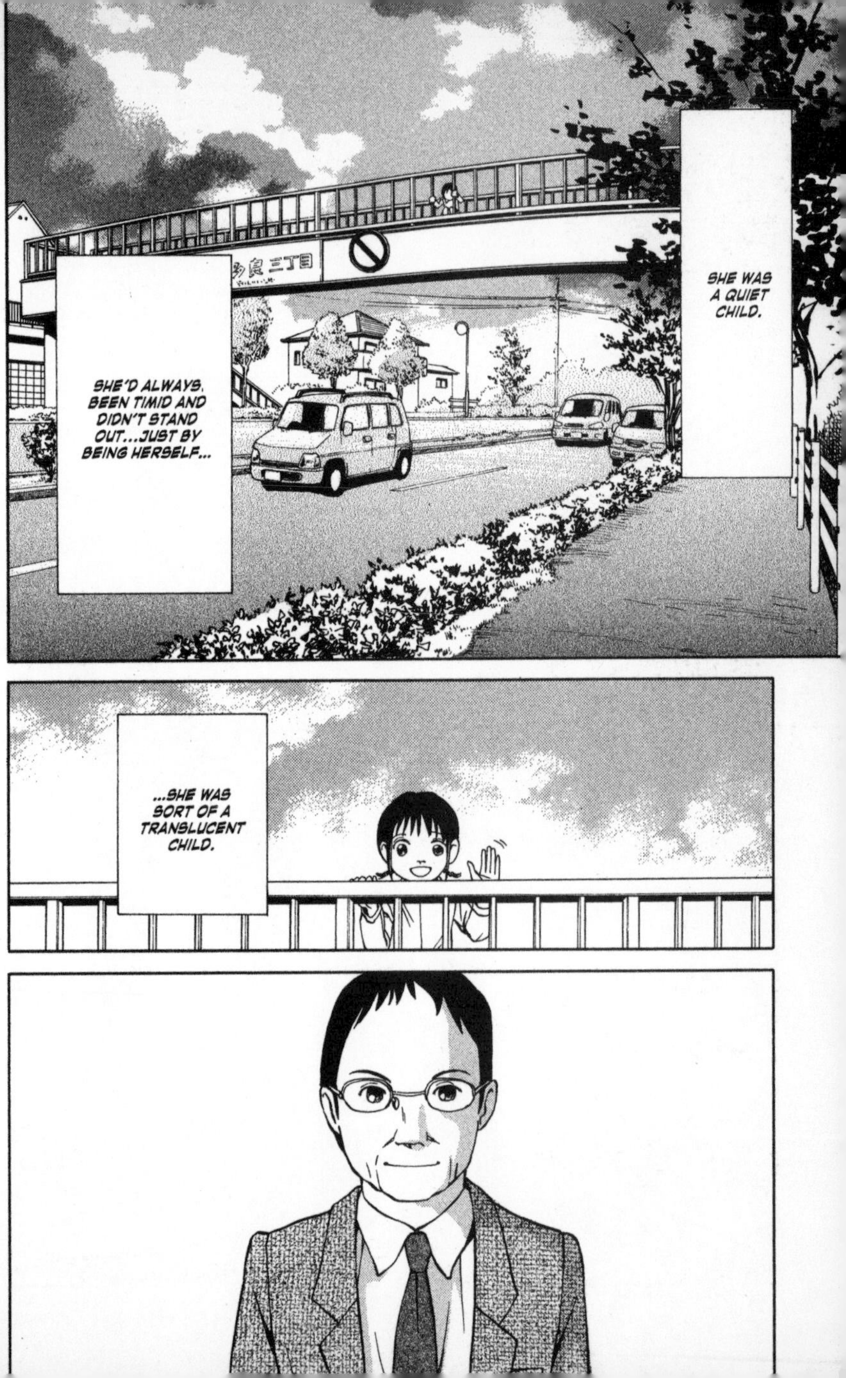
SHE WAS A QUIET CHILD.
多良 三丁目
SHE'D ALWAYS BEEN TIMID AND DIDN'T STAND OUT...JUST BY BEING HERSELF...
...SHE WAS SORT OF A TRANSLUCENT CHILD.

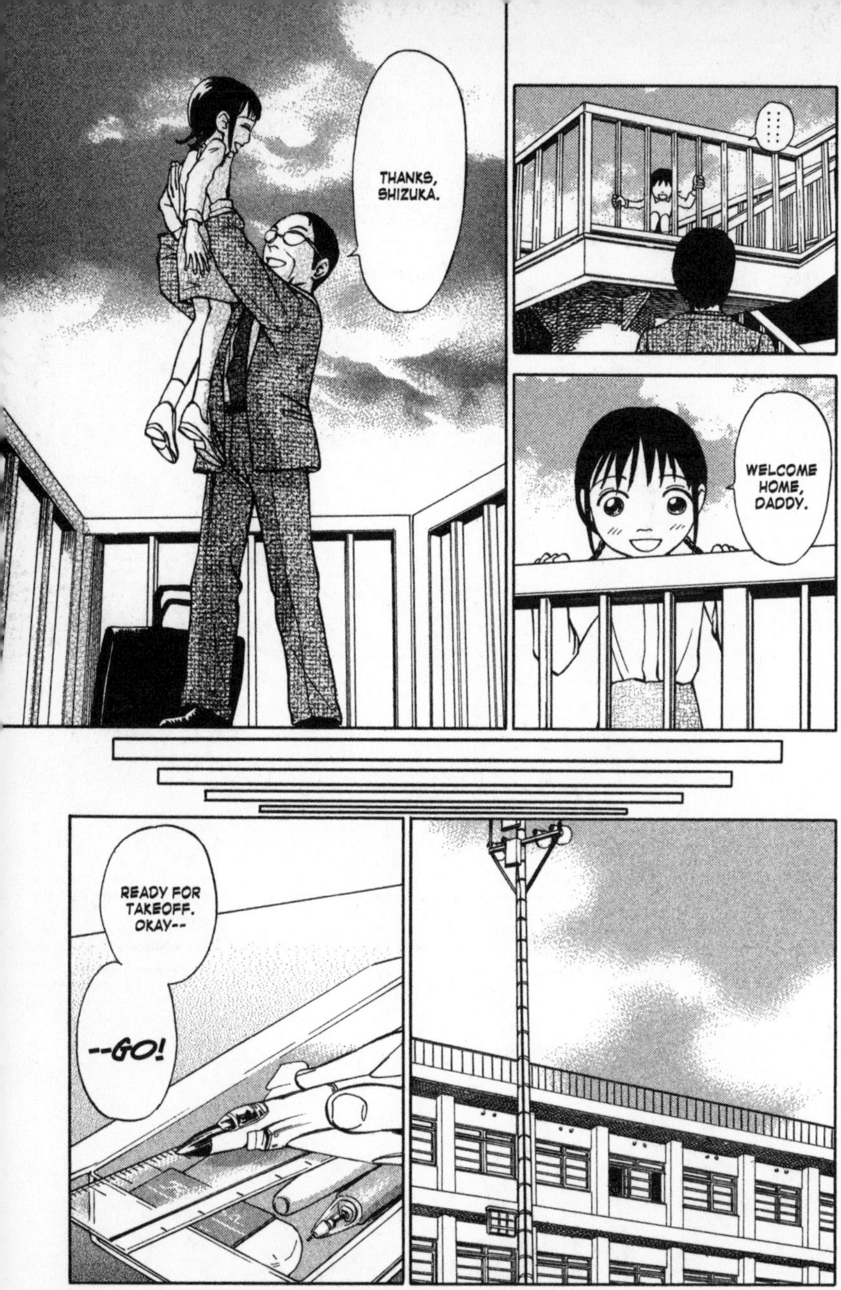
......
WELCOME HOME, DADDY.
THANKS, SHIZUKA.
READY FOR TAKEOFF. OKAY--
--GO!

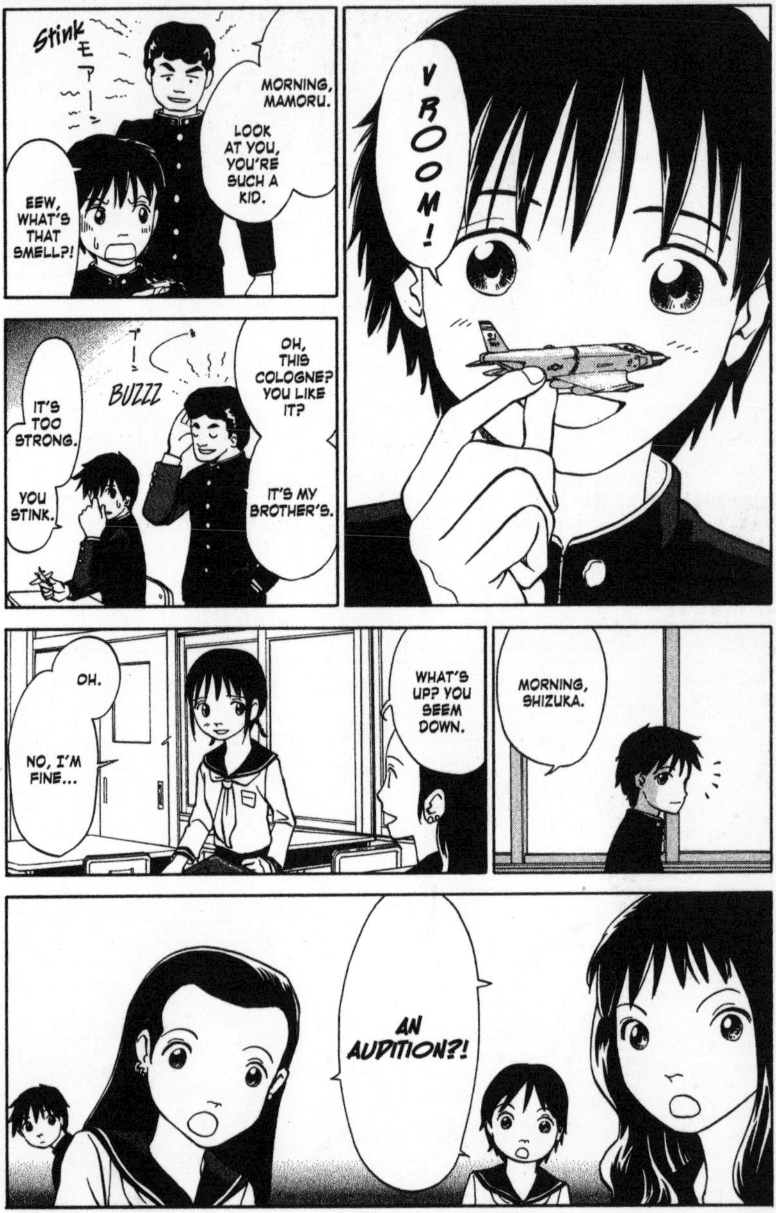
VROOM!
MORNING, MAMORU.
LOOK AT YOU, YOU'RE SUCH A KID.
Stink
EEW, WHAT'S THAT SMELL?!
OH, THIS COLOGNE? YOU LIKE IT?
IT'S MY BROTHER'S.
BUZZZ
IT'S TOO STRONG.
YOU STINK.
MORNING, SHIZUKA.
WHAT'S UP? YOU SEEM DOWN.
OH.
NO, I'M FINE...
AN AUDITION?!

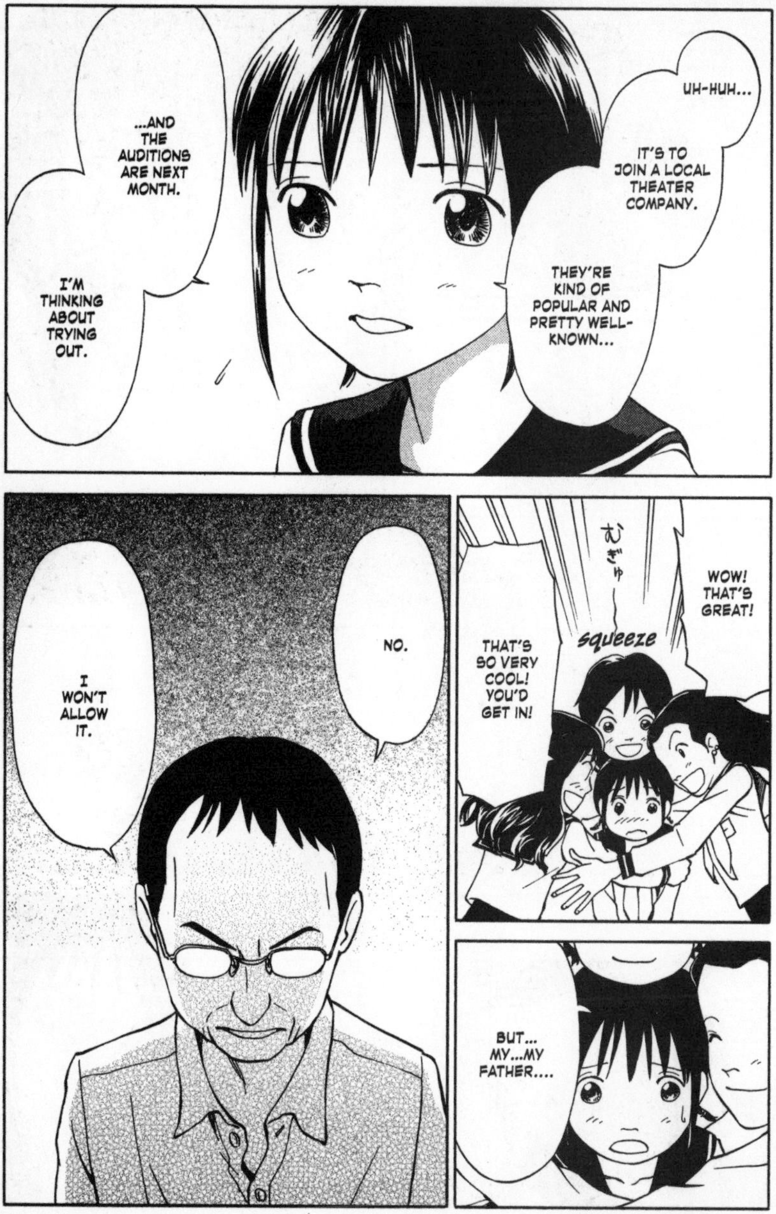
UH-HUH...
IT'S TO JOIN A LOCAL THEATER COMPANY.
THEY'RE KIND OF POPULAR AND PRETTY WELL-KNOWN...
...AND THE AUDITIONS ARE NEXT MONTH.
I'M THINKING ABOUT TRYING OUT.
むぎゅ
squeeze
WOW! THAT'S GREAT!
THAT'S SO VERY COOL! YOU'D GET IN!
BUT... MY...MY FATHER....
NO.
I WON'T ALLOW IT.

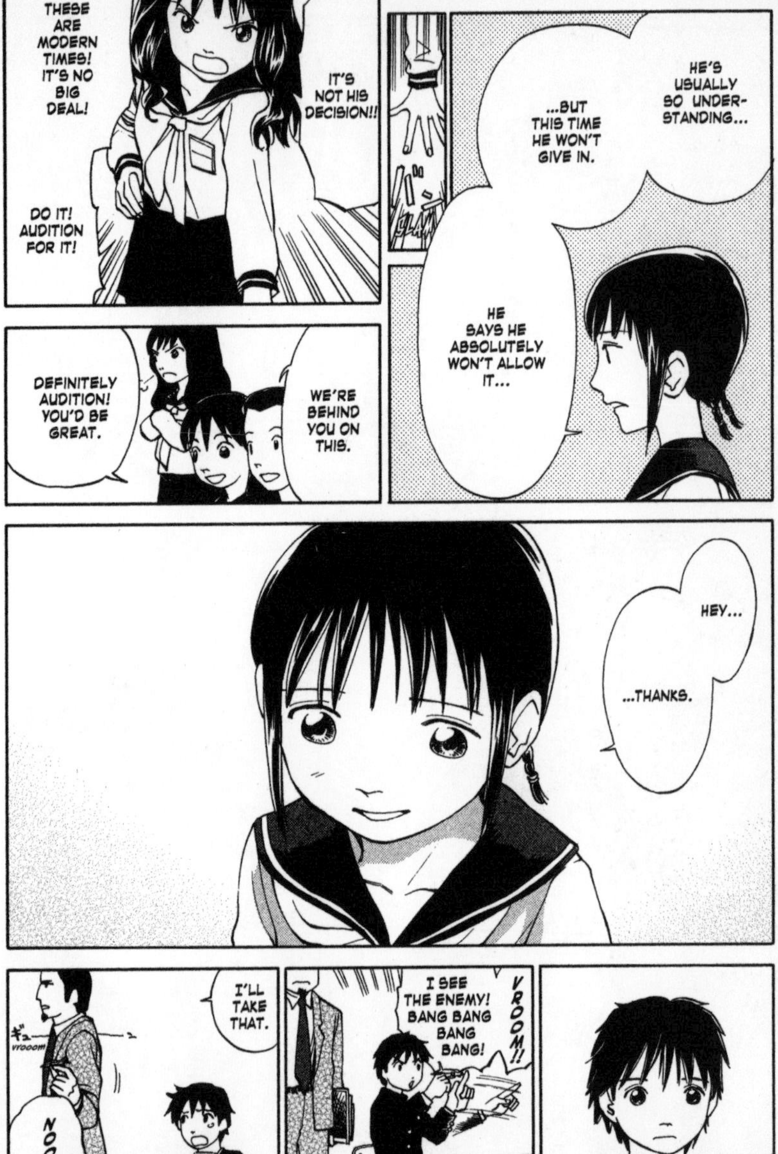
HE'S USUALLY SO UNDER-STANDING...
...BUT THIS TIME HE WON'T GIVE IN.
HE SAYS HE ABSOLUTELY WON'T ALLOW IT...
SLAM
IT'S NOT HIS DECISION!!
THESE ARE MODERN TIMES! IT'S NO BIG DEAL!
DO IT! AUDITION FOR IT!
WE'RE BEHIND YOU ON THIS.
DEFINITELY AUDITION! YOU'D BE GREAT.
HEY...
...THANKS.
VROOM!!
I SEE THE ENEMY! BANG BANG BANG BANG!
I'LL TAKE THAT.
ギュ
VROOOM
NOOOOO!!

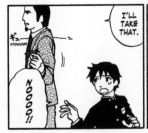

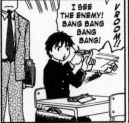

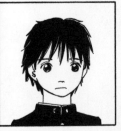

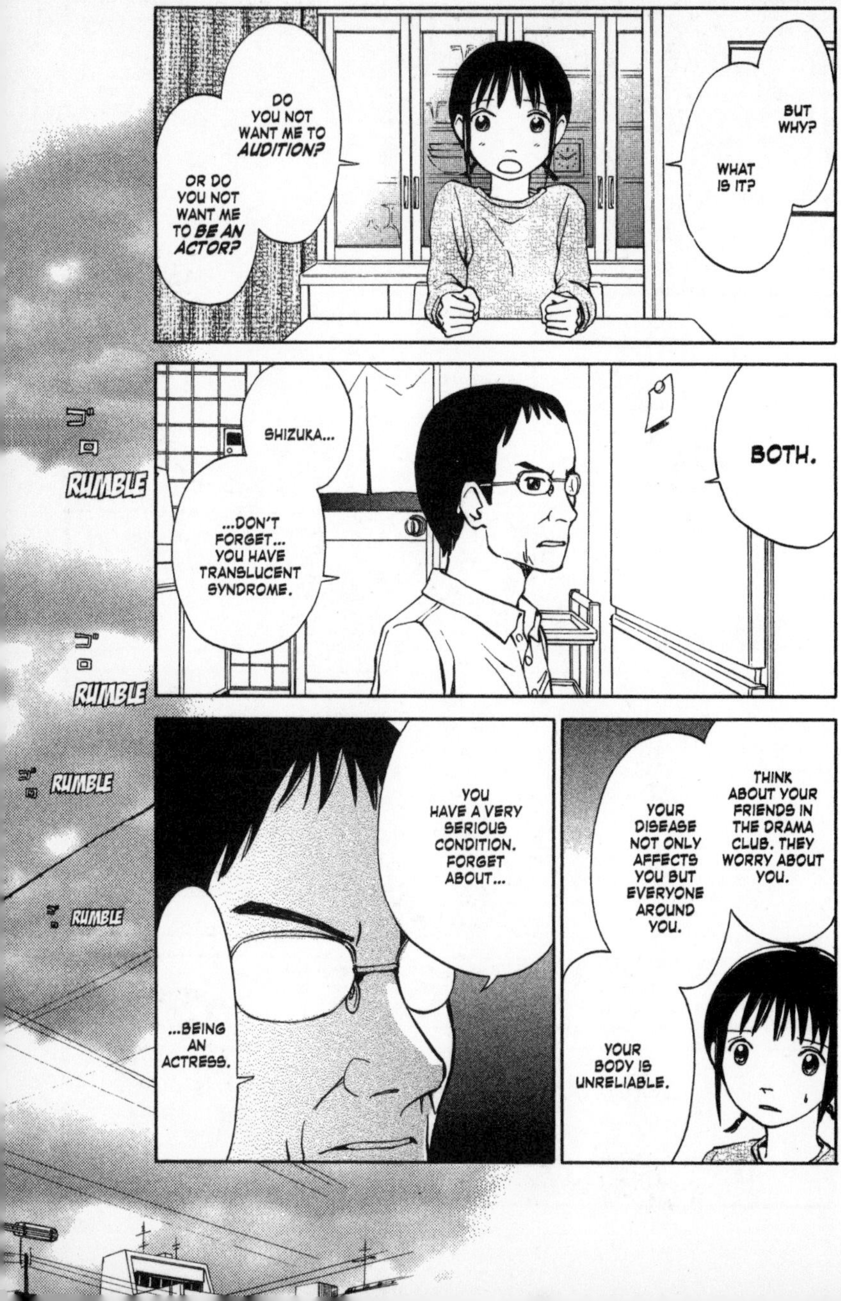
BUT WHY?
WHAT IS IT?
DO YOU NOT WANT ME TO AUDITION?
OR DO YOU NOT WANT ME TO BE AN ACTOR?
BOTH.
SHIZUKA...
...DON'T FORGET... YOU HAVE TRANSLUCENT SYNDROME.
RUMBLE
RUMBLE
THINK ABOUT YOUR FRIENDS IN THE DRAMA CLUB. THEY WORRY ABOUT YOU.
YOUR DISEASE NOT ONLY AFFECTS YOU BUT EVERYONE AROUND YOU.
YOUR BODY IS UNRELIABLE.
YOU HAVE A VERY SERIOUS CONDITION. FORGET ABOUT...
...BEING AN ACTRESS.
RUMBLE
RUMBLE

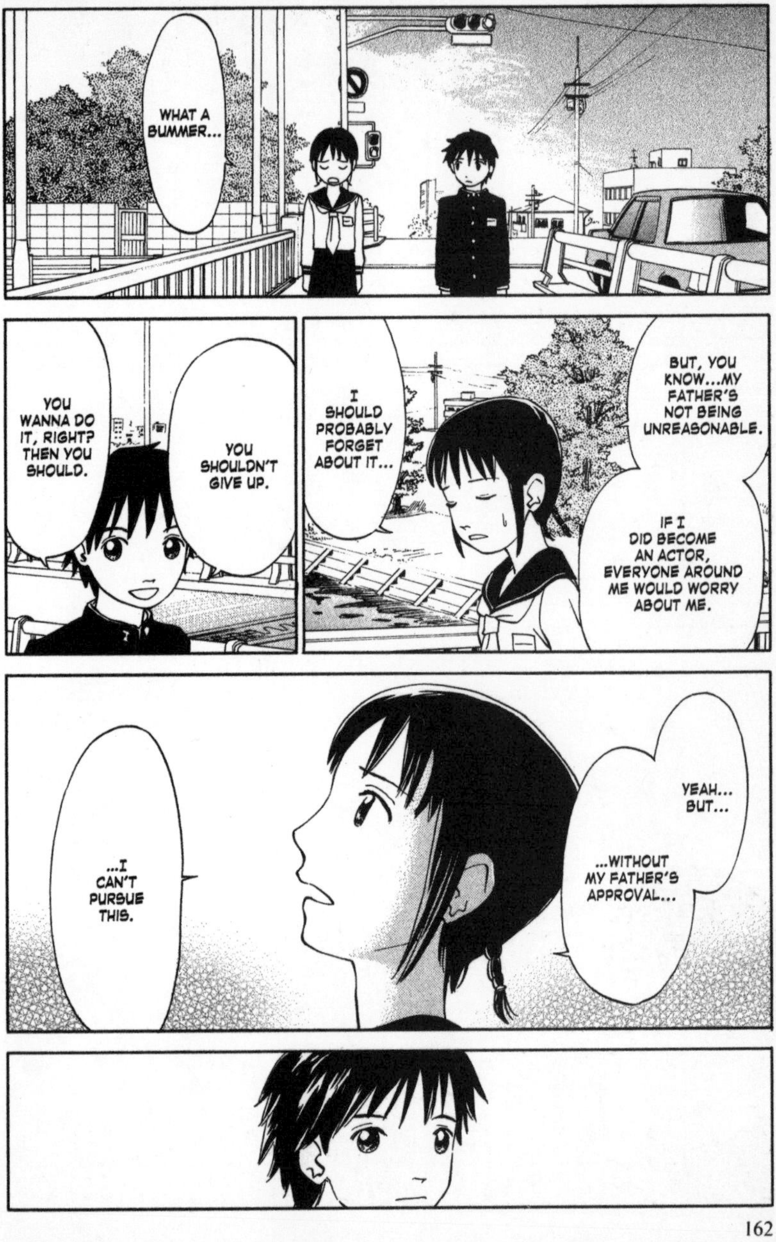
WHAT A BUMMER...
BUT, YOU KNOW...MY FATHER'S NOT BEING UNREASONABLE.
IF I DID BECOME AN ACTOR, EVERYONE AROUND ME WOULD WORRY ABOUT ME.
I SHOULD PROBABLY FORGET ABOUT IT...
YOU SHOULDN'T GIVE UP.
YOU WANNA DO IT, RIGHT? THEN YOU SHOULD.
YEAH... BUT...
...WITHOUT MY FATHER'S APPROVAL...
...I CAN'T PURSUE THIS.

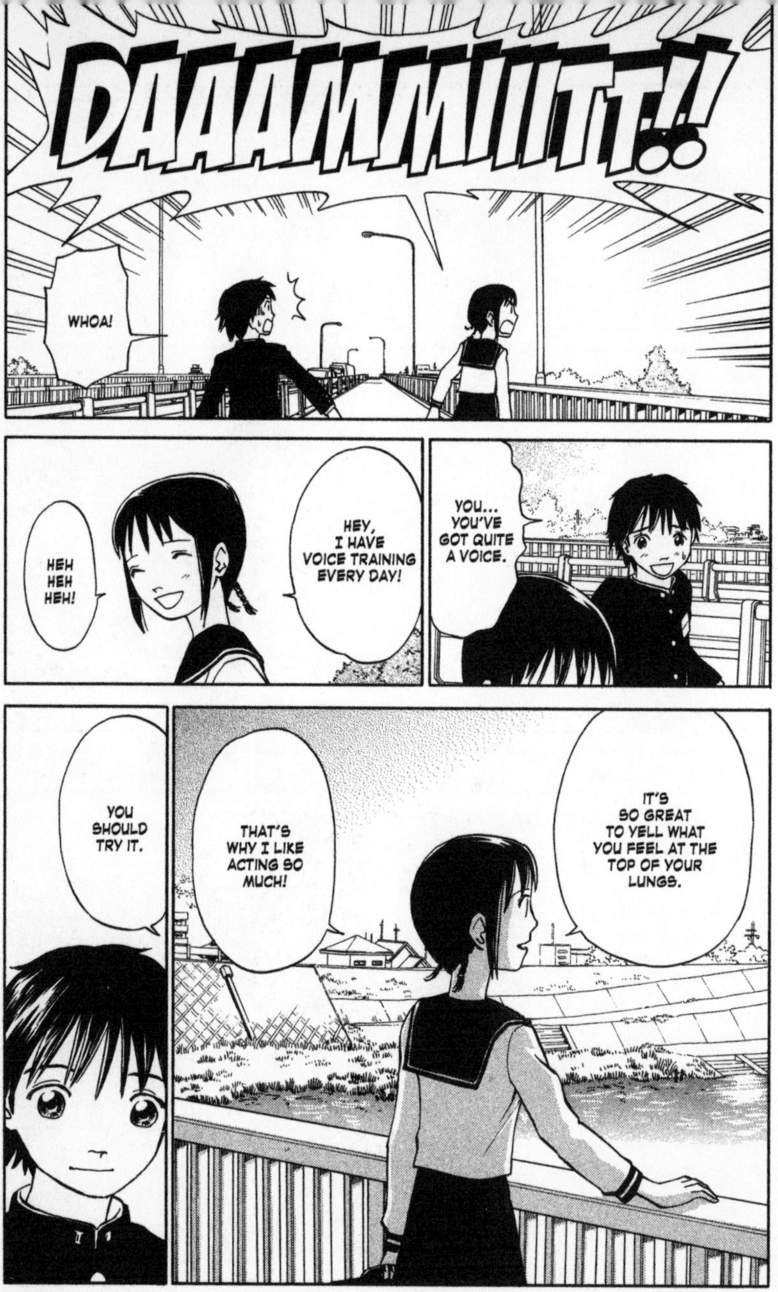
DAAAMMIIITT!!
WHOA!
YOU... YOU'VE GOT QUITE A VOICE.
HEY, I HAVE VOICE TRAINING EVERY DAY!
HEH HEH HEH!
IT'S SO GREAT TO YELL WHAT YOU FEEL AT THE TOP OF YOUR LUNGS.
THAT'S WHY I LIKE ACTING SO MUCH!
YOU SHOULD TRY IT.

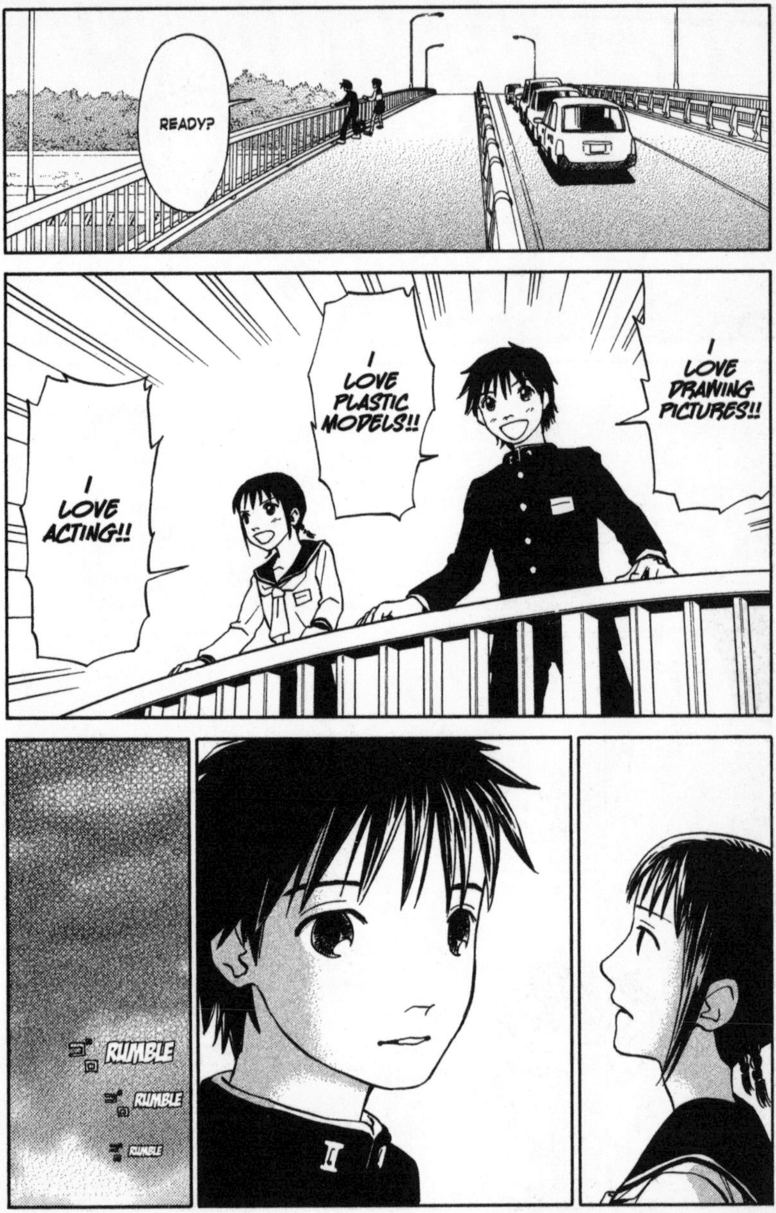
READY?
I LOVE DRAWING PICTURES!!
I LOVE PLASTIC MODELS!!
I LOVE ACTING!!
RUMBLE
RUMBLE
RUMBLE

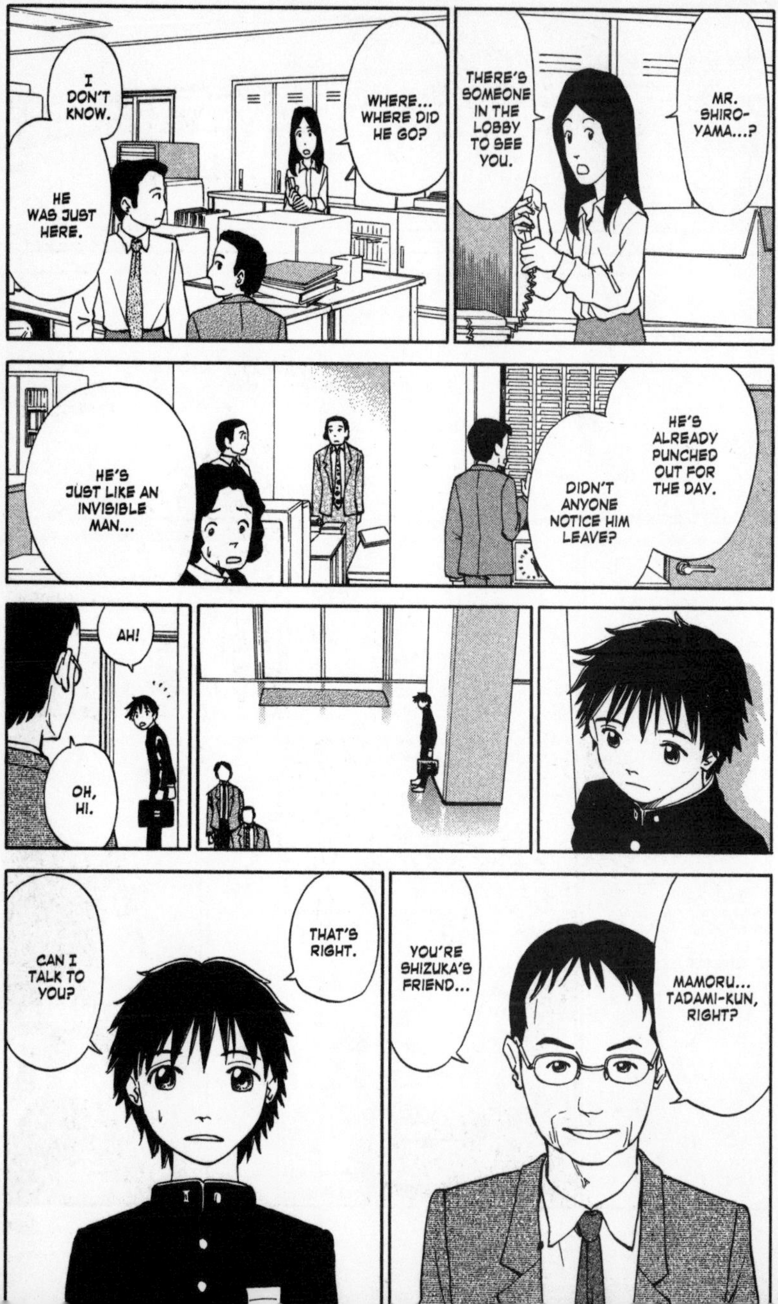

MR. SHIRO-YAMA...?
THERE'S SOMEONE IN THE LOBBY TO SEE YOU.
WHERE... WHERE DID HE GO?
I DON'T KNOW.
HE WAS JUST HERE.
HE'S ALREADY PUNCHED OUT FOR THE DAY.
DIDN'T ANYONE NOTICE HIM LEAVE?
HE'S JUST LIKE AN INVISIBLE MAN...
AH!
OH, HI.
MAMORU... TADAMI-KUN, RIGHT?
YOU'RE SHIZUKA'S FRIEND...
THAT'S RIGHT.
CAN I TALK TO YOU?

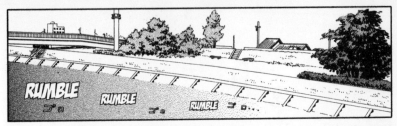

RUMBLE
ゴロ
RUMBLE
ゴロ
RUMBLE
ゴロ...
THIS IS ABOUT SHIZUKA AND THAT AUDITION, RIGHT?
YOU WANT ME TO ALLOW HER TO TRY OUT...
...BUT I CAN'T.
WHY NOT?
THINK ABOUT IT.
SHE HAS TRANSLUCENT SYNDROME, AND NO ONE KNOWS WHEN IT WILL AFFECT HER.
PLUS, AS OF NOW... THERE'S NO CURE FOR IT.
TO BECOME TRANSPARENT MEANS...
...THAT OTHER PEOPLE ARE UNABLE TO SEE YOU.
FOR SOMEONE LIKE THAT TO WANT TO ACT IS AN ISSUE THAT SHOULDN'T BE TAKEN LIGHTLY.

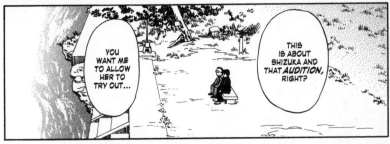

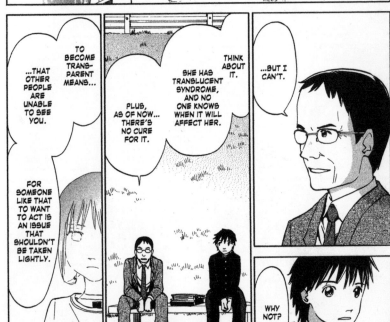

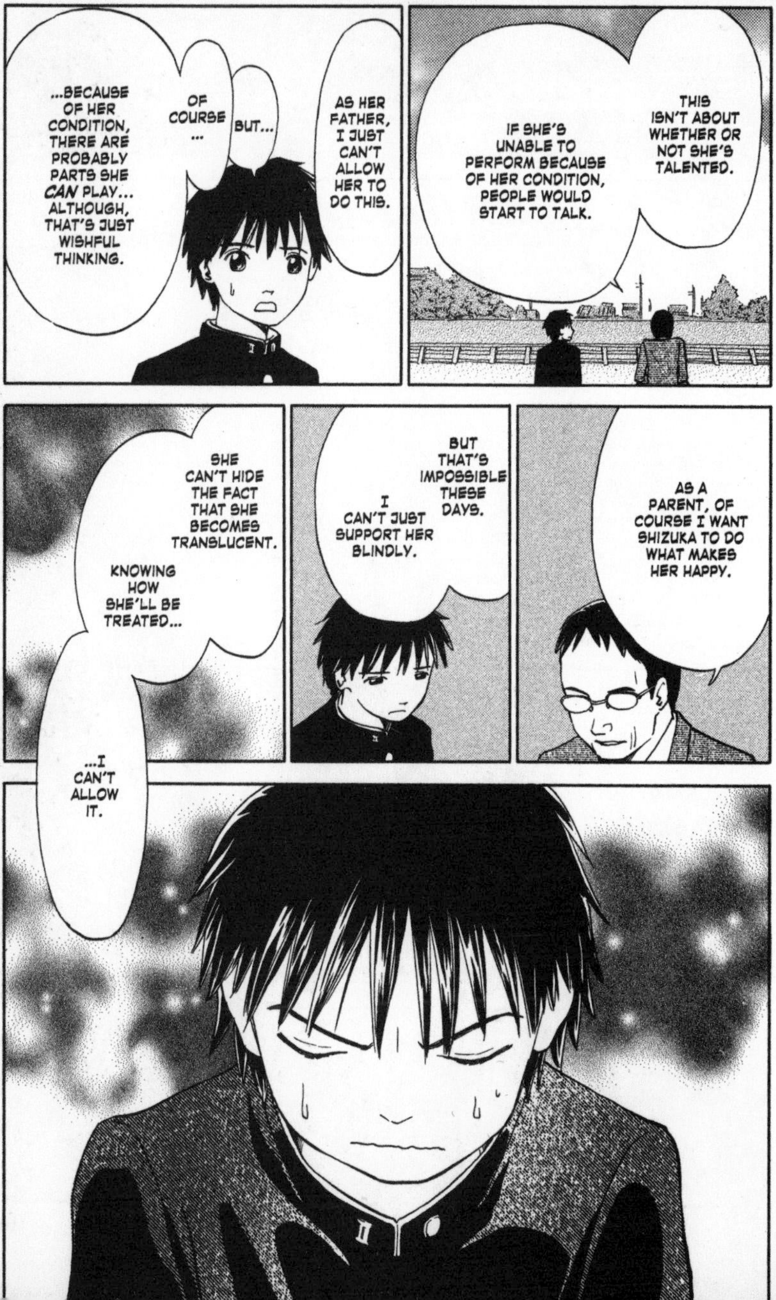
THIS ISN'T ABOUT WHETHER OR NOT SHE'S TALENTED.
IF SHE'S UNABLE TO PERFORM BECAUSE OF HER CONDITION, PEOPLE WOULD START TO TALK.
AS HER FATHER, I JUST CAN'T ALLOW HER TO DO THIS.
BUT...
OF COURSE...
...BECAUSE OF HER CONDITION, THERE ARE PROBABLY PARTS SHE *CAN* PLAY... ALTHOUGH, THAT'S JUST WISHFUL THINKING.
AS A PARENT, OF COURSE I WANT SHIZUKA TO DO WHAT MAKES HER HAPPY.
BUT THAT'S IMPOSSIBLE THESE DAYS.
I CAN'T JUST SUPPORT HER BLINDLY.
SHE CAN'T HIDE THE FACT THAT SHE BECOMES TRANSLUCENT.
KNOWING HOW SHE'LL BE TREATED...
...I CAN'T ALLOW IT.

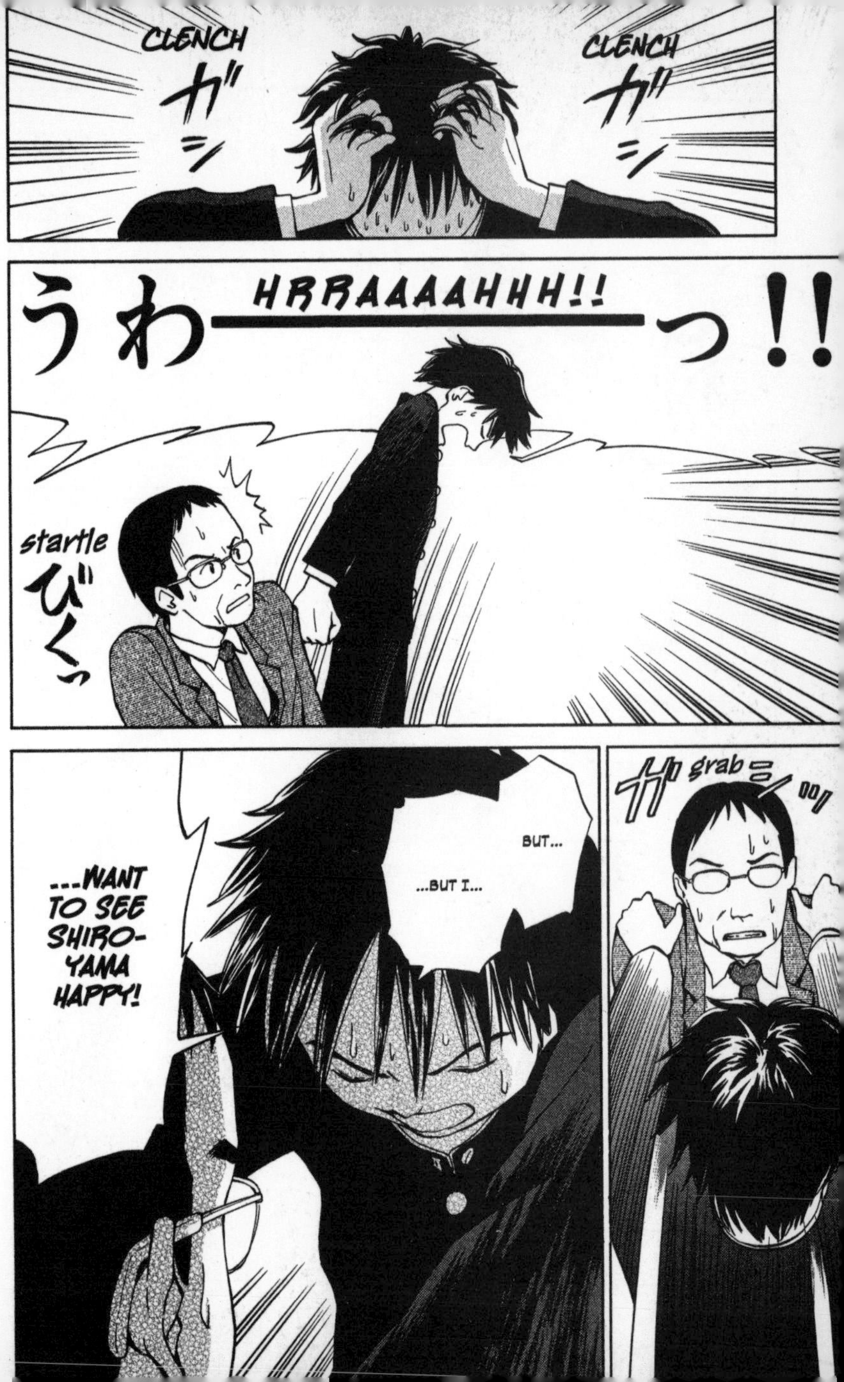
CLENCH
ガッ
CLENCH
ガッ
うわーーっ!!
HRRAAAAHHH!!
startle
びくっ
grab
ガッ
BUT...
...BUT I...
---WANT TO SEE SHIRO-YAMA HAPPY!

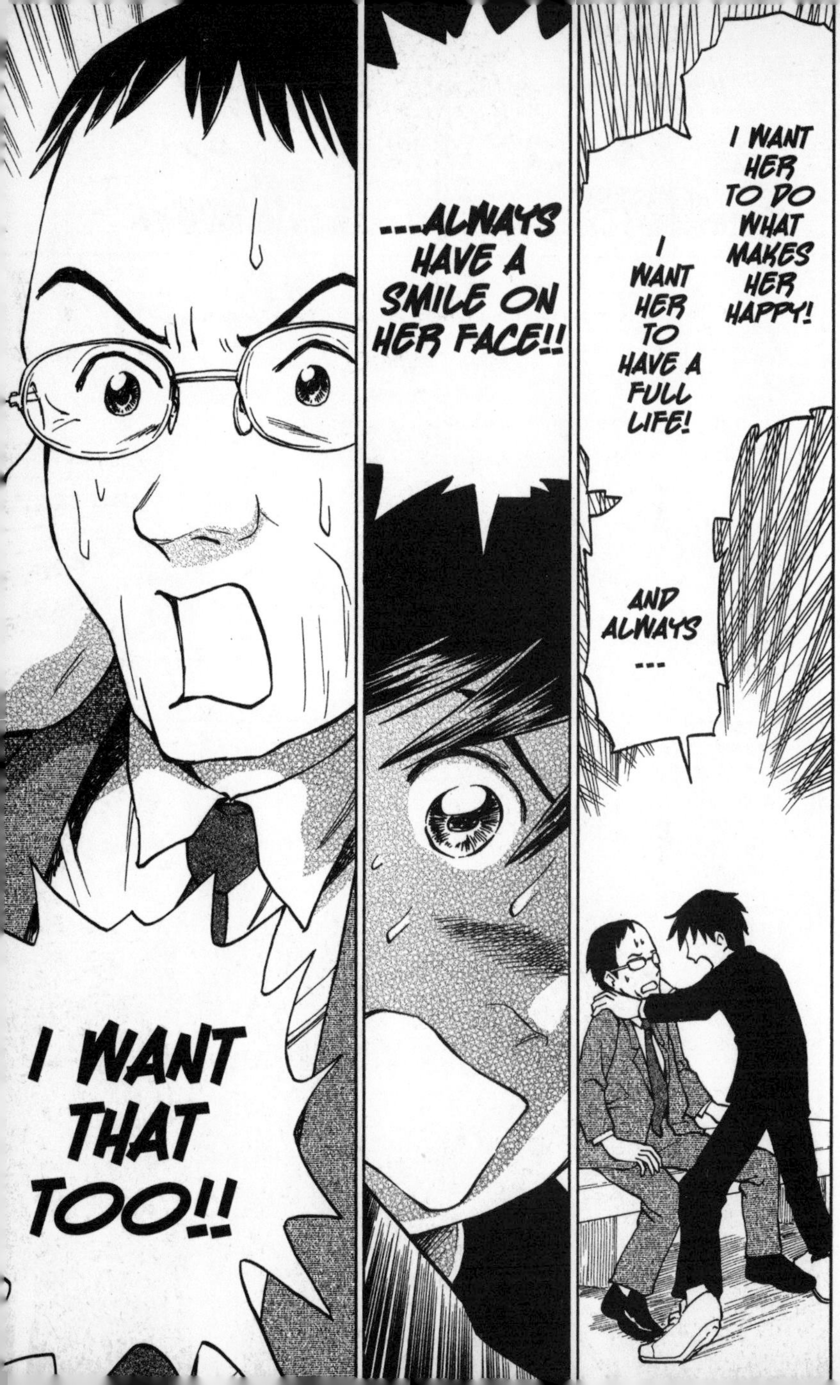
I WANT HER TO DO WHAT MAKES HER HAPPY!
I WANT HER TO HAVE A FULL LIFE!
AND ALWAYS ...
...ALWAYS HAVE A SMILE ON HER FACE!!
I WANT THAT TOO!!

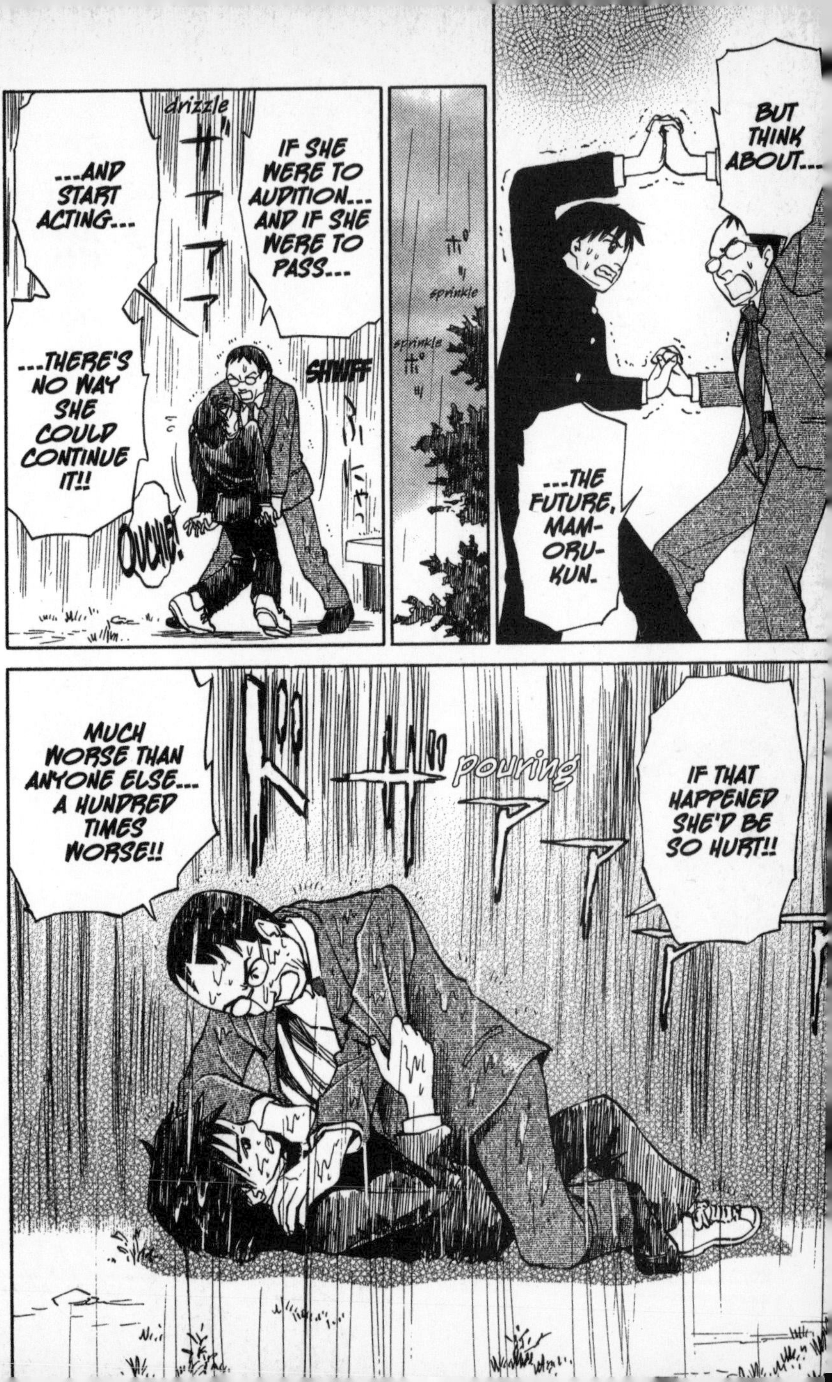
BUT THINK ABOUT...
...THE FUTURE, MAMORU-KUN.
sprinkle
sprinkle
drizzle
IF SHE WERE TO AUDITION... AND IF SHE WERE TO PASS...
...AND START ACTING...
...THERE'S NO WAY SHE COULD CONTINUE IT!!
SHWFF
OUCHIE!
IF THAT HAPPENED SHE'D BE SO HURT!!
pouring
MUCH WORSE THAN ANYONE ELSE... A HUNDRED TIMES WORSE!!

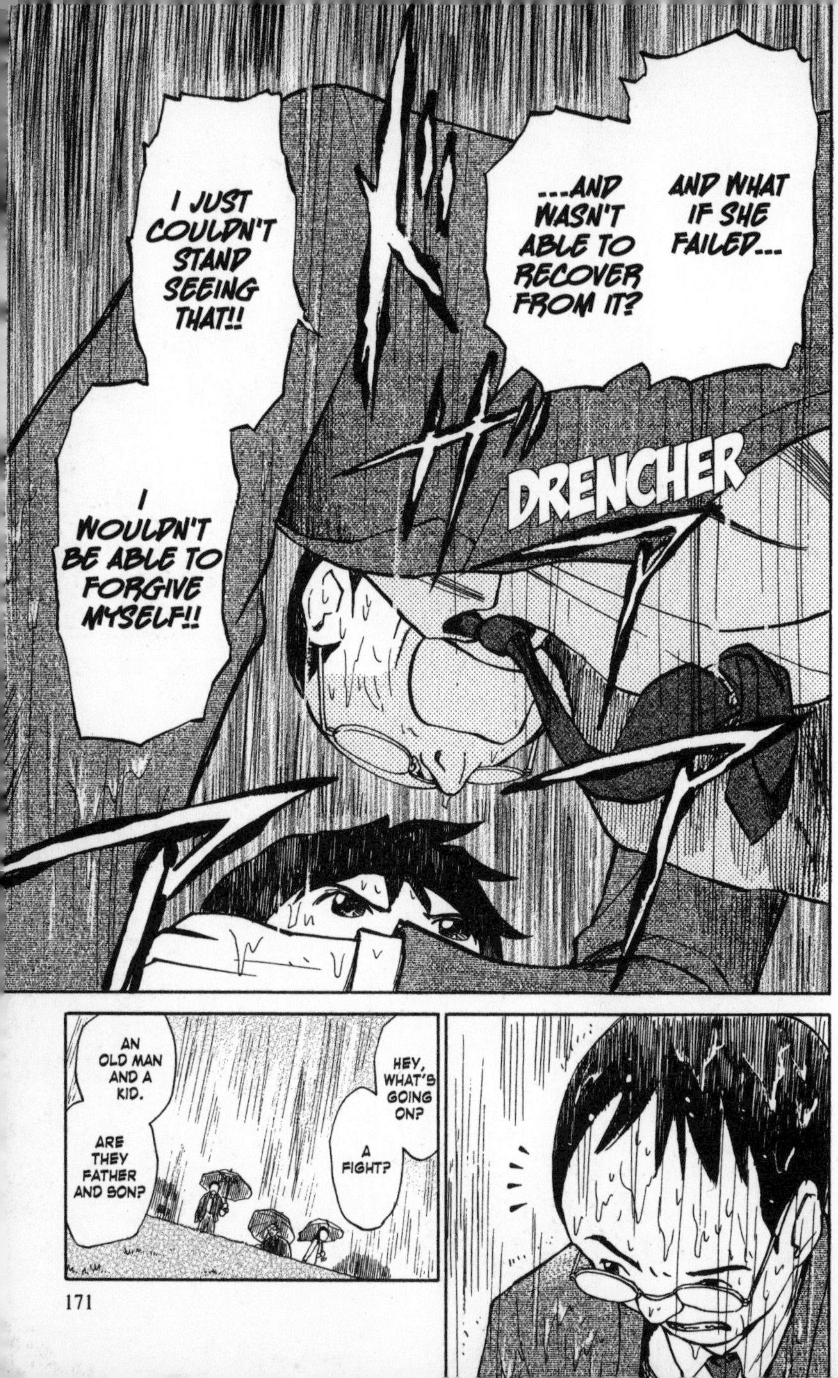
AND WHAT IF SHE FAILED...
...AND WASN'T ABLE TO RECOVER FROM IT?
I JUST COULDN'T STAND SEEING THAT!!
DRENCHER
I WOULDN'T BE ABLE TO FORGIVE MYSELF!!
HEY, WHAT'S GOING ON?
A FIGHT?
AN OLD MAN AND A KID.
ARE THEY FATHER AND SON?

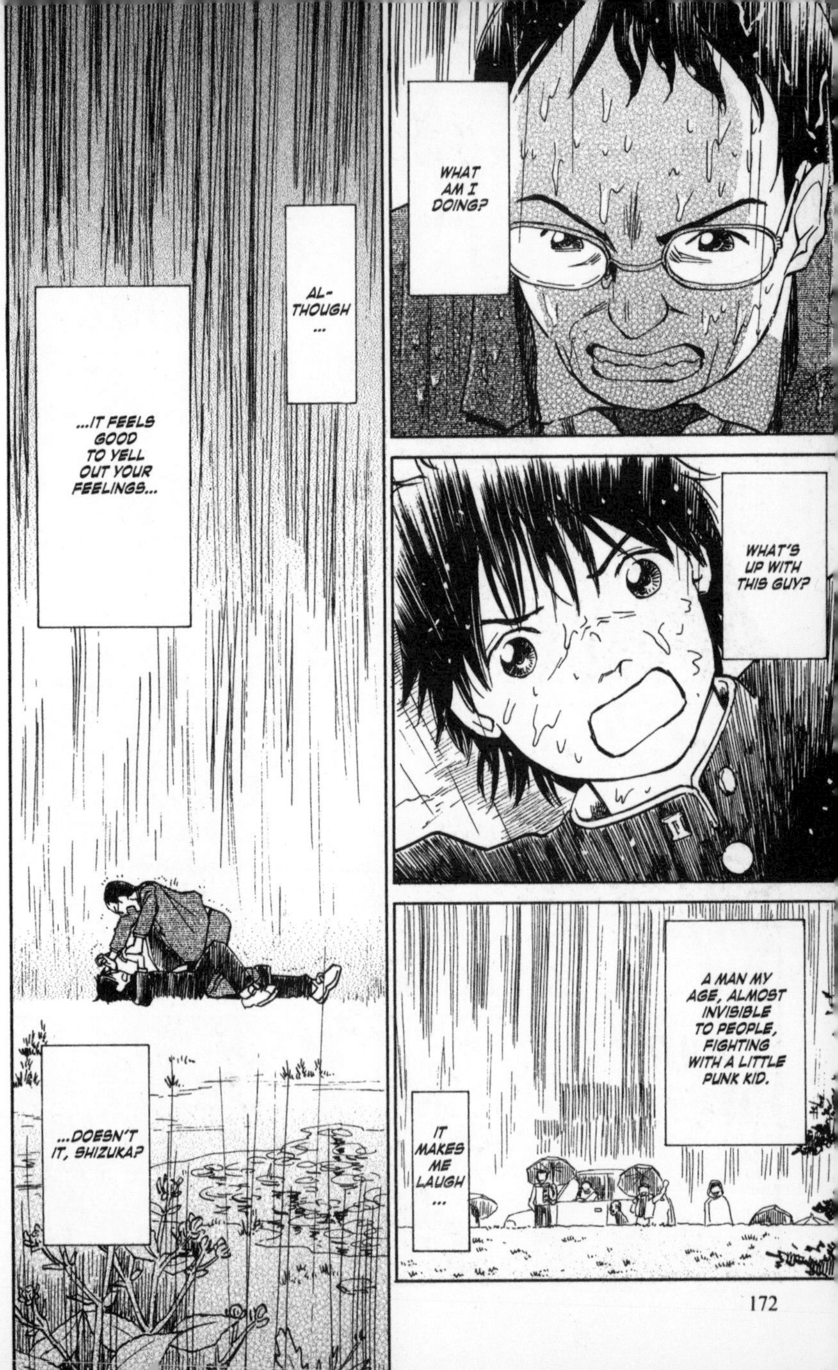

WHAT AM I DOING?
WHAT'S UP WITH THIS GUY?
A MAN MY AGE, ALMOST INVISIBLE TO PEOPLE, FIGHTING WITH A LITTLE PUNK KID.
IT MAKES ME LAUGH ...
AL- THOUGH ...
...IT FEELS GOOD TO YELL OUT YOUR FEELINGS...
...DOESN'T IT, SHIZUKA?

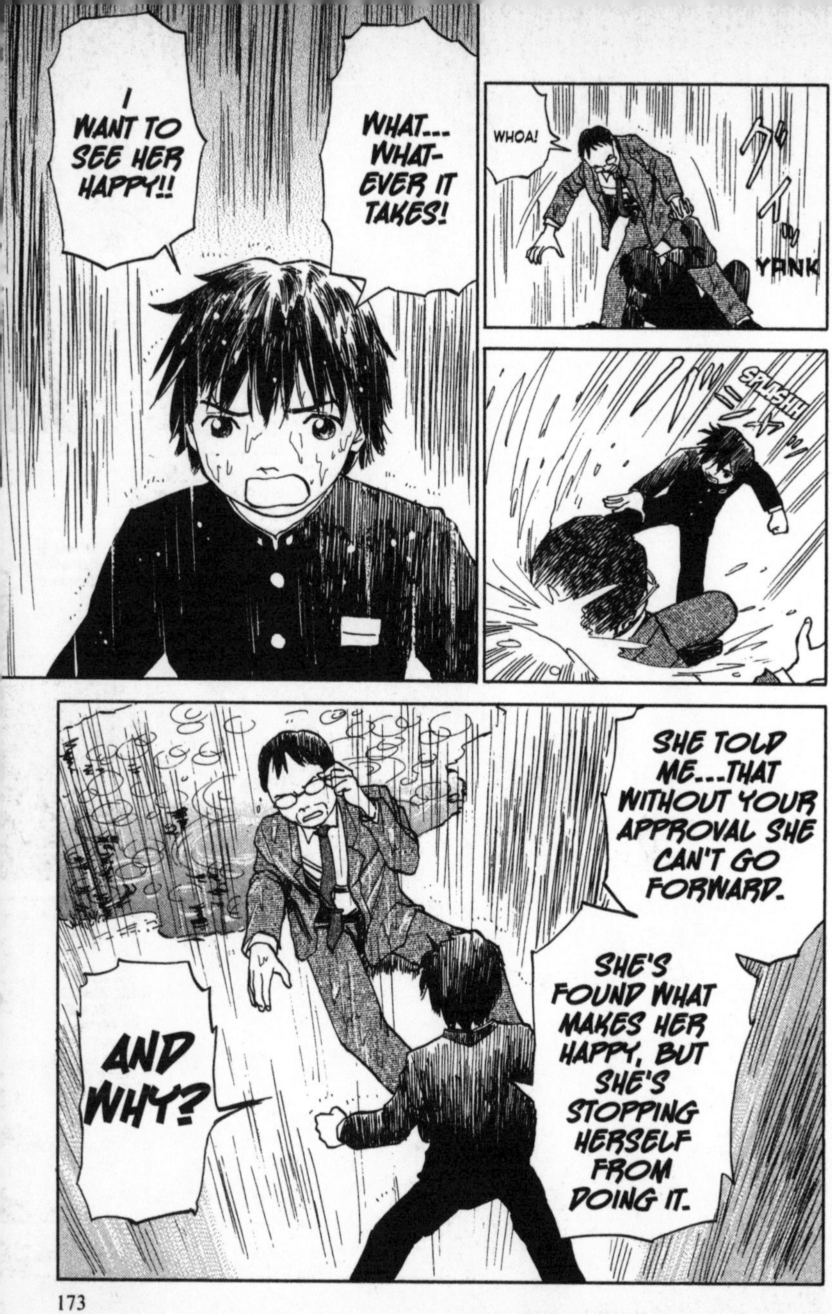
WHOA!
YANK
SPLASHH
I WANT TO SEE HER HAPPY!!
WHAT... WHAT-EVER IT TAKES!
SHE TOLD ME...THAT WITHOUT YOUR APPROVAL SHE CAN'T GO FORWARD.
SHE'S FOUND WHAT MAKES HER HAPPY, BUT SHE'S STOPPING HERSELF FROM DOING IT.
AND WHY?

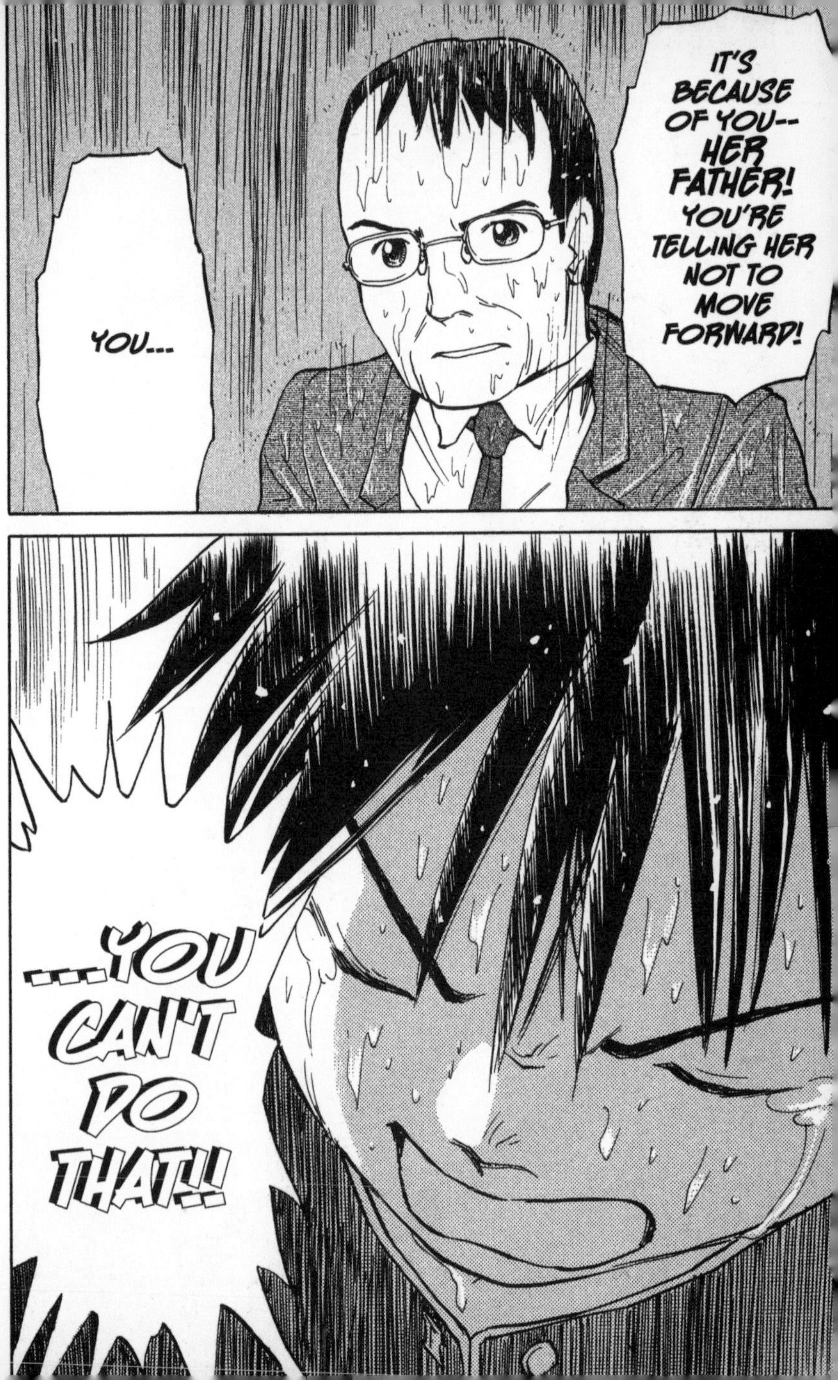
IT'S BECAUSE OF YOU-- HER FATHER! YOU'RE TELLING HER NOT TO MOVE FORWARD!
YOU...
...YOU CAN'T DO THAT!!

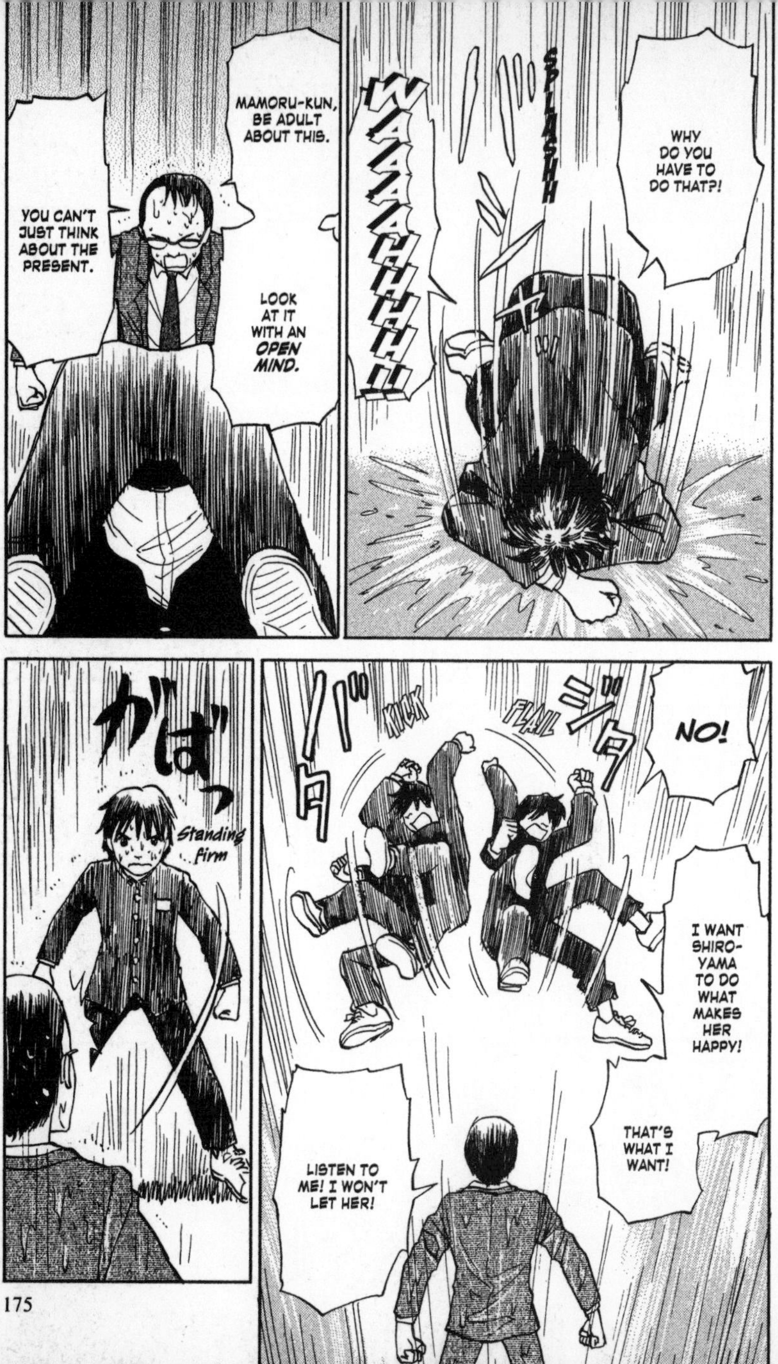
WHY DO YOU HAVE TO DO THAT?!
SPLASHH
WAAAAHHHHH!!
MAMORU-KUN, BE ADULT ABOUT THIS.
YOU CAN'T JUST THINK ABOUT THE PRESENT.
LOOK AT IT WITH AN *OPEN MIND.*
NO!
ジタ
FLAIL
KICK
バタ
I WANT SHIRO-YAMA TO DO WHAT MAKES HER HAPPY!
THAT'S WHAT I WANT!
LISTEN TO ME! I WON'T LET HER!
がばっ
Standing firm

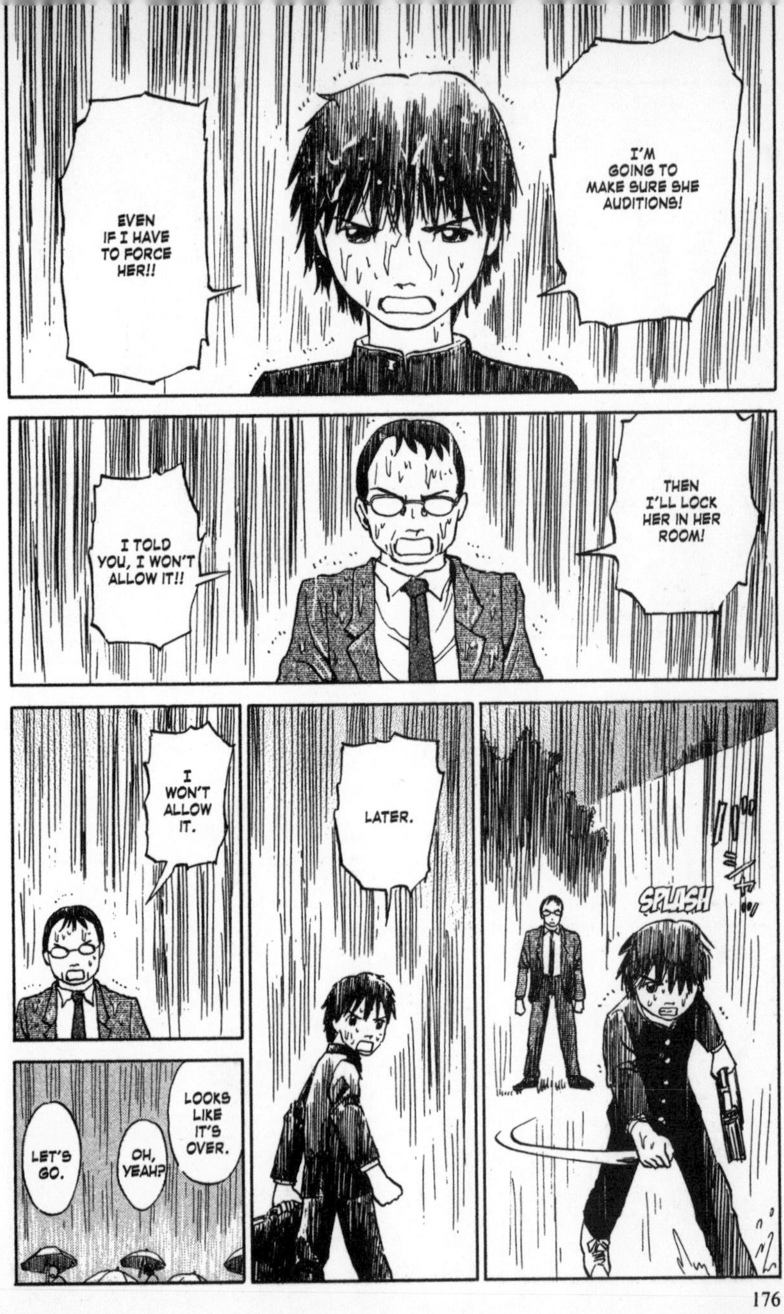
I'M GOING TO MAKE SURE SHE AUDITIONS!
EVEN IF I HAVE TO FORCE HER!!
THEN I'LL LOCK HER IN HER ROOM!
I TOLD YOU, I WON'T ALLOW IT!!
SPLASH
LATER.
I WON'T ALLOW IT.
LOOKS LIKE IT'S OVER.
OH, YEAH?
LET'S GO.

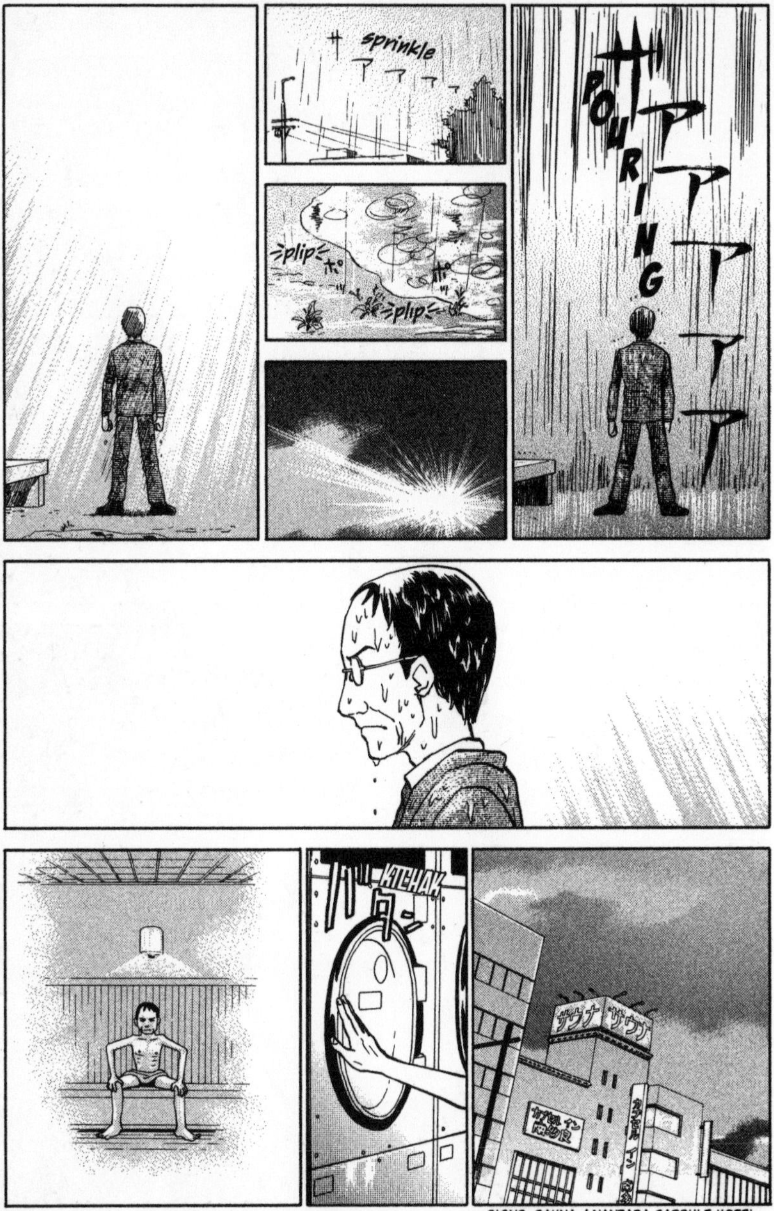
POURING
sprinkle
plip
plip
KTCHAK

SIGNS: SAUNA / NANTARA CAPSULE HOTEL

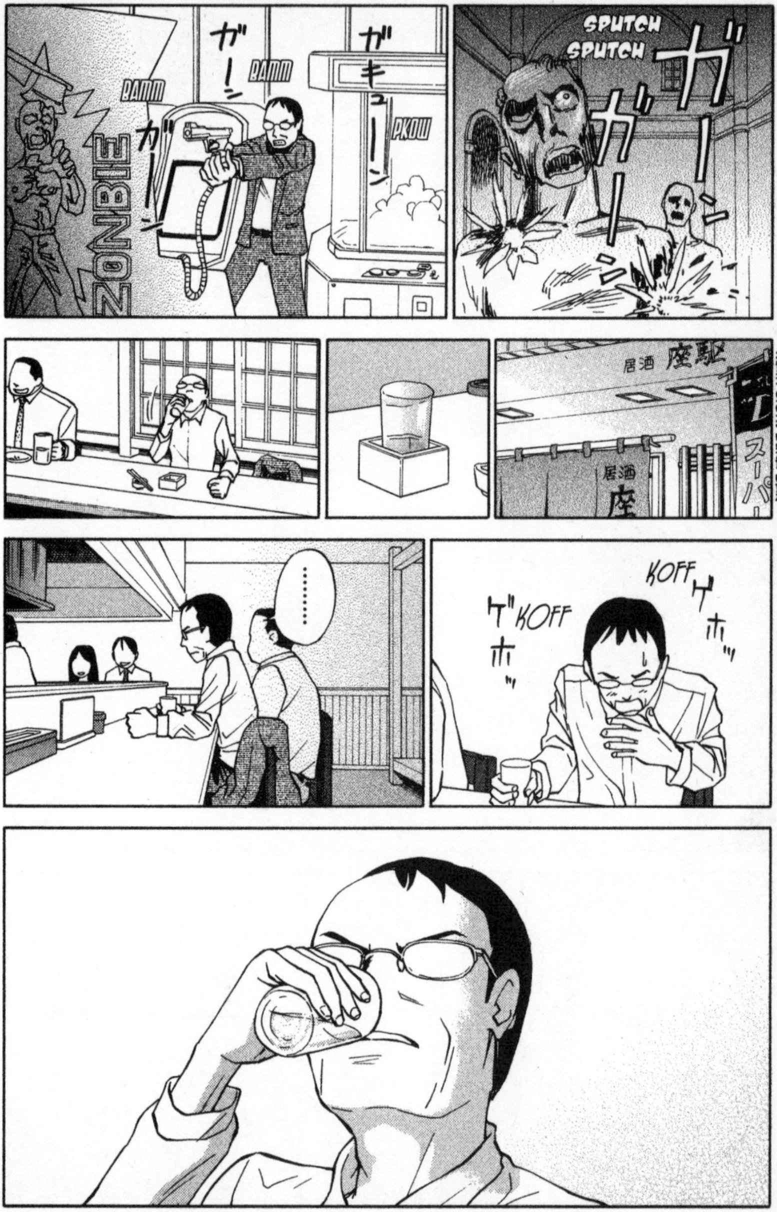
SPUTCH
SPUTCH
ガーン
ガーン
BAMM
ガーン
BAMM
ガキューン
PKOW
ガーン
ZOMBIE
MAIN SIGN: ZUKA BAR
KOFF
ゲホッ
ゲホッ
KOFF
……

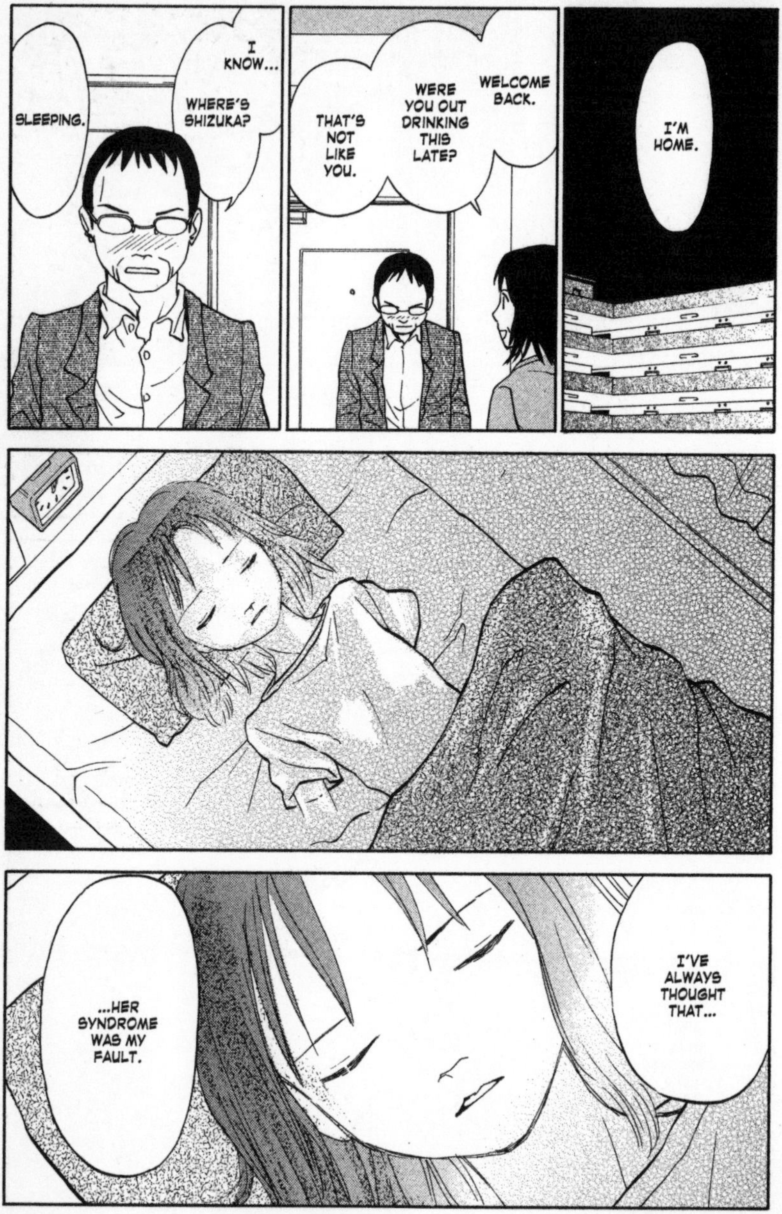
I'M HOME.
WELCOME BACK.
WERE YOU OUT DRINKING THIS LATE?
THAT'S NOT LIKE YOU.
I KNOW...
WHERE'S SHIZUKA?
SLEEPING.
I'VE ALWAYS THOUGHT THAT...
...HER SYNDROME WAS MY FAULT.

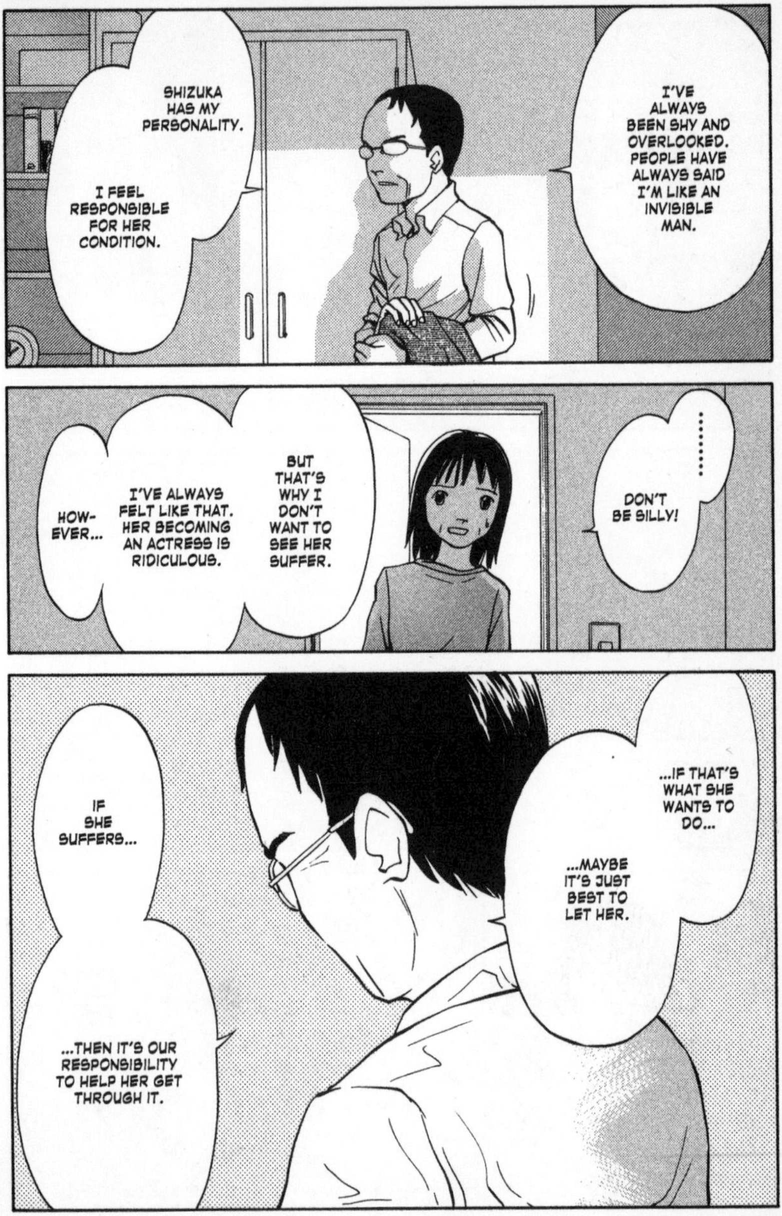
I'VE ALWAYS BEEN SHY AND OVERLOOKED. PEOPLE HAVE ALWAYS SAID I'M LIKE AN INVISIBLE MAN.
SHIZUKA HAS MY PERSONALITY.
I FEEL RESPONSIBLE FOR HER CONDITION.
......
DON'T BE SILLY!
BUT THAT'S WHY I DON'T WANT TO SEE HER SUFFER.
I'VE ALWAYS FELT LIKE THAT. HER BECOMING AN ACTRESS IS RIDICULOUS.
HOW-EVER...
...IF THAT'S WHAT SHE WANTS TO DO...
...MAYBE IT'S JUST BEST TO LET HER.
IF SHE SUFFERS...
...THEN IT'S OUR RESPONSIBILITY TO HELP HER GET THROUGH IT.

SHIZUKA CAN HANDLE IT.

SHE HAS A GREAT FRIEND.

HUH?

～whzzzz～
シャアア

ん？
ど…
に？
Huh? Where?

TADAMI-KUN!

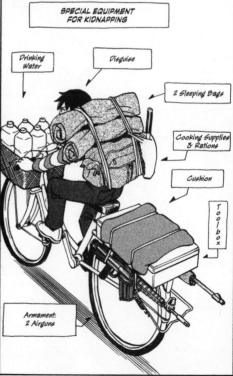

SPECIAL EQUIPMENT FOR KIDNAPPING

Drinking Water

Disguise

2 Sleeping Bags

Cooking Supplies & Rations

Cushion

Toolbox

Armament: 2 Airguns

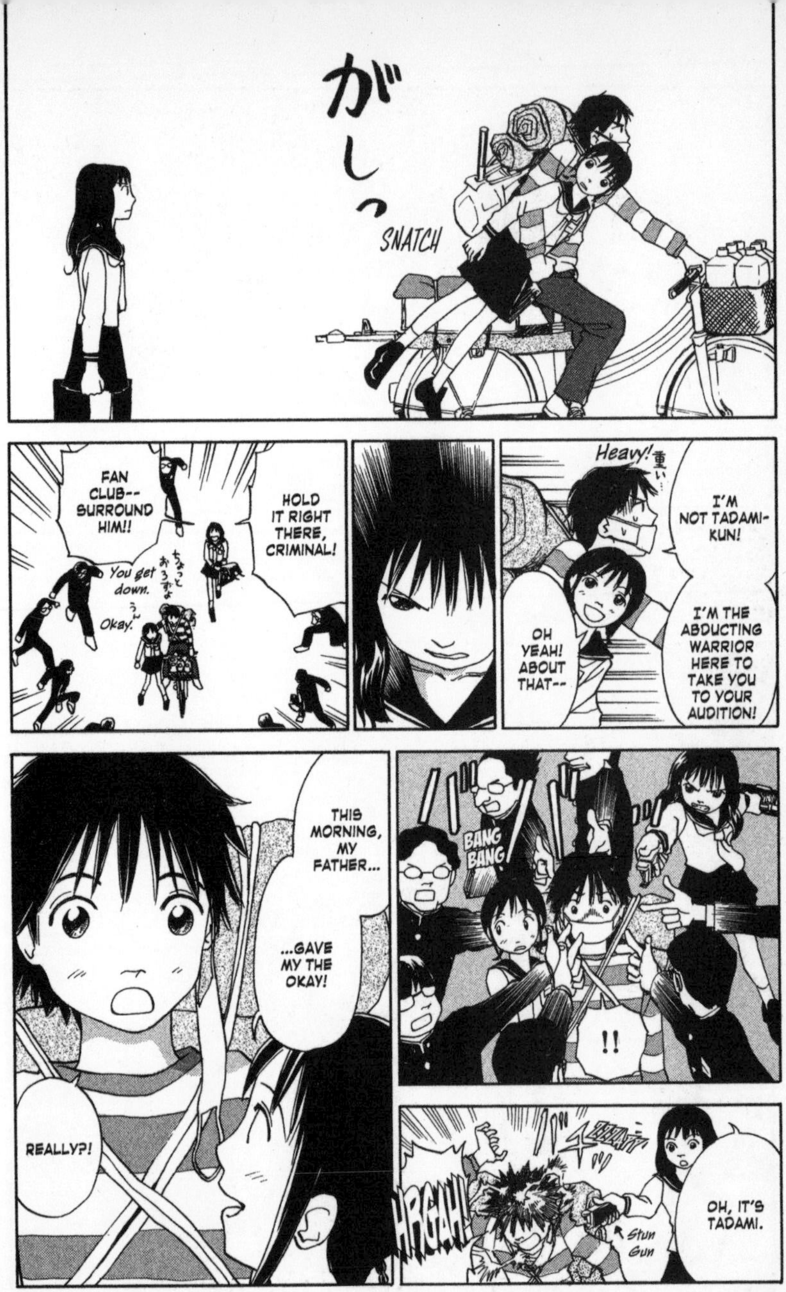
がしっ
SNATCH
Heavy! 重い…
I'M NOT TADAMI-KUN!
I'M THE ABDUCTING WARRIOR HERE TO TAKE YOU TO YOUR AUDITION!
OH YEAH! ABOUT THAT--
HOLD IT RIGHT THERE, CRIMINAL!
FAN CLUB-- SURROUND HIM!!
ちょっとおろすよ
You get down.
うん
Okay.
BANG BANG
!!
OH, IT'S TADAMI.
HRGAH!
Stun Gun
THIS MORNING, MY FATHER...
...GAVE MY THE OKAY!
REALLY?!

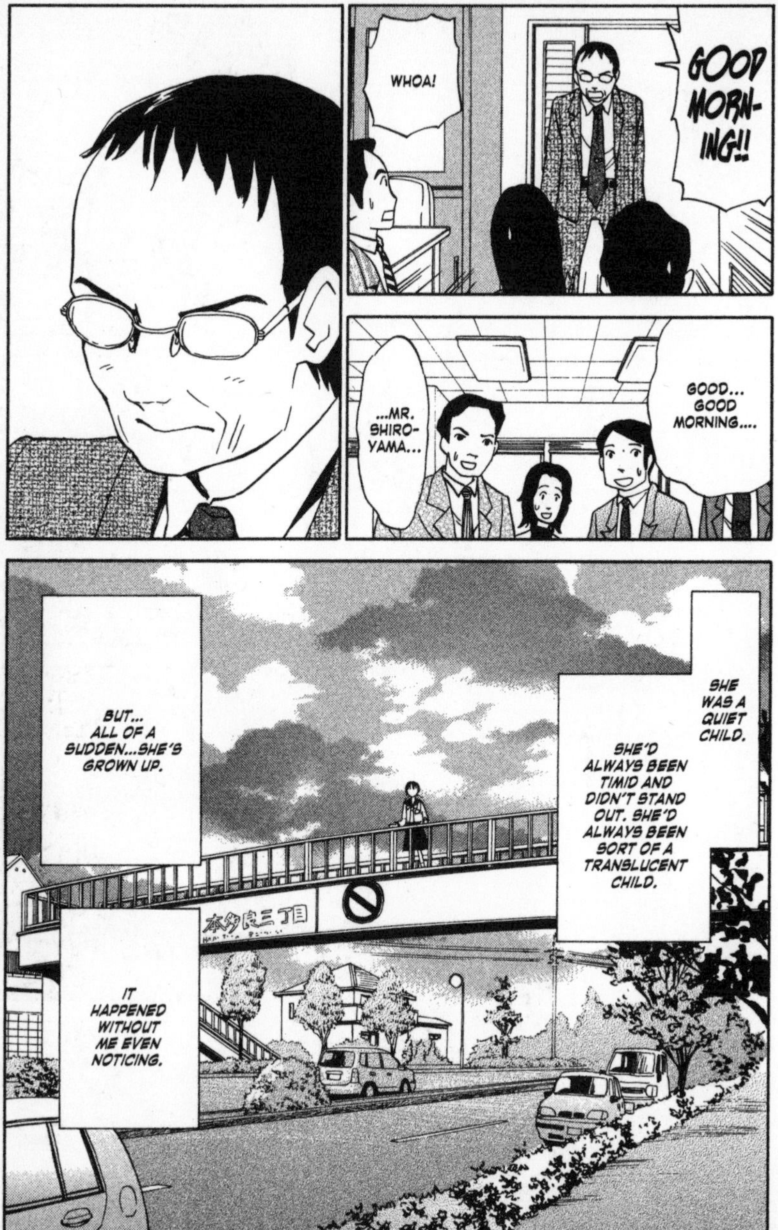
GOOD MORNING!!
WHOA!
GOOD... GOOD MORNING....
...MR. SHIROYAMA...
SHE WAS A QUIET CHILD.
SHE'D ALWAYS BEEN TIMID AND DIDN'T STAND OUT. SHE'D ALWAYS BEEN SORT OF A TRANSLUCENT CHILD.
BUT... ALL OF A SUDDEN...SHE'S GROWN UP.
IT HAPPENED WITHOUT ME EVEN NOTICING.

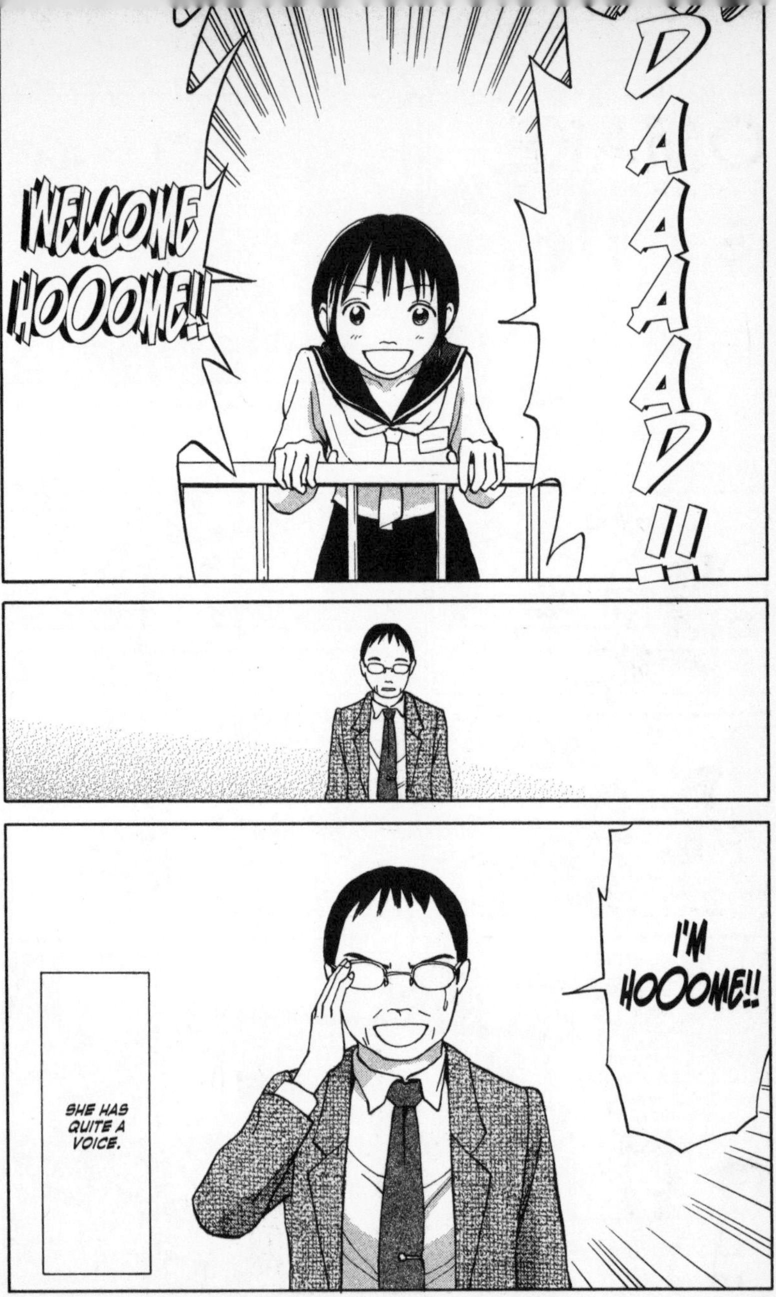
DAAAAD!!
WELCOME HOOOME!!
I'M HOOOME!!
SHE HAS QUITE A VOICE.

OMAKE

ONE-PAGE BONUS MANGA #5

5

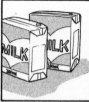

"SMALL BEAUTY"
MILK
MILK
OKOUCHI-SAN, YOU MUST REALLY LIKE MILK.
YOU DRINK IT EVERY DAY AT LUNCH.
OH. YEAH.
push
push
WHAT'RE YOU DOING?
ARE YOU PRAYING?
LEAVE ME ALONE !!
MAKE YOUR BREASTS LOOK BIGGER.
SMALL BREASTS ARE NOT TRAGIC.
EXERCISE TO INCREASE YOUR SIZE.
WHAT ARE YOU READING?
QUIT BUGGING ME!
I PROBABLY SHOULDN'T DO THIS AT SCHOOL.
おうちでやろう
I'll do it at home.
?

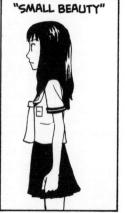

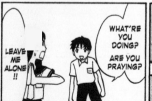

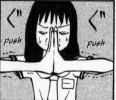

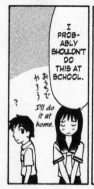

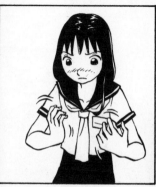

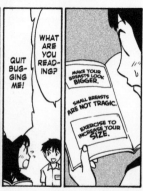

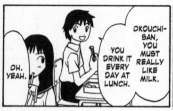

OMAKE

ONE-PAGE BONUS MANGA #6

6

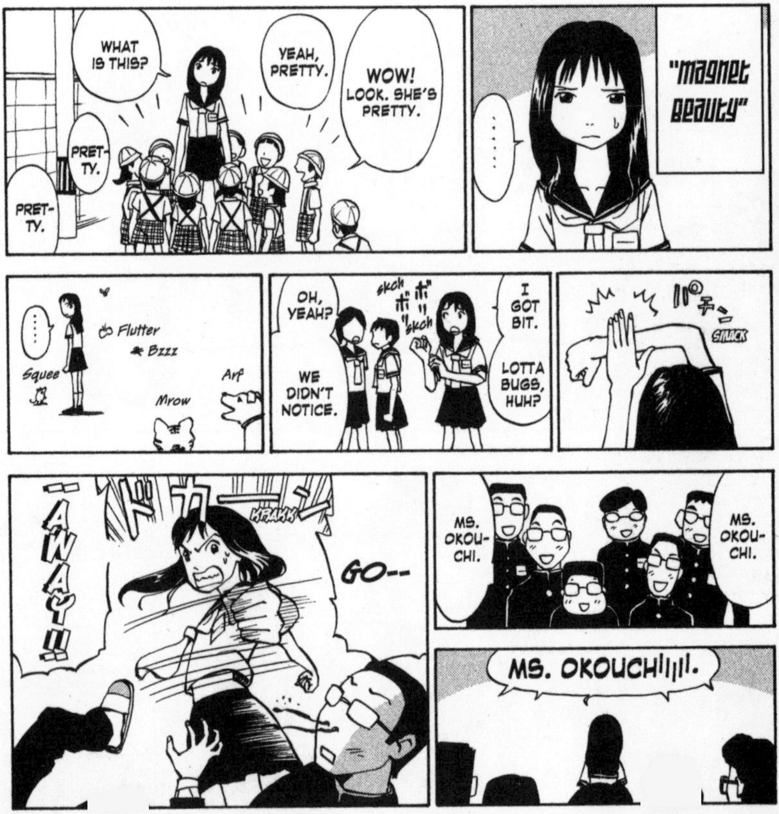

...
"magnet beauty"
WOW! LOOK. SHE'S PRETTY.
YEAH, PRETTY.
WHAT IS THIS?
PRET-TY.
PRET-TY.
SMACK
I GOT BIT.
LOTTA BUGS, HUH?
skch
skch
OH, YEAH?
WE DIDN'T NOTICE.
Flutter
Bzzz
...
Arf
Squee
Mrow
MS. OKOU-CHI.
MS. OKOU-CHI.
MS. OKOUCHIIIII.
KRAKK
GO--
AWAY!!!

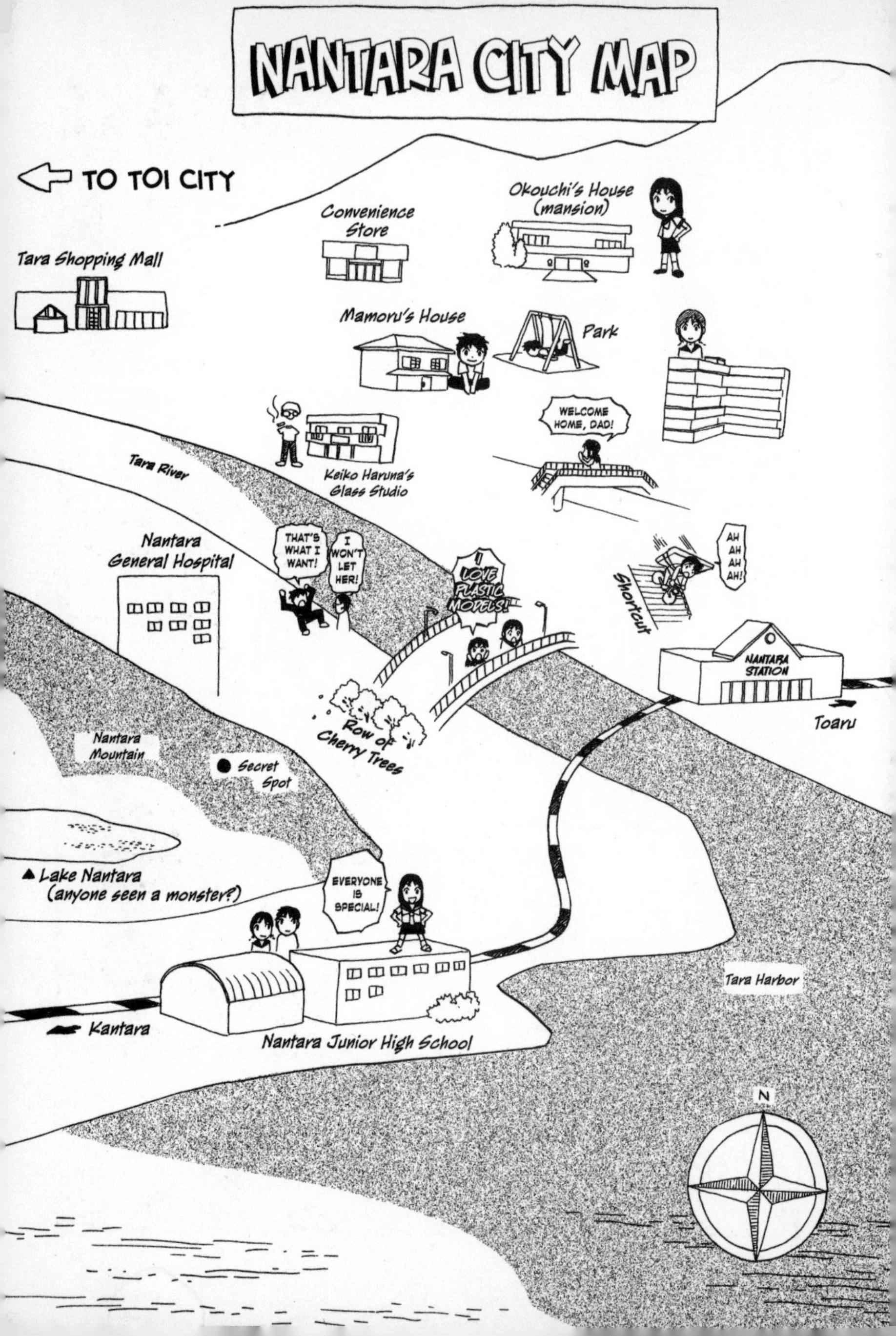
NANTARA CITY MAP
TO TOI CITY
Okouchi's House (mansion)
Convenience Store
Tara Shopping Mall
Mamoru's House
Park
WELCOME HOME, DAD!
Tara River
Keiko Haruna's Glass Studio
Nantara General Hospital
THAT'S WHAT I WANT!
I WON'T LET HER!
I LOVE PLASTIC MODELS!
AH AH AH AH!
Shortcut
NANTARA STATION
Toaru
Row of Cherry Trees
Nantara Mountain
Secret Spot
Lake Nantara (anyone seen a monster?)
EVERYONE IS SPECIAL!
Tara Harbor
Kantara
Nantara Junior High School
N

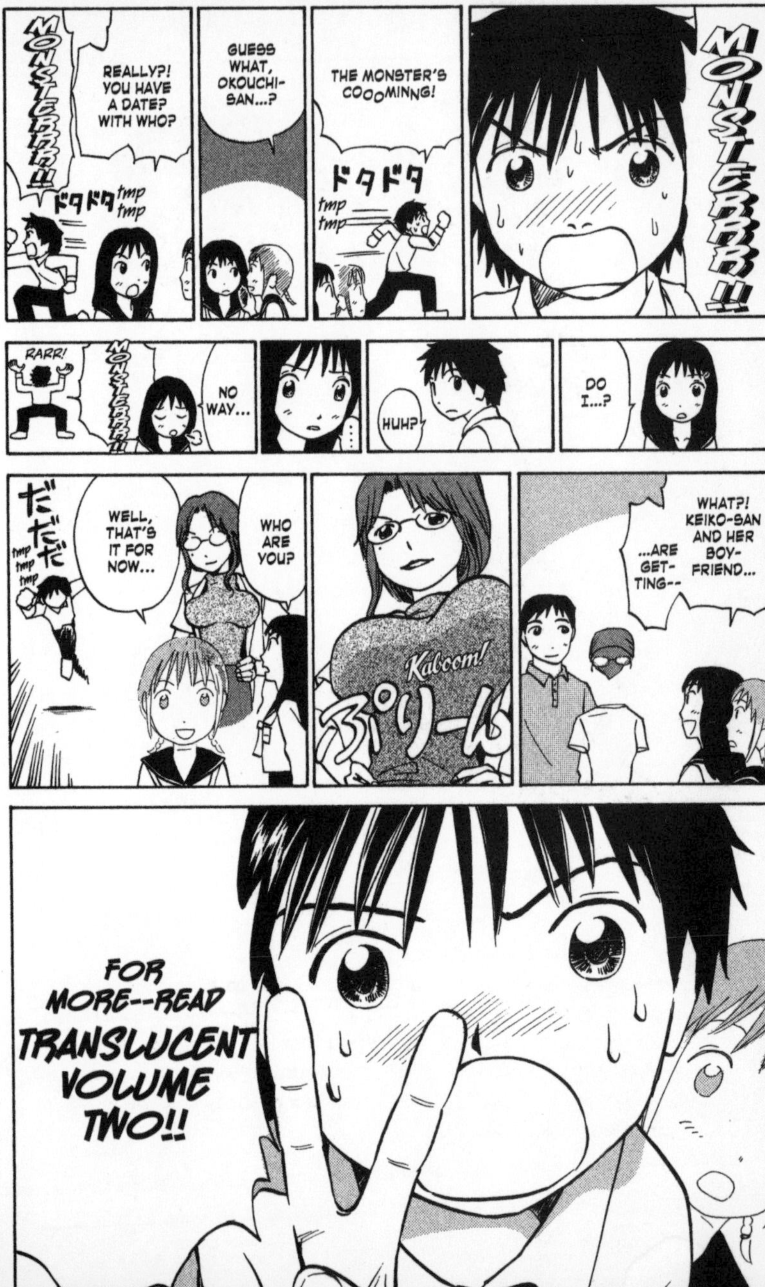
MONSTERRRR!!
THE MONSTER'S COOOMINNG!
ドタドタ
tmp tmp
GUESS WHAT, OKOUCHI-SAN...?
REALLY?! YOU HAVE A DATE? WITH WHO?
MONSTERRRR!!
ドタドタ
tmp tmp
DO I...?
HUH?
...
NO WAY...
MONSTERRRR!!
RARR!
WHAT?! KEIKO-SAN AND HER BOY-FRIEND...
...ARE GET-TING--
Kaboom!
ぷりーん
WHO ARE YOU?
WELL, THAT'S IT FOR NOW...
だだだ
tmp tmp tmp
FOR MORE--READ TRANSLUCENT VOLUME TWO!!

KAZUHIRO OKAMOTO

was born in 1971 in Okayama Prefecture, Japan. In 1995, he received a manga award from the monthly magazine *Afternoon*. *Translucent* was first featured in the March 2003 edition of the magazine *Comic Flapper*, and it became a monthly feature due to its wide popularity. Seventy percent of Mr. Okamoto's body is a plastic model. The other thirty percent is a curry bun.

HANAMI
하나미
International Love Story

Story by **PLUS**
Art by **SUNG-JAE PARK**

Seventeen-year-old Joonho Suk just had the best day of his life. He finally asked out his big crush, and she said yes. But after floating home on cloud nine, he found his family packing up to move to Seoul! Now tossed into a big new city and lovesick for the girl still in Suwon, Joonho runs into weird characters at every turn. Girl troubles and crazy adventures abound! Discover one of the most popular comics Korea has to offer!

VOLUME 1
ISBN-10: 1-59307-737-8
ISBN-13: 978-1-59307-737-2

VOLUME 2
ISBN-10: 1-59307-738-6
ISBN-13: 978-59307-738-9

$9.95 each!

Previews for *Hanami: International Love Story* and other Dark Horse Manhwa titles can be found at darkhorse.com!

AVAILABLE AT YOUR LOCAL COMICS SHOP OR BOOKSTORE. To find a comics shop in your area, call 1-888-266-4226. For more information or to order direct: On the web: darkhorse.com.
E-mail: mailorder@darkhorse.com. Phone: 1-800-862-0052 Mon.-Fri. 9 A.M. to 5 P.M. Pacific Time.

publisher
MIKE RICHARDSON

editor
PHILIP SIMON

editorial assistant
RYAN JORGENSEN

digital production
AREN KITTILSEN

collection designer
TONY ONG

art director
LIA RIBACCHI

Special thanks to Riko Frohnmayer and Michael Gombos.

English-language version produced by DARK HORSE COMICS.

Dark Horse Manga
A division of Dark Horse Comics, Inc.
10956 SE Main Street
Milwaukie, OR 97222

darkhorse.com

To find a comics shop in your area, call the Comic Shop Locator
Service toll-free at 1-888-266-4226

First edition: July 2007

ISBN-10: 1-59307-647-9
ISBN-13: 978-1-59307-647-4

1 3 5 7 9 10 8 6 4 2
Printed in the U.S.A.

STOP!

THIS IS THE BACK OF THE BOOK!

This manga collection is translated into English but oriented in a right-to-left reading format at the creator's request, maintaining the artwork's visual orientation as originally published in Japan. If you've never read manga in this way before, take a look at the diagram below to give yourself an idea of how to go about it. Basically, you'll be starting in the upper right corner and will read each balloon and panel moving right to left. It may take some getting used to, but you should get the hang of it very quickly. Enjoy!

1
C-COACH, I'M HERE!
2
OH, THERE YOU ARE.
3
I DIDN'T SEE YOU THERE, TRANSLUCENT GIRL.
4
HA HA HA HA
5
IT LOOKS LIKE YOU'RE BECOMING MORE TRANSPARENT AGAIN.
6
YEAH.
7
SUPPOSE IT WON'T BE LONG NOW...
8
...'CAUSE I USUALLY GO COMPLETELY TRANSPARENT EVERY FOUR WEEKS.
9
MY FACE AND RIGHT WRIST ARE THE LAST TO GO.

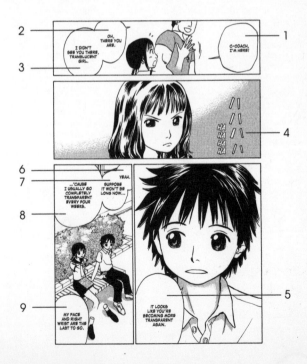